CICS

The Macmillan Database/Data Communications Series
Jay Ranade, Series Editor

Cave/Maymon: *Software Lifecycle Management*

Fadok: *Effective Design of CODASYL Data Base*

Ha: *Digital Satellite Communications*

Ranade/Ranade: *VSAM: Concepts, Programming, and Design*

Singer: *Written Communication for MIS/DP Professionals*

St. Amand: *A Guide to Packet-Switched, Value-Added Networks*

Towner: *The ADS/Online Cookbook*

Forthcoming

Kohn: *Practical Algorithms for Numerical Analysis*

McGrew/McDaniel: *In-House Publishing in a Mainframe Environment*

Potter: *Local Area Networks: Applications and Design*

Ranade: *VSAM: Performance, Design, and Fine Tuning*

Samson: *MVS*

Stallings: *Handbook of Computer-Communications Standards*
       I. The Open Systems Interconnection Standards

Stallings: *Handbook of Computer-Communications Standards*
       II. Local Network Standards

Stallings: *Handbook of Computer-Communications Standards*
       III. Department of Defense Protocol Standards

Towner: *Automate Plus*

Towner: *IDMS/R*™ Cookbook

CICS
Application Development and Programming

Arlene J. Wipfler

Macmillan Publishing Company
NEW YORK

Collier Macmillan Publishers
LONDON

> *Dedicated to*
> *the memory of my brother,*
> *Louis Epstein*

The following are reprinted by permission of International Business Machines Corporation—**page 101,** Figure 5-1, **244,** Figure 10-5, **403,** Figure G-1, **404,** Figure G-2, and **405,** Figure G-3, copybook members included in compiled CICS COBOL programs: Exec Interface COBOL Working Storage Area, DFHAID, DFHEIBLK, and DFHBMSCA (c) 1985; **181,** Figure 8-1, adapted from a diagram on page 343 of *IBM CICS Application Programmer's Reference Manual (Command Level)* (SC33-0241) (c) 1985; and **239,** Figure 10-4, and **402,** figure in Appendix F, chart on page 12 from the *3270 Information Display System Reference Summary* (GX20-1878) (c) 1979.

Macmillan Publishing Company
866 Third Avenue, New York, New York 10022

Collier Macmillan Canada, Inc.
Collier Macmillan Publishers ● London

Library of Congress Cataloging-in-Publication Data

Wipfler, Arlene J.
  CICS application development and programming.

  (The Macmillan Database/Data Communications Series)
  Includes index.
  1. CICS (Computer system) I. Title. II. Series.
QA76.76.T45W56 1987   005.4′42   87-5662
ISBN 0-02-949930-5

Printing: 1 2 3 4 5 6 7 8   Year: 6 7 8 9 0 1 2 3 4

PREFACE

The Customer Information Control System/Virtual Storage (CICS/VS) is IBM's premiere teleprocessing monitor. Because of the ever-increasing popularity of online systems and the versatility of CICS/VS, it remains one of the most popular and widely used software products. CICS/VS is used in almost all large computer installations where IBM mainframes are utilized. CICS/VS is, in reality, a large control system with numerous facilities, and it is very easily tailored to the requirements of each installation's needs in terms of online systems development and implementation. Because of the scope of CICS/VS, the process of learning to design CICS systems and write online programs can be somewhat overwhelming.

Often programmers pick up a little of the coding and manage to write some programs. However, in order to develop efficient programs, it is necessary to do more than code CICS commands. A good understanding of how to use CICS and related programming considerations is critical. Efficiency is particularly important in online design and programming, because being able to provide timely responses to terminal operators is critical to the successful use and operation of the system. This book was written to address not only command coding and program debugging, but also the special considerations involved with online programming and design. It is the author's intention to provide under one cover all of the information needed to teach readers to be successful CICS programmers and designers.

HOW THIS BOOK CAME INTO BEING

This book has grown out of my experience as a CICS technician, course developer, and instructor. During the last seven years I have taught CICS courses in large corporations as an outside teaching consultant. Teaching specific skills in industry is a very challenging enterprise, because the ultimate measure of success is that students be able to work effectively as a result of the instruction. To that end, I have had the joy of seeing the success and professional advancement of my former students. Undoubtedly, I have benefited immeasurably from this experience. It has given me a perspective on what information people need to know, and how to convey it. During the years many students have suggested that I write a textbook on CICS because they felt it would be an invaluable reference. This book came into being as a result.

WHO THIS BOOK IS WRITTEN FOR

This book is intended for batch programmers who want to learn CICS programming, debugging, and design. However, it should also prove quite useful to experienced CICS technicians, because topics are discussed in sufficient depth that new insights and techniques can be learned.

A COMMENT REGARDING THE WRITING STYLE

I have endeavored to write this book as if I were teaching CICS in a relaxed classroom environment. The writing style is my speaking style as an instructor. I have also attempted to incorporate humor and simplicity. It is my fond wish that you will find this text easy and clear reading.

WHAT IS COVERED IN THIS BOOK

Part I provides an overview of CICS. It begins with a discussion of the differences between batch and online systems. Then the concepts and facilities of CICS are discussed. The major parts of CICS are explained so that the reader gains a firm grasp of the scope and capabilities of the system.

Part II presents application programming under CICS. Each of the programming-oriented facilities is discussed with regard to commands, command syntax, and examples. The special considerations for command use and program structure are emphasized. Program debugging and application design facilities are likewise included, and the concluding chapter presents a sample of CICS application design.

ACKNOWLEDGMENTS

There are so many people who helped me in preparing the material that ultimately became this text, that I hardly know where to begin.

First, to all of the students who participated in my CICS classes: The many excellent questions you asked gave me insights not only into CICS, but also into what people need to know about the subject to work effectively as online programmers. Thus, in teaching you, I learned, and I have attempted to incorporate what you taught me into this text.

Second, to Maria Zimmerlein and Howie Bobish: Maria patiently and tirelessly helped me to improve the effectiveness of my courses and presentation skills over the last seven years. Howie was my technical guru in preparing the CICS courses that ultimately became this text. He expended much time and effort advising me on course contents. Without their efforts, this book certainly would not have come into being.

Third, to Heinz, Becky, Julia, Michael, and Kranie, whose love and encouragement egged me on.

Finally, to Jay Ranade, who carefully edited and checked the original manuscript. His excellent suggestions have all been incorporated into this final version.

CONTENTS

chapter 3 # More Concepts and Facilities   **50**

chapter 9 Introduction to Basic Mapping Support 206

chapter 12   # Application Design Facilities   **325**

one
AN OVERVIEW OF CICS

chapter *1*

Introduction

1.1 INTRODUCTION TO CICS

The execution of an online computer system transforms batch computing into an interactive workaday tool that enables nontechnical business personnel to perform their daily jobs in a more effective manner. Information can be retrieved or stored in a matter of seconds, as opposed to the hours or days common in the batch environment. This results in more efficient, cost-effective business operation and, as a consequence, online system development is proceeding at a rapid pace. In an IBM mainframe environment the development of an online system is greatly facilitated by using IBM's teleprocessing monitor, the Customer Information Control System (CICS).

CICS is referred to as a Data Base/Data Communication (DB/DC) control system. This means that CICS controls application program access to file information and data arriving over a communications network. From the previous statement one might get the impression that CICS is made up of access methods enabling it to access such data. However, this is not so. CICS runs under the control of a host operating system such as MVS or VSE and utilizes the file and telecommunications access methods of the host operating system.

In order to understand what CICS does, it is first necessary to differentiate between two aspects of an online computer system. The first is that part which provides the intelligence to do particular application processing. As an example, let's consider a customer service system that enables telephone operators in a customer service department to respond to phone calls and answer questions by using video terminals to inquire into a company's data files. Application programs are required to perform application-specific work, such as selecting and formatting appropriate data items that are to be displayed on a terminal screen.

In addition to application-dependent functions, however, there are also environmental issues that must be addressed. These environmental issues comprise the second aspect of an online system. For example, an interactive system by definition must support the exchange of information between application programs running in a computer and people using computer terminals in offices. In order to accomplish this communication, there must be software to interact with a network of terminals.

This control function must be performed regardless of the nature of the application. Terminal management is not dependent upon the type of information being displayed. The same terminal management can be used to display customer service or inventory control information. In other words, terminal management is independent of the application. Terminal management is only one control function required for online processing. However, before we go on to discuss online control functions, let's focus on the key point that control functions are necessary regardless of the application, and control functions can be independent of the application.

CICS is a generalized solution for managing all of the control or environmental aspects involved with online system execution. Application development can proceed without concern for environmental issues. CICS creates and controls an executing online environment into which application-specific programs can be inserted. Since CICS controls the online environment, application programs can be coded to address solely the requirements of the application. CICS handles the control aspects in a general manner and can therefore be used to implement any online application.

In order to understand exactly what CICS does, we must examine the characteristics of the online environment that CICS manages. This can be accomplished by contrasting online processing with batch processing.

1.2 BATCH VS. ONLINE

In batch processing data requests are collected from offices where people work. The same kinds of data items are batched together, converted into a machine-readable format, and brought to a central computer for processing. Figure 1-1 depicts batch processing. Two separate user areas are illustrated. In the customer service office, customer service representatives answer telephone calls and respond to customer inquiries. After soliciting appropriate customer information, the telephone operator informs the customer that the query will be looked into and continues answering calls from other customers. For each call, the customer service operator fills out

Figure 1-1. Diagram depicting batch processing.

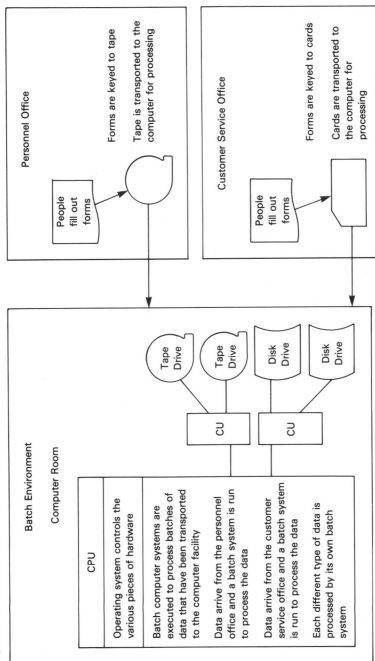

Personnel Office

People fill out forms

Forms are keyed to tape

Tape is transported to the computer for processing

Customer Service Office

People fill out forms

Forms are keyed to cards

Cards are transported to the computer for processing

Batch Environment

Computer Room

Tape Drive

Tape Drive

Disk Drive

Disk Drive

CU

CU

CPU

Operating system controls the various pieces of hardware

Batch computer systems are executed to process batches of data that have been transported to the computer facility

Data arrive from the personnel office and a batch system is run to process the data

Data arrive from the customer service office and a batch system is run to process the data

Each different type of data is processed by its own batch system

After data are brought to the computer, a batch system processes. Processing and error reports are created by the batch system. It takes one or more days for processing and delivery of reports.

5

a form with customer information that might include the customer's name, address, and account number. At periodic intervals—perhaps daily—the forms are collected and brought to a place where the information on them can be keyed to a computer-readable format such as cards, tape, or disk.

The machine-readable information is then sent to a computer facility, where the customer service system is executed. As a result, reports providing current information about appropriate customers are created. These reports are then delivered to the customer service office and the customer's query can be answered. Any data collected from the personnel office are not processed by the batch customer service system. A separate system is needed for the processing of personnel data.

An online computer system, illustrated in Fig. 1-2, represents a revolutionary departure from batch processing. A computer terminal is placed on the office desk, thereby bringing computing directly to the end user. Requests for data can be entered via the terminal and processed immediately. The telephone operator in the customer service department enters a code word (called a transaction identifier) requesting customer service information and a customer number directly into the terminal. This request is conveyed via a data communications network to the online computer system, and the request is processed immediately. An output response is created for the request, and this response is conveyed back to the terminal through the network. The terminal operator thus receives a rapid answer to his or her query. Instead of waiting one or more days, information is available almost immediately. However, this "virtual" description of how an online system works does not take into account the complex combination of hardware and software required to make possible the exchange of information between a mainframe application program and a person in a user department who is armed with a computer terminal.

Data communications hardware and software are required to support a network of distant terminals. In Figure 1-2 an IBM 37X5 communications controller or front end is depicted. The communications controller serves as a dedicated processor that handles some of the network management functions; this frees the mainframe software from responsibility for low-level detail functions involved with data communications. This, of course, removes some of the details of processing from the host and thereby increases the availability of the host CPU for application processing. The mainframe is not totally isolated from communications work, however.

The mainframe must contain an appropriate telecommunications access method to interact with and oversee the operation of the communications controller. The telecommunications access method can be thought of as analogous to the director of a mail service or delivery system. Such access methods include the *Virtual Telecommunications Access Method* (VTAM) and the *TeleCommunications Access Method* (TCAM). The access method is concerned not with the application content of data

Figure 1-2. Diagram of online processing.

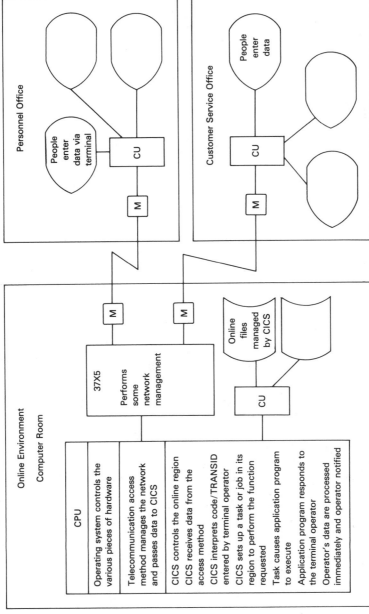

Terminal operators receive information via terminals connected to the CICS system. Response is immediate. People don't have to wait one or more days for access to data.

messages, but rather with the correct distribution of them. On the input side, the access method is responsible for seeing that input terminal messages received from the communication controller are delivered to the appropriate application subsystem where such messages can be processed. A CICS region with appropriate application programs is an example of an application subsystem. On the output side, the access method is responsible for ensuring that output responses are properly directed to the appropriate terminals. The access method is the "director" of the communications system and uses the communications controller to actually handle the details of message delivery.

Returning to Figure 1-2, we can see that there are two communication links emanating from the 37X5 communications controller: one is a link with the personnel office; the other is connected to the customer service office. These links serve as a physical path over which data can be transmitted. At each end of the communications link is a little box containing the letter "M." These boxes represent modems that in a physical sense make communication possible.

Very often the telephone network is used to connect the mainframe host computer to terminals located in geographically distant user departments. The modem is required to transform computer data into a signal that is appropriate to the type of data circuit or "line" being utilized. The telephone network was built for the transmission of the human voice and as such is not appropriate to the conveyance of computer digital data. For sending, the modem changes the computer's digital information into a signal that can be transmitted over the data circuit. For receiving, the modem changes the signal back into computer digital information that can be understood by the terminals. Through the use of modems the standard telephone network can be utilized for data transmission between computers and remote terminals.

Assuming that all of the appropriate data communications hardware and software have been duly installed and are operational, we can build an interactive environment that supports conversations between one or more user departments and application programs running in the host computer. What is the role of CICS in this dialog? CICS is responsible for managing and controlling the application subsystem. As part of this function, CICS must interact with the telecommunications access method and obtain terminal input requests. Having received terminal input, CICS recognizes the request code or transaction identifier and relates this to an application program that processes the particular request. Both the customer service and personnel offices are connected to a single CICS system, and the system provides services for both user areas. Each area may have one or more functions that they can request online. CICS must be able to distinguish between different requests and select the right application program to process each query.

The appropriate program is invoked by CICS. The program does its application-specific processing to create an output response. These data are passed to CICS, which assumes responsibility for interacting with the telecommunications access method so that the user's response is displayed on the terminal's screen. A customer service representative using an online system such as the one in Figure 1-2 is able to enter a request into a terminal on his or her desk and receive an answer directly. The effectiveness of online processing is quite obvious from the vantage points of both the customer and the individual working in the customer service office. Online processing is far more responsive to information needs than is a corresponding batch system. Online system requirements differ from those of batch processing in a variety of ways, and as a result there are unique issues that must be addressed in an online control system such as CICS. These issues center around performance measurement, system scheduling, security considerations, system availability requirements, and considerations for building a recovery/restart system.

1.2.1 Performance Measurement

A batch system is called a data-driven system because it is scheduled and executed when there are data to be processed. The batch customer service system is not run when there are no preexisting data. Furthermore, the batch system terminates execution as soon as it has handled all of the data. We measure a batch system by the amount of data that can be processed in a given interval of time or system "throughput." The faster the processing, the less computer time is used and the more cost effective the system is. Furthermore, each type of data is processed by a separate batch system. Accounts payable, customer service, personnel, and accounts receivable all have separate batch systems. In the batch world we never combine different kinds of data for processing, because each system is designed to handle only a specific kind of information.

An online system is called a transaction-driven system because the processing of an online system is determined by the entry of transaction identifiers or service requests by terminal users. The number of transactions that can be processed in a given amount of time is certainly important, but it is not the primary measure of the performance of an online system. Rather, our main concern for online processing is that the system be able to satisfy information needs in a timely fashion. The amount of time it takes for the system to respond to a request for service is the real measure of the effectiveness of an online system.

This interval is called *"response time,"* and it should be rapid enough so that the terminal user is not impeded in the performance of his or her job. Remember that an online system is supposed to be an effective workaday tool; a sluggish tool may prevent a user from working effectively. An online system that is perfection itself in terms of ease of use and quality of information available is not an effective system unless it responds to user requests within a satisfactory time interval. The degree to which the system response slows down the user's work determines how ineffective the system is.

Although one might like to think of response time in absolute terms as a finite measure of time, this is not a realistic approach. The response time required for a particular function is dependent on the nature of the work being done by the individual requesting service. The more time required on the part of the terminal operator for processing, thinking, or data entry, the slower the system's response can be without seriously affecting the person's work. Response time of one to three seconds is generally desired, but this is not an absolute value. There are different types of online transactions, and they each have different requirements for response time. Let's take a look at two different types of transactions.

Our customer service system is primarily an inquiry/response type of system. The terminal operator enters a code word such as 'INQ1' and a customer number and depresses the ENTER key on the terminal. The system responds by presenting the appropriate customer information. In this type of processing very rapid response time is needed for the system to be effective. The operator is not going to require much time for thinking or data entry for each transaction. Rather, in customer service the phones are ringing away and the terminal operator wants to answer the customer's questions as quickly as possible and get on to the next phone call. If the system takes several minutes to display information, the operator can put the waiting customer on hold but there is no meaningful work that the operator can perform. Rapid response time on the order of one to three seconds would be desired for this type of transaction.

Another type of transaction might be an online shipping transaction in which a terminal operator in a warehouse enters a shipping transaction request such as 'SHP1' and an order number. The system's response would be to display a customer order from the order image file. The terminal operator would then arrange to have merchandise rounded up and placed on a loading platform for shipping. When all of the available ordered merchandise has been collected and staged together, the terminal operator would enter the quantities of merchandise being shipped. This is not a brief transaction, and would typically take at least 10 minutes to be processed. A response time longer than one to three seconds would not affect the ability of the individual in the warehouse to perform his or her job. As a matter of fact a response time of up to 30 seconds might not present a problem. With data entry transactions, operator processing time results in fewer transactions performed in a given time period, so a slower response is not as injurious.

An online system that supports several different functions or transactions should be able to distinguish between functions in terms of prioritizing them for processing. This is easily accomplished in CICS because there is a highly flexible mechanism for prioritizing work to be done in the CICS region. CICS can distinguish between different terminal users, different terminals, and different transactions or requests. Priorities can be established for any combination of the above.

The issue of good response time is compounded by the fact that for a particular transaction or function the response time should be even across the terminal network. It is not sufficient for one person to have good response time while everyone else doing the same function has to sit and wait for progressively longer periods of time. Yet, if we have 25 terminals in the customer service department it would be conceivable for all of them to be in use concurrently. The online system must be capable of receiving and processing requests and giving timely responses to all terminal users.

This is accomplished in CICS through multitasking. CICS receives incoming requests and sets up a unit of work or a "task" for each. It also dispatches or permits tasks to be processed concurrently. Multitasking within the CICS region or partition is handled by CICS and is not apparent to the operating system or application programs that run under CICS's control. In order to accomplish multitasking, CICS keeps all tasks in a list and allows the one with the highest priority to execute. When a processing task requires a service for which it must wait, such as obtaining file information, CICS uses this Input/Output (I/O) wait time to allow other tasks within the region or partition to process. Each task represents a user's request, and through internal task switches or multitasking numerous terminal users can be serviced concurrently. In this way an online system controlled by CICS can give good even response time to all terminal users.

1.2.2 System Scheduling

A batch system is executed when there are data to be processed. When all of the batch data items have been processed, the system ends and another system can be run to process other types of data. Again, the online environment is different. The online system must provide good response time, and therefore we do not wait until there is a request for service before starting up the execution of the online system. There would be no system to receive the request. Furthermore, after processing a request from a terminal operator, we can't bring down the system and wait for the next request. **An online system is typically brought up in the morning when the business day is about to begin and executes for the entire day.**

The online system sits and waits for transactions or requests to be entered by terminal operators. In a mainframe environment, this means that an entire region or partition is dedicated every business day to an online system. For a single department the cost of an online system can therefore be prohibitive. Instead of paying for the computer time required to process collected batch data, the department must pay for the use of a mainframe region or partition for every business day. This problem is resolved by providing support within one online system for several user areas.

One online system might support customer service, personnel, and online shipping functions. The user's advantage here is that the cost associated with the online system can be shared by several different departments and the prorated cost may be less than or equal to the cost of batch processing. From the vantage point of the systems area, however, we can see that this makes for a more complex operating environment. Instead of allowing the online system to be dedicated to processing a single kind of data, it is necessary for all of the data from supported areas to be processed by the same system. This means that numerous application programs providing different functions for supported user areas need to be available in the online system. These different programs must be allowed to process concurrently in support of user requests.

The online system should be able to distinguish between request codes or transaction identifiers and relate these different requests to the appropriate application programs. CICS handles this aspect of online processing. It keeps track of different transaction identifiers and the programs that process each of them. It also keeps track of where programs are located and monitors program use within the online region.

CICS multitasking allows a variety of application programs to execute concurrently, resulting in a dynamic environment. The system is driven by transactions as they arrive from terminal users. At any given moment we cannot predict exactly what the job mix in the online region will be. Any of the application programs may be in use based upon the requests that have entered the system. After a while we may begin to see statistical trends in online processing, but the system must be prepared to do any of the supported functions at any time, and it must give good response time as well.

1.2.3 Security Considerations

The security considerations for an online system are far more numerous than those for a batch system. In the first place, a person in the batch environment has to have physical access to the computer information. The chances of a security breach are limited to those people who can get into the computer room itself or who have access to computer reports. Beyond this, surreptitious retrieval or modification of data requires that the individual have certain technical skills.

If, for example, one brought an intelligent but computer-illiterate man to a computer room and told him that he had carte blanche to do whatever he wanted to do (except pull plugs), the likelihood of his being able to breach security would be almost negligible. He wouldn't speak Job

Control Language and would probably think that a utility provides electrical power. Quite obviously, it would be quite a long time before he would be able to access or modify information stored in computer files. In the batch world, one needs physical access and a level of technical proficiency in order to represent a potential security problem.

Now let's consider the online world. Terminals are moved into offices and placed on people's desks. In some instances there may be access security, but in many cases anyone can simply walk in. Even where there is physical access security, it is quite often possible to follow an authorized person through locked doors.

Online systems are designed to be used by nontechnical personnel in the performance of their daily jobs, and are consequently called "user-friendly" systems. This means that one does not have to possess technical know-how to use an online customer service system. We don't want to spend two years training business personnel to become technicians so that they can work in the customer service department and use an online system. The user-friendly system accommodates nontechnical business personnel by providing such things as menu screens and simple English language messages.

Menu screens list functions that the system can perform. In customer service, for example, there might be several functions or transactions that can be utilized. A customer might not know his or her account number. Anticipating this situation, the system developers could provide an alphabetic search function that could look up a customer's number based upon the customer's name. Once we have the customer's number, there may be several types of information that can be sought.

The customer service system might provide access to billing, payment, or purchase information for customers for several months. There may be indicative information about the customer, such as home address or place of business. A customer may call and request that indicative information be changed because of a change of residence. On the other hand, a customer may call because a bill does not reflect a recent payment. Each of these different functions is usually considered a different transaction to the online system. It would not normally be desirable for an operator to have to remember half a dozen different function codes or transaction identifiers. Therefore, a menu screen such as the one in Fig. 1-3 might be presented to the user. The user could make a selection from the menu.

Now, sit our computer illiterate down before this menu screen; he could gain access to information very easily by merely selecting a function described in the menu. Yet, he might not be a bona fide system user. Valid users should be defined to the system and each user should have to provide some sort of identifying information such as a name and password before being allowed to use the system. This type of security is called "sign on

```
                        CUSTOMER SERVICE SYSTEM


    ENTER YOUR CHOICE: ____



        AND CUSTOMER NAME: _____

        OR CUSTOMER NUMBER: _____




            1.  ALPHABETIC SEARCH OF CUSTOMERS
            2.  BILLING INFORMATION — MOST RECENT
            3.  BILLING INFORMATION — PRIOR MONTH
            4.  PAYMENT HISTORY
            5.  PURCHASE HISTORY
            6.  COMPLAINT HISTORY
            7.  GENERAL INFORMATION
```

Figure 1-3. Sample customer service menu screen.

security," and most online systems require that sign on security be used. Sign on processing is provided within CICS, and there is no application code required to implement this function.

However, sign on security is not the only type of security required for many online systems. Consider a system that supports numerous functions across several different business areas. A person who works in customer service would be a valid system user. Such a person would have a valid system sign on. Yet, after signing on to the system, this individual should not be able to perform every function available within the system. Customer service transactions might include a function that allows a customer service representative with the appropriate authorization to change a customer's balance or remove an erroneous charge. Would it be advisable for everyone in the customer service department to be able to perform this function? Clearly the answer is NO.

The plot becomes even thicker in an online environment where several departments share a single online system. For example, suppose that customer service and personnel share a single online system. The system provides application support for both areas to reduce the cost for each department. It would clearly not be desirable to allow someone in the customer service area to use personnel transactions to obtain confidential salary information or give themselves promotions or raises. An additional level of security called transaction security is required to forestall such a security breach. A valid terminal user should be limited in terms of those functions or transactions that he or she can actually perform.

There are obviously business concerns here. However, there may also be legal considerations as well. A person's credit history or personnel records should not be available to anyone who happens to enter the appropriate code. An online system must provide security appropriate to the resources being accessed within the system; normally transaction security is a requirement. In CICS each transaction or function can have a security level defined for it. CICS checks transaction security prior to allowing the request to be serviced. An operator is limited by his or her assigned security level.

1.2.4 System Availability

The online system typically supports several user areas, and when the system is down everyone is aware of the fact. Thus, availability becomes a real issue for online processing. In batch, if we are implementing a change to a system and an error is detected in an application program, the system is not run until the error has been resolved. In the online system, however, several user departments cannot be deprived of their systems because a program for one of the areas is not operating properly.

If a particular customer service program is abending with a data check, we do not want the entire online system to end. The online system should be able to recover from the failure of a single application program or transaction and not terminate processing. We might hasten to fix the abending program, but we would want the portions of the system that are unaffected to be left up and running. In CICS an error in an application program does not necessarily or even typically result in system termination. Unless the integrity of the CICS address space is compromised, CICS can recover from the error, purge the application task, and continue with online processing. There is no application code required for this function to be implemented.

1.2.5 Recovery/Restart Considerations

A system abend or crash can result from a software error, a hardware malfunction, or a power failure. In the batch environment, if a system goes down we can usually restart the system from a checkpoint within a particular step or go back to a prior step. In a worst case scenario it would be necessary to rerun the entire system from the beginning. This would mean that we might have to do some rescheduling. For example, testing might be canceled for the morning or other batch systems might have to be rescheduled. User areas might notice a delay in the receipt of reports.

In contrast, the online system abend is far more dramatic. Users are sitting with terminals on their desks and are very aware of the fact that the system is not up because when the system is down their terminals become expensive paperweights. Depending on the nature of the online system, restarting may be a simple matter or it may involve a recovery operation. In batch we have all of our data sitting on a data volume and we always have a backup copy of our files. After the batch system completes, backup copies of modified files are made.

The online environment is different. When the online system is brought up at the start of the day we normally have backup copies of the files as they exist at system startup. If the online system is merely an inquiry/response type of system, then the files are never changed online. After a system failure we merely fix the problem and bring the system back up again. A recovery operation is not required.

If, on the other hand, online processing modifies file information, we are confronted with a more complicated situation. Consider a system in which telephone operators enter orders for merchandise online. In the event of a system crash we would want to get the system up as soon as possible. Suppose, however, that we had suffered a head crash during the system abend and had lost the order image file. We would normally have a backup copy of the file taken prior to bringing up the online system. This backup copy of our file would not, however, reflect information collected online. Do we call up the user department and tell them to pretend that the day never occurred? What happens to the lost orders? Do we wait for irate customers to call back to find out when they are going to receive their merchandise?

In online processing we must not wait until the system is shut down at the end of the day to save copies of modified data records. As file information is altered online it is necessary to save a backup copy of file changes. This ongoing logging/journaling must be done while the system is processing. In this way, if physical damage results in the loss of a file, we can apply file modifications to a backup copy of the file and thereby recover online updates.

Furthermore, certain transactions or online functions may change multiple resources. The processing of the online shipping transaction discussed above would result in several different files being updated. After an order is completely processed, we would update the order image file to indicate that the order had been shipped. Also, we would typically update our inventory files for each of the separate products shipped and perhaps generate inventory replenishment information as well. If each order could process up to 20 different inventory items, our shipping transaction might involve updating three files, two of those files multiple times.

In this environment we would have even more complex considerations for recovery/restart, because if a system crash occurred while one or more inventory requests were being processed, our three files could in fact become out of synchronization with each other. We might have updated the order image file saying that the order was shipped, but not have completed our inventory or merchandise replenishment updates. In this case, we would want to have the synchronization of our files restored. Once again, this is something that CICS manages without application code.

The recovery/restart considerations for an online system are a function of what the system is doing. In an inquiry/response type of system we don't have to be concerned with recovery; we merely have to restart the system. If we are updating resources online we must be certain that physical file damage does not result in the loss of data collected online. If the system involves transactions that update two or more resources, we must make sure that our recovery system resynchronizes modified resources. This requirement of an online system is easily handled within the executing environment provided by CICS. There are tools that enable application developers to implement a recovery/restart system utilizing services and facilities that come as a part of CICS.

1.3   THE STRUCTURE OF CICS

CICS can be described as a modular system. It consists of a collection of control programs called management modules. The management modules are the executing code of CICS, and represent a functionalized division of responsibility for online system management. In other words, CICS is a collection of control programs, and each control program manages a particular aspect of the online environment. In this regard one might say that CICS is a union shop, since each aspect of the online environment is controlled by a separate management module or collection of management modules.

CICS addresses general or environmental issues that are normally involved in any online system regardless of the specifics of the application. What are some of the online management capabilities of CICS? As mentioned above, CICS interacts with the telecommunications access method of the host operating system. This interaction is centered on a collection of control programs known as the terminal control programs. These modules are concerned solely with managing this particular aspect of CICS. In other words, terminal control does whatever needs to be done to receive input from and send output to the telecommunications access method.

After input has been received into the CICS region, it is necessary to process the data and create a response for the terminal user. CICS is concerned with environmental issues and relies on application programs to perform application-specific processing. Therefore, CICS relates an input request to a particular application program. CICS initiates a unit of work, called a task, which executes within the application program, thereby creating a response. Terminal management obtains input from the telecommunications access method and passes the data to the CICS Task Control Program. It is the function of Task Control to create a task for each input request, keep track of all of the tasks in the system, and dispatch the highest-priority task ready to execute.

In order to accomplish this, the *tasK Control Program* (KCP) keeps a prioritized list of all of the tasks within CICS. New tasks are added to the list and completed tasks are removed. This is really very similar to the way in which a person might keep track of things that need to be done. As soon as CICS has updated its list by adding or removing a task, it looks for the highest-priority task that is ready to execute. The selected task is allowed to process until it needs a resource for which it must wait. An example of this is a file record that must be retrieved from a *Direct Access Storage Device* (DASD) file. CICS schedules the retrieval of the requested resource, and the task is placed into a wait state until the Input/Output has completed. During I/O wait time, Task Control (being a glutton for work) reexamines its list and finds the next highest-priority task that is ready to process. Terminal operator requests do not queue up and wait until one request has completed processing. Concurrent task execution or multitasking allows CICS to support fairly large terminal networks. Task Control accomplishes multitasking by using the I/O wait time of one task to dispatch other tasks in the system. The use of I/O wait time is thus critical to CICS performance.

Before we get too involved with the functioning of this one facility, let's get back to the main point, which is the modular structure of CICS. Task Control manages multiple tasks in the region, and in order to do so it must have *control blocks* to keep track of each task. In other words, Task Control needs storage or memory within the CICS region so that it can create control blocks. Task Control is the supervisor of the CICS region, but it is concerned solely with providing a safe multitasking environment. Task Control is not concerned with storage management.

Storage management is handled by the Storage Control Program, which allocates storage when needed. This includes storage needed internally by CICS. Therefore, when Task Control needs storage to create a control block for a task, it interacts with Storage Control to obtain the allocation. Storage Control is also responsible for taking back allocated storage when a task is completed. Consider the processing of a customer service request. A user enters a transaction identifier and a customer number into a terminal. CICS Terminal Control receives the input and passes the data along to Task Control. Task Control relates the transaction identifier to an application program and initiates a task to process the request. Task processing will not be of long duration; the task will be finished after it has read a record from a file, created an output response, passed the response to CICS, and informed CICS that it has been completed. The task will process for less than the typical one- to three-second response time interval. The nature of online processing demands that storage be reused for subsequent tasks. Storage Control allocates needed storage when a task begins and frees storage upon task termination.

Other resources of the system, such as application programs, must also be managed. As discussed above, a CICS system may be used to support multiple user areas, and consequently may have many application programs available to service different transaction requests. Application programs are managed by the CICS Program Control Program (PCP). Program Control keeps track of where programs are located; if a program is not resident in the CICS region when needed for online processing, Program Control fetches the program into memory.

Thus terminals, tasks, storage, and programs are some of the resources requiring CICS management. Each resource within the CICS environment is controlled by a specific management module, which has its own unique role to play in CICS processing. What we see as a functioning real time CICS system is actually the interaction of these separate management modules. Yet the module is concerned only with its own particular area or domain of online system management. Terminal Control, Task Control, Storage Control, and Program Control are but a few of the control programs or management modules in the CICS system. The central point in discussing them here is not to list all of the management modules or elucidate how they work, but to point out the modular structure of CICS.

The management modules come complete as a part of CICS software, and are unique to CICS as a system. Every installation that uses CICS will have approximately the same set of management modules (although some optional characteristics can be selected during the system generation process). Yet CICS can be used to support the processing of a variety of very different online systems.

Typically each major part of the CICS system consists of two types of components: one or more generalized management modules that manage an aspect of real time execution, and a system table that provides the specific information about what is being managed. The characteristics of an installation's online system are defined in system tables that drive the various management modules. The system tables are unique to each installation and define the resources, functions, and requirements of that installation.

In an installation there are specific terminals that may be connected to CICS. There are terminal operators who are to be allowed to sign on to and use the CICS system. There are transaction identifiers that invoke CICS services. There are application programs that provide the application-specific intelligence to create responses to operator requests. These separate aspects of an installation's environment are defined in CICS system tables. Valid CICS terminals are defined in a *Terminal Control Table* (TCT). The terminal operators are specified in a *Sign oN Table* (SNT). The transaction identifiers are described in a *Program*

Control Table (PCT). The application programs are named in a *Processing Program Table* (PPT). Each of these tables contains all of the information needed by CICS to manage and control these resources.

Generally, a systems programmer is responsible for creating and maintaining the system tables. This can be done by coding macro instructions provided specifically for the generation of system tables. After the macro instructions have been coded, this source code is assembled and link edited. If this process is performed without serious error, a load module is created. Each table is a separate load module, and the various system tables and management modules are brought into memory during system initialization.

Certain CICS tables can be altered online. A CICS system transaction "CEDA" is used for this purpose. Use of "CEDA" is called *Resource Definition Online* (RDO). RDO can be used to dynamically define and install information into an executing CICS system.

CICS is not the only online control system. There are several others, such as *Task Master,* the *Airline Control Program-2,* and *Intercom.* Also, most data base management systems have an online capability. For example, IBM's *Information Management System* (IMS) has a data communication facility called IMS/DC. However, CICS is the most widely used of the online control systems.

1.4 SUMMARY

We have described CICS thus far as a **modularly constructed table-driven online control system.** The various functions performed during CICS execution are handled by separate control facilities. Each control facility consists of one or more management modules and typically has a system table to define installation-specific information. Each management module and system table is a separate load module. During real time execution it is the functionalized interaction of the separate CICS programs that provides the executing real time environment.

The virtue in the way CICS is built or designed is that it results in a system that is particularly easy to maintain and change. For example, if a new terminal operator is hired, the systems programmer merely creates a new SNT entry and reassembles the table. When CICS is brought up again it has this new version of the SNT, and the operator has been added to the system.

It also means that CICS can be tailored to each installation's requirements very readily. If there is a CICS facility that is not required in a particular installation, the unneeded facility can be omitted. For example, consider an online system that is purely an inquiry type of system. The recovery function needed is very minimal. We do not need to create ongoing backup of file modifications because there are none. In this case the recovery facilities within CICS need not be used, and as a matter of fact the Recovery/Restart facility within CICS need not even be generated.

REVIEW EXERCISE

Mark each of the following statements True (T) or False (F).

_____ 1. CICS creates an executing online environment into which application programs can be inserted.

_____ 2. Security is more of an issue for batch systems than for online systems.

_____ 3. CICS consists of data base and data communications access methods.

_____ 4. CICS can be used to build an online system that supports several different user departments. The primary motivation for this is to make the online system more cost effective.

_____ 5. CICS application programs must contain code to provide multitasking of requests from numerous terminal operators.

_____ 6. An online system is considered a transaction-driven system because its processing is in response to requests from terminal operators.

_____ 7. Response time must always be within the range of one to three seconds.

_____ 8. It is a good practice to save a copy of file modifications (logging/journaling) while the online system is processing.

Provide a short answer to each of the questions below.

1. What is the difference between sign on security and transaction security?
2. Cite two types of recovery considerations that we may have to be concerned with in a system which permits file updates online.
3. What is meant by the term user-friendly system?
4. What is meant by the statement that CICS controls the online environment? How is this a benefit in terms of developing an online system?
5. What is the primary measure of online system performance?
6. Why is an online system called a transaction-driven system?
7. CICS consists of two types of components. What are they?
8. How is installation-specific information defined to CICS?
9. Why does the storage used by tasks in a CICS system have to be reclaimed when the tasks end?
10. What is the name of the CICS management module that manages application programs?
11. Which management module is responsible for CICS multitasking?

12. What is the relationship between I/O wait time and CICS multitasking? Is multitasking important to CICS performance? Why?

    Match the CICS tables listed below with the information defined in each.

_____ 1. Sign oN Table (SNT)
_____ 2. Processing Program Table (PPT)
_____ 3. Terminal Control Table (TCT)
_____ 4. Program Control Table (PCT)

    A. Contains information about the terminals in CICS's network.
    B. Contains information about the operators who are to be allowed to sign on to the CICS system.
    C. Contains information about the application programs that are to be used within a CICS system.
    D. Contains information about the transaction identifiers or TRANSIDs that can be used by terminal operators to request services of CICS.

ANSWERS TO REVIEW EXERCISE

    Mark each of the following statements True or False.

___T___ 1. CICS creates an executing online environment into which application programs can be inserted.
___F___ 2. Security is more of an issue for batch systems than for online systems.
___F___ 3. CICS consists of data base and data communications access methods.
___T___ 4. CICS can be used to build an online system that supports several different user departments. The primary motivation for this is to make the online system more cost effective.
___F___ 5. CICS application programs must contain code to provide multitasking of requests from numerous terminal operators.
___T___ 6. An online system is considered a transaction-driven system because its processing is in response to requests from terminal operators.
___F___ 7. Response time must always be within the range of one to three seconds.
___T___ 8. It is a good practice to save a copy of file modifications (logging/journaling) while the online system is processing.

Provide a short answer to each of the questions below.

1. What is the difference between sign on security and transaction security?

   Sign on security requires that an operator provide identifying information such as a name and password before being allowed to sign on and use the system. Transaction security tests operator authority to perform each transaction. It is assumed that an operator performing transactions has already signed on to the system.

2. Cite two types of recovery considerations that we may have to be concerned with in a system which permits file updates online.

   First, we want to ensure that file updates accomplished during online processing are not lost if files are destroyed because of a head crash or other catastrophe. This is accomplished by saving a copy of file modifications as they are performed. If an online file is physically damaged, the saved file changes are applied to a backup copy of the file.

   The second recovery consideration involves the processing of online transactions that update two or more resources. If such a transaction is interrupted during processing, our resources may be out of synchronization. One file, for example, may have been updated while the second was not. In this instance it would be desirable to resynchronize the files by backing out the update performed.

3. What is meant by the term user-friendly system?

   A user-friendly system is one that can easily be used by nontechnical business personnel. Such a system may use menu screens to present the user with a list of functions that can be performed and explain user errors in a nontechnical manner.

4. What is meant by the statement that CICS controls the online environment? How is this a benefit in terms of developing an online system?

   CICS processing manages the environmental aspects of an online system. For example, the application interface to the terminal network is handled by CICS. Multitasking and storage management are also provided within CICS. It is therefore easier to develop an online system using software such as CICS. Application developers can concentrate on application processing issues and rely on CICS to manage the online environment.

5. What is the primary measure of online system performance?

   The single most important measure of an online system is its ability to provide good response time.

6. Why is an online system called a transaction-driven system?

An online system is referred to as transaction driven because the processing done within the online region is in response to requests for service or transactions entered by system users.

7. CICS consists of two types of components. What are they?

CICS consists of management modules or control programs that each handle a particular aspect of online processing, as well as system tables that define the resources to be managed.

8. How is installation-specific information defined to CICS?

Information about an installation is defined to CICS management modules in a collection of system tables. For example, CICS terminals are defined in a table called the Terminal Control Table.

9. Why does the storage used by tasks in a CICS system have to be reclaimed when the tasks end?

Tasks are of short duration. If storage were not reclaimed and reused for subsequent tasks, the system would run out of storage after a short time.

10. What is the name of the CICS management module that manages application programs?

The Program Control Program.

11. Which management module is responsible for CICS multitasking?

The Task Control Program.

12. What is the relationship between I/O wait time and CICS multitasking? Is multitasking important to CICS performance? Why?

CICS uses the I/O wait time of one task to allow another task to process. Multitasking is important to CICS performance because it allows multiple tasks to process concurrently and thereby more than a single operator's request can be handled at a time.

Match the CICS tables listed below with the information defined in each.

___B___ 1. Sign oN Table (SNT)
___C___ 2. Processing Program Table (PPT)
___A___ 3. Terminal Control Table (TCT)
___D___ 4. Program Control Table (PCT)

chapter 2

CICS Concepts
and Facilities

In the previous chapter we discussed some of the unique characteristics of an online system, defined CICS as an online control system that provides an executing environment for application-specific programs, and introduced the structure or architecture of CICS. In this chapter we will examine how the particular facilities of CICS work and what their capabilities are. The reader is advised that a thorough understanding of the information contained in this chapter, while important, is not essential to being able to code CICS application programs.

2.1 SIGN ON MANAGEMENT

Sign on management consists of the Sign oN Table (SNT) and the Sign oN Program (SNP). The Sign oN Program processes sign on requests from CICS terminal operators.

2.1.1 The Sign oN Table (SNT)

The SNT is used to define the operators who are to be allowed to sign on to CICS. The SNT entry contains the operator's name or USERID and password, as well as operator security and priority information and the operator ID. This information defines the operator to CICS. The operator's name or USERID and password are used during sign on processing.

The operator's security information defines what the operator may do once signed on to CICS. There are actually two types of security information that can be defined for a CICS terminal operator. The first is called **transaction security** and is used to determine which functions or transactions an operator can perform. A transaction security key is defined with one or more numeric values from 1 to 64. An operator's transaction security key can contain multiple values or security levels. From the perspective of CICS these different levels are mutually exclusive values, and there is no implied increased security level for higher numbers.

Each transaction is defined to CICS with a transaction security level. Let's say that the transaction "WI01" is defined as having a security level of 10. An operator would be required to have the number 10 in his or her security key in order to perform this transaction. The operator's security key could possess a higher number, but higher numbers do not denote higher security levels. The operator must have the exact value in his or her security key or CICS detects an attempted breach of security. In the event of a security violation, the operator is sent a message to that effect and CICS saves an indication of the attempt. When the system is shut down a report of daily processing is produced, and attempts to violate security are noted.

In addition to transaction security, CICS allows a **resource security** key to be defined for an operator. Resource security is handled in a similar manner as transaction security, except that resource security values may only be from 1 to 24. Each resource in the CICS system may be defined with a particular resource security level. Resources can include files, programs, transaction identifiers, journals, and queues defined to CICS.

Once the operator's transaction is initiated, CICS can be requested to check the operator's resource security key against the security level of each resource accessed on the operator's behalf. Resource security level checking is not possible for all transactions. CICS programs may be written using macro instructions (Macro Level programs) or commands (Command Level programs) to request CICS services. Resource security level checking is applicable only when the transaction uses a Command Level program. In addition, resource security level checking must be requested for each transaction for which it is desired. In most cases transaction security is sufficient for user transactions because resources are accessed under application program control. If the operator can be permitted to utilize the transaction, then the program will do the appropriate functions.

However, the CICS system transaction "CECI" permits CICS commands such as those used in application programs to be entered directly into a video terminal. A command is first checked for syntax and if it is correct the operator can elect to have it executed. "CECI" creates an "open sesame" in terms of modifying resources online. One can literally alter file data or access any other CICS resource available to an application program. This transaction is an invaluable tool for application programmers because test data can be generated online by simply entering CICS commands. Data generation that might require several hours or more to accomplish using batch utilities can be done in a matter of minutes with "CECI." However, its dynamic nature could lead to a breach of security if there were no control over individual resources. In many installations "CECI" is defined and used only in test CICS systems, as the security risks in a production environment are quite obvious.

With resource security level checking, an operator can be allowed to use "CECI" but only operate upon those resources allowed by his or her resource security key. Thus for test systems supporting multiple application development areas, resource security checking could be used in addition to transaction security. All application programmers would be given transaction security keys that permit them to perform the "CECI" transaction. By specifying different resource security keys, programmers are limited under "CECI" to looking at or changing resources associated with their respective application areas.

The operator's priority is an ingredient used in determining the priority of tasks initiated on behalf of the operator. CICS uses three different priority values. In addition to operator priority, there are priority values that can be defined for each transaction in the Program Control Table (PCT) and for each terminal in the Terminal Control Table (TCT). When a task is initiated by an operator, CICS adds the three priority values and thus derives the executing priority of the task. This corresponds to the task's placement in CICS's list of tasks; the higher in the task list the more likely the task is to be dispatched or allowed to execute quickly.

All three of these values can be from 0 to 255. CICS priority is likewise from 0 to 255, with 255 being the highest priority. In the event that the addition of the three priority values exceeds 255, the task gets a priority of 255. This would be very rare, however, because normally low priorities and small increments in priority are used to differentiate between different transactions, operators, and terminals.

By allowing these three specifications to establish priority, CICS prioritization can be quite flexible. If certain transactions or functions require rapid response time, this can be defined. If, on the other hand, certain terminal operators require rapid response, this can be specified. If terminals in a particular location demand quick response, this can also be accommodated. The typical procedure, however, is to use only one of the three priority values within CICS, because use of all three frequently makes system tuning more complex. Normally transaction priority alone is used, and then only after the system has been properly tuned. This is because it is generally easier to tune a CICS system before priorities are introduced.

The CICS task chain or list is not in physical sequence. Forward and backward address pointers are used between adjacent tasks. Therefore, the insertion of the new task will merely result in adjacent tasks having address pointers adjusted to include the additional task. During a dispatch cycle Task Control starts at the top of the task chain and examines each task to determine whether the task is ready to process. Therefore, a task's priority is significant. Higher-priority tasks are examined more often than lower-priority ones.

Within the same priority CICS treats tasks on a First-In-First-Out (FIFO) basis. Figure 2-1 illustrates the addition of a task with a priority of 10 to the task list. Since a task with that priority is already present, CICS places the new task after it but before the next task, which has a priority of 6. From this example we can see that if we desire a FIFO system this can easily be accomplished by giving all elements the same (or no) priority. All tasks are then treated on a first-in-first-out basis.

The operator ID can and should be a unique value assigned to each operator. This value is quite useful in the creation of audit trails, which are critical in a system that allows resource modification online. Normally an audit trail record is created for each modification to an online resource such as a file or data base. An audit trail contains information indicating the nature of the change. It is normally desirable to save the date and time of the change as well as the name of the terminal (TERMID), the transaction identifier, and the ID of the operator who was signed on to the terminal. The date, time, terminal ID, and transaction identifier are readily available to each task. The operator ID can be requested using an ASSIGN command. Many CICS systems support processing in different

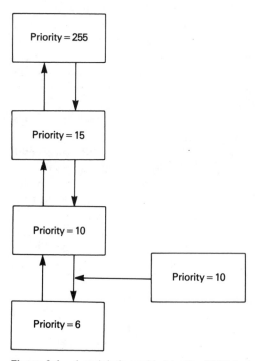

Figure 2-1. A task being added to the CICS task list.

locations, and by including the above information we can pinpoint all of the particulars for any breach of security.

The Sign oN Table (SNT) can be used to request that external security be utilized. External security means that a security package such as IBM's Resource Access Control Facility (RACF) is to be used in place of CICS security. This can be requested on an individual operator basis, with some operators having CICS security and other operators having external security. Figure 2-2 illustrates a typical SNT entry. The parameters are explained below.

OPNAME is the name by which CICS knows the operator. This name may be up to 20 characters in length, and should be unique in the table. During sign on processing the Sign oN Table (SNT) is searched on the basis of operator's name.

OPIDENT is an internal three-character ID assigned to the terminal operator. This value should be unique for audit control purposes. The operator's ID is reported when there is a breach of security. Additionally, application programs can request the operator ID during processing, and this information should be saved in audit trails.

PASSWRD is the password associated with the operator. The password can be up to eight characters in length. The longer the password, the less likelihood there is that someone will be able to guess a password and sign on with another's identity. Therefore, in a production environment the full eight-character password should be utilized.

OPPRTY is the operator priority, which may be from 0 to 255 and is one of three priority values used in the calculation of priority for any requests entered by the operator.

SCTYKEY is the security key associated with the operator. Multiple values may be coded; valid values are from 1 to 64. Each transaction defined in the PCT can have a transaction security level. When an operator enters a transaction identifier, the transaction's security level is compared against the operator's security key. If the operator's security key does not contain the value associated with the transaction, CICS recognizes an attempted security breach.

RSLKEY is the resource security key associated with the operator. Multiple values may be coded; valid values are from 1 through 24. Each resource in the system may have a resource security value associated with it. Command Level transactions can have resource security level checking defined for them. In such cases CICS checks the operator's resource security against each resource's security requirement.

```
DFHSNT TYPE=ENTRY,OPNAME='ARLENE WIPFLER',
       OPIDENT=027,PASSWRD=SCRT,OPPRTY=10,
       SCTYKEY=(1,2,3,4,5,6,7,64),
       RSLKEY=(1,2,4,12,24)
```

Figure 2-2. A typical Sign oN Table entry.

2.1.2 The Sign oN Program

Sign on processing is handled by the CICS Sign oN Program. Sign on is accomplished utilizing the CICS system transaction "CSSN." In MVS systems either "CSSN" or a newer "CESN" transaction may be used. "CSSN" uses the operator name and password for sign on processing. "CESN," in contrast, uses the eight-character USERID and password.

2.2 THE TERMINAL CONTROL FACILITY

The Terminal Control Facility is in many ways the most complex and variable facility in CICS. This is a result of the fact that different telecommunications access methods can be used. The three major IBM telecommunications access methods are the *Basic Telecommunications Access Method* (BTAM), *TeleCommunications Access Method* (TCAM), and *Virtual Telecommunications Access Method* (VTAM). CICS can use any of these access methods, and the exact functions performed by CICS differ on the basis of the access method employed. CICS also supports the *Graphics Access Method* (GAM), but its use is not as common as the other access methods listed above.

2.2.1 The Terminal Control Table (TCT)

The Terminal Control Table contains the information that the CICS Terminal Control Facility needs in order to support the communications between CICS application programs and terminals in the network. This information varies based upon the access methods utilized. It is typical for a single access method to be used in a CICS system, but in some cases more than one communications access method can be utilized. Use of multiple access methods may affect performance.

In a BTAM environment the information defined in the Terminal Control Table includes a complete network definition, that is, each of the communications lines and the terminals that are accessible via the respective lines are defined. This is because in a BTAM environment the CICS Terminal Control Facility actually manages the network. BTAM is a low-level type of access method that requires CICS to assume network management functions.

In contrast, TCAM and VTAM provide far more service to CICS and relieve CICS of the necessity of actually managing a network. In a TCAM or VTAM environment CICS deals with an access method that owns and manages the network. CICS is an application subsystem that can use the facilities provided by the access method, and the information in the Terminal Control Table reflects the way in which CICS is to interact with the telecommunications access method employed.

Regardless of the access method, the Terminal Control Table contains entries for terminals. A sample Terminal Control Table entry for a

```
DFHTCT TYPE=TERMINAL,ACCMETH=VTAM,TRMIDNT=T001,
       TRMTYPE=3270,TRMMODL=2,TRMPRTY=1,
       TIOAL=2000,DEFSCRN=(24,80),NETNAME=N013T009,
       TRMSTAT=(TRANSCEIVE, 'OUT OF SERVICE')
```

Figure 2-3. Sample 3270 Terminal Control Table entry.

3270 terminal is shown in Fig. 2-3. TYPE and ACCMETH indicate that this is a VTAM terminal entry. The TRMIDNT provides the CICS four-character name for the terminal (TERMID). The systems programmer provides this name when the terminal's entry in the table is created. TRMTYPE and TRMMODL indicate a 3270 and model-type information, respectively. Terminal priority is defined by TRMPRTY. (As described previously, the terminal's priority is used as one of the ingredients in the calculation of priority for tasks initiated from the terminal.)

TIOAL indicates an input buffer size that is to be passed to the application program. DEFSCRN specifies that the terminal screen is 24 by 80. NETNAME defines the terminal's name within the network. TRMSTAT indicates the terminal's status. A terminal may be in or out of service during real time execution. A terminal that is out of service to CICS cannot be used for CICS processing. The status of a terminal may be changed dynamically while CICS is running using the Master Terminal Facility. There are two CICS system transactions for the Master Terminal Facility, "CSMT" and "CEMT." Either of these transactions can be used to place terminals in or out of service.

"CSMT" is an older transaction, and is more difficult to use because it requires the entry of appropriate syntax and correct spelling of keywords. "CEMT" is far easier to use because it prompts the terminal operator, displays lists of choices available, and allows full screen operation. Because "CEMT" uses the full screen capability for its displays, its use presupposes a video terminal such as the IBM 3270 display station. "CEMT" also utilizes the Program Function (PF) keys of the 3270. For example, PF keys can be used to page through a display of CICS resources. The only "difficult" thing about using "CEMT" is remembering how to exit from this function: it is necessary to press PF3 or PF15 and then clear the screen.

The Master Terminal Facility is an extremely useful and important part of CICS because it allows the status of nearly all of the system's resources to be altered during real time operation. As such, we will be talking about the Master Terminal in conjunction with other aspects of CICS.

2.2.2 Terminal Control Programs

The terminal control programs use the Terminal Control Table as a definition of the CICS network, and these programs are generated in accordance with the telecommunications access method being used. Regardless of the access method, terminal management and that which has to be done in support of terminal interaction are, by and large, transparent to the application programmer under CICS. Conversions from one telecommunications access method to another *normally* do not involve application program changes. The systems programmer has to regenerate the Terminal Control Programs and the Terminal Control Table but, since the interface is within CICS, application programs are not usually affected.

2.3 TASK MANAGEMENT

CICS task management is handled by the *tasK Control Program* (KCP) using the Program Control Table as a complete definition of any application transactions that are to be processed under CICS. Certain CICS system transactions, such as the master terminal transactions or the "CECI" transaction, are also defined in the Program Control Table. Task Control is responsible for initiating tasks, terminating tasks when complete, and managing task execution.

In the previous chapter we touched upon the fact that multitasking is important to CICS's ability to manage a large network of terminals and still provide good response time. However, multitasking requires a number of control measures to ensure that there is never a loss of data integrity. Allowing multiple tasks to execute and share resources within a single region is rather like opening a Pandora's box. Task Control, however, not only provides multitasking but also addresses these potential problems.

2.3.1 The Program Control Table (PCT)

The Program Control Table (PCT) contains an entry for each transaction identifier that CICS can recognize and process. The information in each Program Control Table entry includes everything that CICS needs to know about the transaction, namely transaction security and priority requirements, the name of the first program that processes the transaction, transaction status, and a specification of whether dynamic recovery is required.

CICS security and priority were discussed in the section dealing with the Sign oN Table, and we will not review them again. The name of the first program that processes a transaction is defined in the Program Control Table so that CICS knows which program to invoke. The Program Control Table thus enables task management to translate a transaction identifier or request code into the name of a program that services the request. Linkage to subsequent programs can be accomplished by CICS commands that pass control between application programs. Common subroutines can be developed and invoked from different application programs using these commands. Such interprogram linkage, however, requires application code because CICS is only aware of the first application program associated with each transaction identifier.

A transaction's status reflects whether the TRANSID is enabled or disabled. A disabled transaction cannot be performed. A terminal user who enters a TRANSID that is disabled receives a message to that effect from CICS. Using the master terminal transactions "CEMT" or "CSMT," a transaction's status can be altered dynamically.

The Program Control Table entry also indicates whether *Dynamic Transaction Backout* (DTB) is to be used for a transaction. Dynamic Transaction Backout is applicable to transactions that update two or more protected resources. Consider the online shipping transaction discussed earlier. This transaction updates an order image file to reflect the completion of order processing. The inventory file is also updated to indicate decreased inventory and perhaps an inventory replenishment file is likewise updated. During the execution of this transaction, a program check or other abnormal termination could result in file problems. If abnormal termination occurs after the order image file is updated but before the other file updates are complete, our files are no longer in synchronization. Either all of the work of this transaction must complete successfully or we need to reverse or backout any updates. The CICS Recovery/Restart subsystem accomplishes this type of backout after a system crash. However, in this instance a single task fails but the system remains up.

Dynamic Transaction Backout can be used to accomplish individual task backout, and no application code is required. Dynamic Transaction Backout is to a single task what the Recovery/Restart Subsystem is to the entire system. Both DTB and Recovery/Restart work solely when resource recovery is explicitly requested. A resource for which CICS recovery is requested is termed a *protected resource*. A protected resource *must* be defined as such, and not all resources can be protected. An example of a protected resource is a file for which recovery is requested in CICS's File Control Table.

If DTB=YES is specified in the Program Control Table entry for a transaction, then CICS builds a task-unique dynamic storage log for each invocation of the TRANSID. This log is actually allocated when the task first updates a protected resource. "Before update" information is saved in this task-unique memory log; if a task failure occurs CICS performs the appropriate backout.

The shipping transaction is an obvious candidate for Dynamic Transaction Backout. In this case we must request "DTB=YES" in the transaction's Program Control Table entry. Additionally, the three files must be defined as protected resources in the File Control Table. Assuming that the table entries have been properly defined, a shipping transaction failure would result in a reversal of task updates to protected files. Our files would thus remain in synchronization and not reflect any incomplete updating done by a failed unit of work. A note of caution should be injected here: if

DFHPCT TYPE=ENTRY,TRANSID=XI01,TRANSEC=8,
        PROGRAM=XI01P01,TRNPRTY=10,DTB=YES,RSLC=NO

Figure 2-4.   A sample PCT entry for a transaction.

one of our files were not defined as a protected resource, CICS would NOT perform backout for it. CICS performs backout only for protected files. Figure 2-4 illustrates a sample Program Control Table entry.

TRANSID is the one- to four-character transaction identifier that CICS is to recognize. Only transactions defined in the PCT can be used in CICS systems.

TRANSEC is the level of security associated with the transaction. The value is checked during task initiation to ascertain that the terminal operator should be allowed to perform the transaction. The value may be from 1 to 64.

PROGRAM names the first program that processes the transaction. Since the program name is associated with the TRANSID, CICS is able to pass control to the appropriate application program. In the above table entry there is an attempt to relate the TRANSID (XI01) and program name (XI01P01). This standardization is helpful in keeping track of the association between transactions and programs. However, this is by no means required by CICS. TRNPRTY defines the priority associated with this TRANSID. DTB specifies whether the Dynamic Transaction Backout facility is to be used on behalf of this transaction. We have specified "DTB=YES" for this TRANSID; therefore, if the transaction abnormally terminates, CICS will back out any modifications to protected resources done by the abending task.

RSLC defines whether resource security level checking is to be used for a TRANSID. During transaction initiation CICS checks the transaction security against the operator's security key; if transaction security is valid, a task can be initiated. As resources are accessed during task execution, CICS checks the resource security level associated with accessed resources against the operator's resource security key if RSLC=YES is coded. This is applicable to command level transactions only.

2.3.2   Task Control Program

The tasK Control Program (KCP) is the effective supervisor of the CICS region and provides multitasking within CICS. However, there is more to multitasking than maintaining a list of tasks in the region and passing control to the one with the highest priority that is ready to process. In a multitasking region there are a large number of dangerous situations that can occur unless proper preventive measures are taken. For example, if two tasks were allowed to update a resource at the same time, a loss of data integrity could result. Many other complications could result from the transaction-driven nature of the online system. The exact task mix in a CICS system is an outcome of the transactions entered by terminal operators; we cannot predict exactly which tasks will be present together in the system at any given time. Tasks have to share resources, and these resources are ultimately finite. Resource-related problems could have dire consequences if left uncontrolled. Task Control addresses all of the potential problems incurred as a result of multitasking. Task Control consists of two functional areas: the task dispatcher that performs CICS multitasking, and the application service processor that allows resources to be reserved or enqueued on behalf of a single updating task.

2.3.3 Task Control as Application Service Processor

Task Control permits a resource to be exclusively reserved for a task that is modifying it. Resource reservation means that no other task may have update access to the resource. After the owning task accomplishes its modification, the reservation is removed and the resource is then available for update processing by another task in the system. Thus, when required, Task Control can be used to make shared resources serially reusable. A serially reusable resource is one that can be shared by many tasks but which can be used for modification purposes by only one task at a time.

2.3.4 The Dispatcher

The dispatcher maintains a prioritized list or chain of tasks within CICS, and performs task switches to enable multiple tasks to process concurrently. Tasks are examined in priority sequence, and the first or highest priority task that is not waiting for something is selected to execute. When this task encounters a situation that causes it to wait, the dispatcher reexamines the task chain and dispatches another task. Situations that may cause task waits include file I/O. Time is required for file information to be transferred from a peripheral device into memory, and CICS assumes that the requested data are needed before the task can continue processing. Only one task can process at any given moment if there is only one CPU, but CICS provides multitasking by using I/O wait time to interleave task processing.

Once a task has been dispatched, CICS normally does not interrupt its execution. A task is passed control and allowed to execute until it requires a CICS service. CICS is an interface to all system resources; it owns or controls access to almost everything. Therefore, application tasks are constantly returning control to CICS. The type of multitasking done by CICS is called noninterrupt-driven multitasking. For example, CICS dispatches a task that has a priority of 10. During that task's execution an event completes for which a higher-priority task is waiting. CICS does not interrupt the lower-priority task's execution; the executing task continues to process until it requires an online service. The task invokes CICS requesting the service. CICS initiates the request, places the task into a wait state, and passes control to the dispatcher. The dispatcher finds the highest priority task that is then ready to process and performs a task switch.

There is, however, a danger inherent in this type of multitasking, because a task that executes in an enclosed program loop could conceivably not return control to CICS. This looping task would in effect be a runaway task, and the continued execution of such a task would impair CICS's ability to provide a safe multitasking environment. As a matter of fact such a task would execute to the exclusion of CICS and all other application tasks. The system would appear to be up and running from the vantage point of CPU utilization, but there would be no terminal responses. The system would appear to be locked out.

In order to prevent this situation, CICS uses a *Runaway Task Interval* to limit task processing time. The systems programmer defines the "Runaway Task Interval" in a CICS table called the System Initialization Table (SIT), but the value can be changed during real time execution using either of the Master Terminal transactions. When entering a dispatch cycle, the dispatcher sets the runaway interval. If a dispatched task executes beyond the runaway interval, it is interrupted and flushed from the system. A message is sent to the appropriate terminal indicating the abnormal termination, and a unique abend code of "AICA" is included to indicate the reason for the task termination.

Although CICS performs noninterrupt-driven multitasking, this is not the case with the host operating system. Multiple regions or partitions are controlled by the operating system, and a priority is associated with each region. The operating system always favors higher-priority regions/ partitions. If a region with lower priority is executing and an event completes for a higher-priority one, the operating system interrupts the execution of the lower-priority region and allows the higher-priority one to process. If we are running a telecommunications access method such as VTAM in one region, production CICS in a second, and production batch in a third, the relative priority of CICS is very significant to online system performance. The VTAM region is not considered an application region since it is performing network management. As such, VTAM would have the highest priority in the system. However, the CICS and batch regions are application regions, and in determining their relative priority CICS should be favored.

Running CICS as the highest-priority application in the system ensures that CICS effectively utilizes all of the CPU resources required to service terminal operator requests and provide good response time. When there are no application tasks that are ready to process within the CICS region and there is no internal work for CICS, Task Control returns control to the host operating system. The operating system can then allow lower-priority regions or partitions to process. During the execution of a lower-priority region, CICS waits until an event occurs that causes it to be reinvoked. Such an event might be an input from any of the CICS terminals.

The systems programmer can define a time value that limits the interval for which CICS passes control back to the operating system. This value is known as the partition or region exit time and is defined in the *System Initialization Table* (SIT). The purpose of this value is to keep CICS from being paged out during periods of network inactivity. CICS can be page fixed or the region exit time can be used to cause the operating system to reinvoke CICS periodically. Reinvoking CICS keeps the most important parts of the system resident in memory. When a transaction is ultimately entered, CICS system response will not be slowed down by an extensive amount of paging. The partition/region exit time is particularly applicable to CICS systems with small networks and intermittent activity. In these circumstances there could be long periods of time between reinvocations of CICS to process terminal input.

Tasks are allowed into the CICS system up to a defined limit. This limit is referred to as the maximum task value, and is defined by the systems programmer in the System Initialization Table. This value affects performance. All active tasks must share the resources of the system. If the maximum task value is greater than the system can accommodate, too many tasks compete for the finite resources of the system. Resource-related problems, such as excessive Virtual Storage paging or extensive file waits, could adversely affect response time. On the other hand, a maximum task value smaller than that which can be efficiently supported results in underutilization of the online region. Fewer tasks than the system can support are allowed to execute, and during periods of peak system usage response time could suffer. Quite simply, terminal inputs could queue up waiting for task initiation. The maximum task limit is one of the values that is tuned by the systems programmer. This value is altered until an ideal level is reached. Maximum efficient use of the system is the goal. The maximum task value can be altered dynamically using the Master Terminal Facility.

Actually, there are two separate maximum task values. The first limits the number of tasks that can be in the system. This is a high watermark for the region, and is known as "MXT." Additionally, a maximum task value can be used to limit the number of tasks that are to be examined by the dispatcher during a dispatch cycle. This means that active tasks within the region are given more of an opportunity to process because the CPU resources are shared among a subset of dispatchable tasks. This is beneficial in several ways. First, tasks are in and out quickly, freeing up resources for other tasks in the system. Second, by limiting the number of tasks that can execute, paging becomes less of a problem than if every task were given an equal opportunity at execution. This second value is called "AMXT."

The purpose of favoring high-priority active tasks is to enable them to complete processing quickly and be terminated. Ideally the CICS system should be like a revolving door for tasks. The more tasks that CICS has to manage, the more overhead there is just for the system to handle a large number of tasks. As the number of tasks increases, so do the overhead and the likelihood of resource-related problems.

In addition to the maximum task values that are described above, CICS allows specific transactions to be limited. Let's say that we have a transaction that is particularly resource sensitive. If we allow too many of these transactions into the system at one time, resources may become too tight for efficient execution. Therefore, we want to ensure that only a certain number are allowed into the system at one time.

We define the transaction as having a unique class. This is done in the Program Control Table using a TCLASS parameter. The System Initialization Table parameter "CMXT" can specify limits for up to ten classes of tasks. There are ten positional values of CMXT, and each corresponds to a limit for transaction classes from 1 to 10, respectively. As an example, a resource-sensitive transaction might be defined as being a TCLASS=3. To limit Class 3 tasks to two (meaning that only two of this class of task would be allowed into the system concurrently), we would specify CMXT=(4,6,2,,9,,8,8,4,2) in the System Initialization Table. The third positional value of CMXT is 2, and therefore this serves as a limitation for the number of Class 3 tasks. The same TCLASS can be specified for multiple TRANSIDs. If multiple transactions use the same resources, we are able to limit the total number of tasks using specific resources even across different TRANSIDs. This can be helpful in heading off system problems that result from having many tasks waiting for resources.

In a transaction-driven system such as CICS, it is possible for the work load to be such that tasks in the system cannot execute because they require resources owned by other tasks. A task deadlock situation could result. Depending on the number of deadlocked tasks, it is conceivable for the entire system to stall. A system stall means that the dispatcher runs its chain of tasks and finds nobody ready to process. During a stall system resources are spread very thin or they are exhausted. The probability of recovery without taking some kind of corrective action is nil. If this were allowed to continue indefinitely nothing would get done, and as a consequence CICS is prepared to perform triage.

The systems programmer defines a stall interval in the System Initialization Table. CICS keeps track of how long it has been since an application task could be dispatched; when that length of time exceeds the stall interval CICS takes recovery measures that may include purging one or more tasks. Thus, when caught in a desperate stall situation, CICS is prepared to kill individual tasks so that the system can recover. Not all transactions, however, can be purged. When creating a Program Control Table entry for a transaction, the systems programmer defines whether it is a candidate for a stall purge. Only transactions that are defined in the table as being stall purgeable are killed by CICS.

2.4 PROGRAM MANAGEMENT

The CICS Program Control Facility consists of the Program Control Program and the Processing Program Table. The Program Control Facility manages the use of application programs by fetching required programs into storage when needed, monitoring program use, and providing a mechanism for passing control between application programs during task execution.

2.4.1 Processing Program Table (PPT)

The Processing Program Table contains an entry for each program that is to be loaded into the CICS region or executed under CICS. The systems programmer specifies the program's name, programming language, resource security level, and residency requirements. It is important that the correct programming language be specified because CICS uses different interfaces to assembler language programs than it does to high-level language programs. The resource security level is a value from 1 to 24 used to limit the operator's use of the program through resource security level checking (described above).

A program's residency status indicates whether the program is to be permanently resident or nonresident. A resident program has storage set aside for it during system initialization, and is kept permanently resident once loaded into memory. A program is actually loaded when it is first used during real time execution. A nonresident program does not have storage allocated during system initialization. Nonresident programs are loaded when needed and may be released from storage when CICS detects that it is running short of storage.

Figure 2-5 is a sample program entry in the Processing Program Table. PROGRAM provides the name of the load module in the CICS program library or core image library (DOS). RES=YES specifies that this is to be a permanently resident program; RES=NO indicates that the program is to be nonresident. PGMLANG specifies that this is a COBOL program, as opposed to assembler language or PL/I. In DOS entry-level systems RPG may also be used.

In addition to the information defined by the systems programmer in the Processing Program Table, there is also information dynamically obtained by CICS. CICS ascertains the program's size and disk location

```
DFHPPT TYPE=ENTRY,PROGRAM=XI01P01,RES=YES,
       PGMLANG=COBOL
```

Figure 2-5. A sample processing program table entry.

during system initialization. The size is needed so that CICS knows how much storage to allocate when a program is to be loaded. The program's disk location is a TTR (Track, Track, Record) address within the CICS Relocatable Program Library.

In MVS systems the relocatable library is a partitioned data set with the DDNAME of DFHRPL. The CICS job stream must contain a DD statement named DFHRPL. DFHRPL may be concatenated to encompass several disk libraries. All application programs must reside within DFHRPL. During system initialization CICS reads the directory of DFHRPL and obtains size and location information about all of the programs defined in the Processing Program Table. The BLDL macro is used for this purpose. By having all program disk locations determined prior to real time processing, CICS cuts down on search time when a program is needed. The Processing Program Table also contains storage addresses of modules that are resident within CICS main storage, and thereby serves as a kind of link list enabling CICS to keep track of the locations of numerous application programs.

2.4.2 Program Control Program

Application program use is managed by the CICS Program Control Program. Program Control loads programs into memory when they are needed for online processing, and also provides mechanisms for passing control between programs. A TRANSID tells CICS which application program is required to process a user's request. However, the TRANSID only takes us to the program that is to begin transaction processing. In many cases this will be the only module to process the request. However, it is sometimes desirable to invoke a subsequent program. Program Control provides two mechanisms that can be used to pass control between application programs. The first, a transfer of control, passes control to a module without an implied return to the caller. The second, a link, branches to a program with an implied return. When the linked to module completes processing, CICS returns control to the calling program at the next instruction after the link request. Use of link and transfer of control allow application designers to functionalize CICS applications so that commonly used code can be placed in submodules and invoked from two or more application programs. Redundant application code can thereby be avoided. However, a note of caution should be mentioned. Linking and transferring between application programs do involve system overhead, and modularization should be approached wisely. There should be a real functional reason for building a subroutine, and the subroutine should embody a fair amount of processing.

Only one copy of a program is kept in storage, and many tasks may execute concurrently in an application program. The advantage of this is obviously the conservation of storage, which does not have to be filled with redundant copies of application programs. If 20 operators in a customer service department enter the same TRANSID to do customer service inquiries, there will be 20 tasks in the system but they will all be executing in the same copy of the application program. This concept is called multithreading. Figure 2-6 illustrates multithreading.

Figure 2-6. Illustrating the concept of multithreading.

Application Program

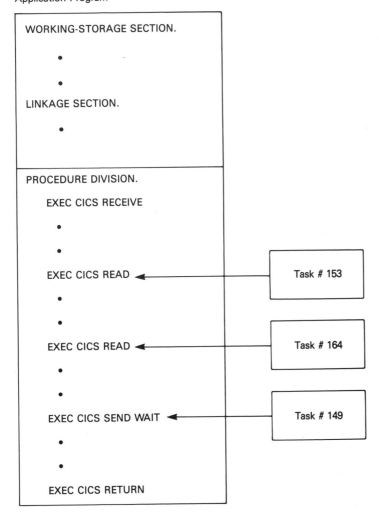

There are three tasks depicted executing in this CICS Command Level application program. Multithreading requires that CICS application programs be reentrant or serially reusable.

Multithreading requires that a program be reentrant or serially reusable. This means that a CICS application program must not permanently alter instructions or data within itself. For example, it would be necessary for a CICS COBOL program not to use the Working-Storage Section contained within the load module itself. There are two application programming interfaces to CICS: Command Level and Macro Level. Program reusability is handled differently in each interface. For high-level language programs using the Command Level interface, reusability is assured. This is because a task-unique work area is acquired by CICS. The Command Level COBOL program has Data Division storage acquired on a dynamic basis so that each task has its own dynamic Working Storage acquired on a task by program basis. In COBOL internal pointers or registers called Base Locators are used to address Working Storage. The COBOL Base Locator cells are set so that it appears to the executing task that it is utilizing the load module's Working Storage and Data Division, but in reality each task is using its own dynamic copy of the Data Division. Therefore, what the tasks are really sharing is the Procedure Division. This concept is illustrated in Fig. 2-7.

Figure 2-7.   Dynamically acquired Task Storage for Command Level CICS tasks.

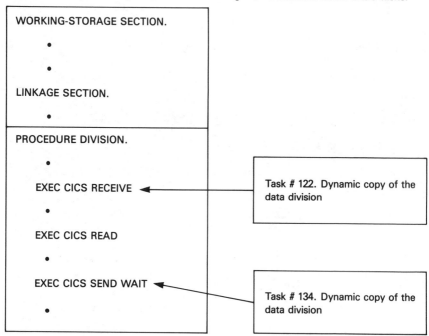

Each Command Level task that executes in a CICS program has its own dynamic copy of the Data Division. Therefore, modifiable data can be saved in Working Storage without affecting the program's reusability. The load module's Data Division is not used by any task. The Procedure Division is the only part of the program that is actually shared.

In terms of coding a CICS Command Level COBOL program, there is no need to be cognizant of the fact that the load module's Working Storage is not being utilized. However, when debugging a CICS transaction dump, the load module's Working Storage will not contain any pertinent task data. At this point it becomes necessary to be aware of the dynamically acquired copy of the COBOL Data Division. Register 6 points to the task-unique Working Storage.

Command Level PL/I programs have a unique storage area acquired on a task-by-program basis. Likewise, Command Level assembler programs have dynamic DSECT storage acquired by CICS. Command Level assembler modules should save modifiable data fields in this dynamic DSECT area. It is mandatory that the contents of altered data fields within the body of an assembler language program (within the CSECT) be restored prior to issuing a CICS command.

Since CICS normally does not interrupt task execution, the program will be refreshed before CICS permits another task to execute in the module. It is best, however, not to place modifiable data fields within the CSECT of an assembler language Command Level Program, because if the task is interrupted as a runaway task the program might not be refreshed. **A program that alters itself (data or instructions within the load module) but resets such altered fields prior to invoking CICS is termed a serially reusable or quasi-reentrant program. A reentrant program is one that changes nothing within the load module during execution.**

For Macro Level CICS programs, the programmer must take special precautions to code programs so that they will be serially reusable or reentrant. As mentioned previously, Command Level programs have a dynamic work area acquired on a task-by-program basis. This is not true of Macro Level programs. Working Storage or any data fields defined within Macro Level programs are part of the load module, and there is no dynamic Working Storage acquired for separate tasks. There is only one copy of such storage regardless of the number of tasks multithreading within the program. Therefore, in Macro Level programs storage within the load module, such as the COBOL Working Storage, must be used for read only data constants.

Variable data fields for Macro Level programs must be kept in a special CICS area called a *Transaction Work Area* (TWA). The Transaction Work Area is a user appendage of the *Task Control Area* (TCA), the control block that CICS uses to control a task's execution. There is one TCA for every task in the system regardless of the fact that two or more tasks may be sharing an application program. Since there is a Task Control Area for each task, there is also a TWA for each task if requested. The size of a required TWA is defined in a transaction's Program Control Table entry. Typically, Command Level programs do not use the TWA, so none is requested for TRANSIDs associated with Command Level programs. Command Level programs use their dynamic storage instead. Since there is

Figure 2-8. Use of the Transaction Work Area in Macro Level.

Macro Level Application Program

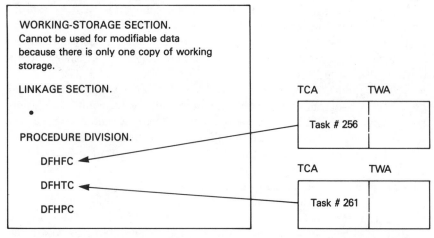

There is only a single copy of Working Storage for Macro Level programs, and therefore it is used for read only data. Task-unique data can be kept in the Transaction Work Area, which is a user appendage of the Task Control Area or the main control block governing a task's execution under CICS. The TWA size is defined in the Program Control Table transaction entry.

no dynamic storage for Macro Level programs, they utilize the Transaction Work Area. TRANSIDs associated with Macro Level programs typically have a TWA size defined in their Program Control Table entries. Since there is a Transaction Work Area for each executing Macro Level task, modifying data within the TWA does not affect the reusability of a Macro Level program. Figure 2-8 illustrates the use of the Transaction Work Area in a Macro Level program.

Multiple tasks may share a CICS application program; for a nonresident program it is imperative that CICS not release it from storage unless the module is not currently in use. Program Control monitors task execution within CICS programs and keeps a count of tasks utilizing each program. This "resident use count" is kept in the program's Processing Program Table entry. When a task starts, CICS increments the resident use count of the program used by the task. As a task terminates, CICS decrements the resident use count. Nonresident modules are released from memory when CICS is short of storage, but only if the program is not currently in use as reflected by the program's resident use count.

REVIEW EXERCISE

Provide a short answer to each of the questions below.

1. What is defined in the Sign oN Table (SNT)?
2. What does CICS do when a security violation is detected?

3. An operator's security key contains the following values: 1,2,4,8,22, 36,58,64. The following list of transactions are defined in the Program Control Table (PCT). Next to each TRANSID is its security level. Next to each TRANSID place an "A" if the operator would be allowed to perform the transaction, or a "V" if the transaction would result in a security violation.

_____ WY01,8	_____ AAMP,9	_____ XI01,36
_____ WY02,37	_____ JJMP,7	_____ XI02,19
_____ WY03,23	_____ YYMP,11	_____ XI03,46
_____ WY04,2	_____ WEMP,7	_____ XI04,10
_____ WY05,4	_____ WOMP,4	_____ XI05,22
_____ WY06,60	_____ AA01,3	_____ XI06,58

4. How is a task's priority determined in CICS? What are the values that go into the priority calculation?

5. In a CICS environment where BTAM is used as the telecommunications access method, CICS Terminal Control manages the network. In a system utilizing TCAM or VTAM, the access method runs in its own region and relieves CICS of network management. Does this mean that a conversion of telecommunications access method from BTAM to TCAM or VTAM will result in changing application programs?

6. There are two master terminal transactions: CEMT and CSMT. What are the differences between them?

7. How does one terminate the use of CEMT?

8. What are the two major areas of CICS Task Control?

9. What is the Runaway Task Interval used for in CICS? If a task times out because of the Runaway Task Interval, is there an indication provided to the terminal operator?

10. How does CICS relate a TRANSID entered by a terminal operator to the appropriate application program that actually performs the transaction?

11. What is Dynamic Transaction Backout?

12. What is the partition/region exit time? In what way is this useful to CICS?

13. What is meant by enqueuing or reserving a resource? Why is this capability important for a CICS system in which resources such as files are being modified online?

14. What is the stall interval, and what does it address?

15. What is the maximum task value?

16. What is the difference between resident and nonresident application programs?

17. What is the CICS Relocatable Program Library?

18. Are there facilities under CICS that permit control to be passed between application programs? If so, cite two ways to accomplish this and specify how they differ.

ANSWERS TO REVIEW EXERCISE

Provide a short answer to each of the questions below.

1. What is defined in the Sign oN Table (SNT)?

    The Sign oN Table defines the terminal operators or users who will be allowed to sign on to the CICS system. Operator security and priority information are included in the information defined in the Sign oN Table.

2. What does CICS do when a security violation is detected?

    When a security violation is detected, CICS terminates the task. A message is sent to the terminal operator and an indication of the attempted breach is saved. When CICS is shut down, any attempted security breaches are noted.

3. An operator's security key contains the following values: 1,2,4,8,22, 36,58,64. The following list of transactions are defined in the Program Control Table (PCT). Next to each TRANSID is its security level. Next to each TRANSID place an "A" if the operator would be allowed to perform the transaction or a "V" if the transaction would result in a security violation.

A	WY01,8	V	AAMP,9	A	XI01,36
V	WY02,37	V	JJMP,7	V	XI02,19
V	WY03,23	V	YYMP,11	V	XI03,46
A	WY04,2	V	WEMP,7	V	XI04,10
A	WY05,4	A	WOMP,4	A	XI05,22
V	WY06,60	V	AA01,3	A	XI06,58

4. How is a task's priority determined in CICS? What are the values that go into the priority calculation?

    A task's priority is determined by adding together the priorities defined for the operator in the Sign oN Table, the terminal in the Terminal Control Table, and the transaction identifier in the Program Control Table.

5. In a CICS environment where BTAM is used as the telecommunications access method, CICS Terminal Control manages the network. In a system utilizing TCAM or VTAM, the access method runs in its own region and relieves CICS of network management. Does this mean that a conversion of telecommunications access method from BTAM to TCAM or VTAM will result in changing application programs?

    Normally there will be no required changes to CICS application programs because the interface to the telecommunications access method is within CICS. The systems programmer will, however, have to change Terminal Control.

6. There are two master terminal transactions: CEMT and CSMT. What are the differences between them?

   CEMT is the newer of the two master terminal transactions, and is far easier to use. CSMT requires the use of exactly spelled keywords, whereas CEMT prompts the user and provides full screen displays.

7. How does one terminate the use of CEMT?

   CEMT is terminated by pressing PF3/PF15 and clearing the screen.

8. What are the two major areas of CICS Task Control?

   Task Control consists of the dispatcher, which handles CICS multitasking, and the application request processor, which handles requests for resource serialization.

9. What is the Runaway Task Interval used for in CICS? If a task times out because of the Runaway Task Interval, is there an indication provided to the terminal operator?

   The Runaway Task Interval is a time limit placed upon application task execution. If a task exceeds this limit it is purged from the system or timed out. When a task is timed out, a message including an abend code is sent to the terminal operator.

10. How does CICS relate a TRANSID entered by a terminal operator to the appropriate application program that actually performs the transaction?

    CICS looks in the Program Control Table, which defines each of the TRANSIDs that can be utilized. In the TRANSID's table definition the application program is named.

11. What is Dynamic Transaction Backout?

    Dynamic Transaction Backout (DTB) is a CICS facility that provides recovery for a failing application task. If the TRANSID is defined as requiring DTB and there is a task abend, CICS will back out changes to protected resources such as files defined as requiring recovery.

12. What is the partition/region exit time? In what way is this useful to CICS?

    The partition/region exit time defines the maximum amount of time for which CICS will pass control back to the operating system when there is no work for CICS to perform. In CICS systems with small networks and light volume this keeps CICS from being paged out during periods of inactivity.

13. What is meant by enqueuing or reserving a resource? Why is this capability important for a CICS system in which resources such as files are being modified online?

    Enqueuing or reserving a resource means that the resource is held exclusively for a specific task. In CICS systems multiple tasks may attempt to update a resource at the same time. If this were permitted a loss of data integrity could ensue. Therefore, CICS provides a resource reservation mechanism so that shared resources can be held by a single updating task.

14. What is the stall interval, and what does it address?

    The stall interval is a limit CICS uses to determine whether the system is deadlocked. Many tasks can simultaneously attempt to use finite system resources; if tasks have to wait for resource availability, the system as a whole could become bogged down with nonexecutable tasks. When the stall interval indicates that the system is stalled, CICS takes emergency action and attempts to kill stall purgeable tasks.

15. What is the maximum task value?

    The maximum task value is a high watermark for the number of tasks that CICS can accept into the system. This is used to prevent CICS from accepting more tasks than can be processed with the resources allocated for the system.

16. What is the difference between resident and nonresident application programs?

    A resident application program is one that is not normally released from storage during CICS execution. Storage is set aside for resident programs during system initialization, and they are loaded when first used. After being loaded into CICS, resident programs are not released. Nonresident programs can be released from storage if CICS needs the storage and the program is not then in use. Storage for nonresident programs is acquired when the program is needed, and must therefore be loaded.

17. What is the CICS Relocatable Program Library?

    The Relocatable Program Library is the load library that contains any programs which are to be used during CICS execution. In DOS systems this is the Core Image Library. In MVS a DD statement named DFHRPL in the CICS job stream identifies this load library.

18. Are there facilities under CICS that permit control to be passed between application programs? If so cite two ways to accomplish this and specify how they differ.

Program Control supports two mechanisms for passing control between CICS application programs. The first, a link request, passes control to a module with an implied return to the linking program. The second, a transfer of control, branches to another program without implying a return to the invoking module.

chapter 3

More Concepts and Facilities

In this chapter we will continue our examination of CICS and discuss its other facilities. Again, the reader is advised that the material contained in this chapter, while helpful, is not required for application programming.

3.1 TRANSACTION VS. PROGRAM VS. TASK

In the previous chapter we discussed the CICS Program Control Facility and used the terms TRANSACTION, PROGRAM, and TASK. At this point it is necessary to formally define these three terms. It is very important that these concepts be understood because there are significant differences between these entities in comparison with the batch environment.

3.1.1 Transaction

A transaction is a service request that can be made from any user terminal in CICS's network. The transaction is represented within CICS by a Transaction Identifier or TRANSID, and the TRANSID can be utilized to request a particular service or function. In this sense a transaction is really conceptual, in that it defines a potential service that can be requested of the online system by any system user. However, before any particular transaction can be performed one or more application programs must be coded. The program(s) actually contain(s) the instructions or code detailing the processes to be performed to accomplish the work of the transaction.

3.1.2 Program

A CICS application program is written to detail how to perform a transaction. As such, a program is a body of executable code that potentially can be used to specify the processes that have to be accomplished in order for a transaction to be processed in the CICS system. The word "potentially" is used to point out the fact that the program is invoked when the transaction code or TRANSID is entered by a terminal operator. A transaction or function becomes available to system users when the program is placed into production and the appropriate CICS table updates have been performed.

In batch, a program is brought into memory and executed. It is thought of as a processing entity. In CICS, however, we separate the program from the executing entity. CICS programs can be viewed as dry, lifeless bodies of code. This is derived from the fact that CICS permits multiple tasks to execute concurrently in a single copy of an application program. We defined this concept of allowing multiple executing threads to process within a single copy of a program as multithreading. Multithreading in Command Level programs results in CICS acquiring a unique work area, such as a dynamic copy of a COBOL program's Data Division, for each executing thread. Therefore, the executing entity embodies more than just the program.

3.1.3 Task

The executing entity is called a task. When a user enters a TRANSID, CICS creates a unit of work called a task. Internally, a task is represented to CICS by a Task Control Area (TCA). The TCA is the main control block used by CICS to govern a task's execution and keep track of all of the resources "loaned" to the task during its processing. Each task has its own unique task number assigned by CICS. An application task executes in an application program and utilizes the dynamically acquired work area for modifiable task data. The task can thus be thought of as a combination of a CICS application program, the dynamic work areas allocated for task execution, and the CICS data areas (such as the TCA). CICS sees the world in terms of tasks. This can have implications for designing CICS transactions or functions, as we shall discuss later.

3.1.4 Summary

The relationship between a transaction, a program, and a task can be likened to the process of preparing dessert. The idea of preparing a chocolate cake for dessert is similar to the transaction. This idea is a functional capability that some people may wish to perform. However, in order to prepare a chocolate cake one needs to use a recipe. A recipe with explicitly detailed instructions can be compared to a program.

Having a recipe does not automatically result in a chocolate cake. Let's say Mrs. X has a famous recipe for chocolate cake. When she is in her kitchen using her stove and cooking equipment (her task-unique work areas) she can use her recipe to bake a chocolate cake. The same recipe can be used concurrently by other people in different kitchens, and they will all produce separate cakes. The preparation of an actual chocolate cake is the equivalent of a CICS task. A task uses the program or set of instructions and has a dynamic work area, just as Mrs. X has her famous chocolate cake recipe and works in her work area or kitchen. The task is the executing entity that results in work actually being done.

3.2 STORAGE MANAGEMENT

Dynamic storage within the CICS region is managed by the *Storage Control Program* (SCP). There is no table associated with storage management because CICS takes everything it can get. In systems using the eXtended Architecture (XA), the CICS Storage Control Program directly manages the storage up to the 16-megabyte line. (Above the 16M line Storage Control interfaces with the host operating system to obtain storage.) Storage Control uses a storage map called the Page Allocation Map (PAM) to keep track of storage up to 16M. As pages are allocated the PAM is updated to reflect the fact that the storage is currently in use; when the storage is freed the PAM is altered to indicate that the page may be reallocated.

Storage management in CICS is quite sophisticated in that different algorithms are used in storage allocation. These algorithms are implemented by having different subpools for storage allocation. This means that CICS can make storage allocations based upon how the storage is to be used and how long it is to remain allocated. There is a major difference between application task storage and work areas acquired for CICS's internal use. This type of storage management results in more efficient use of this system resource, the machinations of storage management being transparent to application programmers.

Before we discuss storage management any further, we should address how CICS comes to be in control of most of the storage within its region/partition. This occurs during the initialization of the CICS system, which is performed by a subsystem within CICS. When we wish to bring up CICS we submit a job stream in which data sets used by CICS are defined. The program named in the CICS JCL is called DFHSIP (System Initialization Program). Actually, DFHSIP is the first of several modules that process system initialization, it being a fairly complex process. Resources needed for real time processing are prepared during initialization. Dynamic storage within the CICS partition/region is one of these resources.

During system initialization an operating system GETMAIN is performed so that the system initialization subsystem can gain control of region/partition storage up to the 16M line. A small part of this storage is released back to the operating system. This storage (called OSCORE in MVS systems) is used by the operating system during its interactions with CICS. CICS does not contain its own access methods and therefore relies on the operating system for access to telecommunications and file data. In support of these interactions the operating system must have a small amount of storage within the CICS region.

System Initialization loads the individual CICS management modules into storage and creates address pointers to each module's location. This enables the separate CICS programs to communicate with each other during online execution. The various system tables are also loaded into the region, and address pointers are likewise created for each table. CICS control blocks are formatted, and storage is set aside for resident application programs. After all of the parts of CICS have been loaded or created and storage has been set aside for resident application programs the storage remaining in the region is called the Dynamic Storage Area (DSA). During real time processing this area is managed by the Storage Control Program. Storage Control manages the allocation, initialization, and de-allocation of the Dynamic Storage Area. These functions are performed in support of the various tasks that enter the CICS system during online execution.

A request for storage allocation is serviced by Storage Control as long as there is sufficient dynamic storage available. When storage is needed on behalf of an application task, Storage Control not only makes the allocation, it also constructs storage accounting areas that are used to chain all task storage together. A Task Control Area (TCA) points to the most recent storage area allocated to the task, and each separate allocation points to a previously allocated area if there is one. Thus one can follow a task's storage chain from its Task Control Area and consequently locate all of the separate pieces of storage given to a task, as depicted in Fig. 3-1. When a task completes processing and returns control to CICS for task termination, Storage Control is invoked to free the task's storage. CICS follows the task's storage chain and returns the storage to the Dynamic Storage Area.

Available storage in the Dynamic Storage Area is a CICS resource, and it would be quite conceivable for storage to become tight as the number of tasks in the system increases. There is a maximum task value, as discussed above, but it is possible to run short of storage if some tasks have extensive storage requirements. Therefore, a storage cushion is used to monitor the availability of storage within the region. The size of this storage cushion is defined by the systems programmer in the System Initialization Table (SIT). The size of the storage cushion can be altered during online processing using the Master Terminal Transactions.

The storage cushion is insurance that CICS will not run completely out of storage. This possibility would have dire implications for the region

Figure 3-1. Application Task Storage chained from a Task Control Area (TCA).

Task Control Area (TCA)

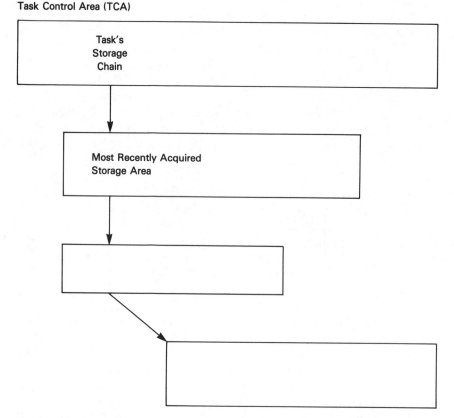

By maintaining all of the separate storage allocations given to a task on a task-unique storage chain, CICS is able to reclaim all Task Storage when the task ends.

as a whole and for all of the tasks in the system. In making storage allocations, Storage Control is mindful of the size of the cushion and of the amount of storage remaining unallocated in the region. When the available dynamic storage falls below the cushion size, CICS enters an emergency state known as a "Short on Storage" or SOS.

Actually, it's more like "Save Our System" because during an SOS no new tasks are initiated. Tasks within the system are allowed to continue processing and the storage in the cushion is used to satisfy task storage needs. New transaction requests received from terminal operators are responded to with a message indicating that the SYSTEM is UNDER STRESS. Operators are directed to wait several minutes before trying to initiate transactions again. When emergency actions and normal task completions have released enough storage to restore the cushion, Storage Control turns off the SOS indicator and CICS resumes normal processing.

3.3   DATA MANAGEMENT FACILITIES

CICS has three data management facilities: File Control, Temporary Storage, and Transient Data. File Control provides access to standard user data sets, Temporary Storage provides a dynamic scratch pad, and Transient Data is a queuing facility.

3.3.1   File Control Facility

CICS File Control Facility supports application program requests for file access *and* provides access to VSAM and BDAM data sets. The VSAM support allows Key Sequenced Data Sets (VSAM keyed files), Entry Sequenced Data Sets (VSAM sequential files), and Relative Record Data Sets (VSAM direct files) to be accessed. CICS also supports the use of VSAM Alternate Indexes. File Control supports reading, adding, deleting (where applicable to the type of data set), updating, and browsing of multiple records in sequence.

File Control, however, provides more than just data set access capability. The File Control Facility serves as a central control point for file access to ensure file sharing and data integrity in a multitasking environment. The data sets to which CICS controls access are defined in the File Control Table (FCT); the File Control Facility uses this table as a definition of the files and processing requirements for file access. CICS is responsible for opening files. This normally occurs when the first access request is made against the file. The File Control Table (FCT) can be used to request that a file be opened subsequent to system initialization before a first access request is received, but the default is for the opening to be deferred until the file is needed online. Also, a file can be opened or closed dynamically under CICS using the Master Terminal Facility.

3.3.1.1   File Control Table (FCT)   The File Control Table contains an entry for each standard OS or DOS data set for which CICS File Management is to provide access. Application programs that run under CICS do not contain file definition statements such as DCBs, DTFs, or FDs and SELECTs. Files are defined in the File Control Table and application programs gain access to file information by using CICS file access commands. The COBOL application program seeking to read a file, for example, would issue a command such as:

```
EXEC CICS READ DATASET('APPFILE')
      INTO(MY-USER-AREA)
      LENGTH(MY-REC-LEN)
      RIDFLD(MY-SEARCH-ARGUMENT)
      END-EXEC.
```

CICS interprets the data set DDNAME defined with the DATASET option as a DDNAME of a file defined in the File Control Table. In response to the preceding command, the File Control Table is searched for an entry with the appropriate DDNAME, in this case APPFILE. If an entry is located, CICS has all of the information it needs to access the file. In the CICS-run JCL there may be a DD statement for a file defined in the File Control Table. In this case the run JCL might contain the following DD statement:

//APPFILE DD DSN=MY.USER.FILE,DISP=OLD

In MVS systems, data set name and disposition information can also be defined in the file's entry in the File Control Table. If this is done there need not be a DD statement in the JCL. The advantage of naming the DSNAME and DISP in the table and not including a DD statement in the JCL is that the DSNAME and DISP can be changed by using the Master Terminal Facility or by using a SET command in a program. This permits dynamic allocation[1] of files during CICS execution. If a DD statement is included in the CICS job stream, then DSNAME and disposition information defined in the JCL takes precedence.

By centralizing file information in the File Control Table, file access is made available to all of the tasks that are running under CICS. Thus, application programmers neither have to code file definition statements or be aware of the type of data set being accessed. The information defined in the File Control Table includes the DDNAME, the data set organization, the file access information, the resource security level of the file, and the recovery requirements of the data set. Optionally the data set name and file disposition may also be defined in the file's entry. The data set organization may be VSAM or BDAM. The resource security level may be from 1 to 24, and is checked against operator resource security when resource security level checking is used.

The recoverability status of the data set defines what recovery information CICS is to save for the file. In the batch environment, a backup of modified files is made as soon as a batch system completes execution. However, we can't wait until the online system comes down to back up files modified during CICS execution. To this end, the File Control Table can be used to request that CICS journals copies of file modifications to a separate journal data set. In the event of physical destruction of the file, it is merely necessary to apply copies of file updates collected online to a backup copy of the file to be recovered. This brings our file forward to reflect online processing, so this type of recovery is called forward recovery.

---

1. Dynamic allocation allows a file to be dynamically acquired by CICS while the system is running. Without dynamic allocation it would be necessary to know in advance of CICS execution all of the files to be used during CICS processing. Since normally all of the files to be used are known in advance of bringing up CICS, dynamic allocation is the exception and not the rule. However, there may be instances when a user's request for information requires that we acquire a file not already allocated to CICS.

The type of information saved is called an afterimage, meaning that the afterimage of an updated record is journaled.

Another type of recovery is also needed. If we have a system crash, our files may have to be resynchronized to reflect only complete task processing, as discussed earlier. A task that was processing at the time of a system crash is called an inflight task, and what we want to accomplish is either the completion of the task's updates or the reversal of any updates done by the incomplete unit of work. CICS Recovery/Restart backs out any updates to protected files by inflight or incomplete tasks. This is done by saving an image of what a file record looked like before it was updated. During an emergency restart the before image is used to replace the updated record and therefore backout of incomplete work is accomplished. This type of recovery is called inflight backout.

The File Control Table defines the protection status of online files. A file may be defined as a protected resource. Making a file a protected resource means that CICS assumes responsibility for saving before images and reapplying them in the event of a system crash and subsequent recovery/restart of the system. If a file is not a protected resource, CICS can be requested to save before images of updated records, but the installation must provide the recovery/restart processors to use such journaled information. Remember also that Dynamic Transaction Backout (DTB) is applicable only to protected files.

The indicative information about a file allows CICS to access the data set. Such information includes the block or VSAM control interval size so that CICS knows the size of a storage buffer to acquire for file I/O. The logical record size, key length, relative key position, and record format are also included in an FCT entry.

In a subsequent section of this chapter we will be discussing CICS Intercommunication which permits two or more separate CICS systems to share resources such as files. A file can be owned by one CICS system and accessed from another. This is accomplished by shipping a file access request between the CICS systems in question. The system that owns the file contains a complete definition of file information in the FCT. The system that accesses a file in another CICS system may contain an FCT entry for the remote file with enough information so that a file access request can be created and sent to the owning CICS system.

3.3.1.2 The File Control Program The File Control Program is the control point for access to standard user data sets defined within the File Control Table. The FCT is used as a definitive source of information about our processing requirements for file access. The type of access permitted for each data set is specified, and each time that an application task seeks to access a data set the type of request is validated against the data set's FCT entry. File Control provides automatic logging or journaling of modifications to files if requested in the file's entry in the table. This type of logging or journaling is transparent to the application program and requires no application coding.

In support of file access, File Control interfaces with the appropriate access method, blocks and deblocks records, manages the use of I/O areas, synchronizes I/O operations with task processing, and ensures data integrity during update operations. File updating under CICS presents a unique logistical problem because multiple application tasks are executing concurrently. Two or more tasks could attempt to update the same record or two records within the same block or VSAM Control Interval. If multiple tasks were allowed to update such resources concurrently, we could lose one of the updates and thereby have a loss of data integrity. Figure 3-2 illustrates the potential problem graphically.

Two tasks are executing concurrently within an online region. Task 1 reads logical record "123" with the intention of updating an inventory on-hand field by subtracting 5 from this quantity. CICS File Management is invoked and the access method read is issued. Once the input operation is scheduled the requesting task is placed into a wait state. Control passes to the task dispatcher and Task 2 gains control. Task 2 seeks to read the same record with the intent of subtracting 10 units from the inventory on-hand field. Subsequent to the second task's input operation, both tasks have copies of the record in storage.

Task 1 performs its update and causes the record to be rewritten to the file. Task 1 sends a message to the terminal indicating the success of its processing and ends. Note that the record being processed by Task 2 still has the old value in the inventory on hand field. When Task 2 updates and rewrites its copy of the record to the file, we have lost the modification done by Task 1. Obviously, this loss of data integrity cannot be allowed to happen.

CICS prevents loss of data integrity through exclusive control during update processing. This means that in CICS Task 1 would be required to inform CICS of its update intentions when reading the file record. This is accomplished by including the "UPDATE" option in the READ command as follows:

```
EXEC CICS READ UPDATE DATASET('PRODMST')
     RIDFLD(STOCK-NO) INTO(PROD-REC)
     LENGTH(PROD-LENGTH)
     END-EXEC.
```

CICS File Control recognizes the UPDATE option as requiring exclusive control on behalf of the task issuing the request. Exclusive control means that no other task is allowed update access. Therefore, Task 1 is given exclusive control and completes its update before the Task 2 request for update access is honored. The Task 1 update is safely stored in the file

Figure 3-2. Potential loss of data integrity in multitasking.

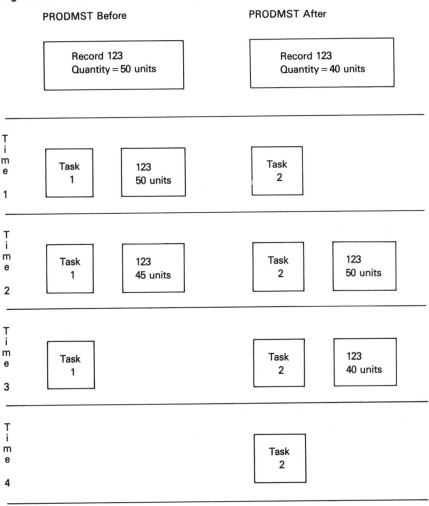

Time 1: Two tasks are in the CICS system. Task 1 READs the PRODMST file to retrieve record 123. CICS issues the read and passes control to Task 2 while the input operation for Task 1 is completing.

Task 1's input completes while Task 2 issues a READ for the PRODMST file to retrieve record 123.

Time 2: Task 1 regains control while the read for Task 2 is completing.

Task 1 subtracts 5 units from its record and REWRITEs the record to the PRODMST file.

Task 2 receives control while the REWRITE of Task 1 is completing.

Time 3: Task 2 subtracts 10 from the units figure in its record. Task 2 REWRITEs the record to the PRODMST.

Task 1 gains control and sends a message to the terminal indicating the successful completion of the transaction.

Task 1 terminates its processing by passing control back to CICS.

Time 4: Task 2 regains control and sends a message to the terminal indicating successful transaction processing. Task 2 terminates by returning control to CICS.

Time 5: Nobody knows it, but the PRODMST file does not reflect the update done by Task 1.

before the record is retrieved for Task 2. Exclusive control is used to make file records serially reusable resources so that there can be no loss of data integrity.

Actually, exclusive control is slightly more complex than the above paragraph would imply. During actual update processing there is an access method-dependent enqueue. For VSAM files, exclusive control is on the control interval containing the record to be updated. The BDAM enqueue is on the block. The access method-dependent enqueue is used ONLY during update processing. In the following code this level of enqueue is used from the READ UPDATE through the REWRITE commands.

```
EXEC CICS READ UPDATE DATASET ('PRODMST')
    INTO (PROD-RECORD) LENGTH (PROD-RECL)
    RIDFLD (PRODUCT-NUMBER) END-EXEC.

SUBTRACT QTY-SHIPPED FROM PROD-QUANTITY.

EXEC CICS REWRITE DATASET ('PRODMST')
    FROM (PROD-RECORD) LENGTH (PROD-RECL)
    END-EXEC.
```

Recall that a file can be defined as either a protected or an unprotected resource. For unprotected files this level of enqueue is the only type of protection utilized. However, if a data set is defined as a protected resource there is an additional level of exclusive control used in addition to the access method-dependent enqueue during update processing.

For protected files CICS also uses an internal enqueue to lock the logical record until the update is committed. Work is automatically committed when a task ends, but there is a CICS command (SYNCPOINT) that can be used to commit all task processing without ending the task. The additional enqueue for protected resources prevents a subsequent task from modifying a record that is potentially a candidate for backout. CICS backout is accomplished by replacing an updated record with a "before update" record image. If a subsequent task were permitted to update an uncommitted record, then CICS Recovery/Restart or *Dynamic Transaction Backout* (DTB) could inadvertently back out the work done by the subsequent task. This would also represent a loss of data integrity, and therefore necessitates the additional type of exclusive control for protected files.

3.3.2 Temporary Storage Facility

The Temporary Storage Facility consists of the *Temporary Storage Program* (TSP) and an optional *Temporary Storage Table* (TST). The Temporary Storage Table is optional because temporary queues can be built and accessed whether or not they are defined in the table. The table is used only if there is some particular requirement, such as queue recoverability.

The Temporary Storage Facility provides a useful scratch pad for the storage of temporarily needed information. This temporary data can be saved in main storage or within a disk data set based upon an option specified by the application program. There is one physical data set used for all disk or auxiliary Temporary Storage. This data set is a VSAM ESDS and is represented in the CICS JCL by a DD statement named "DFHTEMP." DFHTEMP is dynamically suballocated and managed by the Temporary Storage Program (TSP).

Data saved in Temporary Storage is logically organized into sequential queues. The queue is given a logical name within the application program when the first data item is saved, and queue data can subsequently be retrieved by the queue name. Data in Temporary Storage can be updated, retrieved sequentially, or retrieved randomly by specifying the relative item number within the queue. Data in Temporary Storage are not permanent, but CICS does not know their shelf life and therefore it relies on an application code to actually delete any Temporary Storage queues. This, of course, does not have to be done in the program or task that builds the queue.

3.3.3 Transient Data Facility

The Transient Data Facility consists of the *Transient Data Program* (TDP) and the *Destination Control Table* (DCT). The Destination Control Table defines each of the queues to be created or accessed by CICS application programs. Transient Data is a queuing facility within CICS, but it really consists of two very different types of queues. The two types are Extrapartition and Intrapartition Transient Data queues. From the vantage point of coding, the difference between these two types of Transient Data is transparent; from a functional perspective they are almost like separate facilities.

Extrapartition Transient Data is actually a mechanism for accessing or creating standard sequential data sets. Extrapartition queues can be input to or output from CICS, and any media supported by QSAM can be used for Extrapartition Transient Data. Extrapartition queues are actually sequential data sets, and as such they can be accessed by other regions beside CICS. Extrapartition Transient Data is normally used to provide a shared DASD capability between a CICS region and a batch region.

Extrapartition queues can be written to tape, disk, or a printer. On the input side, tape or disk can be used. Usually, however, disk is used for extrapartition queues because extrapartition support utilizes the Queued Sequential Access Method (QSAM). **When using the queued access tech-**

nique, the access method causes a requesting task to wait until the input or
output operation is complete. From the operating system's perspective the
CICS region/partition is one task. The fact that there are multiple CICS
application tasks is transparent to the operating system.

Therefore, when the Transient Data Program initiates a QSAM I/O,
the task (from the operating system's perspective) waits. This means that
the CICS region—not a single CICS application task—waits. In this case
CICS is unable to use the I/O wait time to perform its own internal
multitasking. Excessive use of Extrapartition Transient Data can cause
performance degradation for a CICS system. The wait implicit with
Extrapartition Transient Data means that disk is really the only suitable
option. It could be quite a long wait for the CICS region when an end of
volume on a tape file was reached. An extrapartition queue is really a
sequential data set, and therefore requires a DD statement in the CICS
JCL. The DDNAME is defined in the Destination Control Table information for the extrapartition queue.

Intrapartition Transient Data is totally different. There is no wait for
Intrapartition Transient Data access because Intrapartition Transient Data
uses VSAM. There is one VSAM data set that is dynamically divided to
accommodate all Intrapartition Transient Data queues. This intrapartition
data set is represented in the CICS JCL by a DD statement with the
DDNAME of "DFHINTRA." Because all intrapartition queues are dynamically constructed within one physical data set, there is no way for a batch
region to access a particular Intrapartition Transient Data queue.

However, these queues can be utilized to collect one or more data
elements and trigger tasks to process queue data. This is referred to as
Automatic Transaction Initiation (ATI), and this facility allows an application task to be triggered when the appropriate number of data records
have been saved to an intrapartition queue. This means that task initiation
in CICS can be accomplished as a result of batching of one or more data
elements in an Intrapartition Transient Data queue.

Normally, data in Transient Data queues are not reusable; that is, as a
data item is read the pointer to it is deleted and the item cannot be reread.
Neither is updating possible for Transient Data queues. Access is strictly
sequential in terms of both input and output operations. There is no
random access capability for Transient Data queues as well.

3.4 MISCELLANEOUS CICS FACILITIES

In this section we will examine miscellaneous facilities within CICS. These
include Interval Control (which provides time services), Intercommunication (which allows two CICS systems to communicate), debugging aids
such as Dump and Trace Control, Basic Mapping Support, and recovery-
oriented facilities.

3.4.1 Interval Control Facility

The Interval Control Facility is managed by the *Interval Control Program* (ICP). Interval Control provides time services within the CICS system. There are two main capabilities provided within Interval Control: delay of a task's execution and initiation of tasks at particular times. Time services are requested using CICS commands within application programs. The "time" may be specified as an interval or as an exact wall time based upon command coding.

The DELAY command is used by an application task to request that its execution be delayed. This can be included to cause an ongoing or repeated function to occur at particular intervals. CICS ensures that the task is reawakened when requested so the application program need not be concerned with checking time.

The START command initiates a task based upon time. Data can be passed to the started task, and the task can be requested for a particular terminal. If we want an event to occur routinely at a particular time in the day, this is very handy. For example, we might wish to initiate tasks at 5:00 PM every day to poll point-of-sale terminals and collect sales/inventory information. CICS ensures that Interval Control-initiated tasks are started at the appropriate time, and also acquires and synchronizes use of any required terminals. In other words, CICS detects when a terminal becomes available, and reserves it prior to initiating an Interval Control task.

When a request is made to Interval Control, it creates a small control block called an *Interval Control Element* (ICE). The Interval Control Element contains all pertinent information needed to perform the request when the appropriate time comes. The Interval Control Elements are kept in a chain or list sequenced by expiration time. Therefore, if the first Interval Control Element in the chain has not expired, CICS need not check any other ICE. When the task dispatcher enters a dispatch cycle to look for the highest priority task ready to execute, it checks to see if the first Interval Control Element in the ICE chain is due for scheduling. If so, the Interval Control Processor is invoked and performs the requested time service.

3.4.2 Intercommunication

CICS Intercommunication facilities allow the sharing of resources between CICS systems. There are two types of intercommunication: *MultiRegion Operation* (MRO) and *InterSystem Communication* (ISC).

3.4.2.1 MultiRegion Operation (MRO) MultiRegion Operation (MRO) allows two CICS systems running in different regions/partitions in the **same** machine to communicate with each other. Using this facility, it is

possible to have a CICS region dedicated to terminal management, while another CICS region can process as a file server, and two more CICS regions can be transaction processors. Transaction requests received in the "Terminal Region" can be routed to the appropriate transaction processing region. For example, a very large CICS system has to be broken into two smaller systems because of security or integrity reasons; use of MultiRegion Operation could be used to resolve conflicts or redundancies (Which region gets shared files? Do we define the same files for both regions with all of the potential problems implied by anything other than read only access for everybody?). Likewise, redundant terminal definitions can be avoided using MRO.

3.4.2.2 InterSystem Communication (ISC) InterSystem Communication is oriented toward distributed processing through CICS. Using InterSystem Communication, resources can be shared by CICS systems in **different** machines. The objective of InterSystem Communication is to make resources available to CICS users whether the resource is contained within their local CICS system or another CICS system. Appropriate telecommunications software such as Advanced Communication Function Virtual Telecommunications Access Method (ACF/VTAM) must be utilized.

3.4.3 Dump Control Facility

The *Dump Control Facility* in CICS is a debugging aid. Abnormal task terminations result in formatted dumps being written to a CICS Dump Data Set. Actually, there are two dump data sets that are used in a flip-flop manner. When the currently used Dump Data Set is filled, CICS flips and uses the other. Storage dumps can be printed using a batch program called the *Dump Utility Program* (DFHDUP). The DDNAMEs for the two dump data sets are DFHDMPA and DFHDMPB.

3.4.4 Trace Control Facility

Trace Control provides a general trace facility within CICS. Trace information is saved in a memory trace table. Trace entries are created when CICS commands are executed. There are also application program commands that can be used to create trace entries. When all of the entries in the memory trace table have been used, tracing wraps around and the table is reused. Therefore, in some cases the storage trace table may not contain all of the needed information in order to resolve a particular problem. In this case an auxiliary storage data set known as the Aux Trace Data Set can be used to capture the information saved in the trace table. The information saved in the trace data set is identical to that saved in the storage trace table. Auxiliary tracing is turned on or off using the Master

Terminal Facility. Data recorded to the aux trace data set can be printed with a CICS batch program named the Trace Utility Program (DFHTUP).

3.4.5 Basic Mapping Support

Basic Mapping Support (BMS) is a facility that makes program interaction with a video display terminal considerably easier than if the application program were coded to create a device-dependent data stream. Using Basic Mapping Support terminal screen maps can be created; the use of these maps allows terminal data formatting to be greatly simplified. Additionally, paging or storing of multiple display pages for subsequent operator retrieval is supported.

3.4.6 Recovery-Oriented Facilities

Recovery facilities can be considered from two perspectives: those that are oriented to capturing failing tasks within a CICS system, and those that are utilized if the online system itself crashes.

3.4.6.1 Task Recovery Facilities   During system initialization processing, two operating system macros [SPIE and (E)STAE] are used to inform the operating system that program checks or task abends should not result in an abnormal termination of the CICS region. These macros name a CICS program [the System Recovery Program (SRP)] as an abend exit. Therefore, if there is a program check during CICS execution the operating system passes control to the System Recovery Program. SRP attempts to recover by purging failing application tasks from the system. A formatted dump is written to the CICS Dump Data Set and a message with the abend code of ASRA is written to the appropriate terminal. If Dynamic Transaction Backout has been requested for the TRANSID, then backout of modifications to protected resources is also performed. Not all online abends can be recovered. If, for example, the abend occurs during the execution of the Task Control Dispatcher, then the System Recovery Program permits the system to crash. Such an abend would probably indicate the corruption of one or more CICS data areas, and this therefore precludes recovery.

3.4.6.2 System Recovery Facilities   The system recovery facilities include a facility to record recovery information while CICS is up and running, as well as a recovery/restart subsystem that processes an emergency restart of the CICS system. While CICS is running, the Journal Control Facility is the primary mechanism for collecting the required information for dealing with a system crash. During an emergency restart the major processors are the Recovery Utility Program (DFHRUP) and transaction backout programs.

3.4.7   The Journal Control Facility

The Journal Control Facility consists of the *Journal Control Table* (JCT) and a collection of Journal Control programs. The main program of Journal Control is the *Journal Control Program* (JCP). The Journal Control Table contains an entry for the system log and each of the user journals utilized to collect user recovery information. The first entry in the Journal Control Table is the entry for the system log. CICS Recovery/Restart uses only information from the system log.

Journals and the system log can be recorded to disk or tape. Each entry in the Journal Control Table can have one or two data sets specified for it. If there are two data sets defined, then there are two tape data sets or two separate disk data sets that can be used in a flip-flop manner. When one fills up, CICS switches to the other. Each Journal Control Table entry must be represented by one or two DD statements in the CICS job stream. The DDNAME reflects the journal's relative entry number within the table and whether it is for the first or second of the two possible data sets per JCT entry. The format of the DDNAME is DFHJnn1 where "nn" is the journal's relative JCT entry number and "1" is A or B for the first and second data sets, respectively. As an example, the DDNAMES for a system log requesting two data sets would be DFHJ01A and DFHJ01B. Had the entry defined only one data set, then DFHJ01B would not be needed in the CICS JCL.

During real time processing Journal Control is invoked to record information regarding modifications to protected resources. Journal Control saves this information on the system log. This information is used if a subsequent emergency restart of the system is performed.

3.4.8   The Recovery Utility Program

During an emergency restart of CICS, the Recovery Utility Program reads and collects recovery information from the system log. This information is written to a data set called the Restart Data Set. The DDNAME of the Restart Data Set is DFHRSD. After DFHRUP has built the Restart Data Set, control is passed to transaction backout programs, which perform the inflight backout requisite for resynchronizing protected resources.

3.5   STARTING UP CICS

CICS is brought up by submitting a job stream naming the System Initialization Program (DFHSIP) as the program to execute. DFHSIP is the first of a series of overlay processors that prepare the region for real time execution. The remaining JCL statements in the job stream define CICS system data sets, extrapartition transient data queues defined in the Destination Control Table, and, optionally, user data sets defined in the

File Control Table. The data sets defined in the CICS job stream are depicted in Fig. 3-3.

CICS startup can be accomplished in several ways. The type of startup can be specified by the installation, or CICS can determine the type of startup to perform. There are three types of startups: a COLD start, a warm start, or an EMERgency restart. A cold start results in CICS being brought up with no information from prior executions. The system is thus totally reinitialized such that CICS "remembers" nothing from any earlier execution.

In contrast, a warm start prepares selected CICS facilities so that they reflect their status from a prior execution of the system. Most of the CICS facilities can be warm started, and the warm start is philosophically similar to a checkpoint restart in that the system can pick up from where it left off. The warm start information is obtained from the *Restart Data Set* (DFHRSD). As part of normal shutdown CICS saves warm start information in the Restart Data Set, and therefore a warm start can only be accomplished after a normal system shutdown. In addition to information needed to warm start various facilities, a "startup token" is also saved in the Restart Data Set. This token indicates that the system can be warm started. In any other type of shutdown this "warm start OK" token is not written. CICS can be requested to perform an AUTO startup; in this case the initialization subsystem examines the startup token in the Restart Data Set and determines whether to do an emergency restart or a warm start. A warm start cannot be requested by an installation; rather, CICS is AUTO started and decides that it can do a warm start.

An emergency restart is performed after a system crash, and begins with a cold start of the system. After the system is partially initialized, control passes to the Recovery/Restart Subsystem. As a result of an emergency restart, protected resources are restored to a synchronized state reflecting only committed work. Protected resources can include user data sets so defined in the File Control Table, Auxiliary (disk) Temporary Storage Queues defined as recoverable in the Temporary Storage Table, and Intrapartition Transient Data queues defined as "logically recoverable" in the Destination Control Table.

Regardless of the type of startup, user programs can be given control during system initialization. This is accomplished by naming such programs in a *Program List Table for Program Initialization* (PLTPI). User programs are given control subsequent to initialization, so most facilities of CICS are available (with the notable exception of the Terminal Control Facility).

3.6 SYSTEM SHUTDOWN

The CICS system can come down in one of three ways: a normal shutdown, an immediate shutdown, or a system crash. The first two types of shutdown are accomplished by utilizing the Master Terminal transac-

DDNAME	Purpose of Data Set
STEPLIB	Names the library containing the system initialization programs.
DFHRPL	Names the library that contains the CICS management modules, system tables, and application programs. This partitioned data set can be concatenated.
DFHRSD	Names the restart data set. This data set contains startup information including a control record that indicates the type of startup to perform. Subsequent to a normal shutdown there is also warm start information that can be used to warm start selected facilities. During an emergency restart of CICS the restart data set is used by the Recovery Utility Program (DFHRUP) to save backout information for subsequent backout processing by the transaction backout programs.
DFHTEMP	Names the Auxiliary Temporary Storage Data Set. This data set is dynamically carved up by the Temporary Storage Program to accommodate Temporary Storage queues.
DFHINTRA	Names the Intrapartition Transient Data Set. This data set is dynamically managed by the Transient Data Program to accommodate Intrapartition Transient Data queues.
DFHSTM + DFHSTN	Names the automatic statistics data sets. These data sets are used to collect CICS statistics. CICS statistics are printed out when the system is brought down. The statistics provide information about the use of CICS resources during online execution. The information in the statistics report is quite valuable in pinpointing resource-related problems.
DFHAUXT + DFHBUXT	Names the auxiliary trace data sets. The Aux Trace can be turned on and off via the master terminal transactions. When on, trace information saved in the storage trace table is also recorded in an Aux Trace data set. Trace information in the Aux Trace data set can be printed by the CICS batch utility program DFHTUP.
DFHDMPA + DFHDMPB	Names the CICS Dump Data Sets. Application programs can issue dump requests using dump commands. Additionally, when a task abends a dump is written to the active Dump Data Set. The dumps are formatted and all data areas are clearly labeled. The contents of a Dump Data Set can be printed with the CICS batch utility program DFHDUP.
DFHJnnA	Names first data set defined for journal entry "nn."
DFHJnnB	Names second data set defined for journal entry "nn."
DFHCSD	Names the CICS System Definition file where table information dynamically defined with the CEDA transaction is saved.
DDNAME(s)	Names user data sets defined in the File Control Table. The table entry specifies the DDNAME. The inclusion of file control data sets is optional as DSNAME and DISP can be defined in the File Control Table.
DDNAME(s)	Names Extrapartition Transient Data queues defined in the Destination Control Table. DDNAMEs are assigned in the DCT.

Figure 3-3. Data sets in the CICS job stream.

tion to enter a shutdown command. In a normal shutdown, CICS is quiesced or brought down in stages. All of the tasks in the system are permitted to end normally; then the files and queues are closed and the terminal network is quiesced. At this point warm start information is saved in the Restart Data Set so that a subsequent warm start can be accomplished. Lastly, CICS passes control back to the operating system.

In an immediate shutdown, CICS is not quiesced; the "plug is pulled" and any tasks in the system are not allowed to continue. Control passes back to the operating system immediately, and no warm start information is saved. After an immediate shutdown we can either cold start or attempt an emergency restart.

A system crash occurs because of a hardware, software, or power failure. Application software failures do not normally result in system crashes. Instead, the System Recovery Program purges a failing application task and the system continues. However, application errors can affect the integrity of the CICS region (for example, overlaying a CICS data area or control block). In this case, recovery may very well not be possible.

As with system initialization, user programs can be passed control during normal system shutdown. Such programs are named in a *Program List Table for Shut Down* (PLTSD). The programs named in the beginning of the table execute during the first quiesce when the tasks in the system are being allowed to complete processing. The second half of the table names programs to run in the second quiesce of the system (when the terminal network is being shut down). Second quiesce programs cannot use the Terminal Control Facility. The two halves of the PLTSD are indicated by a table entry for a program named DFHDELIM. Modules named before this entry are executed in the first quiesce, and those that follow DFHDELIM are scheduled in the second quiesce.

REVIEW EXERCISE

Provide a short answer to each question listed below.

1. Define the terms transaction, program, and task as they relate to CICS application processing.
2. How does file-exclusive control differ based upon file protection status?
3. How is a file made a protected resource?
4. Why is it necessary to keep an enqueue on an updated record in a protected file until the update is committed?
5. What types of files are supported by the CICS File Control Facility?
6. Since there are no file definition statements in a CICS application program, how are data records accessed?

7. Why does extensive use of Extrapartition Transient Data queues hamper CICS performance?
8. Must all Temporary Storage queues be defined in the Temporary Storage Table?
9. Cite two places where Temporary Storage Queue data may be saved.
10. Which of the facilities discussed in this chapter can be used to trigger a task automatically?
11. Cite three types of CICS startup and explain how they differ.
12. What is a normal shutdown, and how does it occur?

Match each of the following with a description below.

_____ 1. PLTSD   _____ 6. PLTPI
_____ 2. Interval Control   _____ 7. Journal Control
_____ 3. Dump Control   _____ 8. Intercommunication
_____ 4. DFHRUP   _____ 9. DFHSIP
_____ 5. Basic Mapping   _____ 10. DFHSRP

A. Allows tasks to be STARTed at specific times.
B. Provides formatted storage dumps for tasks that abend.
C. First program to process during CICS initialization.
D. Allows CICS resources to be shared by CICS systems in different locations.
E. Simplifies creation of video terminal data streams.
F. Intercepts program checks in the CICS region and prevents a system crash if possible.
G. Reads the system log and creates the Restart Data Set during an emergency restart of CICS.
H. Manages the system log and any user journals.
I. Names application programs to process during system startup.
J. Names application programs to process during system termination.

Match each of the DDNAMES listed below with a description of the data set's use in CICS.

_____ 1. DFHJ01A   _____ 5. DFHJ01B
_____ 2. DFHRPL   _____ 6. DFHDMPA
_____ 3. DFHINTRA   _____ 7. DFHTEMP
_____ 4. DFHRSD   _____ 8. DFHSTM

A. Contains all application program load modules.
B. Used to build Aux Temporary Storage Queues.
C. Contains warm start information.
D. Used to build all Intrapartition Transient Data queues.
E. Used for formatted transaction dumps.

F.   The first data set defined as the system log.
G.   The second data set defined as the system log.
H.   Used to save CICS statistics.

ANSWERS TO REVIEW EXERCISE

Provide a short answer to each question listed below.

1. Define the terms transaction, program, and task as they relate to CICS application processing.

A transaction is a service that can be requested at any CICS terminal. Thus, the transaction represents a functional capability that can be provided to CICS terminal users.

A program contains the code/instructions to provide the service requested by a transaction. The program represents what has to be done.

A task is a unit of work that CICS creates when a user enters a transaction identifier or request for service. The task is the actual executing entity. It is composed of task-unique work areas and uses the code in a program to drive execution.

2. How does file-exclusive control differ based upon file protection status?

For unprotected files, exclusive control consists of an access method-dependent enqueue upon the block or control interval during file update access. Once the update is completed, this type of exclusive control is released.

For protected files, there are two types of exclusive control provided. The first is the update access exclusive control provided for unprotected files. The second consists of an enqueue upon the logical record until the file modification is committed.

3. How is a file made a protected resource?

A file is made a protected resource by requesting protection status in the file's FCT entry. The systems programmer codes LOG=YES.

4. Why is it necessary to keep an enqueue on an updated record in a protected file until the update is committed?

CICS will potentially back out modifications to protected files. Backout is accomplished by saving a before update image of a file record. As long as the potential exists for the first updating task to require backout, any subsequent modifications could be backed out as well.

5. What types of files are supported by the CICS File Control Facility?
   BDAM and VSAM (KSDS, ESDS, RRDS, and AIX).

6. Since there are no file definition statements in a CICS application
   program, how are data records accessed?
   *Files are defined in the File Control Table. Application programs
   use CICS access instructions to access such files. In the CICS access
   instruction the DDNAME of the file is specified. CICS uses this
   DDNAME to determine the actual file to be accessed.*

7. Why does extensive use of Extrapartition Transient Data queues
   hamper CICS performance?
   *Physical reads and writes to Extrapartition Transient Data
   cause the CICS region to wait, as opposed to a single CICS task
   waiting. Consequently, CICS is not able to perform multitasking
   during the I/O wait time.*

8. Must all Temporary Storage queues be defined in the Temporary
   Storage Table?
   *No. Only Temporary Storage queues with special requirements
   such as recovery or resource security level checking are defined in the
   TST.*

9. Cite two places where Temporary Storage Queue data may be saved.
   *TS Queues may be saved in main storage (MAIN) or within a
   DASD data set managed by Temporary Storage (AUX).*

10. Which of the facilities discussed in this chapter can be used to trigger a
    task automatically?
    *Intrapartition Transient Data queues can be defined with a
    trigger level and a TRANSID. When the number of records in such a
    queue reaches the trigger level, CICS will automatically initiate a task
    based upon the TRANSID.*
    *Interval Control can be used to request automatic transaction
    initiation based upon time.*

11. Cite three types of CICS startup and explain how they differ.
    COLD, AUTO, EMERgency.
    *A COLD start begins CICS as if it had never been up before.
    That is, CICS has no information about any prior executions.*
    *An EMERgency restart is used subsequent to a system crash.
    During an emergency restart, protected resources such as files are
    restored to reflect only completed units of work.*
    *An AUTO startup allows CICS to determine how it should
    start up. Based upon a startup token in the Restart Data Set, CICS*

*determines whether it must perform an emergency restart or if a warm
start of the system is possible. A warm start allows CICS to recall
information about prior executions. In other words, CICS is able to
remember the status of things like Temporary Storage Queues or
unexpired Interval Control requests.*

12. What is a normal shutdown, and how does it occur?

    *A normal shutdown results from the master terminal transaction
being used to request that CICS shut down normally. During a normal
shutdown, tasks already in the system are allowed to complete processing. When all tasks are done, warm start information is saved in the
Restart Data Set so that the system can next be warm started.*

Match each of the following with a description below.

J	1. PLTSD		I	6. PLTPI
A	2. Interval Control		H	7. Journal Control
B	3. Dump Control		D	8. Intercommunication
G	4. DFHRUP		C	9. DFHSIP
E	5. Basic Mapping		F	10. DFHSRP

Match each of the DDNAMES listed below with a description of the
data set's use in CICS.

F	1. DFHJ01A		G	5. DFHJ01B
A	2. DFHRPL		E	6. DFHDMPA
D	3. DFHINTRA		B	7. DFHTEMP
C	4. DFHRSD		H	8. DFHSTM

two

APPLICATION PROGRAMMING

chapter 4

Application Programming Considerations

In this part we will examine how to write CICS Command Level programs. However, before we begin examining the commands of CICS that allow application programs to request online services, there are programming considerations that should be examined. These considerations include: writing programs that will execute efficiently in a virtual storage environment; the two application interfaces to CICS; COBOL options that should be avoided in a CICS program; using the COBOL Linkage Section for efficient data input; using a special technique called pseudoconversational programming for terminal communications; and dealing with unusual conditions that occur during program execution.

4.1 VIRTUAL STORAGE CONSIDERATIONS

Virtual Storage (VS) is a software mechanism for improving the utilization of real computer memory. Let's say that in our region we have a fixed amount of real memory of 1 million bytes. However, we want to use this storage as if it were 2 million bytes. Through the use of a virtual storage operating system this is possible. Software in the operating system maps real storage and storage in a page data set on a peripheral disk, and treats this total amount of storage as if it were the available storage in the region. Storage in both places is divided into fixed size pages which are usually 4096 bytes. Through the manipulations of paging software it appears to processing programs that there are 2 million bytes of storage in computer memory. Note, however, that a program cannot act upon information that is physically in the page data set. Data must be in real storage for it to be truly available for program processing. At first this might appear to be a bit of a shell game because there are still only 1 million bytes of real memory. However, the paging software switches pages between real storage and the storage in the page data set so that we may use 2 million bytes of memory. Figure 4-1 illustrates the use of Virtual Storage (VS).

If there is a page of storage in real memory that is not being used and has not been referenced for a while, the system can write the contents of this area to the page data set and use the real storage for something else. If we refer to information which is in a page that has been written to the page data set, then the operating system will release another page and bring the needed page into memory. Through this technique (called paging) we can

Figure 4-1. Virtual Storage.

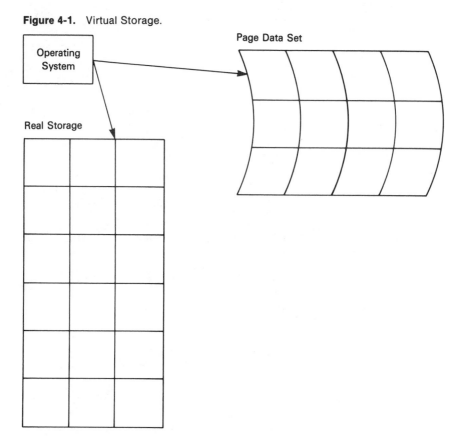

Storage in real memory and the storage in a page data set are mapped into "pages" that are typically 4096 bytes in size. A program executing in a Virtual Storage region can only operate on data that are physically in computer memory, so the operating system pages in and out of real storage. In this way it appears that the combination of real storage and the storage in the page data set is the amount of available storage. This combination is called Virtual Storage.

use the combination of storage in real memory and storage in the page data set as if the combination of both areas were one large memory area called Virtual Storage. The practical use of Virtual Storage relies on the fact that there will be some areas of memory that will be used infrequently and therefore need not be kept in real storage continuously. Virtual Storage, therefore, allows us to make better use of the real storage in a computer region by allowing programs to use all of Virtual Storage. If, however, program execution must refer to a lot of pages in Virtual Storage that are not physically present in main memory, the amount of paging increases and overall efficiency decreases. If the operating system is spending lots of time paging things in and out of real storage, then our problem program cannot execute.

CICS runs in a Virtual Storage environment, which is why it is called CICS/VS. We have thus far examined only a small part of the total CICS system, but already we can see that CICS is not a small system. There are numerous management modules, system tables, and system control blocks that are part of CICS. Moreover, we have to consider that there will be numerous application programs in addition to CICS itself.

There are many things in CICS that are oriented toward making its execution efficient in a Virtual Storage environment, and there are options that the systems programmer has to tailor CICS based upon the way in which a particular installation uses it. However, we must be concerned that our application programs operate efficiently. If the operating system is busy paging in parts of the CICS region because of inefficient operation of application programs, CICS and application tasks are not executing. Writing efficient CICS programs involves structuring programs so that program execution necessitates as little paging as possible.

In a Virtual Storage environment, program execution can be kept efficient by keeping the number and combination of VS pages used during execution to a minimum. The number and combination of pages used during execution are called the **working set**. We want to keep the working set as small as possible because the fewer pages referenced, the less likelihood there is of paging. It is also important to keep program references as local as possible. If we alternately reference data areas that exist in different pages, there is a greater likelihood of paging than if we make all of our references to the data in one page and then make all of our references to the data in another page. Now, what can we do in terms of application programming?

First, it is helpful to keep our application programs small so that they do not occupy a lot of pages of Virtual Storage. This means that we try to design CICS systems and programs that are functionalized. Large functions (such as extensive editing routines or lengthy error handling processes that are done in several programs) can be broken down into submodules. Coding should be done with efficiency in mind; it is desirable to **avoid using high-level language instructions that generate large subroutines.** In COBOL, for example, it is best not to use variable MOVE or EXAMINE instructions because these COBOL statements create subroutines. Normally we can code specific routines ourselves that are smaller and operate more efficiently than the subroutines generated by the compiler.

Second, we want to modify the type of program structure that we use in batch. There are two major approaches to writing application programs: structured programming and straight-line programming. In the straight-line program we do not create many subroutines. Our program consists of instructions that process data in their entirety down the path of the program; when we have completed our straight-line execution, we go back to the beginning of the program and process the next data record. In other words, our program consists of all of the details without an overview of processing. However, such programs are difficult to maintain because one is forced to jump right into the details of processing without an overview of what the program does. The major cost associated with a program during its useful life is maintenance due to changing business practices and legal requirements. Straight-line programs are more difficult to change and keep up to date; therefore most installations frown upon straight-line coding.

In structured programming, subroutines are used extensively. A structured program consists of a mainline that provides an overview of the major aspects of processing. The mainline is kept free of processing details, which are coded within subroutines that are invoked or called from the mainline. In COBOL we perform subroutines. Subroutines are small enclosed units of code that perform a particular detail function. There should be one entry point and one exit point within a subroutine. Because the mainline represents an overview of processing, it is considerably easier to get an idea of what the program is doing. If it is necessary to change a structured program, one looks at the mainline and determines which subroutines are affected. Altering subroutines involves small units of code, so maintenance is greatly facilitated.

When writing batch programs we normally write highly structured code in which subroutines invoke smaller subroutines. If a function is performed in several different places, it is quite common to make the function into a subroutine even if it contains only a couple of instructions. Of primary concern is the logical structuring of the program. The execution of a highly structured program may result in a great deal of paging because processing is hopping from place to place within the program. We start in the mainline and branch to a subroutine that reads a file. We return to the mainline and branch to another subroutine that reads another file to obtain a matching record. We come to the mainline and invoke another subroutine that performs some validation, and so forth. By branching to these subroutines during execution, we increase the likelihood of paging. The execution of a highly structured program normally results in more paging than the execution of a straight-line module.

You are probably beginning to wonder if you are about to be told to write straight-line programs under CICS. *No way!* But one should modify structuring techniques that are used in batch programming. Although CICS programs are structured to facilitate writing, debugging, and maintenance, online programs should not be quite as highly structured as batch programs. Make subroutines a little meatier. Instead of having subroutines branch to smaller subroutines, consider duplicating small amounts of code *in* several places rather than having a small subroutine that is invoked *from* several different places. This enables us to keep processing as sequential as possible without compromising program structure and legibility. We still want a mainline which provides an overview of processing, but we want fewer and meatier subroutines. The order of subroutine placement is also important. Infrequently used subroutines should be placed at the end of the program. Such routines might be error processing routines that are not executed often. Conversely, frequently used subroutines should be close to the mainline. If a subroutine is near the mainline it may occupy the same page of Virtual Storage. Place subroutines that are used together near each other for the same reason. You are not going to count bytes and calculate which routines are together in which pages. However, if some thought is given to subroutine placement the program will be more efficient. In this regard, reflect on what will be the most common path through a program, and place subroutines accordingly. A few minutes of planning program organization results in a more efficiently executed module.

In a batch program we normally start off with an initialization or housekeeping routine in which we initialize all of the data areas used by a program. This type of approach results in less efficient online operation, because data is referenced once during initialization and again when the area is used. In a CICS program a work area should be initialized immediately before it is used. Continued reference to an area already in memory does not cause paging. In contrast, if an area is used during initialization, not referred to for a while, and then used again, the likelihood of paging is increased.

Another goal is to keep the program's Working Storage as small as possible. For Command Level programs each task that uses the program has its own unique copy of Working Storage, so any inefficiency is compounded by multiple tasks. Try to avoid putting data constants in Working Storage. It is better to define constants as literals in instructions where they are used. For example, a program could contain the following COBOL code:

```
DATA DIVISION.
WORKING-STORAGE SECTION.
77 MSG1          PIC X(41)
        VALUE 'ZIP CODE INCORRECT FOR STATE CODE
        ENTERED'.
```

```
01 TERMINAL-OUT-MSG.
   04  CUR-DATE   PIC X(8).
   04  CUR-TIME   PIC X(8).
   04  SV-CODE    PIC X(4).
   04  ERRMSG     PIC X(41).
     .
PROCEDURE DIVISION.
     .
   MOVE MSG1 TO ERRMSG.
   EXEC CICS SEND FROM (TERMINAL-OUT-MSG)
      LENGTH (61)  END-EXEC.
```

In this case every task's copy of Working Storage would contain the 41-byte field called "MSG1." However, if the message were a literal value in a MOVE instruction, the "literal" would be contained in the program's literal pool, and there is only one copy of the literal pool per program. Therefore, the following would be a more efficient way to code the module:

```
DATA DIVISION.
WORKING-STORAGE SECTION.
01  TERMINAL-OUT-MSG.
    04  CUR-DATE   PIC X(8).
    04  CUR-TIME   PIC X(8).
    04  SV-CODE    PIC X(4).
    04  ERRMSG     PIC X(41).
      .
PROCEDURE DIVISION.
      .
    MOVE 'ZIP CODE INCORRECT FOR STATE CODE
       ENTERED' TO ERRMSG.
    EXEC CICS SEND FROM (TERMINAL-OUT-MSG)
       LENGTH (61)   END-EXEC.
```

Consider the use of application tables separate from application programs. For example, common error messages can be placed in a storage table that is available for all CICS tasks. Program Working Storage will be smaller. As an added benefit, there will be a consistency in error messages. The same error message will be used for the same error regardless of the program issuing the message. This makes life easier for the user. Such tables can be resident in memory in one place and referenced as needed by application programs.

When using tables or similar data areas, try to organize information such that a formula or an algorithm can be used to directly locate specific entries or items. In other words, avoid storing and searching sequentially for specific table entries. Sequential searches are costly because, as the program steps through successive entries, the likelihood of paging increases. If you can get directly to a desired data element, instruction execution and storage references are minimized. As an example of how this could be done with an error message table, different error conditions could be equated with different error numbers, and the error number could serve as the basis for directly locating an error message within the table.

4.2 CICS PROGRAMMING INTERFACES

CICS application programs do two major types of processes. They operate on data (performing validation and formatting operations), and they interface with CICS to obtain the online services when needed. There are two ways of interfacing with CICS: the *Macro Level Interface* and the *Command Level Interface*.

4.2.1 Macro Level Programs

The Macro Level Interface is the older of the two approaches. Macro Level derives its name from the fact that assembler language macros are used to invoke the services of CICS. Macro Level programs can be written in PL/I, COBOL, or assembler language, but they are most oriented to assembler language because of the use of macro instructions to talk to CICS. However, Macro Level is more than just the use of macros. With Macro Level the application program interfaces directly with the numerous management facilities of CICS. If a file service is required, the Macro Level program invokes CICS File Control Facility and passes File Control the appropriate parameters that define the type of service, the name of the data set (DDNAME), and the address of the field containing the key or other search argument.

If a service is required of storage management, Storage Control is invoked. Storage Control is likewise passed parameters that tell it the amount and type of storage requested, as well as whether or not the storage is to be initialized. If a Program Control link or transfer of control is desired, the same approach is used. So, in essence, the application program is interfacing with a collection of different CICS management facilities in order to obtain services. When a management facility is through processing a request, it passes back appropriate information to the application. For example, File Control passes back the address of a file record that has been read, or Storage Control presents the address of a piece of dynamically acquired storage. Figure 4-2 illustrates the interaction of a Macro Level program with each of the management facilities of CICS.

There must be a data area that can be shared by CICS management modules and the application program so that parameters can be passed back and forth. This area is the Task Control Area (TCA), the main control block CICS uses to govern a task's execution. So, if a task requires

Figure 4-2. Macro Level interface to CICS.

Macro Level Program

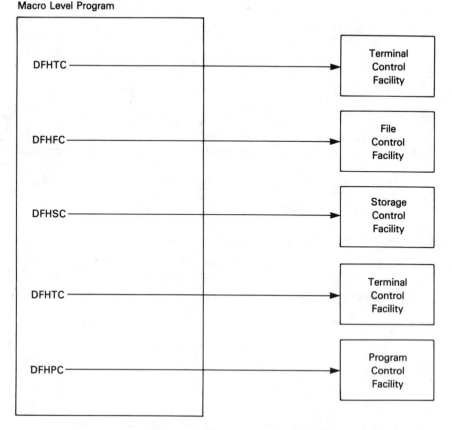

Macro Level CICS programs not only use assembler language macro instructions to communicate with CICS, but also interact with each of the separate management facilities on a one-to-one basis. This low-level interface is not used for the development of new CICS applications, but there are Macro Level systems in many installations that still must be maintained.

a piece of storage, it formats appropriate parameters in the TCA. These parameters include the amount of storage required. This size information is placed in the "TCASCNB" or Task Control Area Storage Control Number of Bytes field. When Storage Control returns to the task, the address of acquired storage can be found at the "TCASCSA" or Task Control Area Storage Control Storage Address field. The application programmer writing Macro Level CICS programs must have a good knowledge of the use of fields within the Task Control Area, and must know something about CICS internal processing. It is rather like a batch program interfacing with MVS by calling specific routines within that operating system and using the *Task Control Block* (TCB) to exchange information with MVS. Macro Level programming is obviously very detailed.

The Command Level program is readily reusable because CICS acquires a task-unique storage area, such as a COBOL Data Division. The Macro Level programmer must be very careful to make a program reentrant or serially reusable, because all tasks threading through a Macro Level program share the single copy of Working Storage contained within the load module. This Working Storage cannot be used for modifiable data without compromising the reusability of the program. Modifiable data must be kept in a task-unique work area, and typically the Macro Level program utilizes a user appendage of the TCA called the *Transaction Work Area* (TWA). Figure 4-3 illustrates the use of the Transaction Work Area in a Macro Level task. Since there is a Task Control Area for every task, the user appendage of this control block can be used for modifiable

Figure 4-3. Use of the TCA/TWA in a Macro Level task.

Macro Level Program

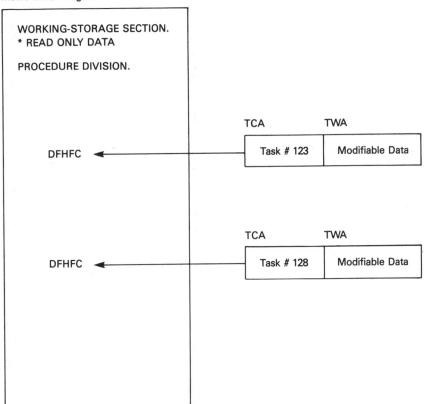

Since there is only one copy of Working Storage, this area must be used for read-only data or the Macro Level program will not be reusable. Therefore, a data area other than program Working Storage is needed for task-unique modifiable data. There is a Task Control Area (TCA) for every task in the CICS system, and the TCA can have a user appendage called the Transaction Work Area (TWA). In Macro Level programs the TWA is used for task-unique data. The size of a required Transaction Work Area is defined in the Program Control Table entry for a Transaction Identifier requiring a TWA.

data without affecting the program's reusability. It is important to remember the use of the Transaction Work Area if you are going to be called upon to maintain Macro Level programs.

We have discussed the use of the Task Control Area in Macro Level programs, but the TCA is not the only CICS data area used by Macro Level programs. The Macro Level task must also obtain addressability to its terminal's entry in the Terminal Control Table in order to obtain the address of terminal input. On the output side, the address of an output message is placed in the terminal's entry in the Terminal Control Table prior to output requests. All in all, the Macro Level application programmer must know a lot about CICS. Familiarity with some CICS control blocks and knowledge of interfacing with a collection of different management facilities are needed. It is also necessary to use assembler language macros with correct assembler language syntax, even if writing a high-level language program. In philosophy the Macro Level is more oriented toward assembler language programming.

4.2.2 The Command Level Interface

Now, the good news. The Command Level interface removes most of these obstacles. With Command Level, high-level language type commands are used to request services of CICS. The commands invoke an interface called the Execute Interface, which is exactly what its name implies. The Execute Interface is an executing interface between the Command Level application program and the rest of CICS. The Command Level application program does not use the Task Control Area to pass parameters to a collection of different management modules. Rather, commands invoke the executing interface, and the interface translates high-level commands into the unique requirements of all of the different management facilities of CICS.

The trail of command processing is depicted in Fig. 4-4. The issuance of a command results in the invocation of the Execute Interface. The Execute Interface determines which control facility is needed to service the command, primes the applicable areas, and invokes the appropriate CICS management facility. After the facility has serviced the request, control passes back to the Execute Interface, which obtains information from CICS data areas and passes this information back to the Command Level application task. The structure and nature of CICS control blocks are thus transparent to Command Level programs. Command Level is considerably easier to learn and use. There is no need to utilize the Transaction Work Area for modifiable data. COBOL programs use their task unique Working Storage, as depicted in Fig. 4-5.

4.3 COBOL RESTRICTIONS

There are some differences between batch and online programs. First, there are no file definitions within CICS programs. Remember, all files are defined

Figure 4-4. Command processing.

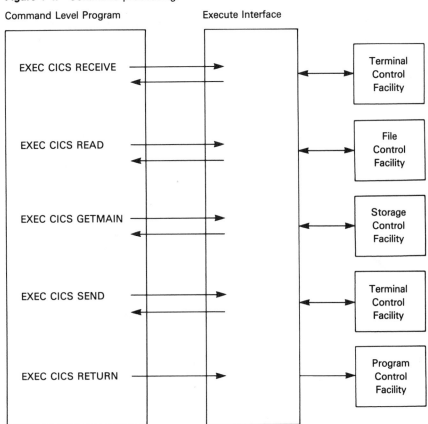

With the Command Level interface there is an executing interface that translates application program service requests into the requirements of each different CICS facility. The Execute Interface provides a programmer-friendly interface to the rest of CICS.

in the File Control Table (FCT), and application access to files involves using CICS commands. Therefore, the CICS COBOL program does not have entries in the Environment or Data Divisions associated with data management. COBOL file access instructions (such as READ, WRITE, OPEN, or CLOSE) are not used. The files are opened by CICS. Once opened, files are generally left open for continuing online operation, and therefore the application program never closes them. CICS commands are used to request file access, so the EXEC CICS READ replaces the COBOL READ, and EXEC CICS WRITE replaces the COBOL WRITE. Anything that you can do with COBOL file access instructions has a corresponding CICS equivalent.

COBOL special features such as SORT or REPORT WRITER should not be used. This is normally not an issue because of the type of processing done online. Typical programs are invoked by an operator's transaction

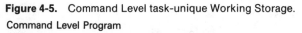

Figure 4-5. Command Level task-unique Working Storage.

Command Level Program

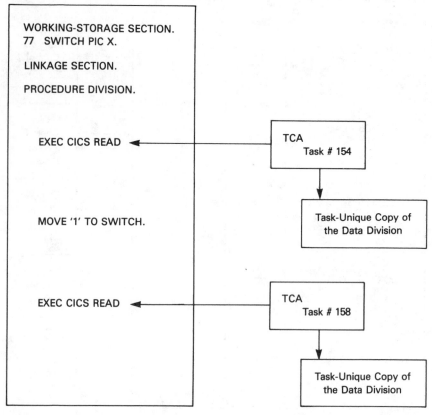

In Command Level each task has its own dynamic copy of the Data Division, including a unique Working-Storage Section on a task-by-program basis. Therefore, the Command Level CICS COBOL programmer can use Working Storage for modifiable data. CICS handles the acquisition, initialization, and addressing of the task-unique Working Storage. From a programming perspective this is totally transparent to the application programmer. In actuality, the Procedure Division is the part of the COBOL Command Level program that is shared by tasks. There are two tasks sharing this Command Level program, but when the instruction "MOVE '1' TO SWITCH." is executed for Task # 154, its own unique copy of Working Storage will be acted upon. When Task # 158 executes this instruction, its task-unique area will likewise be affected. No task uses the load module's copy of Working Storage.

identifier, and then process a customer or an order or an employee. There is obviously not much to sort or report about.

Lastly, you should not use instructions that require operating system intervention. Such commands as ACCEPT, CURRENT-DATE, DIS-PLAY, or TIME cause the application task to invoke the operating system—this is bad for CICS performance. CICS multitasking is based upon the fact that CICS is able to schedule things and use the I/O wait time to allow other waiting tasks to process. Remember that the CICS system is one task to the operating system; if the operating system is invoked with an implied wait, then all of CICS waits and is not able to perform multitasking.

Invariably people ask if CICS can monitor application programs to ensure that these prohibitions are not violated. The answer is *no*. If you write a program that has file SELECTs and FDs and you OPEN and READ files with COBOL access instructions, CICS is not going to be aware of it. You won't even have compile errors, and your program will be executable under CICS. What happens is that system performance degrades—the more processing of this type, the greater the degradation.

4.4 USING THE LINKAGE SECTION IN A COBOL PROGRAM

The Linkage Section is a mechanism that provides the COBOL program with a way of accessing storage areas outside of the load module. Figure 4-6 is an illustration of a load module in memory. The executable program occupies a particular area in storage, and since this is a Command Level CICS program, we are already addressing a data area outside of the load module. We are using a dynamic copy of our Data Division that CICS has obtained for us, but this is transparent because the COBOL BASE LOCATORs that address Working Storage have been set to point to the dynamic area without our having to do anything.

When we place a data area in Working Storage there is real physical storage set aside based upon the size of the data area. If the following were coded in Working Storage, there would be 500 bytes of storage allocated because the area is 500 bytes in length:

```
01   EMPL-MASTER-RECORD.
     05   EMPL-NUMBER      PIC X(10).
     05   EMPL-NAME        PIC X(40).
     05   EMPL-ADDR-1      PIC X(30).
     05   EMPL-ADDR-2      PIC X(30).
     05   EMPL-ADDR-3      PIC X(30).
     05   FILLER           PIC X(360).
```

If the above area were defined within a COBOL Command Level program, every task executing within the program would have a dynamic Working Storage with this 500-byte allocation.

The Linkage Section is a collection of Base Locators for Linkage or BLL cells. A BLL cell is a 4-byte area that can contain the address of data which exist somewhere else in memory. In Figure 4-6 the Linkage Section contains seven such 4-byte areas. In batch, if a program is called and data are passed to it via the COBOL CALL . . . USING statement, the Linkage Section is used to address passed data. Figure 4-7 depicts batch use of the Linkage Section in a called program. The actual data being passed reside within the calling program (load module). The CALL . . . USING invokes the called program and places in a Linkage Section BLL cell the address of

Figure 4-6.   Command Level COBOL load module.

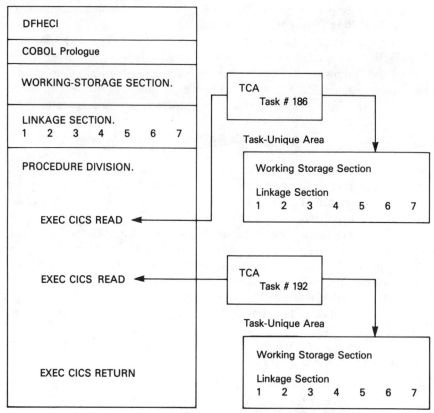

Command Level Load Module

The Command Level COBOL load module begins with a Control Section (CSECT) called DFHECI. This is a stub of the interface, and the presence of the stub indicates that this is a Command Level program. The stub is used during the execution of calls to the Execute Interface. After DFHECI there is the standard COBOL prologue code to initialize processing. The load module then contains the Data Division of the program. In the Linkage Section of the load module the numbers 1–7 are shown. These numbers represent seven BLL cells that are present in the load module and likewise present in the task-unique work areas. The BLL cells are 4-byte areas that can contain a storage address and are used as the means to gain addressability to data outside of the task-unique work area.

the data in the calling program's Working Storage. Using the Linkage Section, the called program gains access to data outside of the load module. A work area is defined in the called module's Linkage Section but this area is conceptually an overlay providing field lengths and displacements. What this means is that the only real physical storage that is allocated in the Linkage Section consists of the 4-byte BLL cells that are used to contain the addresses of data. Data areas defined in the Linkage Section do not cause real storage to be allocated. Such data areas are a way of looking at data that are addressed via the BLL cell.

Now, why would we want to use the Linkage Section in a COBOL Command Level program? The reason is really quite simple. There are cases when input operations are more efficient if the Linkage Section is used. Let's consider file input. There is a file defined in the File Control Table (FCT) called PRODMST. PRODMST contains records about the products that a company offers. There is a user transaction which permits terminal operators to request inventory information on various products by product number. In the application program, CICS file access commands are used to access data from this file. The COBOL program is not going to have any SELECT or FD statements for the PRODMST, but a data structure or record area is needed so that the program can access the data record passed by CICS.

There are two places where the data record can be located, corresponding to the two modes of input that can be used in CICS programs.

Figure 4-7. Batch use of the Linkage Section.

CALLing Module   CALLed Module

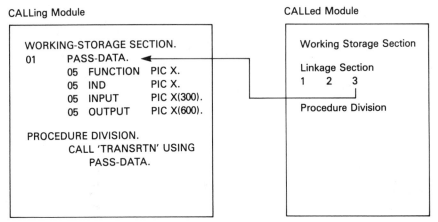

```
WORKING-STORAGE SECTION.
01    PASS-DATA.
      05  FUNCTION  PIC X.
      05  IND       PIC X.
      05  INPUT     PIC X(300).
      05  OUTPUT    PIC X(600).

PROCEDURE DIVISION.
      CALL 'TRANSRTN' USING
          PASS-DATA.
```

```
Working Storage Section

Linkage Section
1    2    3

Procedure Division
```

CALLed Module's Linkage Section Contains
the Following Source Code:

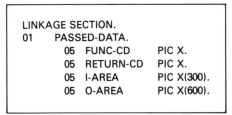

```
LINKAGE SECTION.
01    PASSED-DATA.
      05  FUNC-CD    PIC X.
      05  RETURN-CD  PIC X.
      05  I-AREA     PIC X(300).
      05  O-AREA     PIC X(600).
```

When the CALLed module is invoked by the operating system, it will have addressability to the passed data in the CALLing program's Working Storage. The CALLed module can use these data fields because of the Linkage Section mechanism in COBOL. Note, however, that the CALLed program is actually using the storage in the CALLing program. There is no actual storage set aside in the CALLed program's Linkage Section. BLL 3 in the CALLed program has the address of the passed data.

Figure 4-8. MOVE mode example of file access.

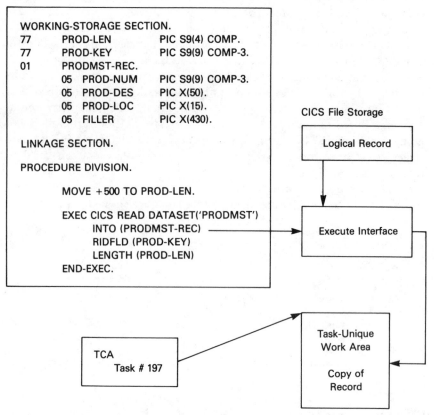

MOVE mode is indicated by the use of the INTO option. The EXEC CICS READ command invokes the
Execute Interface. The Execute Interface invokes File Control, which actually schedules the record retrieval.
File Control acquires storage for the record retrieved, and passes the address of the logical record to the
Execute Interface. The Execute Interface copies the file record from the CICS storage area into the dynamic
copy of Working Storage for Task # 197. The task's Working Storage is larger by the amount of storage
reserved for the PRODMST-REC.

The two modes of retrieval are MOVE and LOCATE. MOVE mode uses
the Working-Storage Section and LOCATE mode uses the Linkage
Section.

Figure 4-8 is an example of a program that uses MOVE mode to
access a file record. Note that in the program the 01-PRODMST-REC
area is defined in the Working-Storage Section. The READ command in
the Procedure Division uses the word INTO and names PRODMST-REC.
This command invokes the CICS Execute Interface. The Execute Interface
invokes File Control. File Control uses the File Control Table and
ascertains all of the information needed in order to access the file. One of
the things that File Control has to do is acquire storage for use as an input
area. File Control acquires storage and schedules the input operation.

When the data transfer from the peripheral device into memory is complete, File Control deblocks the logical record into a storage work area. File Control then passes the logical record address to the Execute Interface. The Execute Interface copies the logical record into the task's copy of Working Storage—the logical record now exists in two areas from which it can be used. It is contained in the CICS work area and is also within the task's Working Storage. This is true for all of the tasks that execute in the application program. Every task automatically gets a Working Storage with space for the PRODMST-REC.

Figure 4-9 is an example of file access using LOCATE mode. Note that a record area is not defined in the program's Working-Storage Section. Rather, the record area is defined in the Linkage Section in conjunction with a BLL cell that is called FILE-BLL in the program. The names are not fixed, and any data name could have been used in place of FILE-BLL. Coding the BLL cell in the COBOL Linkage Section results in a 4-byte area being allocated. However, the associated 01-level data area that is also in the Linkage Section does not result in any storage being allocated. This 01-level record area is nothing more than a collection of field names that we can use to view the data addressed by the BLL cell. In response to the read instruction with the SET option naming FILE-BLL, the Execute Interface invokes File Control to read the file. When the input operation is complete, File Control passes the Execute Interface the address of the logical record. However, instead of copying the record into an area in Working Storage, LOCATE mode results in the execute interface placing the address of the file record into the appropriate BLL cell. The 01-PRODMST-REC allows the program to look at various fields at relative offsets from the starting address in the BLL cell. The Working Storage of the load module is smaller in the LOCATE mode example by 500 bytes. However, we are not so much concerned with a single load module. Every task executing in this program has its own Working Storage, which is smaller by the additional 500-byte area. If there were 20 tasks executing in the program, the savings would be 20 × 500 (10,000) bytes. If this were a heavily used transaction, the extra storage requirement could affect performance, especially in a CICS region suffering from storage constraints.

It is recommended that LOCATE mode be used for file input because of this storage savings. The more heavily used the program and the larger the file record, the greater the potential savings. Therefore, it is desirable to learn all about coding Linkage Sections in CICS application programs.

There is a distinction that must be made regarding the version of the COBOL compiler being used. Three compilers are supported for CICS programs: OS Full COBOL, OS/VS COBOL, and VS COBOL II. The VS COBOL II compiler which supports 31-bit addressing does not require that BLL cells be coded, but the other two COBOL compilers require explicit BLL cell definitions. First we'll discuss Linkage Section coding for the

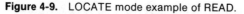

Figure 4-9. LOCATE mode example of READ.

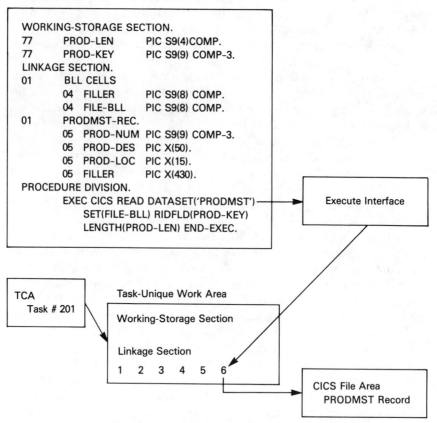

```
WORKING-STORAGE SECTION.
77      PROD-LEN      PIC S9(4)COMP.
77      PROD-KEY      PIC S9(9) COMP-3.
LINKAGE SECTION.
01      BLL CELLS
        04  FILLER    PIC S9(8) COMP.
        04  FILE-BLL  PIC S9(8) COMP.
01      PRODMST-REC.
        05  PROD-NUM  PIC S9(9) COMP-3.
        05  PROD-DES  PIC X(50).
        05  PROD-LOC  PIC X(15).
        05  FILLER    PIC X(430).
PROCEDURE DIVISION.
        EXEC CICS READ DATASET('PRODMST')
             SET(FILE-BLL) RIDFLD(PROD-KEY)
             LENGTH(PROD-LEN) END-EXEC.
```

Execute Interface

TCA
Task # 201

Task-Unique Work Area

Working-Storage Section

Linkage Section
1   2   3   4   5   6

CICS File Area
PRODMST Record

LOCATE mode is indicated by the use of the SET option. The EXEC CICS READ command invokes the
Execute Interface. The Execute Interface invokes File Control, which actually schedules the record retrieval.
File Control acquires storage for the record retrieved and passes the address of the logical record to the
Execute Interface. The Execute Interface places the address or location of the record in CICS's storage area into
the named BLL. FILE-BLL is the sixth BLL-cell in this module and consequently the pointer to the data record
is contained in BLL number 6. The first two BLLs in a COBOL module are not used in CICS. BLLs 3 and 4 are
used to address work areas associated with CICS Command Level programs that we will be discussing in the
next chapter. BLL 5 is associated with the FILLER BLL defined in the Linkage Section of this program and
BLL 6 is for the next or FILE-BLL. After successful execution of the READ SET command, the program can
use the PRODMST-REC record description defined in the Linkage Section to reference the data in the CICS
area. The task's unique Working Storage does not have room set aside for the PRODMST-REC.

COBOL compilers that require BLL cells, and then we'll look at the
differences for the new VS COBOL II compiler.

4.4.1   OS COBOL Linkage Section

There are two entities that are used to gain linkage or addressability to a
data area outside of dynamic Working Storage. Those two things are a
BLL cell and an 01-level record area defined in conjunction with the BLL

cell. The BLL cells are coded together within one BLL cell parameter list in the Linkage Section. If one were planning to use four BLL cells, the Linkage Section BLL parameter list might look like this:

```
LINKAGE SECTION.
01 BLLCELL-PARMLIST.
      04  FILLER            PIC S9(8) COMP.
      04  FIRST-BLL         PIC S9(8) COMP.
      04  SECOND-BLL        PIC S9(8) COMP.
      04  THIRD-BLL         PIC S9(8) COMP.
      04  FOURTH-BLL        PIC S9(8) COMP.
01 FIRST-RECORD-AREA.
      04  whatever fields exist in this area
01 SECOND-RECORD-AREA.
      04  whatever fields exist in this area
01 THIRD-RECORD-AREA.
      04  whatever fields exist in this area
01 FOURTH-RECORD-AREA.
      04  whatever fields exist in this area
```

The names given to BLL cells are selected by the programmer at will. Any valid COBOL name can be used. Note that the BLL cells are binary fields, and are indicated by the usage of COMP. Also, PIC S9(8) in COMP is a 4-byte binary area which we need in order to contain an address. Even though we specified the use of four BLL cells, five are actually coded. This is because the first is needed for CICS. The "FILLER" BLL is required by the software; if a Linkage Section is coded without providing this BLL, then CICS takes the first one anyway. The first BLL doesn't have to be called FILLER, but it is TAKEN by CICS. The four remaining BLLs can be used (unmolested by CICS) in commands that are coded in LOCATE mode; the SET option causes appropriate addresses to be placed in them. There are four 01-level data areas following the 01 for the BLL parameter list. These four 01-level areas correspond on a one-to-one basis with each of the BLL cells. The software knows which address (BLL) goes with which 01-level area by their relative placement.

When using BLL cells, it is important to remember that a BLL cell can address a data area that is a maximum of 4096 bytes. It is necessary to code one or more additional BLLs for larger areas. The programmer must also prime the second or subsequent BLLs. Figure 4-10 is an example of a Linkage Section using three user BLL cells. Note that the first BLL (FILLER) is used by CICS. The second and third BLLs (user BLLs 1 and 2) are used for the same 01-level record, because the area is larger than that which can be addressed by one BLL. In the Procedure Division, after the READ command which sets the FIRST-FILE-BLL, there is an instruction to prime the second BLL:

ADD +4096 TO FIRST-FILE-BLL GIVING SECOND-FILE-BLL.

Figure 4-10. Linkage Section with three user BLL cells to address two data areas.

```
WORKING-STORAGE SECTION.
77    FILE-KEY-1       PIC 9(9).
77    FILE-KEY-2       PIC 9(7).
77    FILE-LEN         PIC S9(4) COMP.

LINKAGE SECTION.
01    BLLS.
      04  FILLER            PIC S9(8) COMP.
      04  FIRST-FILE-BLL    PIC S9(8) COMP.
      04  SECOND-FILE-BLL   PIC S9(8) COMP.
      04  THIRD-BLL         PIC S9(8) COMP.

01    FILE-RECORD.
      05  KEY-FIELD         PIC 9(9).
      05  FILLER            PIC X(4090).
01    THIRD-BLL-DATA        PIC X(100).

PROCEDURE DIVISION.

      EXEC CICS READ DATASET ('FILEDD')
         RIDFLD (FILE-KEY-1) SET (FIRST-FILE-BLL)
         LENGTH (FILE-LEN) END-EXEC.

      ADD +4096 TO FIRST-FILE-BLL GIVING SECOND-FILE-BLL.
```

Because the FILE-RECORD area is larger than 4096, a second BLL cell is needed to address the area beyond 4096. CICS SETs the first BLL cell as a result of the execution of the READ command. However, the application programmer must ensure that the second BLL cell is properly initialized. The software is smart enough to realize that THIRD-BLL-DATA is the data area associated with THIRD-BLL.

THIRD-BLL is correctly associated with the second user 01-level record area named 01 THIRD-BLL-DATA. If a data area is one byte larger than that which can be addressed by a BLL cell, an additional BLL cell is needed. Each 4096-byte part of a record requires a BLL cell.

One additional point must be mentioned regarding Linkage Section use. When the OS Full COBOL compiler is used it is necessary to add a SERVICE RELOAD instruction subsequent to the CICS command that sets the BLL cell. This ensures that correct addressability is obtained to the dynamic area. An example of the SERVICE RELOAD is illustrated below.

```
WORKING-STORAGE SECTION.
77 FILE-KEY-1    PIC 9(9).
77 FILE-LEN      PIC S9(4) COMP.
LINKAGE SECTION.
01 BLLS.
   04  FILLER            PIC S9(8) COMP.
   04  FIRST-FILE-BLL    PIC S9(8) COMP.
```

```
01  FILE-RECORD.
    05  KEY-FIELD          PIC 9(9).
    05  FILLER             PIC X(4000).
PROCEDURE DIVISION.
    EXEC CICS READ DATASET ('FILEDD')
         RIDFLD (FILE-KEY-1) SET (FIRST-FILE-BLL)
         LENGTH (FILE-LEN) END-EXEC.
    SERVICE RELOAD FILE-RECORD.
```

4.4.2 VS COBOL II Linkage Section Coding

The VS COBOL II compiler eliminates the need to code BLL cells in the Linkage Section. A Linkage Section for this compiler is illustrated below.

```
WORKING-STORAGE SECTION.
77  FILE-KEY-1      PIC 9(9).
77  FILE-LEN        PIC S9(4) COMP.
LINKAGE SECTION.
01  FILE-RECORD.
    05  KEY-FIELD       PIC 9(9).
    05  FILLER          PIC X(4090).
PROCEDURE DIVISION.

    EXEC CICS READ DATASET ('FILEDD')
         RIDFLD  (FILE-KEY-1)
         SET     (ADDRESS OF FILE-RECORD)
         LENGTH (FILE-LEN) END-EXEC.
```

Note that even though the data area illustrated in the Linkage Section is larger than 4096, it is not necessary to do anything other than execute the read. Addressability is automatically acquired to the entire area. Also note that there is no SERVICE RELOAD instruction. SERVICE RELOAD is never needed for this compiler.

REVIEW EXERCISE

Provide a short answer to each of the questions below.

1. What is the difference between a straight-line program and a structured program? Which type of program do we want to write for CICS systems? How might we alter batch programming style to suit the CICS/VS environment?
2. Why is the Command Level interface far easier to learn than the Macro Level?
3. How does one define files in a COBOL CICS program?

4. Explain the difference between MOVE mode input and LOCATE mode input.

5. What is the Linkage Section, and what is its use in a COBOL CICS program?

6. CICS utilizes a technique called multithreading to allow multiple tasks to share a single copy of an application program. This means that a CICS program must be reusable. How does this affect Command Level program coding? Macro Level program coding?

ANSWERS TO REVIEW EXERCISE

Provide a short answer to each of the questions below.

1. What is the difference between a straight-line program and a structured program? Which type of program do we want to write for CICS systems? How might we alter batch programming style to suit the CICS/VS environment?

   A straight-line program does not contain many subroutines. Such programs consist of instructions that process in a straight-line path through the program. A straight-line program consists of a list of detailed instructions without inclusion of an overview of processing. A structured program, in contrast, makes extensive use of subroutines. The structured program contains a mainline that serves as an overview of processing. The mainline calls up subroutines, which are small enclosed units of code that actually handle the details of processing. Since structured programs are far easier to maintain, we want to write structured programs for both batch and CICS systems. However, since paging may be more of a problem in a CICS system, we want to alter batch programming style to use fewer but larger subroutines.

2. Why is the Command Level interface far easier to learn than the Macro Level?

   Command Level presents a single face to the application programmer. CICS commands invoke an executing interface that translates high-level language commands into service requests for the many different facilities contained in CICS. Macro Level involves interaction with each separate facility of CICS and an understanding of how to pass and receive information in order to request and receive services of CICS.

3. How does one define files in a COBOL CICS program?

   Files are not defined in a COBOL CICS program. All files are defined in the File Control Table.

4. Explain the difference between MOVE mode input and LOCATE mode input.

During file input operations, CICS places the logical record retrieved into a CICS work area and passes the work area address to the Execute Interface. In MOVE mode operations, the Execute Interface copies the logical record from the CICS work area into the task's unique Working Storage. In LOCATE mode, the Linkage Section is used to address the logical record in the CICS work area. The Execute Interface places the address of the data record into a BLL cell named in the input command. Use of LOCATE mode reduces the size of the task-unique Working Storage.

5. What is the Linkage Section, and what is its use in a COBOL CICS program?

The Linkage Section is used to obtain addressability to data areas. In batch, this allows a program to access data outside of the load module. In CICS COBOL programs, this permits use of data contained outside of the task unique working storage. By using the Linkage Section in a CICS program, it is possible to use data in CICS work areas and therefore have fewer work areas defined in Working Storage. Thus, use of LOCATE mode and the Linkage Section means that programs require less Working Storage.

6. CICS utilizes a technique called multithreading to allow multiple tasks to share a single copy of an application program. This means that a CICS program must be reusable. How does this affect Command Level program coding? Macro Level program coding?

CICS Command Level programs are normally reusable because the Execute Interface acquires a dynamic work area for each task. For COBOL programs each task has a unique copy of the Data Division on a task-by-program basis. However, with Macro Level programs there is no task-unique copy of program Working Storage. Therefore, for the Macro Level Program to be reusable, Working Storage should be used for read-only data.

chapter **5**

More Programming Considerations

5.1 THE TRANSLATOR

In the last chapter we looked at various examples of COBOL CICS code. You may have noticed that there is source code in a CICS Command Level Program that is not recognizable by any COBOL compiler. In order to compile a CICS Command Level program successfully, this non-COBOL code must be translated into something that is recognizable by COBOL. This is accomplished via a translator. The translator is a preprocessor that converts CICS-specific code into source code statements that can be compiled. The process of creating an executable CICS Command Level load module is thus a three-step process: (1) the translator processes CICS-oriented code; (2) the COBOL compiler creates an object module; and (3) the Linkage Editor creates a load module. There is a preprocessor or translator for each programming language, and normally it is relatively transparent to the application programmer because the translator is invoked from a CICS JCL Compile procedure.

The translator prepares CICS-specific source code for processing by the compiler. The COBOL translator does a couple of things to a source module. First, it places a collection of 01-level work areas as the last thing in Working Storage. This area is not used in application programming, but since it is present in compiler listings we might as well show you what it looks like and explain why it is there. This area appears as shown in Figure 5-1. The commands that are used to call CICS (the Execute Interface) are translated into COBOL CALL . . . USING statements. These inserted Work-

16.39.10   NOV 18,1986

```
*
 01    DFHLDVER PIC X(22) VALUE 'LD TABLE DFHEITAB 170.'.
 01    DFHEID0 PICTURE S9(7) COMPUTATIONAL-3 VALUE ZERO.
 01    DFHEIB0 PICTURE S9(4) COMPUTATIONAL VALUE ZERO.
 01    DFHEICB  PICTURE X(8) VALUE IS '        '.

 01    DFHEIV16   COMP PIC S9(8).
 01    DFHB0041   COMP PIC S9(8).
 01    DFHB0042   COMP PIC S9(8).
 01    DFHB0043   COMP PIC S9(8).
 01    DFHB0044   COMP PIC S9(8).
 01    DFHB0045   COMP PIC S9(8).
 01    DFHB0046   COMP PIC S9(8).
 01    DFHB0047   COMP PIC S9(8).
 01    DFHB0048   COMP PIC S9(8).
 01    DFHEIV11   COMP PIC S9(4).
 01    DFHEIV12   COMP PIC S9(4).
 01    DFHEIV13   COMP PIC S9(4).
 01    DFHEIV14   COMP PIC S9(4).
 01    DFHEIV15   COMP PIC S9(4).
 01    DFHB0025   COMP PIC S9(4).
 01    DFHEIV5    PIC X(4).
 01    DFHEIV6    PIC X(4).
 01    DFHEIV17   PIC X(4).
 01    DFHEIV18   PIC X(4).
 01    DFHEIV19   PIC X(4).
 01    DFHEIV1    PIC X(8).
 01    DFHEIV2    PIC X(8).
 01    DFHEIV3    PIC X(8).
 01    DFHEIV20   PIC X(8).
 01    DFHC0084   PIC X(8).
 01    DFHC0085   PIC X(8).
 01    DFHC0320   PIC X(32).
 01    DFHEIV7    PIC X(2).
 01    DFHEIV8    PIC X(2).
 01    DFHC0022   PIC X(2).
 01    DFHC0023   PIC X(2).
 01    DFHEIV10   PIC S9(7) COMP-3.
 01    DFHEIV9    PIC X(1).
 01    DFHC0011   PIC X(1).
 01    DFHEIV4    PIC X(6).
 01    DFHC0070   PIC X(7).
 01    DFHC0071   PIC X(7).
 01    DFHC0440   PIC X(44).
 01    DFHC0441   PIC X(44).
 01    DFHDUMMY   COMP PIC S9(4).
 01    DFHEIV0    PICTURE X(29).
 LINKAGE SECTION.
```

Figure 5-1. Execute Interface Working-Storage work areas.

ing-Storage fields contain the variables that are passed to the Execute Interface. Appropriate values are placed into this parameter area by MOVE statements generated as a result of translator processing of CICS commands. Although not used by the application programmer, this area must be present for successful compilation and execution.

Immediately after the beginning of the Linkage Section the translator inserts a Command Level control block called the Execute Interface Block (EIB). The EIB is a *read-only* control block, which means that it is used solely to pass information to the application task. The Macro Level program shares CICS data areas such as the Task Control Area (TCA). As such, the Macro Level task has access to much information that is useful in these areas. This information is not routinely available to the Command Level task because the Command Level task does not share CICS data areas. In order to make application-oriented information from CICS data areas available to the Command Level task, CICS summarizes such information in the Execute Interface Block. Types of information that can be found in the EIB include: the name of the terminal to which the task is attached (EIBTRMID); the transaction identifier that initiated the task (EIBTRNID); the name of the terminal key used to cause a device interrupt and have the terminal send data to the computer (EIBAID); the location of the cursor on the terminal screen when the device interrupt occurred (EIBCPOSN); the date and time when the task was initiated (EIBDATE and EIBTIME); a code indicating the last command issued by the application task to CICS (EIBFN); and the return code from the last command (EIBRCODE). There are more fields in the EIB, and we will refer to this data area in subsequent discussions.

You can see from the above that the EIB contains useful application-oriented information. The EIB is like free lunch. You don't need to code anything to obtain it, and it is available as soon as the program gains control initially. The first instruction in your program could access an EIB field if you wanted.

The next thing that is in the Linkage Section is a communications area called DFHCOMMAREA. The communications area is used for passing information between CICS application programs or for passing information between tasks that follow each other at the same CICS terminal. The latter part of the last statement will be explained when we discuss the RETURN command. For now let's concentrate on the coding rules for the COMMAREA. If using the COMMAREA in a program, its definition is placed as the first item coded after the beginning of the Linkage Section. Below is an example of how this is done:

```
LINKAGE SECTION.
01 DFHCOMMAREA.
    04 whatever fields you are expecting to be passed.
```

In batch programming, if data are being passed between two modules, both the calling and the called programs must agree on the data format and contents. Since this is also true of the COMMAREA, the data anticipated in the COMMAREA are totally dependent upon the application.

If the COMMAREA is not being used in a CICS program, there is no need to code the 01 DFHCOMMAREA in the Linkage Section. In this case the translator inserts the following:

```
01 DFHCOMMAREA PIC X.
```

This is done because a COBOL Command Level CICS program has a BLL cell in the Linkage Section for the COMMAREA whether or not it is used. Since the BLL cell is present, there must be an 01-level description that corresponds to the BLL.

Figure 5-2 is an example of a Linkage Section for a program that uses a COMMAREA. The 01 DFHCOMMAREA is coded *before* the 01 for the user BLL cells (if your compiler requires that they be coded).

Figure 5-3 illustrates a Linkage Section of a program that is not using a COMMAREA. The first thing coded by the programmer after the words LINKAGE SECTION is the 01-level description of the linkage BLL cell parameter list. In this latter case, the translator will insert an 01 for the DFHCOMMAREA. The next definition after DFHCOMMAREA in the Linkage Section is the BLL parameter list.

Figure 5-2. Linkage Section coding with a COMMAREA.

Program Code

Dynamic Task Area

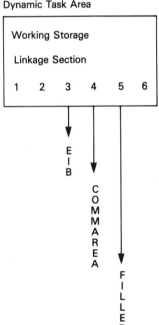

```
WORKING-STORAGE SECTION.

LINKAGE SECTION.
*   TRANSLATOR INSERTS EIB
*   TRANSLATOR WON'T INSERT AN
*   01 FOR THE DFHCOMMAREA
*   SINCE ONE IS CODED IN THE
*   PROGRAM.
01      DFHCOMMAREA.
        05  PASSED-FIELD    PIC X.
        05  PASSED-KEY      PIC X(9).
01      BLLS.
        05  FILLER       PIC S9(8) COMP.
        05  USER-BLL     PIC S9(8) COMP.
01      USER-DATA-AREA  PIC X(100).
```

In CICS programs, COBOL BLLs 1 and 2 are not used. The remaining BLL cells are used as follows:

BLL 3 addresses the Execute Interface Block. This BLL is set by CICS.
BLL 4 addresses the DFHCOMMAREA if one is present. CICS provides automatic addressability.
BLL 5 is the "FILLER" BLL used by CICS. This BLL contains its own storage address.
BLL 6 is the first user BLL named USER-BLL in the sample. A valid address is placed in this BLL during the successful execution of a CICS LOCATE mode command.

Had there been more user BLLs coded, then there would be additional BLLs present in the load module and in the dynamic copy of the Data Division.

Figure 5-3. Linkage Section coding without a COMMAREA.

Program Code   Dynamic Task Area

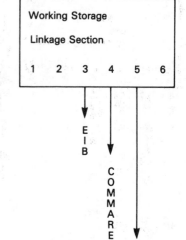

```
    WORKING-STORAGE SECTION.

    LINKAGE SECTION.
  *  TRANSLATOR INSERTS EIB
  *  TRANSLATOR INSERTS AN 01
  *  FOR THE DFHCOMMAREA SINCE
  *  ONE IS NOT CODED IN THE
  *  PROGRAM.
    01      BLLS.
                05  FILLER        PIC S9(8) COMP.
                05  USER-BLL      PIC S9(8) COMP.
    01      USER-DATA-AREA    PIC X(100).
```

In CICS programs COBOL BLLs 1 and 2 are not used. The remaining BLL cells are used as follows:

   BLL 3 addresses the Execute Interface Block.
   BLL 4 addresses the DFHCOMMAREA if one is present. Since we are not using one, this BLL contains X"FF000000."
   BLL 5 is the "FILLER" BLL used by CICS.
   BLL 6 is the first user BLL named USER-BLL in the sample. A valid address is placed in this BLL during the successful execution of a CICS LOCATE mode command.

   Had there been more user BLLs coded, then there would be additional BLLs present in the load module and in the dynamic copy of the Data Division.

The translator changes the PROCEDURE DIVISION statement to PROCEDURE DIVISION USING DFHEIBLK, DFHCOMMAREA. This gives you automatic addressability to these two areas. There is a field in the Execute Interface Block that defines the length of a passed COMMAREA (EIBCALEN). If you are expecting a COMMAREA to be passed to you, it is possible to test EIBCALEN to make sure that your COMMAREA is there and is the size you are expecting.

The translator then goes through the Procedure Division statements looking for CICS commands. These commands begin with the words EXEC CICS. CICS commands are coded in agreement with the coding rules of the respective programming languages. For example, in COBOL it is quite acceptable to begin the command anywhere after the beginning of the B Margin. The commands are free format within the rules of the respective programming language, meaning that parameters can be coded in any order that suits you. In COBOL, parameters are separated from each other by one or more spaces, and commands may be continued on successive lines. If a parameter is to name an option, the option is enclosed in parentheses and no space or one or more spaces may separate the option from its parameter. For example, here is the READ command:

```
EXEC CICS READ DATASET('PRODMST')
     RIDFLD(MY-KEY) INTO (WS-RECORD)
     LENGTH (WS-LEN) END-EXEC.
```

This command could have been coded with the parameters in different order. A single parameter per line could have been coded, or more parameters could have been strung across a line as long as the ending margin was not exceeded. Note that between the parameter DATASET and its option naming PRODMST there is no space, but between the INTO parameter and its option naming the place where the record is to be placed there is one space. The commands are free format, except that they must abide by the rules of the programming language and always begin with EXEC CICS.

Before we leave the topic of abiding by the rules of respective programming languages, a word must be said about the options that are coded within CICS commands. In many cases we can use either a field name or a literal value within CICS commands. Consider the following commands, both of which are valid:

```
EXEC CICS READ DATASET('APPFILE') RIDFLD(KEY)
     SET(FILE-BLL) LENGTH (FILE-LEN) END-EXEC.

EXEC CICS READ DATASET(FILE-NAME) RIDFLD(KEY)
     SET (FILE-BLL) LENGTH(FILE-LEN) END-EXEC.
```

The DATASET option is specified differently in the above commands. The first specifies the data set DDNAME as a nonnumeric literal value, and is consequently enclosed in single quotes. The latter command uses the name of a field that contains the value of the DDNAME. In this option either a literal value or a field name may be used. Other options are not so flexible. The SET option, for example, must name a BLL cell. The INTO option must name a data area. In the case of output commands, the LENGTH option can name either a data area or a numeric literal. On the other hand, the LENGTH option used in input commands must name a data field, since CICS returns length information and a literal cannot be used for this purpose. However, if a mistake is made in command coding, the translator flags the error during translation so that a correction can be made and the program recompiled.

In COBOL, commands end with END-EXEC. This is not applicable to assembler or PL/I. The reason for END-EXEC is so that CICS commands can be stacked within a COBOL IF . . . ELSE statement. The period is used to end a COBOL statement, such as the IF statement, but the END-EXEC terminates a CICS command. The two can coincide, and a command can end "END-EXEC." or the CICS command can terminate and the COBOL statement continue. Below is an example of a COBOL IF statement that contains several CICS commands:

```
IF FUNCTION-CODE IS ADD
      EXEC CICS GETMAIN
            LENGTH (WS-LENGTH)
            INITIMG (WS-SPACE)
            SET (FILE-BLL)
      END-EXEC
      MOVE NAME TO FILE-NAME
      MOVE ADDR TO FILE-ADDRESS
      MOVE NUMBER TO FILE KEY
      EXEC  CICS WRITE DATASET ('APPFILE')
            FROM (FILE-RECORD)
            RIDFLD (NUMBER)
            LENGTH (WS-LENGTH)
      END-EXEC
ELSE
      EXEC  CICS READ UPDATE DATASET ('APPFILE')
            RIDFLD (NUMBER)
            SET (FILE-BLL)
            LENGTH (WS-LENGTH)
      END-EXEC
      MOVE NAME TO FILE-NAME
      MOVE ADDR TO FILE-ADDRESS
      EXEC  CICS REWRITE DATASET ('APPFILE')
            FROM (FILE-RECORD)
            LENGTH (WS-LENGTH)
      END-EXEC.
```

The use of END-EXEC makes this stacking of commands possible and aids in building structured COBOL programs. Don't be concerned at this time about the syntax of illustrated commands or where referenced data fields are defined. These points will be covered shortly. Right now, the major issue is the use of the END-EXEC in COBOL. CICS commands are translated into calls to the Execute Interface and pass parameters in the Working-Storage data area that have been inserted by the translator. By and large, the translator is transparent to the application programmer. It works because the translate step is included in the compile procedure, and normally one doesn't have to worry about it. You must, however, use a CICS Compile JCL procedure, because without the translate step to process CICS-oriented code the compile step will not stand a chance of completing without serious error. The one problem that people encounter with the translator is that they forget about its existence and neglect to look at its messages. If the translator detects a command that cannot be translated properly because the command is missing a required parameter or contains some other coding fault, it produces a diagnostic message; you must look at translator diagnostics as well as those produced by COBOL.

5.2   UNUSUAL CONDITIONS DURING COMMAND EXECUTION

CICS command execution can result in the occurrence of an unusual condition. For example, a task attempts to read a file but the record requested is not on the file. In this case the NOTFND condition occurs. Unusual conditions can be treated in one of three ways in a CICS application program: we can allow the default course of action to occur; we can ask CICS to IGNORE the fact that the condition occurred; or we can request that the processing program HANDLE the unusual condition in a programmer-specified paragraph.

The typical default course of action for the Execute Interface to take is for the task to be abended. The chain of events is as follows: The processing program issues a CICS command such as READ. The command causes the Execute Interface to be invoked. The Execute Interface primes the appropriate work area and invokes File Control. File Control attempts to retrieve the record indicated and finds that the record is not on the file. File Control returns to the Execute Interface with a return code indicating that the record is not on the file. If the default course of action is allowed to occur, the Execute Interface terminates the task with a unique abend code ("AEIM") that specifically indicates the NOTFND condition. The abend code is written to the terminal along with a message that the transaction has abended, and the abend code is included in a formatted dump that is written to the CICS Dump Data Set. We could print the dump, but essentially we know why it occurred—the record requested wasn't on the file. The main point that is critical to remember here is that control does not return to the Command Level application program after the unusual condition occurs, because in this case the default course of action is to terminate the task.

Most unusual conditions result in task abends unless otherwise trapped by the application program, but there are a number of cases when this is not so. The display of an abend code is not a particularly friendly way for the user to find out that the record is not on the file, but if the abend is well documented in a user manual it may be an acceptable situation in some applications.

However, let's take a look at another example to see how this default abend could be problematic. Consider a transaction that enables a terminal operator to inquire about an employee on the employee master file. This transaction also permits the updating of employee information, the adding of new employee records, and the deleting of employee data. The user enters a transaction identifier, a function code that indicates what type of operation is to be performed, and an employee number. Figure 5-4 illustrates a sample input request that might be used to initiate the transaction. The default course of action would result in a task abend if a record sought were not found in the file. This might be passable in the case of change, delete, or inquiry functions.

However, for the addition of a new record the Execute Interface default processing could present a real problem. For ADD function, we could simply send a data entry screen with field titles so that the terminal operator could enter information. However, if the user entered data regarding someone who had already been added to the file, the data entry operation would be a waste of time; when we attempted to add the record we would discover that the data were already on the file. A transaction that allows someone to spend 5 or 10 minutes entering redundant information is certainly not user friendly. Therefore, for add processing we would want to determine whether the record was already on the file. This is accomplished by attempting to read the file for the record in question. If a record were found we would receive control back at the next sequential instruction after the READ command, and would know that there was a duplicate record on the file. In this event we could display the file

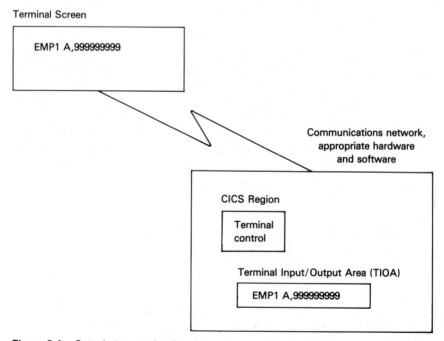

Figure 5-4.   Sample transaction input.

information with a message indicating that the record already exists. The user is then spared the needless work of duplicate data entry.

If a record were not found on the file, the NOTFND condition would occur, and by default the Execute Interface would abend the task with a unique abend code. During add processing the user would never have an opportunity to enter information for new records. We would not want the default course of action for the NOTFND condition in this case. Therefore, we would use a CICS mechanism to alter the default course of action.

5.2.1 Handling Unusual Conditions

The HANDLE CONDITION statement can be used to specify certain conditions that the program is to handle. In the HANDLE CONDITION statement, one or more specific conditions are named, as are paragraphs within the program. The named paragraph for a condition indicates a routine within the program where the condition is processed. One routine or paragraph can be named for multiple CONDITIONs being handled. For the add transaction described above, we might specify the following HANDLE CONDITION statement:

```
EXEC CICS HANDLE CONDITION
      NOTFND (B300-CHECK-IF-ADD)
END-EXEC.
EXEC CICS READ DATASET('APPFILE')
      RIDFLD(MY-KEY)
      SET(FILE-BLL)
      LENGTH(FILE-LENGTH)
END-EXEC.
```

This HANDLE CONDITION statement informs the Execute Interface that if the NOTFND condition occurs during subsequent CICS command execution, control is to pass to the paragraph named B300-CHECK-IF-ADD. Any other unusual condition is to be treated in the default manner. Note that the HANDLE CONDITION statement must be executed prior to the CICS command in which the condition is to be trapped. Otherwise, the Execute Interface is unaware of the intention to override the default at the time of command execution. In this example the HANDLE CONDITION is coded immediately before the actual READ command. However, HANDLE CONDITION can be placed anywhere in the program as long as it is executed prior to the appropriate CICS command.

In the case illustrated above, the HANDLE CONDITION causes the Execute Interface to build a table for the task that relates the occurrence of the NOTFND condition with return of control to the program at the paragraph named in the HANDLE CONDITION. HANDLE CONDITION processing functions as a GO TO . . . DEPENDING ON. Therefore, when the READ command is executed, the return point in the program is dependent on the outcome of reading the file. If a record is found on the file, control returns to the application program at the next sequential instruction after the READ command. If the NOTFND condition occurs during READ processing, then control returns to the program at a paragraph named B300-CHECK-IF-ADD. If any other unusual condition occurs, the Execute Interface abends the task with a unique abend code.

A HANDLE CONDITION statement may include up to 16 different conditions; once defined, the processing of each condition remains in effect until specifically changed with subsequent condition handling statements. The following example illustrates a more complex case using the HANDLE CONDITION:

```
EXEC CICS HANDLE CONDITION
    NOTFND(B300-CHECK-IF-ADD)
    DSIDERR(X100-SEND-DSIDERR-MESSAGE)
END-EXEC.

EXEC CICS READ DATASET('CUSTMAST')
    RIDFLD(KEY-FIELD) LENGTH(FILE-LENGTH)
    SET(CUSTMAST-BLL)
END-EXEC.

EXEC CICS HANDLE CONDITION
    NOTFND(X200-SEND-BKORDS-NOTFND)
    DSIDERR
END-EXEC.

EXEC CICS READ DATASET ('BKORDS')
    RIDFLD (BK-KEY) LENGTH (FILE-LENGTH)
    SET (BKORD-BLL)
END-EXEC.
```

Since a HANDLE CONDITION may name up to 16 conditions, a single statement can set multiple conditions. In the first HANDLE CONDITION we indicate that two different conditions are to be trapped. However, we only want these conditions to be processed for the first READ of the "CUSTMAST" file. Since the conditions HANDLEd are in effect until specifically reset, the second HANDLE is used to alter particular conditions as required for the processing of the BKORDS file. Note that in the second HANDLE CONDITION statement the unusual condition DSIDERR (data set name error) has no paragraph specified after it. This resets the condition to the default course of action.

The flow of processing is as follows: The first HANDLE establishes that if the NOTFND condition occurs control is to return to the paragraph named B300-CHECK-IF-ADD, and that if the DSIDERR condition results the paragraph named X100-SEND-DSIDERR-MESSAGE is to be invoked. When the CUSTMAST file is read, if a record is found then control passes to the next sequential instruction after the READ command. If an unusual condition other than NOTFND or DSIDERR occurs, then the default course of action is taken by the Execute Interface. If NOTFND occurs, control is returned to the program at B300-CHECK-IF-ADD. If DSIDERR occurs, the program is reinvoked at X100-SEND-DSIDERR-MESSAGE.

Suppose that a record had been found on the CUSTMAST; we next want to read the BKORDS file. However, we no longer wish to have unusual conditions treated in the same manner, so the second HANDLE condition is used to alter condition handling for the next READ command. We have elected the same conditions, but could have specified other conditions as well. The second HANDLE CONDITION resets the DSIDERR condition to the default course of action, and the processing of NOTFND is changed so that if this condition occurs the X200-SEND-BKORDS-NOTFND paragraph is invoked.

Conditions specified in HANDLE CONDITION commands can be temporarily ignored for the execution of a single command. A NOHANDLE option can be included in a CICS command to indicate that any unusual condition resulting from command execution is to be ignored. The program receives control back at the next instruction after a command with the NOHANDLE option. It would then be necessary to check the Execute Interface Block return code (EIBRCODE) to determine if an unusual condition resulted from command execution. In the following READ command, the NOHANDLE is used to specify that, regardless of any unusual condition occurring, control is to pass back to the program at the next sequential instruction after the READ:

```
EXEC CICS READ DATASET ('PRODMST') RIDFLD(PROD-NUM)
     SET(PRODUCT-BLL) LENGTH (REC-LEN) NOHANDLE
END-EXEC.
```

In contrast, the IGNORE CONDITION statement causes specific conditions to be ignored for every command until IGNOREd conditions are reset via a condition handling statement. With the IGNORE CONDITION statement, named conditions are ignored and control passes back to the program at the next sequential instruction after each CICS command for which an IGNOREd condition occurs or a normal response is indicated. The application program should interrogate the EIBRCODE to determine if an error occurred during command execution. The following is an example of using the IGNORE CONDITION:

```
EXEC CICS IGNORE CONDITION
     NOTFND DSIDERR
END-EXEC.
```

```
EXEC CICS READ DATASET('CUSTMAST')
    SET(CUST-BLL)  LENGTH(FILE-LENGTH)
    RIDFLD(CUST-NUMBER) END-EXEC.
IF EIBRCODE = LOW-VALUES
    THEN MOVE CUST-NAME TO SCREEN-NAME
ELSE
    PERFORM C100-FORMAT-ERROR-MESSAGE.
```

The EIBRCODE is interrogated because NORMAL processing, NOTFND, and DSIDERR all result in control being returned at the next sequential instruction after the read.

There is also a general error catch-all that can be specified. For example, if we don't want to have four-character abend codes displayed on the screen under any circumstances, it is possible to HANDLE or IG-NORE specific conditions and/or the general ERROR condition.

```
EXEC CICS HANDLE CONDITION
    NOTFND (B200-CHECK-IF-ADD)
    ERROR(X500-SEND-USER-FRIENDLY-MESSAGE)
    END-EXEC.
```

Subsequent to this HANDLE CONDITION, the following will occur during CICS command execution: If the NOTFND condition occurs, control will pass to the appropriate routine. If any other unusual conditions occur, control will pass to the routine named in the ERROR option of the HANDLE. Since this is a general ERROR routine, we may want to know which command was last processed by the Execute Interface. This is contained in the EIBFN field. If EIBFN indicates that a file command was the last command executed, the DDNAME of the data set is contained in EIBDS. The EIBRCODE setting indicates the type of error in relation to the last command or EIBFN. By interrogating these fields in the general error routine, the program can send a "user-friendly" message to the screen rather than have the Execute Interface abend with a four-character abend code. One word of caution should be noted about the use of the general ERROR condition. The paragraph named as the general ERROR processor should either not issue CICS commands or should first reset the general ERROR condition. Otherwise, an error encountered in a command issued in the general ERROR routine would result in the reentry into this routine, and a loop might very well result. The condition can be reset by issuing the following command:

```
EXEC CICS HANDLE CONDITION ERROR END-EXEC.
```

All conditions HANDLEd can be temporarily suspended with the PUSH HANDLE instruction. The POP HANDLE restores all handled conditions suspended by a prior PUSH HANDLE. An example of the use of PUSH and POP is given below:

```
EXEC CICS HANDLE CONDITION NOTFND (B200-CHECK-ADD)
    END-EXEC.
EXEC CICS READ DATASET ('PRODMST') RIDFLD (PROD-NUM)
    SET (PRODMST-BLL) END-EXEC.
EXEC CICS PUSH HANDLE END-EXEC.
EXEC CICS READ DATASET('BKORDS') RIDFLD(ORDER-NUMBER)
    SET(BKORD-BLL) END-EXEC.
EXEC CICS POP HANDLE END-EXEC.
```

The conditions being HANDLEd up to the PUSH HANDLE instruction are temporarily suspended for the READ of BKORDS. No conditions are in effect for this READ. Subsequent to the READ, the POP HANDLE restores all HANDLEd conditions.

Most unusual conditions result in the termination of the task making the request. However, there are conditions that do not result in task termination. For example, a program issues a request for a dynamic storage allocation using the GETMAIN command. An unusual condition NOSTG is associated with the GETMAIN command. In the event that CICS cannot make the storage allocation because there is no storage available, the NOSTG condition default action results in the task being suspended until storage becomes available. We could use one of the mechanisms described above for overriding condition processing and indicating that we do not want the task to be suspended until the requested resource (dynamic storage in this case) becomes available. For commands that may result in task suspension, we can include the NOSUSPEND option in the command. The effect of the NOSUSPEND in this instance is to make the request conditional; if the resource is not available, CICS returns control to the program and we can use the EIBRCODE to determine if CICS was able to satisfy our request successfully. The following is an example of the use of NOSUSPEND in a CICS command:

```
DATA DIVISION.
WORKING-STORAGE SECTION.
77  STORAGE-SIZE                PIC S(4) COMP
        VALUE +80.
77  INITIAL-VALUE               PIC X
        VALUE LOW-VALUES.
LINKAGE SECTION.
01  BLLS.
        04  FILLER              PIC S9(8) COMP.
        04  DYNAMIC-STG-PTR     PIC S9(8) COMP.
01  DYNAMIC-STORAGE-AREA        PIC X(80).
PROCEDURE DIVISION.

    EXEC CICS GETMAIN LENGTH (STORAGE-SIZE)
```

```
                    INITIMG (INITIAL-VALUE)
                    SET (DYNAMIC-STG-PTR)
                    NOSUSPEND
              END-EXEC.
              IF EIBRCODE = LOW-VALUES NEXT SENTENCE
                 ELSE
                       EXEC CICS ABEND
                            ABCODE ('NSTG')
                       END-EXEC.
```

The GETMAIN command coded above will not result in task suspension even if there is no storage available because of the inclusion of the NOSUSPEND option. Consequently, we must test to make sure that storage was in fact available. This is accomplished by examining the EIBRCODE. In this case we are electing to abend the task with a unique abend code of "NSTG" in favor of having CICS suspend the task.

With NOHANDLE, IGNORE CONDITION, and NOSUSPEND we elect to receive control back at the next instruction after a CICS command, and we must test the EIBRCODE in order to determine the relative success of our request. In the coding examples we have used, we simply wanted a yes or no answer from our interrogation of the EIBRCODE. Therefore, we tested "EIBRCODE = LOW-VALUES." However, we are frequently concerned with having more explicit information, such as if the NOTFND condition occurred or if the unusual occurrence was one of several other conditions. That kind of interrogation gets a little more complex because there are unique settings for EIBRCODE to reflect each different condition.

The use of the HANDLE CONDITION makes life a little easier because we don't have to test for specific conditions in application code. However, there is a price. We are opting for programming convenience at the cost of structured elegance. In structured programming there should be one exit and entry point when branching out of code. Using the HANDLE CONDITION, there are potentially numerous return points for one program exit. There is yet another alternative that can be used. We can include the RESP option on our CICS commands. Functionally, what does this do to the command? It has the effect of NOHANDLE in terms of command execution, so unusual conditions are ignored for command processing. The advantage of RESP is that CICS places a code in a 4-byte binary field named by the RESP option and we can use a CICS function, DFHRESP, to examine the RESP field setting. With EIBRCODE we must test for specific hexadecimal settings, but DFHRESP uses condition names, which makes specific condition testing easier to code. Below is an example of the use of RESP option and the DFHRESP function to test CICS response:

```
DATA DIVISION.
WORKING-STORAGE SECTION.
```

```
77  RSP-FIELD          PIC S9(8) COMP.
77  KEY-FIELD          PIC X(9).
LINKAGE SECTION.
01  BLLS.
    04  FILLER         PIC S9(8) COMP.
    04  FILE-BLL       PIC S9(8) COMP.
01  FILE-DATA-AREA.
    04  FILE-KEY       PIC X(9).
    04  FILE-NAME      PIC X(30).
    04  FILE-ADDR1     PIC X(20).
    04  FILE-ADDR2     PIC X(20).
    04  FILLER         PIC X.
PROCEDURE DIVISION.
    .
    .
    EXEC CICS READ DATASET ('APPFILE')
        RIDFLD (KEY-FIELD) SET (FILE-BLL)
        RESP (RSP-FIELD) END-EXEC.
    IF RSP-FIELD = DFHRESP (NORMAL) NEXT SENTENCE
    ELSE
        IF RSP-FIELD = DFHRESP (NOTFND) GO TO 100-ADD-OK
        ELSE
            EXEC CICS ABEND ABCODE ('FERR') END-EXEC.
*   PROCESS RECORD FOUND HERE.
    .
    .
    .
    100-ADD-OK.
*   PROCESS NOTFND CONDITION HERE.
```

Note that the field named in the RESP option is a 4-byte binary field. Any of the unusual condition names and NORMAL can be used in the DFHRESP function. The advantage of using the RESP option and the DFHRESP function is that we can code structured programs without having to test EIBRCODE for specific hex settings.

5.3 HANDLING TERMINAL ATTENTION KEYS

Another thing that can be HANDLEd is the identification of the Attention IDentifier key entered by the terminal operator. Attention IDentifier is the name of the key that the operator presses to cause a device interrupt. This can be the ENTER, CLEAR, or a PF or PA key. The HANDLE AID command is used to identify paragraph names associated with different Attention IDentifiers. The format of the HANDLE AID is as follows:

```
EXEC CICS HANDLE AID
    AID-id (paragraph-name)
```

The AID-id names the Attention IDentifier to be trapped at the paragraph indicated. Up to 16 options may be named in a HANDLE AID. As with the HANDLE CONDITION, PUSH and POP may be used to suspend and reinstate handling of AIDs. The NOHANDLE option coded on a command also suspends HANDLE AID processing. The AID-id can include the following key options:

OPTIONS	KEY(S) INCLUDED FOR HANDLE AID
ANYKEY	Any device interrupt key other than the ENTER key
CLEAR	The CLEAR key
ENTER	The ENTER key
PA1-PA3	The appropriate Program Attention key(s)
PF1-PF24	The appropriate Program Function key(s)

The actual processing of the HANDLE AID does not occur when the command is executed. Rather, a subsequent request for access to terminal input data results in a branch to a paragraph named in the HANDLE AID according to the AID used by the operator. An example of the HANDLE AID is provided below:

```
EXEC CICS HANDLE AID
      CLEAR (X500-END-TRANSACTION)
      PF19 (B200-PAGE-BACKWARD)
      ENTER (B300-PAGE-FORWARD)
      ANYKEY (B300-PAGE-FORWARD)
END-EXEC.
*        NO BRANCH IS TAKEN HERE. THE HANDLE AID CAUSES
*        THE EXECUTE INTERFACE TO BUILD A GO TO . . .
*        DEPENDING ON TABLE WHICH IS USED FOR THE NEXT
*        REQUEST FOR TERMINAL INPUT DATA.
      EXEC CICS RECEIVE INTO(TERMINAL-INPUT-AREA)
          LENGTH (TRMNL-LENGTH) END-EXEC.
```

As a result of the Terminal Control RECEIVE command, which requests terminal input, the appropriate branch is taken. If the operator presses the CLEAR key, control passes to the routine named X500-END-TRANSACTION. The PF19 key causes a branch to the routine named B200-PAGE-BACKWARD. If any other key (with the exception of the ENTER key) is selected, the ANYKEY option causes control to pass to B300-PAGE-FORWARD. The ENTER option is specifically coded to cause a branch to the same routine as ANYKEY because ENTER is excluded from ANYKEY. As with the HANDLE CONDITION statement, HANDLE AID is not a structured approach to dealing with attention identifiers. There is another way that is more efficient and more structured in approach.

Attention keys can also be handled programmatically by checking the AID field presented in the Execute Interface Block. This is the EIBAID field. Since HANDLE AID results in a table being created by the Execute Interface, it is more efficient in terms of program execution for the programmer to interrogate the EIBAID. There is a copy statement that can be brought into the application program that has data names for the various attention keys. This copy statement named DFHAID is normally copied into CICS application program Working Storage, and the key names defined in DFHAID are used to test EIBAID. An example of the code required to programmatically test the EIBAID field is provided below:

```
WORKING-STORAGE SECTION
01 DFHAID  COPY DFHAID.
*   CONTAINS NAMES FOR EACH OF THE KEYS INCLUDING THOSE USED
*       IN THE CODE BELOW.
PROCEDURE DIVISION.
        IF EIBAID = DFHPF19 GO TO B200-PAGE-BACKWARD.
        IF EIBAID = DFHCLEAR GO TO X500-END-TRANSACTION
        ELSE GO TO B300-PAGE-FORWARD.
```

5.4   CONVERSATIONAL VS. PSEUDOCONVERSATIONAL PROGRAMMING

Online programming grew out of batch. In batch programs if information is to be written to a peripheral device such as a printer, the output instruction is executed and the program continues its execution directly after the output completes. Online programs interact with a terminal as a peripheral device, and this approach resulted in what is called CONVER-SATIONAL programming style. In a conversational program there is a conversation between the terminal operator and the online program. Figure 5-5 illustrates the general structure of a conversational program. Note that output to the terminal is handled in the same manner as output to any peripheral device. We SEND data to the terminal and wait for a response. After receiving and reviewing the information displayed on the terminal screen, the operator enters information and presses a device interrupt key. The conversational program receives the input and continues its processing. The only problem with this approach is the fact that the terminal is not just another peripheral device. The terminal's response is directed by a human being who is much slower than the computer. This disparity results in system resources being held until the slow human user has entered or otherwise processed information.

Pseudoconversational programming style attempts to compensate for the unequal processing speeds of people and machines. Therefore, this technique is applicable only to programs written to interface with people

PROCEDURE DIVISION.	**EXPLANATION**
EXEC CICS RECEIVE	Receives terminal input
VALIDATE INPUT DATA	Test initial input
EXEC CICS READ	Read the file
FORMAT DISPLAY SCREEN	Move fields from file record to program work area
EXEC CICS SEND	Display information on the terminal
W A I T	Task waits for the terminal operator to enter update data and press a device interrupt key
EXEC CICS RECEIVE	Task receives data entered by the terminal operator
VALIDATE ENTERED DATA	Test the input to verify correctness
EXEC CICS READ UPDATE	Read the file in anticipation of updating
UPDATE FILE INFORMATION	Move valid data into retrieved file record
EXEC CICS REWRITE	Rewrite the updated record to the file
FORMAT OUTPUT MESSAGE	Create a message to inform the operator of successful update
EXEC CICS SEND	Display the message on the terminal
EXEC CICS RETURN	Inform CICS that task has completed

Figure 5-5. Structure of a conversational program.

using interactive terminals. For programs conversing with other types of processes (for example, host-to-host communication), this programming style is not utilized. Likewise, when writing a program solely to display or print information on a noninteractive device (such as an online printer), the pseudoconversational style is not indicated.

In pseudoconversational processing, a transaction is broken into a collection of one or more tasks based on terminal output and subsequent input. When a pseudoconversational program sends a screen of information, it RETURNs control to CICS and thereby terminates the task. However, the RETURN command is coded in such a way that CICS is informed that the function is to be continued when there is an input received from the terminal operator. The format of a pseudoconversational program is depicted in Fig. 5-6.

The first thing that is done when we enter the program illustrated in Fig. 5-6 is to determine the mode of entry. Is this the first time this

	EXPLANATION
PROCEDURE DIVISION.	
IF FIRST-TIME NEXT SENTENCE ELSE GO TO SECOND-TIME-IN	Determine the mode of entry. FIRST-TIME means that the operator has just initiated the transaction
EXEC CICS RECEIVE	Receives terminal input
VALIDATE INPUT DATA	Test initial input
EXEC CICS READ	Read the file
FORMAT DISPLAY SCREEN	Move fields from file record to program work area
EXEC CICS SEND	Display information
EXEC CICS RETURN TRANSID	Task ends with execution of the RETURN command. The TRANSID option names a next TRANSID that is to be saved by CICS until there is a subsequent I/P from the terminal. CICS then uses the saved TRANSID to begin a new task to complete the transaction. After task termination the Task Control Area (TCA) and dynamic Data Division are released. No resources are held while the operator enters information.
SECOND-TIME-IN.	Resume transaction processing after operator has entered data
EXEC CICS RECEIVE	Task receives data entered by the terminal operator
VALIDATE ENTERED DATA	Test the input to verify correctness
EXEC CICS READ UPDATE	Read the file in anticipation of updating
UPDATE FILE INFORMATION	Move valid data into retrieved file record
EXEC CICS REWRITE	Update the file
FORMAT OUTPUT MESSAGE	Create a successful update message
EXEC CICS SEND	Display the message
EXEC CICS RETURN	Inform CICS that task and transaction have completed

Figure 5-6. Pseudoconversational program structure.

119

program is being invoked by the terminal operator? Phrased another way, is this the initiation of the transaction? (Don't worry now about how this test can be made; we will go over the details when we discuss Program Control commands.) If this is the first time, then control continues with the next statement and we do the first phase of processing, which is to RECEIVE the terminal input, validate the input to determine if it is correctly formatted, READ a file to retrieve the data record to be displayed for the terminal operator, select data fields from the record and format an output data screen, SEND data to the terminal, and then RETURN to CICS with a TRANSID named. This next transaction identifier is saved by CICS in the terminal's entry in the Terminal Control Table. The task ends but, because of the saved TRANSID, control will pass back to the application program associated with the named TRAN-SID when the operator presses a device interrupt key. Note that CICS is not aware of this continuation in any sense other than the saving of the next TRANSID. The task itself has ended and CICS sees the world in terms of tasks or Task Control Areas. The task's TCA and dynamic storage are released, and when the program is reinvoked, it will have a totally refreshed Data Division and will be a new task from CICS's perspective. The program will be reinvoked at the beginning of the Procedure Division.

As a result of the first phase of transaction processing, data are displayed on the terminal screen and the operator can enter information to update one or more fields. If the operator takes 10 minutes entering and verifying updates, no CICS resources are held waiting for the operator; therefore, CICS resources can be used effectively for other work that has to be performed. After completing working on the screen, the operator depresses a key that causes a device interrupt, such as the ENTER key. When CICS Terminal Control receives the input data from the terminal, it checks to see if there is a "waiting" TRANSID from the last task to process at the terminal. A waiting TRANSID takes precedence over everything else. Therefore, control passes back to the application program. Upon this entry we determine that this is the second time into the module and proceed to the paragraph SECOND-TIME-IN. In this part of the program we complete transaction processing by validating data and updating the file. When the second task RETURNs to CICS, it does not name a TRANSID. This means that the transaction is complete from our perspective. The operator can then clear the screen and proceed with another request. Remember, however, the CICS sees the two tasks in our pseudo-conversational program as two separate and distinct units of work. We use CICS to remember where to go next when the operator has entered data, but CICS doesn't relate the two tasks.

In our example, a single program is used to process both phases of transaction processing. However, a pseudoconversational transaction can be broken into two or more programs. The first phase of transaction processing involves file-to-screen display, whereas the second part consists of data validation and screen-to-file update. There is really very little duplication of processing between the two phases, and if broken into two programs we have two smaller modules which are easier to maintain. One of our objectives in a Virtual Storage environment is to have small programs, and therefore pseudoconversational transactions are normally broken into two modules. The first module uses the TRANSID of the second program in the RETURN TRANSID command, rather than its own. Figure 5-7 shows how the program illustrated in Fig. 5-6 can be

PROGRAM 1

PROCEDURE DIVISION.	**EXPLANATION**
EXEC CICS RECEIVE	Receives terminal input
VALIDATE INPUT DATA	Test initial input
EXEC CICS READ	Read the file
FORMAT DISPLAY SCREEN	Move fields from file record to program work area
EXEC CICS SEND	Display information on the terminal
EXEC CICS RETURN TRANSID OF PROGRAM 2	End Task 1 but ensure that Program 2 will be started when the operator presses a device interrupt key

PROGRAM 2

PROCEDURE DIVISION.	Program 2 is invoked because prior task at the terminal returned to CICS with the TRANSID associated with Program 2
EXEC CICS RECEIVE	Task receives data entered by the terminal operator
VALIDATE ENTERED DATA	Test the input to verify correctness
EXEC CICS READ UPDATE	Read the file in anticipation of updating
UPDATE FILE INFORMATION	Move valid data into retrieved file record
EXEC CICS REWRITE	Rewrite the updated record to the file
FORMAT OUTPUT MESSAGE	Create a message to inform the operator of successful update
EXEC CICS SEND	Display the message on the terminal
EXEC CICS RETURN	Inform CICS that task has completed

Figure 5-7. Two program pseudoconversational transaction.

broken into two smaller modules based upon screen output and subsequent input.

Although pseudoconversational programming conserves CICS resources such as storage, getting used to this programming style takes some adjustment for batch-oriented programmers. We will return to pseudoconversational programming again when we discuss Program Control commands, because the realization of pseudoconversational programming utilizes Program Control functions. We will also relate pseudoconversational considerations to file access and integrity when File Control is discussed. At this point it is merely necessary to understand the structure and purpose of pseudoconversational design.

REVIEW EXERCISE

Provide a short answer to each of the questions below.

1. What are the three steps needed to create an executable CICS load module once the source code has been written?
2. List the things that the COBOL Translator does to a COBOL source module.
3. What is the Execute Interface Block? What does the application programmer do to obtain it?
4. What is the purpose of the END-EXEC command terminator in a COBOL program?
5. How may unusual conditions be handled in a CICS program?
6. What does the HANDLE AID instruction do?
7. What is pseudoconversational programming, and why is it used for transactions that involve video terminal interaction?

CODING EXERCISE

1. Code a Linkage Section to process the following data areas: Four files are used in LOCATE mode. The PRODMST record is 110 bytes, the BKORDER record is 250 bytes, the INVMST is 400 bytes, and the ORDIMG is 320 bytes. No COMMAREA is being used.
2. Code the linkage section for number 1 using a COMMAREA of 500 bytes.

The following CICS code is used to READ four files; the subsequent exercises are based upon this sample code:

```
PROCEDURE DIVISION
    EXEC CICS READ DATASET ('ORDIMG')
        SET (ORD-BLL) LENGTH (ORD-LENGTH)
        RIDFLD (ORD-KEY) END-EXEC.
```

EXEC CICS READ DATASET ('PRODMST') RIDFLD (PROD-NUM)
LENGTH (PROD-LENGTH) SET (PROD-BLL) END-EXEC.

EXEC CICS READ DATASET ('BKORDER') RIDFLD (BKOD-NUM)
LENGTH (BK-LENGTH) INTO (BKORDER-RECORD) END-EXEC.

EXEC CICS READ DATASET ('INVMST') SET (INV-BLL)
LENGTH (INV-LENGTH) RIDFLD (INV-NUM) END-EXEC.

3. Code the Data Division statements for file access assuming all file keys to be 9 bytes long and all records to be 100 bytes in length. The record areas for the files are as follows: ORDIMG-RECORD, PRODMST-RECORD, BKORDER-RECORD, and INVMST-RECORD. The key fields named in the RIDFLD command options are to be placed in Working Storage, as are the length fields. Length fields are 2-byte binary fields defined as PIC S9(4) COMP fields.

4. Code the statements to alter processing as follows:
   A. If the NOTFND condition occurs when reading the ORDIMG file, control is to pass to a routine named E100-WRONG-ORDER-NUMBER.
   B. For all other file access, all unusual conditions are to be left to default, including NOTFND.

   Indicate where the above instructions would be placed within the application code provided above (for example, before a particular READ command).

ANSWERS TO REVIEW EXERCISE

Provide a short answer to each of the questions below.

1. What are the three steps needed to create an executable CICS load module once the source code has been written?

   The source module must be translated by a CICS translator. The translator changes the CICS-specific code into compiler-compatible instructions. The translated module is then compiled or assembled, and then it is link edited.

2. List the things that the COBOL translator does to a COBOL source module.

   The COBOL translator inserts 01-level Execute Interface work areas into the module's Working Storage. These areas are used by the translator to pass parameters during CICS calls. The translator alters the Linkage Section by inserting the Execute Interface Block and, if not coded by the programmer, an 01-level for DFHCOMMAREA. The Procedure Division statement is altered to include USING DFHEIBLK,

DFHCOMMAREA. Within the Procedure Division, the Translator replaces EXEC CICS statements with Execute Interface CALLs.

3. What is the Execute Interface Block? What does the application programmer do to obtain it?

    The Execute Interface Block (DFHEIBLK) is a read-only control block passed to a Command Level task. It contains information about the task, such as its terminal, the TRANSID, and the date and time of task initiation. The application programmer does nothing to obtain the Execute Interface Block. The translator inserts the EIB into the Linkage Section and CICS provides automatic addressability to it.

4. What is the purpose of the END-EXEC command terminator in a COBOL program?

    END-EXEC terminates CICS commands. The use of END-EXEC in COBOL permits CICS commands to be stacked within COBOL IF statements. The END-EXEC ends stacked commands, while the period terminates COBOL IF statements.

5. How may unusual conditions be handled in a CICS program?

    Unusual conditions may be captured or ignored using HANDLE or IGNORE CONDITION statements. Also, command options such as RESP can be utilized.

6. What does the HANDLE AID instruction do?

    The HANDLE AID instruction is used to test and branch or GO TO a program paragraph based upon the Attention IDentifier or key pressed by the terminal operator to cause a device interrupt. The HANDLE AID instruction causes CICS to build a GO TO... DEPENDING ON table. The branch is actually taken when the next terminal input instruction is executed.

7. What is pseudoconversational programming, and why is it used for transactions that involve video terminal interaction?

    Pseudoconversational programming is a style of online programming in which a task is terminated with the RETURN command after each terminal output. If the operator has more work to complete, the application program can force a reinvocation of itself or another module by including the TRANSID option of the RETURN command. Pseudoconversational processing is used for update/data entry transactions so that a CICS task will not be kept in the system tying up resources while a human operator enters data.

ANSWERS TO CODING EXERCISE

1. Code a Linkage Section to process the following data areas: Four files are used in LOCATE mode. The PRODMST record is 110 bytes, the BKORDER record is 250 bytes, the INVMST is 400 bytes, and the ORDIMG is 320 bytes. No COMMAREA is being used.

```
LINKAGE SECTION
01  BLL-CELLS.
    04  FILLER          PIC S9(8) COMP.
    04  PRODMST-BLL     PIC S9(8) COMP.
    04  BKORDER-BLL     PIC S9(8) COMP.
    04  INVMST-BLL      PIC S9(8) COMP.
    04  ORDIMG-BLL      PIC S9(8) COMP.
01  PRODMST-RECORD      PIC X(110).
01  BKORDER-RECORD      PIC X(250).
01  INVMST-RECORD       PIC X(400).
01  ORDIMG-RECORD       PIC X(320).
```

The names used in the coding example are arbitrary—any names could have been used.

2. Code the Linkage Section for number 1 using a COMMAREA of 500 bytes.

```
LINKAGE SECTION
01  DFHCOMMAREA         PIC X(500).
01  BLL-CELLS.
    04  FILLER          PIC S9(8) COMP.
    04  PRODMST-BLL     PIC S9(8) COMP.
    04  BKORDER-BLL     PIC S9(8) COMP.
    04  INVMST-BLL      PIC S9(8) COMP.
    04  ORDIMG-BLL      PIC S9(8) COMP.
01  PRODMST-RECORD      PIC X(110).
01  BKORDER-RECORD      PIC X(250).
01  INVMST-RECORD       PIC X(400).
01  ORDIMG-RECORD       PIC X(320).
```

The following CICS code is used to READ four files; the subsequent exercises are based upon this sample code:

```
PROCEDURE DIVISION
    EXEC CICS READ DATASET ('ORDIMG')
        SET (ORD-BLL) LENGTH (ORD-LENGTH)
        RIDFLD (ORD-KEY) END-EXEC.
* COBOL instructions to operate upon file read.
    EXEC CICS READ DATASET ('PRODMST') RIDFLD (PROD-NUM)
        LENGTH (PROD-LENGTH) SET (PROD-BLL) END-EXEC.
```

* COBOL instructions to operate upon file read.
    EXEC CICS READ DATASET ('BKORDER') RIDFLD (BKOD-NUM)
        LENGTH (BK-LENGTH) INTO (BKORDER-RECORD) END-EXEC
* COBOL instructions to operate upon file read.
    EXEC CICS READ DATASET ('INVMST') SET (INV-BLL)
        LENGTH (INV-LENGTH) RIDFLD (INV-NUM) END-EXEC.
* COBOL instructions to operate upon file read.

3. Code the Data Division statements for file access assuming all file keys
   to be 9 bytes long and all records to be 100 bytes in length. The record
   areas for the files are as follows: ORDIMG-RECORD, PRODMST-
   RECORD, BKORDER-RECORD, and INVMST-RECORD. The key
   fields named in the RIDFLD command options are to be placed in
   Working Storage, as are the length fields. Length fields are 2-byte
   binary fields defined as PIC S9(4) COMP.

```
DATA DIVISION.
WORKING-STORAGE SECTION.
77  BK-LENGTH            PIC S9(4) COMP VALUE +100.
77  INV-LENGTH           PIC S9(4) COMP.
77  ORD-LENGTH           PIC S9(4) COMP.
77  PROD-LENGTH          PIC S9(4) COMP.
77  INV-NUM              PIC X(9).
77  BKOD-NUM             PIC X(9).
77  ORD-KEY              PIC X(9).
77  PROD-NUM             PIC X(9).
01  BKORDER-RECORD       PIC X(100).
LINKAGE SECTION.
01  BLLS.
    04  FILLER           PIC S9(8) COMP.
    04  ORD-BLL          PIC S9(8) COMP.
    04  PROD-BLL         PIC S9(8) COMP.
    04  INV-BLL          PIC S9(8) COMP.
01  ORDIMG-RECORD        PIC X(100).
01  PRODMST-RECORD       PIC X(100).
01  INVMST-RECORD        PIC X(100).
```

4. Code the statements to alter processing as follows:
   A. If the NOTFND condition occurs when reading the ORDIMG file,
      control is to pass to a routine named E100-WRONG-ORDER-
      NUMBER.
   B. For all other file access, all unusual conditions are to be left to
      default, including NOTFND.
   Indicate where the above instructions would be placed within the
   application code provided above (for example, before a particular
   READ command).

A. Before the ORDIMG file READ command is executed, the following HANDLE CONDITION statement is inserted.

```
EXEC CICS HANDLE CONDITION
        NOTFND(E100-WRONG-ORDER-NUMBER)
END-EXEC.
```

B. After the ORDIMG file READ but before the next file READ, the following HANDLE CONDITION statement is inserted:

```
EXEC CICS HANDLE CONDITION
        NOTFND
END-EXEC.
```

chapter 6

Terminal Control

6.1 TERMINAL CONTROL COMMANDS

Terminal Control commands enable the application programmer to request terminal management services of CICS. These commands allow a user to SEND data to a terminal, RECEIVE data from a terminal, CONVERSE with a terminal, and WAIT for terminal output to complete. There are several other Terminal Control commands that are used for special devices or specialized purposes, but we will limit our discussion to the more commonly used ones. Although CICS terminal support exists for a wide variety of computer terminals, the most commonly used terminal with CICS applications is the 3270 or 3270-compatible.

The typical CICS program supports the exchange of information between application programs running in the CICS region and video display terminals of the 3270 family being used by terminal operators. The commands of Terminal Control are used only for very simple input and output operations with this type of terminal. More commonly, the screen mapping facility called Basic Mapping Support is used for screen handling, since device data formatting is quite detailed for video terminals. We will discuss screen formatting and Basic Mapping Support in a subsequent chapter.

6.2 THE RECEIVE COMMAND

In the typical CICS program we use the RECEIVE command to receive initial transaction input. A terminal operator enters a TRANSID and optionally other data (such as a function code or an identifying number). The transaction identifier enables CICS to determine which program to invoke; the remaining data are dependent on the application.

Let's consider an example. The following information is entered by an operator seeking to look up information about an employee on the employee master file:

EMP1 067995532

The operator presses a device interrupt key, causing the terminal to transmit the data to the host system and ultimately to CICS. CICS Terminal Control passes the input to Task Control, requesting that a task be attached to process the terminal input. Task Control uses the Program Control Table entry to determine which program is to be invoked and prepares a task that will execute in the appropriate application program. When the task is dispatched, it must obtain the terminal input in order to know which employee number is to be processed. The COBOL source code to RECEIVE this data is illustrated below:

```
IDENTIFICATION DIVISION.
PROGRAM-ID.  SAMPLE1
AUTHOR.    A.J. WIPFLER
REMARKS.    THIS IS A SAMPLE OF CICS CODE DESIGNED TO SHOW
                THE USE OF THE RECEIVE COMMAND IN A PROGRAM.
ENVIRONMENT DIVISION.
DATA DIVISION.
WORKING-STORAGE SECTION.
77   TRMNL-LENGTH              PIC S9(4) COMP VALUE +14.
01   TERMINAL-INPUT-AREA.
      05   TERM-TRANSID          PIC X(4).
      05   TERM-FILLER           PIC X.
      05   TERM-EMPL-NUMBER      PIC X(9).
PROCEDURE DIVISION.
*      UPON ENTRY TO THIS PROGRAM IT IS NECESSARY
*      TO REQUEST THAT CICS PROVIDE THE DATA
*      RECEIVED FROM THE TERMINAL SO THAT WE KNOW
*      WHICH EMPLOYEE NUMBER IS TO BE DISPLAYED
*      FOR THE TERMINAL OPERATOR.
*
       EXEC CICS RECEIVE
            INTO (TERMINAL-INPUT-AREA)
            LENGTH (TRMNL-LENGTH)
       END-EXEC.
```

As a result of the execution of this RECEIVE command, CICS copies the data received from the terminal (and currently in a CICS terminal input buffer) into the dynamic copy of Working Storage associated with this task. The data are placed in the TERMINAL-INPUT-AREA and are then readily available for program processing. Having looked at a sample of how to use the RECEIVE command, let's look at its format and some of the other processing options.

6.2.1 RECEIVE Command Format

The format of the RECEIVE command is:

```
EXEC CICS RECEIVE
        INTO (field-name)        or  SET (bllcell-name)
        LENGTH (field-name)      or  FLENGTH (field-name)
        NOTRUNCATE
        MAXLENGTH (value)        or  MAXFLENGTH (value)
```

For use in a COBOL application program, the command would be terminated with an END-EXEC.

6.2.2 RECEIVE Command Discussion

The mutually exclusive INTO or SET options indicate whether we are going to use the MOVE or LOCATE mode for this input operation. In MOVE mode CICS copies the data from the terminal input area into the dynamic area associated with our task (Dynamic Working Storage). INTO indicates the selection of MOVE mode. The SET option indicates that we want to view the data in CICS's buffer area using the Linkage Section.

The LENGTH or FLENGTH options allow us to specify length information governing the RECEIVE. The use of the length field is different for MOVE and LOCATE mode RECEIVEs. In MOVE mode the LENGTH option tells CICS how much room we have provided in our Dynamic Working Storage for terminal input data. CICS utilizes this length information to determine the maximum number of bytes that the program can accommodate without overlaying adjacent fields in Working Storage. In MOVE mode the LENGTH option provides a maximum size for the data we are prepared to receive. Therefore, the length field must be set to an appropriate value by the application programmer prior to the execution of the RECEIVE command. This can be accomplished either by giving the field a value in Working Storage, or by moving a value into the field prior to command execution.

In LOCATE mode the task looks at data in the terminal buffer, called the CICS Terminal Input/Output Area (TIOA). Therefore, CICS is not concerned with overlaying Working Storage. The program need not preset the length field to a value, and if the field does contain a value it is ignored. The length field in LOCATE mode is used by CICS to tell the task the length of the data area in the terminal buffer area. Execution of a LOCATE mode RECEIVE results in the address of the terminal data being set in the Linkage Section and the length of the data being placed in the named length field.

If the LENGTH option is used, CICS expects the length field to be a 2-byte binary field defined in COBOL as a "PIC S9(4) COMP." If the FLENGTH option is used, CICS expects the length field to be a 4-byte binary field defined in COBOL as "PIC S9(8) COMP." LENGTH and FLENGTH are mutually exclusive options.

NOTRUNCATE informs CICS that the program does not want to have extra data truncated. Perhaps the program has a 14-byte area set aside in Working Storage to RECEIVE data, but the operator enters 16 bytes. In MOVE mode the program provides a length of 14, indicating the size of its work area. If we do not specify the NOTRUNCATE option, one of two things occur. If unusual condition processing for the LENGERR is specified, CICS places the number of bytes of data defined in the length option into the program's Dynamic Working Storage. Any remaining input is truncated and the length field is set to the length of data prior to truncation. CICS processes the length error according to the specification defined by unusual condition processing. If, on the other hand, no provision was made for the unusual condition of LENGERR, CICS terminates the task, sends an abend message to the terminal with the abend code of AEIV, and writes a formatted dump to the current Dump Data Set.

The NOTRUNCATE option tells CICS that we do not want data truncated and that the data may well exceed the size of the work area defined in the program. If NOTRUNCATE is used CICS does not truncate data, and successive RECEIVE commands provide the program with additional data. If NOTRUNCATE is used, the end of input data is indicated by CICS setting the EIBCOMPL field to X'FF' or high values.

MAXLENGTH or MAXFLENGTH is used to define a maximum data size. As with the LENGTH and FLENGTH options, this maximum data length can be expressed as a 2- (MAXLENGTH) or 4-byte (MAXFLENGTH) binary field. A MAXLENGTH option included in a MOVE mode RECEIVE command takes precedence over the LENGTH option. If used in a LOCATE mode RECEIVE, a MAXLENGTH option can define the amount of data the task wants passed. This serves as an upper limit on data for a single RECEIVE SET. If NOTRUNCATE is included, then successive RECEIVE commands can be used to obtain any remaining data. This permits the application programmer to define the maximum amount of data to be passed in response to each LOCATE mode RECEIVE. If NOTRUNCATE is omitted in a RECEIVE SET with a MAXLENGTH option, CICS raises the LENGERR condition and truncates the data.

A sample locate mode RECEIVE is provided below.

```
IDENTIFICATION DIVISION.
PROGRAM-ID.  SAMPLE2.
AUTHOR.      A.J. WIPFLER.
```

```
REMARKS.         THIS IS A SAMPLE LOCATE MODE
                 RECEIVE COMMAND IN THE CONTEXT OF
                 A COBOL PROGRAM.
ENVIRONMENT DIVISION.
DATA DIVISION.
WORKING-STORAGE SECTION.
77  TRMNL-LENGTH                     PIC S9(4) COMP.
LINKAGE SECTION.
01  BLL-CELLS.
    05     FILLER                    PIC S9(8) COMP.
    05     TERMINAL-BLL              PIC S9(8) COMP.
01  LS-TERMINAL-INPUT-AREA.
    05     TRANSID                   PIC X(4).
    05     FILLER                    PIC X.
    05     EMPLOYEE-NUMBER           PIC X(9).
PROCEDURE DIVISION.
    EXEC CICS RECEIVE
        SET (TERMINAL-BLL)
        LENGTH (TRMNL-LENGTH)
        END-EXEC.
```

As a result of the execution of this command, CICS places the address of
the start of input data in its terminal input/output buffer into the BLL cell
named in the command. The 01-level data area defined in conjunction with
this BLL cell (LS-TERMINAL-INPUT-AREA) can then be used to reference
the data within the CICS buffer. For other types of data input (such as reading
files), LOCATE mode is more efficient because task Working Storage is
optimized. **In the RECEIVE command it is normally more efficient to use
MOVE mode, since this enables CICS to reuse the terminal input buffer
immediately.**

6.3   THE SEND COMMAND

In a CICS program the SEND command is used to transmit data to a
terminal. The terminal can be an interactive video terminal such as a 3270,
a printer terminal, or an intelligent system such as a host computer. The
SEND command is used when there is little or no video screen formatting
required—for example, when communicating with another host system,
writing to an online printer, or SENDing a simple unformatted output to
an interactive video terminal. We will discuss video screen formatting in
the chapter on Basic Mapping Support.

Let's examine a simple example of when we might use the SEND
command in a CICS program. In the examples discussed under the
RECEIVE command, the operator enters a TRANSID and an employee
number for a file lookup operation. The program reads the appropriate
record from the file and displays a simple message such as

EMPLOYEE:9-digit number   NAME: name field from record

if a record is found on the file. If no record is found for the requested employee number, then the program displays the following message:

EMPLOYEE:9-digit number   NO RECORD FOUND ON EMPLOYEE FILE

These simple one-line messages do not require much data formatting, so we could use the following code to SEND such messages:

```
IDENTIFICATION DIVISION.
PROGRAM-ID.   SAMPLE3.
AUTHOR.       A.J. WIPFLER.
REMARKS.      THIS IS A COBOL CICS SAMPLE DESIGNED TO
              SHOW THE USE OF THE SEND COMMAND IN
              A PROGRAM.
ENVIRONMENT DIVISION.
DATA DIVISION.
WORKING-STORAGE SECTION.
77  TRMNL-LENGTH                PIC S9(4) COMP VALUE +14.
01  TERMINAL-INPUT-AREA.
    05  INPUT-TRANSID           PIC X(4).
    05  FILLER                  PIC X.
    05  IN-NUMBER               PIC X(9).
01  TERMINAL-OUTPUT-AREA.
    05  FILLER                  PIC X(9) VALUE 'EMPLOYEE:'.
    05  EMPL-NUMBER             PIC X(9).
    05  FILLER                  PIC XXX VALUE SPACES.
    05  REST-OF-MESSAGE.
        08  FILLER              PIC X(6) VALUE 'NAME:'.
        08  EMPL-NAME           PIC X(30).
    05  NOT-FND-MSG REDEFINES REST-OF-MESSAGE.
        08  NOT-FOUND           PIC X(36).
LINKAGE SECTION.
01  BLLCELLS.
    05  FILLER                  PIC S9(8) COMP.
    05  FILE-BLL                PIC S9(8) COMP.
01  FILE-INPUT-AREA.
    05  FILE-KEY                PIC X(9).
    05  FILE-NAME               PIC X(30).
    05  FILLER                  PIC X(41).
PROCEDURE DIVISION.
*   RECEIVE TERMINAL INPUT
    EXEC CICS RECEIVE
        INTO (TERMINAL-INPUT-AREA)
        LENGTH (TRMNL-LENGTH)
    END-EXEC.
```

```
*      SET UP HANDLE CONDITION TO TRAP RECORD NOT ON FILE
*      AND CAUSE CICS TO RETURN CONTROL TO PROGRAM AT
*      PARAGRAPH FOR NOT FOUND MESSAGE FORMATTING.
       EXEC CICS HANDLE CONDITION
             NOTFND (A150-RECORD-NOT-FOUND)
             END-EXEC.
*      SET UP PART OF OUTPUT MESSAGE SINCE THE NUMBER
*      DISPLAY IS COMMON TO BOTH DISPLAYS.
       MOVE IN-NUMBER TO EMPL-NUMBER.
*      READ THE FILE USING THE KEY ENTERED BY THE OPERATOR
       EXEC CICS READ
             DATASET ('EMPLMAST')
             RIDFLD (IN-NUMBER)
             SET (FILE-BLL)
       END-EXEC.
*      IF CONTROL PASSES BACK HERE THEN ALL WENT WELL
*      WITH THE FILE COMMAND.
       MOVE FILE-NAME TO EMPL-NAME.
       GO TO A190-SEND-MESSAGE.
A150-RECORD-NOT-FOUND.
*      CONTROL RETURNS HERE IF THE NOTFND CONDITION OCCURS.
       MOVE 'NO RECORD FOUND ON EMPLOYEE FILE' TO NOT-FOUND.
A190-SEND-MESSAGE.
       MOVE +57 TO TRMNL-LENGTH.
       EXEC CICS SEND
             FROM (TERMINAL-OUTPUT-AREA)
             LENGTH (TRMNL-LENGTH)
             ERASE
       END-EXEC.
A200-END-TASK.
       EXEC CICS RETURN
       END-EXEC.
```

As a result of the execution of the SEND command in the above code, CICS copies the message into a terminal buffer and transmits it to the terminal. Let's examine the format and commonly used options of the SEND command.

6.3.1 SEND Command Format

The format of the SEND command is:

```
EXEC CICS SEND
      FROM (area-name)
      LENGTH (size)      or      FLENGTH (size)
      ERASE
      WAIT
```

6.3.2 SEND Command Discussion

The FROM option names the data area containing the message to be sent to the terminal. This area is typically in the Working-Storage Section of a COBOL program, but may be any area to which the program has valid addressability. Therefore, a message may also be built and sent from the Linkage Section.

The LENGTH or FLENGTH options are required to define the length of the message to be sent. As with RECEIVE, LENGTH indicates a 2-byte field containing the length and FLENGTH specifies a 4-byte length field.

ERASE indicates that the terminal screen is to be erased or cleared prior to the display of the output message. This is typically done for the first terminal output from a CICS program, because the screen is used in the exchange of information between the operator and the program. Otherwise, whatever is left on the screen from any prior processing is not removed.

The ERASE option also affects where the message is displayed in that ERASE also positions the cursor at the upper left corner of the screen. When the message is sent to the terminal, it is placed on the screen starting at the current cursor location unless screen formatting information is contained within message. The ERASE option is included in the sample code showing how to use the SEND command; therefore the message is displayed starting in the upper left corner of the terminal screen.

The WAIT option indicates that the program is not to receive control back from CICS until the data have been successfully sent from the CICS region. This option is not required. If omitted, the program is given control back even though the data may not yet have been sent. If data are simply being sent to a video terminal and the program is next going to RETURN to CICS (as occurs in pseudoconversational programming), the WAIT option can be omitted. In this case the task is concluding and there will be no further processing until the data have been received at the terminal and the operator has entered a subsequent request for service. The interactive nature of video terminal processing means that we will not overrun CICS or the terminal with data.

This option should be included when sending data to a noninteractive printer terminal, because this type of device features no interactive processing and we could overrun CICS with data.

Consider the following case: A task is creating output reports for an online printer. A full buffer of information is formatted and sent to the terminal using the SEND command without the WAIT option. The SEND command results in CICS terminal facility saving the address of the data (in a Terminal Input/Output Area) in a field in the terminal's entry in the Terminal Control Table. This data pointer (TCTTEDA) is a single 4-byte field. Terminal Control also sets flags in the terminal's table entry, indicating that there is an output pending for the terminal. Output processing does not immediately result, because CICS attempts to process such operations during regularly scheduled scans of all terminal entries (to handle I/O operations in groups for more efficient operation). This means that CICS saves the data address, sets output pending flags for the terminal, and returns control to the requesting task. The task could then continue processing, build another output buffer of data, and request a second SEND operation before CICS has completed processing the first request. CICS has only one data pointer, and recognizes the presentation of a second output as an error. It will throw away the second buffer full of data and set error flags.

In order to prevent this, the WAIT option can be used. When WAIT is coded, control is passed back to the program only after CICS has actually disposed of the data. Another way of handling printer output that permits the overlapping of output and program processing is to omit the WAIT option from the SEND command and format the next buffer full of output. Prior to issuing the next SEND command, the program can use the WAIT TERMINAL command discussed below.

6.4 THE WAIT TERMINAL COMMAND

The WAIT TERMINAL command is used to delay a task's execution until a prior SEND command has completed. A WAIT is always implied with a RECEIVE operation (except in pseudoconversational mode, where the data have already been received into the CICS region before the program is invoked).

6.4.1 WAIT TERMINAL Command Format

  EXEC CICS WAIT TERMINAL

6.5 THE CONVERSE COMMAND

The CONVERSE command combines an output SEND, WAIT TER-MINAL, and subsequent RECEIVE into one command. This command should not be used when writing pseudoconversational programs. However, not all CICS programs are pseudoconversational. There are times—albeit few in most applications—when a CICS program communicates with another application program, perhaps in another CICS system. In such cases the problem of man vs. machine-processing speed is not an issue and such programs are normally conversational. The advantage of using one CONVERSE command—as opposed to SEND, WAIT TERMINAL, and RECEIVE—is that the execution path through CICS is shorter for one single CONVERSE command.

6.5.1 CONVERSE Command Format

The format of the CONVERSE command is:

```
EXEC CICS CONVERSE
      FROM (area-name)
      FROMLENGTH (size)   or   FROMFLENGTH (size)
      ERASE
      INTO (area-name)    or   SET (bll-name)
      TOLENGTH (size)     or   TOFLENGTH (size)
      NOTRUNCATE
      MAXLENGTH (size)    or   MAXFLENGTH (size)
```

Since CONVERSE is a combination of SEND and RECEIVE, the parameters of this command are like the corresponding parameters of the SEND and RECEIVE commands.

6.6 UNUSUAL CONDITIONS ASSOCIATED WITH TERMINAL CONTROL

The LENGERR is the most common terminal error condition. LENGERR occurs with the SEND, RECEIVE, and CONVERSE commands. The LENGERR appears for RECEIVE or the input side of CONVERSE when the command is in MOVE mode and the actual data length exceeds the size of the program work area. The default course of action is for CICS to terminate the task with the abend code of AEIV. This default for LENGERR can be prevented by using CICS condition handling mechanisms. However, unless the NOTRUNCATE option is specified in the RECEIVE or CONVERSE command, the data are truncated to the length defined in the command. Use of NOTRUNCATE prevents the occurrence of LENGERR, and successive input commands can be used to obtain the remaining data. LENGERR appears for SEND or the output side of CONVERSE if the LENGTH option defines a data size that is invalid.

CODING EXERCISE

1. Code a CICS command to RECEIVE terminal input data. The data anticipated consist of a four-character transaction identifier, a space, and a 12-byte key field. The data are to be accepted into a Working-Storage area named TRANS-INPUT. Code any data fields required for the command. Any valid data names can be used for fields not explicitly named in this problem.
2. Code a CICS command to SEND a message to a terminal. The message area is 60 bytes in length, and is contained in a Working-Storage field named OUTPUT-MESSAGE. Code any data fields required for the command. Any valid data names can be used for fields not defined in this problem.

3. Code a CICS command to halt task execution until a prior SEND command has completed.

REVIEW EXERCISE

Match each of the options used in Terminal Control commands with a description of the option provided below.

_____	1. ERASE	_____	6. WAIT
_____	2. INTO	_____	7. MAXLENGTH
_____	3. NOTRUNCATE	_____	8. LENGTH
_____	4. FROM	_____	9. FLENGTH
_____	5. SET	_____	10. MAXFLENGTH

A. Names a 2-byte binary length field.
B. Indicates move mode input.
C. Names a field containing an output message.
D. Names a 4-byte binary length field.
E. Requests that a task's execution be suspended until a terminal output request has completed.
F. Specifies that input data is not to be truncated.
G. Causes the screen to be cleared and the cursor to be positioned in the upper left corner of the terminal screen.
H. Defines a 2-byte maximum length field used in conjunction with the NOTRUNCATE option.
I. Indicates locate mode input.
J. Defines a 4-byte maximum length field used in conjunction with the NOTRUNCATE option.

Provide a short answer to each of the following.

1. When coding an input command to RECEIVE terminal data, the application program can request that data not be truncated. Successive RECEIVEs can be used to obtain additional data beyond that defined in the LENGTH option. How can the application program determine when there are no more data to RECEIVE?
2. When is it appropriate to use the CONVERSE command? What is the advantage of using this command?
3. What is the default course of action for the LENGERR?

ANSWERS TO CODING EXERCISE

1. Code a CICS command to RECEIVE terminal input data. The data anticipated consist of a four-character transaction identifier, a space, and a 12-byte key field. The data are to be accepted into a Working-

Storage area named TRANS-INPUT. Code any data fields required for the command. Any valid data names can be used for fields not explicitly named in this problem.

```
DATA DIVISION.
WORKING-STORAGE SECTION.
77  TRANS-LEN              PIC S9(4)  COMP  VALUE +17.
01  TRANS-INPUT.
      04  TRANS-ID         PIC X(4).
      04  FILLER           PIC X.
      04  TRANS-KEY        PIC X(12).
PROCEDURE DIVISION.

    EXEC CICS RECEIVE INTO(TRANS-INPUT)
         LENGTH(TRANS-LEN)
    END-EXEC.
```

2. Code a CICS command to SEND a message to a terminal. The message area is 60 bytes in length, and is contained in a Working-Storage field named OUTPUT-MESSAGE. Code any data fields required for the command. Any valid data names can be used for fields not defined in this problem.

```
DATA DIVISION.
WORKING-STORAGE SECTION.
77  OUTPUT-LEN             PIC S9(4)  COMP  VALUE +60.
01  OUTPUT-MESSAGE         PIC X(60).

PROCEDURE DIVISION.
*    COBOL INSTRUCTIONS TO FORMAT THE MESSAGE
     EXEC CICS SEND FROM(OUTPUT-MESSAGE)
          LENGTH(OUTPUT-LEN)   ERASE
     END-EXEC.
```

3. Code a CICS command to halt task execution until a prior SEND command has completed.

```
    EXEC CICS WAIT TERMINAL END-EXEC.
```

ANSWERS TO REVIEW EXERCISE

Match each of the options used in Terminal Control commands with a description of the option provided below.

__G__	1. ERASE		__E__	6. WAIT
__B__	2. INTO		__H__	7. MAXLENGTH
__F__	3. NOTRUNCATE		__A__	8. LENGTH
__C__	4. FROM		__D__	9. FLENGTH
__I__	5. SET		__J__	10. MAXFLENGTH

Provide a short answer to each of the following.

1. When coding an input command to RECEIVE terminal data, the application program can request that data not be truncated. Successive RECEIVEs can be used to obtain additional data beyond that defined in the LENGTH option. How can the application program determine when there are no more data to RECEIVE?

   The EIBCOMPL field in the Execute Interface Block can be tested for high values (X'FF').

2. When is it appropriate to use the CONVERSE command? What is the advantage of using this command?

   The CONVERSE command is appropriate to use when a CICS program is communicating with an intelligent process such as a program in another system. The CONVERSE is not normally used with video terminal interaction, because it is the equivalent of SEND, WAIT, and RECEIVE in one command and therefore precludes pseudoconversational processing. The advantage of using the CONVERSE command when appropriate is that the execution path through CICS is shorter for the CONVERSE than it is for the separate SEND and RECEIVE commands.

3. What is the default course of action for the LENGERR?

   The default course for LENGERR is to truncate the message and terminate the task with a unique abend code.

chapter 7

File Control Commands

7.1 IMPORTANCE OF VSAM FILES

VSAM files are the type of files most commonly used in CICS. Appendix A contains some general information about VSAM for those who lack knowledge of this access method. If the reader is not familiar with VSAM, Appendix A should be read before proceeding with this chapter.

7.2 REVIEW OF EXCLUSIVE CONTROL

During update processing CICS exclusive control ensures that a loss of data integrity does not occur due to multiple tasks sharing resources. Actually, there are two levels of protection provided, and the exact nature of exclusive control is dependent upon several factors, including the file access method and the way in which the file is defined to CICS in the File Control Table. One can define a file as a protected or unprotected resource of CICS. Protection status is specified by using the "LOG=" parameter in the file's entry. If LOG=YES is coded, then the file is considered to be a protected resource of CICS and it is a candidate for CICS recovery processing. If LOG=NO is chosen, the file is NOT protected and CICS does not provide file recoverability. Whether or not a file is protected, we can request user journaling of before images (file record images prior to updates) or afterimages (copies of file records updating the file).

    The file's status does, however, affect the type of exclusive control obtained during update processing, as well as the length of time for which exclusive control is maintained. First let's take unprotected files, those for which LOG=NO is specified. During update processing, CICS requires that a program READ with an UPDATE option to indicate its intention to update the record being retrieved. There is an access method-dependent enqueue that is obtained during update processing. For VSAM files the exclusive control is on the control interval. The unit of a VSAM file that is transferred between DASD and Virtual Storage is the control interval, so in that sense the control interval is analogous to the block of non-VSAM files. VSAM's enqueue lasts only during update processing, so as soon as the record is rewritten to the file, VSAM's enqueue is released. For BDAM files the enqueue is on the block. As with VSAM, the enqueue is kept only during actual update processing. For files that are not protected resources, this is the only type of exclusive control used.

For protected files (defined as LOG=YES) the access method-dependent enqueue is used during actual update processing. CICS, however, provides additional protection in the form of a CICS enqueue on the logical record on behalf of the updating task. Unlike the access method-dependent enqueue, the CICS enqueue is for the entire task or logical task. This means that, until a task terminates or tells CICS via a SYNCPOINT that a logical unit of work has been completed, the CICS enqueue is kept. The longer the enqueue, the greater the likelihood that there will be resource waits by other tasks seeking to update the same record. However, CICS has no choice but to keep the enqueue. This is because updates to protected resources may potentially be backed out by CICS recovery processing or Dynamic Transaction Backout. The example discussed below is in terms of Recovery/Restart, but this could also happen due to DTB processing.

Figure 7-1 depicts CICS recovery processing and shows why CICS must maintain its enqueue for an entire logical task. Tasks 1 and 2 are in the system, and both have records on the system log indicating that they were initiated. Task 1 READs for UPDATE a record in a file named PRODMST. The product SKU number updated is 123. During update processing, VSAM maintains integrity by locking update access to the control interval being updated. As a result of the READ for UPDATE, CICS requests that a before image of this record be logged to the system log. Note that the inventory amount contained in this before update image is 146. Task 1 updates the record, debiting the inventory amount to 135. With the completion of the update, VSAM releases the control interval exclusive control.

Next, Task 2 gains control and READs for UPDATE the same record. Task 2 debits the inventory amount by 50 and REWRITEs the record to the file. Task 2 sends a message to the terminal indicating that the transaction has been successful, and then terminates. Task 2 is a completed unit of work which *should not* be backed out. The system abnormally terminates at this point. During a subsequent emergency

Figure 7-1. Illustration of why protected resources cannot be released for reuse until modifications are committed.

System Log Data	PRODMST Contents	Explanation
Start Task 1	SKU=123 INV=146	Task 1 starts
Start Task 2	SKU=123 INV=146	Task 2 starts
PRODMST Task 1 SKU=123 INV=146 (Before Image)	SKU=123 INV=146	Task 1 reads and gains access method exclusive control.
PRODMST Task 1 SKU=123 INV=135 (After Image)	SKU=123 INV=135	Task 1 rewrites and access method exclusive control released
		If no additional exclusive control Task 2 could gain access to logical record to change it.
PRODMST Task 2 SKU=123 INV=135 (Before Image)	SKU=123 INV=135	Task 2 reads and gains access method exclusive control.
PRODMST Task 2 SKU=123 INV=85 (After Image)	SKU=123 INV=85	Task 2 rewrites and access method exclusive control released.
End Task 2		Task 2 ends after informing user of update.
System Crashes	SKU=123 INV=146	Subsequent to an emergency restart, update by Task 1 is backed out as Task 1 is incomplete.

The effect of emergency restart is to back out not only the work done by Task 1 (which is an incomplete task), but also the work done by the completed Task 2. **This cannot actually happen in CICS.** In addition to the access method-dependent exclusive control during update processing, CICS maintains an internal exclusive control on the logical record until the logical task is complete. Thus, until the work done by Task 1 is committed, Task 2 cannot gain update access.

143

restart of the system, CICS determines that Task 1 was inflight or incomplete, and that its processing should be reversed. The before image logged when Task 1 READ for UPDATE is used to back out or reverse the processing done by this task. However, not only is the incomplete unit of work backed out, but the work done by Task 2 is also reversed. **This will not happen in CICS!** It is to prevent such an occurrence that CICS maintains its own internal lock on the logical record for the duration of the entire logical unit of work.

Normally, a unit of work is a complete task. That is, a complete unit of work is typically everything that is done from the point that the task initially gains control until it ends by issuing a RETURN. However, a SYNCPOINT command can be used to tell CICS that, although we are not ending the task, we have completed a Logical Unit of Work (LUW). This is taken as a logical end of task. Although the task physically remains in the system, CICS recognizes that modifications to protected resources are now committed. The SYNCPOINT can be viewed as a task's way of saying to CICS, "Don't back out anything that I've done up to now because my processing is logically complete."

Most interactive terminal-oriented tasks do not use SYNCPOINTs. These types of tasks normally involve processing a single item, such as a customer or an order. Multiple files may be updated during processing, but modifications must be accomplished entirely or backed out completely. Tasks that read and process queues of records normally take SYNCPOINTs when they have finished processing a single record. For a task that does a repeated process for multiple records, the SYNCPOINT command can be used to break the processing of the task into logical units of work that we do not want backed out. It is important to remember that CICS sees only tasks where recovery is concerned. A task is represented by a Task Control Area, and a single task may be broken into logically complete units of work. CICS recovery is concerned ONLY with incomplete logical units of work. **This is true for emergency restart and Dynamic Transaction Backout.**

7.3 FILE CONTROL COMMANDS

File control commands enable the application task to READ, REWRITE (update), DELETE, WRITE (add), and browse file records within files defined in the local CICS File Control Table. Additionally, file commands can name a remote CICS system and thereby access files defined in the remote system. The remote system must, of course, be defined to CICS.

7.4 THE READ COMMAND

The READ command is used to request that CICS retrieve a record from a file defined in the File Control Table. The READ can be used to simply inquire or to READ for UPDATE (meaning that exclusive control is obtained for the task).

7.4.1 READ Command Format

The format of the READ command is as follows:

```
EXEC CICS READ
        UPDATE
        DATASET (ddname)
        RIDFLD (search-arg)
        RBA or RRN
        KEYLENGTH (size)
        GENERIC
        INTO (area-name)   or   SET (bll-cell)
        LENGTH (size)
        GTEQ   or   EQUAL
        SYSID (name)
        DEBKEY   or   DEBREC
```

The optional UPDATE parameter indicates that the task is planning to update the file and therefore requires at least the access method-dependent exclusive control during update processing. If the file is a protected resource, CICS's internal enqueue is also obtained. The CICS lock is held until either a SYNCPOINT occurs or the task terminates. After a READ UPDATE, it is imperative that the completing operation (DELETE, UNLOCK, or REWRITE) be done before any other access is made against the data set by that task.

The DATASET option names the DDNAME of the file as it is defined in the File Control Table.

The RIDFLD is used to provide the name of a field containing the search argument. This is assumed to be a key field unless a qualifier (RBA or RRN) is used to indicate the nature of the search argument. RBA is used for a VSAM Entry Sequenced Data Set or Key Sequenced Data Set to specify that the search argument is a Relative Byte Address. RRN is used for a VSAM Relative Record Data Set to indicate that the search argument is a Relative Record Number. RBA and RRN are coded only if needed to qualify the nature of the search argument.

The KEYLENGTH option specifies a length for the key field. This option is used in two cases. For files accessed from other CICS systems, we specify the SYSID parameter and name another CICS system. The KEYLENGTH parameter tells the local CICS system how large the key field is so that the key can be shipped in its entirety to the system that owns the file. The remote system is defined in the Terminal Control Table so that the local CICS system knows where to ship the file request. The other case in which the KEYLENGTH option is used is for VSAM

GENERIC processing. GENERIC or partial key READ requests are allowed only for VSAM files. In this case, CICS must be told the size of the GENERIC or partial key. In all other cases CICS knows the key size from the File Control Table.

INTO or SET defines the input mode. LOCATE mode is preferable for file access, as it permits the application task to access file records in a CICS work area. This means that the application task's Working Storage section is smaller because it doesn't require storage for the file record. CICS acquires the file area whether we use MOVE or LOCATE mode, so we can optimize program Working Storage by using the file record in the CICS area.

Use of the LENGTH option is based on whether the READ command is in MOVE or LOCATE mode. In MOVE mode LENGTH specifies the program work area size. In LOCATE mode CICS uses the LENGTH field to pass on the length of a variable size record.

The GTEQ or EQUAL option defines whether a record equal to the specified key is the only record that can satisfy the read. EQUAL is the default. GTEQ can be used only for VSAM files, and permits the retrieval of the next greater record if there is no equal record on the file. However, for the ESDS the default is EQUAL, and if the requested RBA is not on the file, the ILLOGIC condition is raised.

DEBKEY or DEBREC are used only for BDAM files to specify BDAM deblocking. DEBKEY indicates that deblocking is to be based upon key. DEBREC requests deblocking based on relative record.

There are a number of options in many CICS commands that are used only for particular cases. The READ command is a good example. If we are reading a BDAM file, we use the DEBKEY or DEBREC option; otherwise it is not applicable. The moral of the story is that one never uses all of the options. As a rule of thumb, "if in doubt leave it out." If a required parameter is omitted, the Command Level translator issues a message and the missing parameter can be inserted.

7.5   THE REWRITE COMMAND

The REWRITE command is used to request that CICS rewrite a record that has previously been READ for UPDATE. It is impossible to use this command without having previously READ the record for UPDATE.

7.5.1   REWRITE Command Format

The format of the REWRITE command is:

```
EXEC CICS REWRITE
      DATASET (ddname)
      FROM (data-area)
      LENGTH (size)
      SYSID (name)
```

The parameters of the REWRITE command are fairly self-explanatory and follow the use of such parameters in the READ command discussed above. The FROM option is new in this file command. It names the data area containing the updated record. This area can be in the program's Working Storage subsequent to a READ UPDATE in MOVE mode, or it can refer to a data area in the Linkage Section if the previous READ UPDATE was done in LOCATE mode. A sample of READ UPDATE and REWRITE is shown below:

```
DATA DIVISION.
WORKING-STORAGE SECTION.
77  EMPLOYEE-NUMBER      PIC X(9).
77  FILE-LENGTH          PIC S9(4)  COMP.
LINKAGE SECTION.
01  BLL-CELLS.
    04  FILLER           PIC S9(8)  COMP.
    04  FILE-BLL         PIC S9(8)  COMP.
01  FILE-RECORD-AREA.
    04  FILE-KEY         PIC X(9).
    04  FILE-NAME        PIC X(30).
    04  FILE-SKILL-CODE  PIC XXX.
    04  FILE-LOCATION-CD PIC X(4).
PROCEDURE DIVISION.
    .
        EXEC CICS READ UPDATE DATASET ('EMPMAST')
            RIDFLD (EMPLOYEE-NUMBER)  LENGTH(FILE-LENGTH)
            SET(FILE-BLL)  END-EXEC.
*   RECORD FIELDS MODIFIED HERE.
        EXEC CICS REWRITE DATASET('EMPMAST')
            FROM(FILE-RECORD-AREA)  LENGTH(FILE-LENGTH)
            END-EXEC.
```

Note that the RIDFLD option is not included in the syntax of the REWRITE command. This means that CICS is rewriting a record that was **previously** READ with the UPDATE option. This limits the Command Level program to one outstanding READ UPDATE against a particular data set. While this may at first seem a limitation, in reality it is a protection, because a CICS program should have only one operation outstanding against a particular VSAM file if a file pointer must be maintained, as is the case with a READ UPDATE.

7.6 DELETE PROCESSING AND VSAM

The DELETE command is used to delete one or more records from a VSAM file where applicable to VSAM processing. There are three types of VSAM files: the *Key Sequenced Data Set,* which is a VSAM keyed file; the *Entry Sequenced Data Set* or VSAM sequential file; and the *Relative*

Record Data Set or VSAM direct file. Delete processing is not permitted against the Entry Sequenced Data Set. This is a VSAM limitation, and not a CICS restriction. Deletes are permitted against the other two types of VSAM files.

7.6.1 DELETE Command Format

The format of the DELETE command is:

```
EXEC CICS DELETE
        DATASET (ddname)
        RIDFLD (search-argument)
        RBA   or   RRN
        GENERIC
        KEYLENGTH (size)
        NUMREC (field-name)
        SYSID (name)
```

7.6.2 DELETE Command Discussion

The DELETE command can be used in two ways. The first way is to READ a record with the UPDATE option and subsequently delete that single record. In this case an existing lock is being held on the VSAM control interval, and CICS has a pointer to the record that we are operating on. Therefore, the only option permissible with this type of DELETE command is the DATASET option. The command sequence would look like this:

```
EXEC CICS READ UPDATE DATASET ('APPFILE')
        RIDFLD (FILE-KEY) SET (FILE-BLL)
        LENGTH (FILE-LENGTH) END-EXEC.
  * COBOL code to examine data record
        EXEC CICS DELETE DATASET ('APPFILE') END-EXEC.
```

If any other options (such as RIDFLD) are included in this type of DELETE command, CICS indicates that the request is invalid. The only other option that we may use in this case is the SYSID option if the file exists in another CICS system.

The second way that the DELETE command can be used is without the preceding READ for UPDATE. In this case we do not need to examine the record prior to deleting it. We may have READ the record and displayed it on the terminal screen in an earlier task. In this case we do not need to see the record again unless we want to make sure that it has not changed in the time between pseudoconversational tasks. In the case where we are not going to examine the record, we can issue the DELETE without first reading the record. As a matter of fact, this is more efficient in terms of file processing.

Deleting without reading means that there is no pointer established before the DELETE command is issued. Consequently, the delete itself must provide record identification information. In this case the remaining options can be utilized. RIDFLD, KEYLENGTH, GENERIC, and SYSID are used in the same manner as the file commands discussed earlier. This use of the DELETE command is illustrated here:

```
EXEC CICS DELETE DATASET ('APPFILE')
    RIDFLD (FILE-KEY)
    END-EXEC.
```

This command deletes a single record from the APPFILE. The key of the record is contained in the FILE-KEY field. However, this type of DELETE may also delete multiple records by utilizing the GENERIC option. GENERIC indicates that we not only have a generic or partial key, but we want all records with this generic key to be deleted. The NUMREC option can be used to name a 2-byte binary field used by CICS to indicate the number of "generic" records actually deleted. NUMREC is optional.

Generic deletes may be useful in some applications. For example, consider a CICS program that prints a report file containing records for each page and line of a report. The file key consists of the report name, page number, and line number. If a user prints a report and wants it deleted from the report file, we could go through and delete each record in turn, or we could use the beginning portion of the key that identifies the report name and do a generic delete to scratch the entire report with one command.

The RBA or RRN option qualifies the RIDFLD. However, VSAM deletes are possible only against KSDS and RRDS. RBAs can be used to access KSDS records. However, this is an option that can lead to trouble. RBAs in a KSDS can change. Record insertions, enlargements, or deletions result in a minireorganization of the control interval so that the collating sequence is maintained. This may cause record RBAs to change. So, deleting a KSDS record on RBA is certainly flirting with danger. (If you don't understand how RBAs in a KSDS can change, see Appendix A on VSAM.)

7.7 THE WRITE COMMAND

The WRITE command is used to add a record to a file. For the VSAM KSDS, additions are added within the body of the file if the key indicates that this is where the record should be placed. If the key is beyond the current high key of the file, then it will be added to the end of the file. For a Relative Record Data Set the slot indicated with the RRN must be empty in order to successfully insert the record. The control information in the back of the RRDS control interval (Record Description Fields) contains an indication of which slots are empty and which ones contain records. Records can also be added after the end of the file. For the Entry Sequenced Data Set, records can ONLY be added after the end of the file.

7.7.1 WRITE Command Format

The format of the WRITE command is:

```
EXEC CICS WRITE
        DATASET (ddname)
        RIDFLD (search-argument)
        RRN  or  RBA
        KEYLENGTH (size)
        SYSID (name)
        FROM (data-area)
        MASSINSERT
```

7.7.2 WRITE Command Discussion

The command options of WRITE are used analogously to the similar options in the other file commands discussed above. Note that RIDFLD cannot name a field contained within the record area named in the FROM option; a separate key field outside of the record area referenced by the FROM option is required. Therefore, if the file is keyed, the key exists in two places. It must be within the area referenced by the FROM option, and should also be contained in the record identification field named in the RIDFLD option. Again, RBA and RRN may be used to qualify the contents of the RIDFLD.

KEYLENGTH for the WRITE command is required only if the SYSID option is used to indicate that the file is not defined locally. In this case, if the search argument is a key, KEYLENGTH informs the local CICS system of the key size. Even for access to a file in a remote system, KEYLENGTH is not necessary if the RIDFLD contains either an RBA or RRN, since RBAs and RRNs are of a known size.

MASSINSERT is a VSAM option that indicates that multiple records are being added to the file. Such records must be in collating sequence for keyed files. This is not a common function in a CICS application because we normally don't add collections of records. MASSINSERT is more efficient for adding records that are in required sequence, because entire control intervals are formatted before a physical write to the data set takes place. There is one note of caution about WRITE MASSINSERT: it must be followed with the UNLOCK command before attempting any other access against the file. Failure to do so could result in an endless task wait or even a loss of data. The following is a sample WRITE command to add a record to a VSAM KSDS.

```
WORKING-STORAGE SECTION.
77  FILE-LENGTH        PIC S9(4)  COMP  VALUE +80.
77  FILE-KEY           PIC X(9).
01  APP-RECORD.
    05  APP-KEY        PIC X(9).
    05  APP-NAME       PIC X(30).
    05  APP-ADDR1      PIC X(20).
    05  APP-ADDR2      PIC X(20).
    05  FILLER         PIC X.
    .

PROCEDURE DIVISION.
    .
    EXEC CICS WRITE DATASET ('APPFILE')
        FROM (APP-RECORD) RIDFLD (FILE-KEY)
        LENGTH (FILE-LENGTH) END-EXEC.
```

Note that the record key field within APP-RECORD is not used as the RIDFLD field. Both the key within the record and the RIDFLD field must be the same or an error results.

7.8 THE UNLOCK COMMAND

The UNLOCK command is used in several ways. When adding records to a VSAM file with the MASSINSERT option, this type of WRITE is ended with the UNLOCK command. Remember that MASSINSERT processing causes a physical WRITE only when a control interval is filled. The UNLOCK ensures that a partially filled control interval is written to the file at the end of the MASSINSERT operation. It also releases VSAM's positioning.

The UNLOCK command also releases exclusive control without actually updating a record READ for UPDATE. This command is rarely used in this context, however, because of the way update programs are structured for online operation. When writing an update program in batch, we read a transaction file and seek a matching record on the master file to be updated. We then proceed to validate transaction file data. As we process, we move validated data into the master file record. If there is an invalid data item, we omit updating only the one field, and include a rejection message in an error report.

In a CICS program we do not structure updating in this manner. It would be easier from a coding perspective to RECEIVE screen input, READ for UPDATE the appropriate file record, and then validate the data from the screen. As fields are validated, we could then move them into the record area. However, the typical online transaction is an "all or nothing" operation. There may be exceptions to this, but usually we update a record only if the operator has entered all information correctly.

An operator certainly does not have to update every field, but those fields that are entered by the operator must be correct. This all-or-nothing approach derives from the fact that the user is at the terminal, can be presented with error messages immediately, and can therefore correct errors interactively. As a result, it isn't worthwhile to do partial data capture and file updating when all of the entered information isn't correct. This philosophy isn't a hard-and-fast rule, but reflects the approach normally taken.

This method of handling updates does not preclude a program from READing for UPDATE and performing validation subsequent to the READ. Entered data could then be validated and moved into the retrieved record. If invalid data were discovered, updating could be bypassed and the record UNLOCKed. However, in this case, ease of coding could severely impact performance. Once we do the READ for UPDATE, the access method enqueue locks other updating tasks out of the portion of the file held under exclusive control. In the case of VSAM, this is the control interval. A control interval may contain numerous records, and this lock represents a potential source of task waits.

In a CICS program we want to use resources sparingly and hold such resources for as short a time as possible. File updating, therefore, is typically handled in a different manner than in batch. In a CICS program we RECEIVE the terminal input and perform full data validation. If all entered information is valid, then and only then do we READ UPDATE, move the validated data into the file work area, and REWRITE the record. The READ UPDATE, updating, and REWRITE are done in as tight a sequence as possible. By updating in this manner, we minimize the potential for having other tasks wait while we have exclusive control. If the screen information contains erroneous data, we do not perform the READ UPDATE at all. Rather, we send an error message to the screen and allow the operator to make the corrections before proceeding. Thus, we defer actual posting until all data entered are correct, and we wait to READ UPDATE until we are certain that we actually want to update.

7.8.1 UNLOCK Command Format

The format of the UNLOCK command is:

```
EXEC CICS UNLOCK DATASET(ddname) SYSID(name)
```

7.9 FILE BROWSING

File browsing permits sequential retrieval of records. Although this is not used in the typical CICS transaction, it is a very handy facility for many applications. As an example, let's consider a customer service system.

Obviously there would have to be an inquiry transaction in which customer information is retrieved by customer number. Sometimes, however, an individual does not know his or her customer number. The system should be able to do an alpha search based on the customer's name. We could have a VSAM alternate index built on customer name information, and use the alternate index to provide access to customer information such as the customer's number. However, we may well have many customers with the same name. An alpha transaction could browse the customer file based upon the alternate index and display a screen of customers' names and account numbers. The terminal operator could then determine the customer's number and retrieve and display the customer's information.

Browsing is a very powerful capability in searching for information. However, file positioning must be maintained during the entire time that a browse operation is taking place. For VSAM files this means that a file string or access path is reserved for a browse operation. The number of file strings is limited. If browsing is a heavily used function, a shortage of file strings may result. If a task attempts to access a file and there are no free strings, the task is made to wait until a string becomes available. Task waits can cause response time problems and result in system overhead. Since browsing holds a file string for a fairly long time, its use should be handled carefully. Don't read this to mean *"Thou shalt not browse files."* What it does mean, simply stated, is that when there is a legitimate need to do such operations, try to do your browsing in a tight execution sequence and terminate the browse as soon as possible.

7.10 THE STARTBR COMMAND

The STARTBR command is used to initiate a browse operation. The execution of this command obtains file buffers and locates appropriate positioning in the file. The STARTBR does not, however, return a record. READNEXT and READPREV are used to actually retrieve records.

7.10.1 STARTBR Command Format

The format of the STARTBR command is:

```
EXEC CICS STARTBR
        DATASET (ddname)
        RIDFLD (search-argument)
        GENERIC
        KEYLENGTH (size)
        RBA  or  RRN
        SYSID (name)
        GTEQ  or  EQUAL
        REQID (id)
```

7.10.2 STARTBR Command Discussion

The options of STARTBR are used in the same way as with other CICS file commands. **In the case of browsing, the default is GTEQ rather than EQUAL.** The REQID parameter is used only when a task is conducting multiple simultaneous browse operations against the same data set. In this case each browse operation is given its own unique identifier; when subsequent record retrieval requests are made, the REQID parameter can be used to indicate which browse is involved. The use of multiple browses within the same data set should be avoided if possible. It is better to browse one part of the file and then reset the browse pointer and browse in the next location, rather than to conduct simultaneous browses. After all, **each browse holds a file string.** An example of a STARTBR command is provided below:

```
WORKING-STORAGE SECTION.
77   TERM-LENGTH              PIC S9(4)   COMP   VALUE +9.
77   GENERIC-KEY-LEN          PIC S9(4)   COMP   VALUE +4.
01   TERM-INPUT-AREA.
     04   TRANS-IN             PIC X(4).
     04   FILLER               PIC X.
     04   WS-PARTIAL-KEY       PIC X(4).
              .
              .
              .
PROCEDURE DIVISION.
     EXEC CICS RECEIVE INTO (TERM-INPUT-AREA)
          LENGTH(TERM-LENGTH)
     END-EXEC.
              .
              .
              .
     EXEC CICS STARTBR DATASET('INVMAST')
          RIDFLD (WS-PARTIAL-KEY)
          GENERIC
          KEYLENGTH(GENERIC-KEY-LEN)
     END-EXEC.
```

7.11 READNEXT AND READPREV COMMANDS

The READNEXT and READPREV commands are used to retrieve records once a browse operation has been initiated. READNEXT reads the next sequential record after a browse pointer has been established, and READPREV reads the previous record. When READPREV is used immediately after a STARTBR, the key used in the STARTBR must be on the file or the READPREV does not work. Rather, the NOTFND condition occurs. If it is necessary to do a READPREV immediately after a STARTBR and the possibility exists that the STARTBR key is not on the file, the program can do a READNEXT. This returns the next greater record. Subsequent to the READNEXT, a READPREV can be used to retrieve the same record as the READNEXT; then it is possible to read backwards from that point with READPREV instructions. Otherwise, one can anticipate the NOTFND condition. If NOTFND occurs, use RESETBR and then follow the procedure outlined above. The problem only occurs if the READPREV is the first record retrieval command after the STARTBR is executed.

There is one exception, and that is if we want to begin reading backward from the end of the file. The file key can be set to high values for the STARTBR request. In this case the positioning is correctly established at the end of file, and READPREV can then be used to read backward. Subsequent to the execution of each READNEXT or READ-PREV, the data field pointed to by the RIDFLD is updated to reflect the repositioning of the browse pointer. The application programmer can change the key value during browse operations to change positioning in the file. **READPREV may not be used immediately after a STARTBR specifying a GENERIC key.**

7.11.1 READNEXT or READPREV Command Format

The format of the READNEXT or READPREV is:

```
EXEC CICS READNEXT or READPREV
      DATASET (ddname)
      RIDFLD (search-argument)
      RBA  or  RRN
      INTO (area-name) or  SET (bll-cell)
      LENGTH (size)
      REQID (id)
      SYSID (name)
```

Below is an example of initiating a browse operation to read forward from the beginning of a file or backward from the end of a file:

```
WORKING-STORAGE SECTION.
77  TERM-INPUT-LEN      PIC S9(4)  COMP  VALUE +6.
77  START-KEY           PIC X(9).
01  TERM-INPUT-DATA.
    04  TRANS-IN         PIC X(4).
    04  FILLER           PIC X.
    04  PROCESS-IND      PIC X.
        88  PROCESS-FORWARD        VALUE 'F'.
        88  PROCESS-BACKWARD       VALUE 'B'.
*   Rest of Working Storage.
```

```
LINKAGE SECTION.
01  BLLS.
     04  FILLER              PIC S9(8)  COMP.
     04  FILE-PTR            PIC S9(8)  COMP.
01  FILE-RECORD.
     .  Field definitions

PROCEDURE DIVISION.
     EXEC CICS RECEIVE INTO(TERM-INPUT-DATA)
          LENGTH(TERM-INPUT-LEN)  END-EXEC.
     IF TERM-INPUT-LEN = 6 NEXT SENTENCE
     ELSE COBOL code to handle error of operator entering
                  the wrong amount of data.
*   more COBOL code to verify correctness of terminal input.
     IF PROCESS-FORWARD
        MOVE LOW-VALUES TO START-KEY
     ELSE
        MOVE HIGH-VALUES TO START-KEY.
     EXEC CICS STARTBR DATASET('MYFILE')
          RIDFLD(START-KEY) END-EXEC.
     PERFORM A100-READ-AND-PROCESS-FILE THRU A100-EXIT
          VARYING I FROM 1 BY 1 UNTIL I > 10.
*   rest of program main-line.
A100-READ-AND-PROCESS-FILE.

     IF PROCESS-FORWARD
          EXEC CICS READNEXT DATASET('MYFILE')
               RIDFLD(START-KEY) SET(FILE-PTR)
               END-EXEC
     ELSE
          EXEC CICS READPREV DATASET('MYFILE')
               RIDFLD(START-KEY) SET(FILE-PTR)
               END-EXEC.

*   COBOL code to process data.
A100-EXIT.   EXIT.
```

7.12 THE RESETBR COMMAND

The RESETBR command is used to reset a browse pointer to another
position within a file. If a file has to be browsed in several different places,
it is far more efficient to do the browsing serially rather than by using
multiple simultaneous browses. Serial repositioning can be accomplished
by doing one STARTBR and then successive RESETBRs to reposition
after retrieving records from each file location.

7.12.1 RESETBR Command Format

The format of the RESETBR command is:

```
EXEC CICS RESETBR
        DATASET (ddname)
        RIDFLD (search-argument)
        RBA  or  RRN
        KEYLENGTH (length)
        GENERIC
        GREQ  or  EQUAL
        REQID (id)
        SYSID (name)
```

7.12.2 RESETBR Command Discussion

The parameters of this command are used in the same manner as those of the STARTBR command. Functionally the only difference is that the STARTBR also initializes a browse by acquiring a file string and buffer area, whereas the RESETBR merely repositions an established pointer.

7.13 THE ENDBR COMMAND

The ENDBR command is used to end a browse operation. This releases the file string and any storage areas associated with the browse. The application programmer must be certain to use the ENDBR to terminate a browse. **The browse must be ended before another request is made against the file being browsed, a SYNCPOINT is taken, or the task ends.**

7.13.1 ENDBR Command Format

The format of the ENDBR command is:

```
EXEC CICS ENDBR
        DATASET (ddname)
        REQID (id)
        SYSID (name)
```

An example of a browse operation is provided below:

```
DATA DIVISION.
WORKING-STORAGE SECTION.
77  BROWSE-KEY        PIC X(9).
LINKAGE SECTION.
01  BLLS.
        04  BLL-FILLER      PIC S9(8)  COMP.
```

```
      04  FILE-PTR         PIC S9(8)  COMP.
   01  FILE-REC            PIC X(100).
   PROCEDURE DIVISION.
          .
          .
          .

        EXEC CICS STARTBR DATASET ('APPFILE')
            RIDFLD(BROWSE-KEY)  END-EXEC.
          .
          .
          .

        EXEC CICS READNEXT DATASET ('APPFILE')
            RIDFLD(BROWSE-KEY)   SET(FILE-PTR)
            END-EXEC.
          .
          .
          .

        EXEC CICS ENDBR DATASET ('APPFILE')
            END-EXEC.
```

7.14 SPECIAL FILE ACCESS CONSIDERATIONS

When writing programs that interact with a terminal operator, we normally use the pseudoconversational programming technique. This programming style has some implications for file updating that must be discussed. Let's consider a sample transaction to illustrate the point. An online system supporting bank branch transactions has been developed. When a customer enters the bank seeking to withdraw money from a demand deposit account, the bank teller uses a teller terminal to inquire about the customer's balance. If the account balance is sufficient, the teller enters the amount of the withdrawal into the screen and presses the enter key. The system debits the customer account and displays a message indicating that the funds are to be paid.

Using pseudoconversational programming technique, this single transaction is divided into two or more CICS tasks. In the first task we accept information entered by the teller (the customer account number and perhaps a function code indicating that a withdrawal is about to be performed). This task would execute in a CICS application program that might:

Validate the correctness of the information entered

Read the demand deposit account master

Format an output screen with balance information

Send the screen to the terminal

Return to CICS to end task processing with a defined next transaction identifier

The bank teller sees customer information displayed on his or her terminal. The teller enters the amount of the intended withdrawal and presses enter. Control passes to the program named by the next transaction identifier option of the RETURN command, and the program determines that this is second time processing. The program at this point begins to process the withdrawal. The program processing might:

Receive the input entered by the operator

Validate that the entered withdrawal is numeric

READ for UPDATE the customer's record from the account master

Subtract the withdrawal from the current balance

Rewrite or update the customer's record

Send a transaction accepted message to the terminal

Return to CICS to end processing

This logic works just fine. However, there is one small problem that we haven't considered; there may be many bank branches and there may be two or more people who can withdraw funds from an account. Suppose that two people were at different bank branches making withdrawals concurrently. In that case, the problem is slightly more complex.

There is a possibility of information changing between the time at which the first task reads and displays file data and the time at which the actual update is to be processed. The problem of a customer's balance is fairly easy to contend with, because we have a numeric value and we can simply subtract the amount of the withdrawal. If the remaining balance is positive the withdrawal is permitted. However, there are applications in which we might be concerned that the operator had entered an update without having the most current information on the file. Consider a brokerage system, for example. If a transaction processes security trades against a customer's account, we would be concerned if the customer's market position had changed, particularly in a margin account where the customer's credit balance could alter because of a change in market position.

There are also applications in which it would not be a concern if information had changed. An example of this might be the updating of personnel information on an employee master file. If someone changed an employee's home address while another operator entered information about a promotion or raise, it would not be of consequence. The central issue is that one must recognize that information can change in a multi-tasking environment. When designing update transactions, the issue of concurrent updates and any resulting application problems must be analyzed.

If the potential for changed information causes an integrity problem to the application, then we must programmatically address this issue.

7.14.1 Programming Techniques for File Modification

There are several techniques that can be used for handling the modification of data during the processing of a pseudoconversational transaction. Let's examine some options and analyze their results. One possibility is to have all tasks READ for UPDATE, meaning that only one task can have access to the record at one time. This does not work for pseudoconversational transactions because a READ for UPDATE and the resulting exclusive control is oriented to a particular task. If a task READs for UPDATE, no other tasks are permitted update access to the record during the period of exclusive control. Once the task returns to CICS, exclusive control is released. Our longest exposure to updates is during the time that the terminal operator is reviewing and changing displayed information; there is no exclusive control if the transaction is pseudoconversational because the task has ENDED.

Another possibility is to incorporate a change flag into the actual file record. In this case the first task of a pseudoconversational transaction READs for UPDATE and actually updates the record to indicate that the record is in the process of being changed. The terminal screen is sent and the task terminates by returning to CICS with a TRANSID specified. While the operator is entering information into the terminal, other tasks in the CICS system are able to check the change flag and discern that someone is already updating the particular record. Such tasks can send a "change in progress" message to terminal operators making access requests. After the operator updating the record has entered data, the next task is started by CICS. During the second task the record is updated and the change flag is reset to indicate that the change had been completed. Although this looks good at first glance, it can cause difficulties.

Consider what happens if the system crashes after the first task has completed but before the second phase of the transaction has updated and turned off the "change indicator." Recovery/Restart would view the first task as complete and the update to turn on the change indicator would not be reversed. After Recovery/Restart, tasks would read the record, find the change flag on, and refuse to update the record. Imagine the reaction of a customer in a bank if the system crashes during the processing of a request to withdraw money. The customer waits patiently for the system to be brought back up, only to discover that the funds cannot be withdrawn because the account is in the process of being updated. It would be very tempting for the customer to consider using a different bank.

Passing information between pseudoconversational tasks is another alternative. If we are concerned with the modification of only a few important fields, we can save the data in the first task and pass the saved information to the second task. Although we have not yet discussed how to do this, there are several ways of passing data between tasks. This topic is examined in the discussion on program control commands. A subsequent pseudoconversational task can compare the contents of passed data with the file record subsequent to reading for update, and in this way determine if information has in fact changed. If a modification has taken place, the update can be aborted and the new file data displayed for the terminal operator.

The problem appears slightly more complex if we want to ensure that nothing in the record has changed between tasks. One mechanism for handling this situation is saving the entire record in the first task and comparing the saved record with the one read for update in a subsequent task. Based on the size of the record, this may or may not be a good alternative. Another approach is to use time stamping. In this technique a time stamp field is incorporated into the file record. Tasks that update data fields in the record also update time and date information in the appropriate time stamp fields. Instead of passing the entire contents of a record between pseudoconversational tasks, only the time stamp information is needed. After READing for UPDATE, the passed time stamp and the time stamp in the record are compared. If they are the same, we know that the record is unchanged and can proceed normally. Otherwise, the appropriate action can be taken. In this context, we find a use for the UNLOCK command. If all data entered by the operator are valid, we READ UPDATE. Yet, we do not know whether there has in fact been a record modification until we actually READ UPDATE and compare appropriate data fields or time stamp information. If the record has been modified during pseudoconversational processing, we bypass updating and use the UNLOCK to release exclusive control without updating the file. In the event that we READ UPDATE and neglect to REWRITE or UNLOCK, CICS remembers to release exclusive control when the task ends. However, it is a good practice to issue the UNLOCK to release the resource as quickly as possible.

7.14.2 More File Considerations

Some CICS transactions involve data entry of multiple input screens. The design of such transactions should take into account the need to use CICS recovery. An example of a multiscreen transaction is the data entry processing of a credit system. A customer fills out a form requesting credit and mails the form to a processing center. Terminal operators enter information from the credit application into terminal screens, and usually there is too much information for a single screen. Therefore, multiple screens of input are used to collect all of the information supplied in the application. As we process each screen of input, we could actually update our online files for each successive collection of data. However, such an approach has several disadvantages.

Information from one screen may have to be correlated with information from another screen, and this cross-screen validation cannot be done until all of the data are captured. If we update files before we have all of the data, we may be saving incorrect information. Furthermore, in the event that the operator cancels the data entry operation, we would have to go back and delete incomplete information from our files. This is obviously not an ideal approach to use. As an alternative, we could save screen data in a temporary work area until all information has been entered and validated. Then, knowing that our information is correct and complete, we could perform file updating.

There are also recovery considerations that recommend this second approach. Both CICS system Recovery/Restart and Dynamic Transaction Backout perform file backout operations for modifications to protected resources made during a single logical task. A logical task is either the work done within SYNCPOINTs in a single task or (in the absence of SYNCPOINTs) a single task in its entirety. The data entry transaction described above involves outputting different screens to the terminal. Pseudoconversational processing results in the transaction being serviced by the execution of multiple tasks. If we collect screen information and update files across several tasks, CICS does not perceive a relationship between the updates. Recovery/Restart or Dynamic Transaction Backout would not know to back out the work of earlier tasks.

Suppose that the data entry transaction is executing and the last task abends. DTB backs out any protected file modifications done within this task, but CICS does not see the relationship between this task and the ones that went before it. When a task is created, CICS formats a Task Control Area or a control block to govern the task's execution. Each separate part of the larger transaction is a separate task due to pseudoconversational processing, and therefore each has its own unique TCA. Separate Task Control Areas are interpreted by CICS as unrelated units of work. CICS sees online processing in task terms, and a task is literally a Task Control Area in the system. Through the use of application SYNCPOINTs, a single task or TCA can be broken into separate logical tasks for recovery purposes, but there is no way to bunch together the work done by two or more tasks as one recoverable unit of work. Deferring file updates until we have all of the information available is beneficial in terms of recovery processing. Any collective updates that we want taken or backed out together must be within one logical task. Therefore, we typically wait to update until the final task of a multiscreen transaction.

Another aspect of file access online that can cause difficulty is the updating of multiple files in online transactions. The potential source of difficulty arises from the fact that, in order to ensure data integrity, CICS must provide an updating task with exclusive control. The combination of exclusive control and multitasking can result in a task deadlock which has the colorful name "deadly embrace."

Figure 7-2 illustrates what happens in the deadly embrace. There are two tasks in our CICS system. Task 1 reads for update record 123 in the inventory file. While this input operation is completing, Task 2 is dispatched. Task 2 reads for update record 123 in the reorder file. While this input completes, Task 1 is dispatched again. Task 1 now attempts to READ for UPDATE the reorder file for record 123, and is placed in a wait state because the record sought is held under exclusive control. Task 2 is dispatched again and issues a READ for UPDATE against the inventory file for record 123. At this point Task 2 is likewise placed in a wait state until the resource it is attempting to obtain is free. Neither task can be dispatched. The tasks are locked together and hence the name **"deadly embrace."**

There are several ways of dealing with a deadly embrace. The first and best way is through programming standards. All programs that update multiple files should perform their updates in a **prescribed file sequence.** The deadly embrace explained above would not have occurred if both tasks had READ for UPDATE the inventory file and then the reorder file. Task 2 would have had to wait until Task 1 completed its processing, but it

Figure 7-2. The deadly embrace.

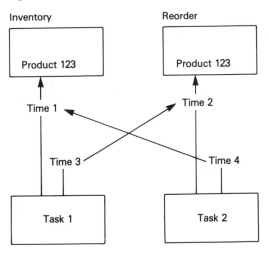

Time 1: Task 1 reads the inventory file for update and gets exclusive control of record 123 on the file.
Time 2: Task 2 reads the reorder file for update and gets exclusive control of record 123 on the file.
Time 3: Task 1 attempts to read the reorder file for update and obtain exclusive control of record 123 but must wait until the resource is available. Task 1 is thus suspended waiting for reorder file record 123.
Time 4: Task 2 attempts to read the inventory file for update and obtain exclusive control of record 123 but must wait until the resource is available. Task 2 is thus suspended waiting for inventory file record 123.

would not have been suspended while owning a record on the reorder file. Task 2 might have had to wait, but the deadly embrace would not have occurred. If a program is to perform multiple updates within the same file, such updates should be performed in a given sequence if possible. The sequence can be ascending or descending, but the likelihood of the deadly embrace occurring is lessened by this technique.

Task lockout can be terminated in some cases by defining transactions in a particular way. In the Program Control Table (PCT) where transactions are defined, we can specify a deadlock timeout value (DTIMOUT=time). If a task defined with a deadlock timeout is suspended while waiting for a resource that CICS manages, then the task is purged when the deadlock timeout elapses. Note, however, that not all resources are managed by CICS. For example, VSAM exclusive control is requested by CICS but managed by VSAM. The deadlock timeout does not affect VSAM locks.

When using the deadlock timeout, it is normally good practice to also request Dynamic Transaction Backout. This is also done in the Program Control Table entry (DTB=YES). In this case CICS purges the task and reverses the task's modifications to protected resources. Optionally, a RESTART parameter in the Program Control Table can be requested so that CICS attempts to restart the transaction internally (RESTART=YES). If task restart is not requested, CICS purges the task, does backout if requested, and writes a message to the terminal operator indicating the abnormal termination and providing a unique abend code (AKCS). If restart is requested, CICS purges the task, performs backout, and attempts to restart. Restart is possible only if the abend results from a deadlock (ADLD abend) and the task has *not* taken a SYNCPOINT. Furthermore, the CICS module that attempts the restart does not check for recursive restarts, and it is recommended that user programming be added for this purpose.

There is one last consideration regarding file modifications online. CICS sign on processing ensures that only authorized users gain access to the system; in addition, there are security packages that can be used with CICS. However, there is always the possibility that an operator's sign on could be compromised or that he or she could step away from a terminal for a couple of minutes. For this reason, we should consider which resources are modified by the system, and perhaps include application program security. In systems where money figures are changed by terminal operators, it is a good idea to have a password field contained right on the terminal screen used to make changes. An operator seeking to change a resource is thus forced to enter a password at the same time that the modification request is made. It is best to have a unique password for this purpose. That is, the password entered on the data entry screen should not be the same one used during sign on processing. The application program should allow only a limited number of retries of the password field. If the terminal user exceeds the number of allowable retries, one can lock out the terminal by placing it out of service (using the Master Terminal Transaction or the EXEC CICS SET command in a program).

7.15 UNUSUAL CONDITIONS ASSOCIATED WITH FILE PROCESSING

There are a large number of unusual conditions that can occur during file processing. Figure 7-3 lists the unusual conditions associated with file commands. Figure 7-4 indicates which conditions are applicable to individual file commands. With unusual file conditions the default course of action is to terminate the task with a unique abend code.

Condition	* * * * * Description * * * * *
DISABLED	The DISABLED condition occurs if the file named in the DATASET option of a file command is disabled. The Master Terminal Facility or the SET command can be used to enable the data set. This condition did not exist prior to release 1.7. In earlier releases a task abend of AFCA would result.
DSIDERR	The Data Set ID ERRor occurs if the file named in the DATASET option of a file command is not defined in the File Control Table. This normally happens because of a spelling error in the command. However, it can also happen because the systems programming staff has not yet added a new file to the File Control Table. The Master Terminal Transaction CEMT can be used to request information about the files defined to CICS by entering "CEMT I DATASET." CICS then lists the FCT data sets, if there is more than a single screen of file information, the PF keys can be used to page forward and backward through the list. This permits the interactive verification of file names.
DUPKEY	The DUPlicate KEY condition can occur when reading a VSAM file by an alternate index. Unlike a prime file, an alternate index can have records with keys that are nonunique. The DUPKEY condition occurs during an input operation that retrieves a record with a nonunique key. Thus, this condition informs the program that there are additional records with the same alternate index key. In order to retrieve all of the records with nonunique alternate index keys, the browse facilities can be utilized. For DUPKEY processing we would use the STARTBR on the alternate key, followed by successive READNEXTs until the DUPKEY condition ceases to occur.
DUPREC	The DUPlicate RECord condition can happen during output operations if a duplicate record is already on the file. The most obvious situation during which this will arise is when an operator WRITES new records. However, DUPREC can also occur when updating VSAM files with alternate indexes. In this case the condition indicates that the alternate index is defined with unique keys and our update is attempting to add a record to the AIX with a key value already in the

Figure 7-3. Unusual conditions associated with file commands.

Condition	* * * * *	Description	* * * * *

DUPREC
continued

index. The CECI transaction can be used interactively to read the appropriate file and determine if the record is indeed a duplicate or if the application program has a bug. In the event that the record is in fact on the file, CECI can be used to browse the file and determine which records are present.

ENDFILE

The END of FILE condition occurs during input operations when there are no more data to retrieve, such as reaching the beginning of the file during a READPREV or the end of the file when executing READNEXT. For VSAM READ processing, the GTEQ option can be used to request the next greatest record if a record EQUAL to the search argument is not on the file. In this instance, if the search argument is greater than the highest key on the file, the ENDFILE can occur. CECI can be used to browse and determine the contents of the file.

ILLOGIC

The ILLOGICal condition can occur during VSAM file processing. This condition is used as a general catchall; a file error that can't be classified as one of the other unusual conditions results in ILLOGIC being raised. An example of what might cause this type of error is if we WRITE a record to a Key Sequenced Data Set and have a disparity between the key contained in the record and the key field pointed to by the RIDFLD.

INVREQ

The INValid REQuest indicates something invalid about a file command. The command is syntactically correct, but is not valid in the context of its execution. For example, we attempt to REWRITE without having executed a prior READ UPDATE, or a STARTBR with the GENERIC option is followed immediately by a READPREV. The DELETE command can also cause this condition. If the RIDFLD option is specified in a DELETE that follows a READ UPDATE, or conversely if the RIDFLD option is omitted from a DELETE command without there being a previous READ UPDATE, we get INVREQ. Also, the DELETE may not be used against all types of data sets. VSAM ESDS and BDAM files do not support DELETE processing, and attempting to use this command for such files results in this condition. The systems programmer is able to limit which requests can be made for each online file. A command may also be invalid because it requests a service that is not allowed for a particular data set.

IOERR

The Input/Output ERRor condition occurs if there is an I/O error during file processing.

LENGERR

The LENGth ERRor condition appears during move mode input operations accessing files with variable length records if the length indicated in the command LENGTH field is exceeded or if the LENGTH option is omitted from the command. In addition, if a length field specifies a size larger than the maximum record size for a file, LENGERR occurs. For files with fixed length records, specifying a length that is inappropriate also causes the LENGERR condition.

NOTFND

The NOT FouND condition occurs if a READ command with the EQUAL option does not locate a record equal to the value contained in the RIDFLD. Attempting to DELETE a record not on the file also

Figure 7.3 continued

Condition	* * * * *	Description	* * * * *

NOTFND
continued
causes this condition, as does a STARTBR with the EQUAL option if a match for the RIDFLD is not found. Last, a READPREV immediately following a STARTBR may result in NOTFND if the RIDFLD search argument of the STARTBR was not on the file.

NOSPACE
The NO SPACE condition results after an attempt to add data to a file when no more space is available. This may occur when adding a record or increasing the size of a record.

NOTOPEN
The NOT OPEN condition occurs in back level releases of CICS when file access is attempted for a file that is not open. The current release of CICS opens closed files as long as the file is enabled. This condition is supported in the current release so that the local CICS system can communicate with a CICS system that is not at the current release.

NOTAUTH
The NOT AUThorized condition is invoked by a resource security check failure. This permits an application program to intercept and deal with this type of violation.

SYSIDERR
The SYStem IDentification ERRor indicates that the system named with the SYSID parameter is invalid, or that the link to the system is closed.

Figure 7.3 continued

Condition	READ	WRITE	REWRITE	DELETE	UNLOCK	STARTBR	READNEXT	READPREV	RESETBR	ENDBR
DISABLED	A	A	A	A	A	A	A	A	A	A
DSIDERR	A	A	A	A	A	A	A	A	A	A
DUPKEY	A			A			A	A		
DUPREC		A	A							
ENDFILE							A	A		
ILLOGIC	A	A	A	A	A	A	A	A	A	A
INVREQ	A	A	A	A		A	A	A	A	A
IOERR	A	A	A	A	A	A	A	A	A	
LENGERR	A	A	A				A	A		
NOSPACE		A	A							
NOTAUTH	A	A	A	A	A	A	A	A	A	A
NOTFND	A			A		A	A	A	A	
NOTOPEN	A	A	A	A	A	A	A	A	A	A
SYSIDERR	A	A	A	A	A	A	A	A	A	A

A = Applicable to Command

Figure 7-4. Matrix of Conditions and File Commands.

7.16 USING CICS AND OTHER DATA BASE SYSTEMS

Application programs running under CICS may need to access data from data base management systems such as IMS, DB2, IDMS, or ADABAS. This is easily accomplished by including commands within the CICS program to invoke the data base and retrieve/modify data. When such commands are used, a preprocessor similar to the CICS translator is used to translate the data base commands. The preprocessor step is typically included in the CICS compile procedure.

REVIEW EXERCISE

Provide a short answer to each of the following.

1. A file's entry in the File Control Table contains the parameter LOG=YES. Because of this, the file is a protected resource of CICS. What levels of exclusive control are utilized for updates to the file? When is exclusive control released? How does a SYNCPOINT command affect exclusive control?
2. In a typical CICS program, file updating is handled in a different manner than would be utilized in a batch update program. How do batch and online programs differ with regard to the logic of file updating? Why is a different approach used in online programs?
3. In a real-time CICS system there are potentially numerous tasks that may be updating online files. Interactive programs are written in the pseudoconversational style. What special concern derives from these facts, and how can this concern be addressed programmatically?
4. The following represents a VSAM data control interval:

A	B	C	D	E	F	G

   A. The file is a Key Sequenced Data Set, and a task issues a DELETE for record D. What happens?
   B. The file is an Entry Sequenced Data Set, and a task issues a DELETE for record D. What happens?
   C. The file is a Relative Record Data Set, and a task issues a DELETE for record D. What happens?
5. Some online functions require that information be collected across two or more screens of input. What unique consideration must be evaluated when designing file updating in a transaction of this sort?
6. The default action for unusual conditions that occur as a result of file command execution is the same for all file unusual conditions. What is this default?
7. If the DISABLED condition occurs as a result of a file request, which CICS system transaction can be used to inquire about the file and alter the file's status?

CODING EXERCISE

    Provide the commands requested in each of the coding samples.

```
1.   IDENTIFICATION DIVISION.
     PROGRAM-ID.  CICSSMP1.
     ENVIRONMENT DIVISION.
     DATA DIVISION.
     WORKING-STORAGE SECTION.
     77  FILE-LENTH-FLD          PIC S9(4)   COMP.
     77  CUSTOMER-NUMBER         PIC X(9).
     LINKAGE SECTION.
     01  BLLCELLS.
         04  FILLER              PIC S9(8)   COMP.
         04  FILE-BLL            PIC S9(8)   COMP.
     01  FILE-RECORD.
         04  FILE-KEY            PIC X(9).
         04  FILE-NAME           PIC X(30).
         04  FILE-ADDR1          PIC X(20).
         04  FILE-ADDR2          PIC X(20).
         04  FILLER              PIC X.
     PROCEDURE DIVISION.


     *   CODE A COMMAND TO READ A FILE NAMED 'CUSTMST.'
     *     THE FILE IS A VSAM KSDS AND THE KEY IS
     *     CONTAINED IN THE FIELD NAMED CUSTOMER-
     *     NUMBER.



     *   CODE ANOTHER COMMAND TO READ THE 'CUSTMST'
     *     FILE IF ONLY THE FIRST FIVE POSITIONS OF
     *     CUSTOMER-NUMBER CONTAIN SIGNIFICANT DATA.



     *   CODE ANOTHER COMMAND TO READ THE 'CUSTMST'
     *     FILE IN WHICH THE NEXT GREATEST RECORD WILL BE
     *     RETURNED IN THE EVENT THAT THE NUMBER
     *     CONTAINED IN CUSTOMER-NUMBER IS NOT ON THE
     *     FILE.


2.   IDENTIFICATION DIVISION.
     PROGRAM-ID.  CICSSMP2.
     ENVIRONMENT DIVISION.
     DATA DIVISION.
     WORKING-STORAGE SECTION.
     77  FILE-LENGTH              PIC S9(4)   COMP.
```

```
77  CUSTOMER-NUMBER      PIC X(9).
01  FILE-RECORD.
        04  FILE-KEY          PIC X(9).
        04  FILE-NAME         PIC X(30).
        04  FILE-ADDR1        PIC X(20).
        04  FILE-ADDR2        PIC X(20).
        04  FILLER            PIC X.
01  OUTPUT-MESSAGE-AREA.
        04  FILLER            PIC X(10) VALUE 'CUSTOMER: '.
        04  CUST-NUM-OUT      PIC X(9).
        04  FILLER            PIC XX VALUE SPACES.
        04  FILLER            PIC X(6) VALUE 'NAME: '.
        04  CUST-NAME-OUT     PIC X(30).
01  FILLER REDEFINES OUTPUT-MESSAGE-AREA.
        04  FILLER            PIC X(21).
        04  NOT-FOUND-MSG     PIC X(20).
LINKAGE SECTION.
PROCEDURE DIVISION.

        MOVE CUSTOMER-NUMBER TO CUST-NUM-OUT.

  *   CODE A COMMAND TO READ THE 'CUSTMST' DATA SET
  *    INTO THE FILE-RECORD. PRECEDE THE FILE ACCESS
  *    COMMAND WITH A COMMAND THAT WILL CAUSE
  *    CONTROL TO PASS TO A100-RECORD-NOT-ON-FILE IN
  *    THE EVENT THAT THE SEARCH ARGUMENT
  *    CONTAINED IN CUSTOMER-NUMBER IS NOT ON THE
  *    FILE. ALSO ADD ANY COBOL STATEMENTS REQUIRED
  *    SO THAT THE READ COMMAND WILL BE VALID.

        MOVE FILE-NAME TO CUST-NAME-OUT.
        GO TO A150-SEND-AND-RETURN.
A100-RECORD-NOT-ON-FILE.
        MOVE 'CUSTOMER NOT ON FILE' TO NOT-FOUND-MSG.
A150-SEND-AND-RETURN.
        EXEC CICS SEND FROM (OUTPUT-MESSAGE-AREA)
            LENGTH (57) ERASE END-EXEC.
        EXEC CICS RETURN END-EXEC.
```

ANSWERS TO REVIEW EXERCISE

1. A file's entry in the File Control Table contains the parameter LOG=YES.
   Because of this, the file is a protected resource of CICS. What levels of
   exclusive control are utilized for updates to the file? When is exclusive
   control released? How does a SYNCPOINT command affect exclusive
   control?

There are two levels of exclusive control used during file updates. First, there is an access method-dependent exclusive control during update processing. For VSAM the control interval is enqueued. For BDAM the block is reserved. Second, CICS maintains an internal enqueue upon the logical record until the update is committed by the task taking a SYNCPOINT. The SYNCPOINT can be explicitly coded in the application program, or it can be implicit when the task ends.

2. In a typical CICS program, file updating is handled in a different manner than would be utilized in a batch update program. How do batch and online programs differ with regard to the logic of file updating? Why is a different approach used in online programs?

In batch, a program typically reads a transaction file containing data to be used to update a master file record. The matching master file record is then read. The program performs validation upon each data item, and if an update is correct, the information is applied directly to the master file record. If the update is invalid, an error message is created for an error report. In CICS, input is coming from the terminal screen. The person seeking to update the master file is sitting within easy reach, and an error message displayed on the terminal can inform the user immediately of the incorrect update attempt. We normally require that all updates requested online be entered correctly before any fields are modified on the master record. Using this approach, we return to the screen with an error message unless all entered fields are correct. In this case, no file updating is performed until entered data have been corrected. Therefore, online programs perform full screen validation before reading for update. If one or more errors are detected, the program sends an error message and terminates the pseudoconversational task by RETURNing TRANSID. The operator can then correct any errors and the next pseudoconversational task can proceed with another full screen validation. This cycle continues until all data are correct. Only when all input passes validation does the program issue the READ UPDATE against the master file. Upon receiving the record from CICS, the program moves the already validated data into the record and REWRITEs in as tight a processing sequence as possible. In this way the update access exclusive control is avoided until all data are correct. Furthermore, exclusive control is maintained for as short a time as possible.

3. In a real-time CICS system there are potentially numerous tasks that may be updating online files. Interactive programs are written in the pseudoconversational style. What special concern derives from these facts, and how can this concern be addressed programmatically?

In a pseudoconversational transaction two or more consecutive tasks processing at the same terminal can display and then update a master file. CICS sees the tasks as separate entities. The first task to be initiated reads the master file, formats an output display, sends the output to the terminal, and then RETURNs TRANSID to CICS. The first task is over and the operator can enter data without there being a task waiting in the system. However, another terminal operator can be updating the displayed data. Therefore, information can change during pseudoconversational processing. People sometimes think that if the first (display) task READs UPDATE, no one else will be permitted update access until the transaction completes. This, however, is not so. When the first (display) task issues a RETURN, any exclusive control held by the task is released. Therefore, READing UPDATE in the first task accomplishes nothing but reserving a resource unnecessarily. If an online application would be affected by the modification, the application program must take this into account. If only one or two fields are crucial, the first task can save such data and pass them to the second task. However, if all or many of the fields are involved, a time stamp can be incorporated into the data record. Each updating task also updates the time stamp field. The contents of the time stamp field can be passed between the first and second tasks. The second task would validate data and, when all updates are correct, READ UPDATE. When the record is thus held under exclusive control, the time stamp passed is tested against the current time stamp in the record. If this field has not changed, the update can proceed.

4. The following represents a VSAM data control interval:

A	B	C	D	E	F	G

   A.   The file is a Key Sequenced Data Set, and a task issues a DELETE for record D. What happens?

   Record D is deleted from the control interval and VSAM shifts the remaining records to the left. This releases the space occupied by record D, which now becomes free space within the control interval.

   B.   The file is an Entry Sequenced Data Set, and a task issues a DELETE for record D. What happens?

   A file error results because deletes are not permitted against an ESDS. This is a VSAM restriction.

   C.   The file is a Relative Record Data Set, and a task issues a DELETE for record D. What happens?

   The slot containing record D is flagged as empty in the control information in the back of the control interval. This slot can then be used for a record insertion.

5. Some online functions require that information be collected across two or more screens of input. What unique consideration must be evaluated when designing file updating in a transaction of this sort?

CICS backout is oriented to a single task (or logical unit of work within a single task that takes one or more SYNCPOINTs). Therefore, data may be collected across multiple screens, but if all updates resulting from this data collection are to be posted or backed out as a set, then actual posting must be done within a single task. In this case data could be passed along through transaction processing, and when all data were collected a single task could perform all file updating.

6. The default action for unusual conditions that occur as a result of file command execution is the same for all file unusual conditions. What is this default?

   The task is terminated with a uniqve abend code.

7. If the DISABLED condition occurs as a result of a file request, which CICS system transaction can be used to inquire about the file and alter the file's status?

   CEMT.

ANSWERS TO CODING EXERCISE

Provide the commands requested in each of the coding samples.

```
1.    IDENTIFICATION DIVISION.
      PROGRAM-ID.  CICSSMP1.
      ENVIRONMENT DIVISION.
      DATA DIVISION.
      WORKING-STORAGE SECTION.
      77   FILE-LENGTH-FLD       PIC S9(4)   COMP.
      77   CUSTOMER-NUMBER       PIC X(9).
      LINKAGE SECTION.
      01   BLLCELLS.
           04   FILLER           PIC S9(8)   COMP.
           04   FILE-BLL         PIC S9(8)   COMP.
      01   FILE-RECORD.
           04   FILE-KEY         PIC X(9).
           04   FILE-NAME        PIC X(30).
           04   FILE-ADDR1       PIC X(20).
           04   FILE-ADDR2       PIC X(20).
           04   FILLER           PIC X.
      PROCEDURE DIVISION.
      *   CODE A COMMAND TO READ A FILE NAMED 'CUSTMST.'
      *     THE FILE IS A VSAM KSDS AND THE KEY IS
      *     CONTAINED IN THE FIELD NAMED CUSTOMER-
      *     NUMBER.
         EXEC CICS READ DATASET('CUSTMST')
              RIDFLD(CUSTOMER-NUMBER)
              SET(FILE-BLL)   LENGTH(FILE-LENGTH-FLD)
```

```
            END-EXEC.
        *   CODE ANOTHER COMMAND TO READ THE 'CUSTMST'
        *     FILE IF ONLY THE FIRST FIVE POSITIONS OF
        *     CUSTOMER-NUMBER CONTAIN SIGNIFICANT DATA.

            EXEC CICS READ DATASET ('CUSTMST')
                RIDFLD(CUSTOMER-NUMBER) GENERIC
                SET(FILE-BLL) LENGTH(FILE-LENGTH-FLD)
                KEYLENGTH(5)
            END-EXEC.


        *   CODE ANOTHER COMMAND TO READ THE 'CUSTMST'
        *     FILE IN WHICH THE NEXT GREATEST RECORD WILL BE
        *     RETURNED IN THE EVENT THAT THE NUMBER
        *     CONTAINED IN CUSTOMER-NUMBER IS NOT ON
        *     THE FILE.

            EXEC CICS READ DATASET('CUSTMST')
                RIDFLD(CUSTOMER-NUMBER) GTEQ
                SET(FILE-BLL) LENGTH(FILE-LENGTH-FLD)
            END-EXEC.

2.      IDENTIFICATION DIVISION.
        PROGRAM-ID.  CICSSMP2.
        ENVIRONMENT DIVISION.
        DATA DIVISION.
        WORKING-STORAGE SECTION.
        77  FILE-LENGTH          PIC S9(4)   COMP.
        77  CUSTOMER-NUMBER      PIC X(9).
        01  FILE-RECORD.
            04  FILE-KEY         PIC X(9).
            04  FILE-NAME        PIC X(30).
            04  FILE-ADDR1       PIC X(20).
            04  FILE-ADDR2       PIC X(20).
            04  FILLER           PIC X.
        01  OUTPUT-MESSAGE-AREA.
            04  FILLER           PIC X(10) VALUE 'CUSTOMER:'.
            04  CUST-NUM-OUT     PIC X(9).
            04  FILLER           PIC XX VALUE SPACES.
            04  FILLER           PIC X(6) VALUE 'NAME:'.
            04  CUST-NAME-OUT    PIC X(30).
        01  FILLER REDEFINES OUTPUT-MESSAGE-AREA.
            04  FILLER           PIC X(21).
            04  NOT-FOUND-MSG    PIC X(20).
        LINKAGE SECTION.
        PROCEDURE DIVISION.
```

```
          MOVE CUSTOMER-NUMBER TO CUST-NUM-OUT.
*    CODE A COMMAND TO READ THE 'CUSTMST' DATA SET INTO
*     THE FILE-RECORD. PRECEDE THE FILE ACCESS COMMAND
*     WITH A COMMAND THAT WILL CAUSE CONTROL TO PASS TO
*     A100-RECORD-NOT-ON-FILE IN THE EVENT THAT THE
*     SEARCH ARGUMENT CONTAINED IN CUSTOMER-NUMBER IS
*     NOT ON THE FILE. ALSO ADD ANY COBOL STATEMENTS
*     REQUIRED SO THAT THE READ COMMAND WILL BE VALID.
          EXEC CICS HANDLE CONDITION
                NOTFND(A100-RECORD-NOT-ON-FILE)
          END-EXEC.
          MOVE +80 TO FILE-LENGTH.
          EXEC CICS READ DATASET('CUSTMST')
                INTO(FILE-RECORD) RIDFLD(CUSTOMER-NUMBER)
                LENGTH(FILE-LENGTH) END-EXEC.
          MOVE FILE-NAME TO CUST-NAME-OUT.
          GO TO A150-SEND-AND-RETURN.
A100-RECORD-NOT-ON-FILE.
          MOVE 'CUSTOMER NOT ON FILE' TO NOT-FOUND-MSG.
A150-SEND-AND-RETURN.
          EXEC CICS SEND FROM (OUTPUT-MESSAGE-AREA)
                LENGTH (57)   ERASE   END-EXEC.
          EXEC CICS RETURN END-EXEC.
```

chapter *8*

Program, Storage, and Task Control Commands

8.1 PROGRAM CONTROL COMMANDS

The commands of Program Control are used to pass control between CICS application programs, ascertain the storage address of a program, or terminate a task and pass control back to CICS.

8.2 THE LINK COMMAND

The LINK command is used to pass control to a program that is functionally a subroutine used by multiple CICS application programs. In this regard the LINK command is the functional equivalent of the COBOL CALL statement. There is a certain amount of overhead in the use of the LINK command, because CICS must acquire a Register Save Area (RSA). The Register Save Area is needed so that the LINKing program's registers can be saved. The Register Save Area enables CICS to return control to the LINKing program. Additionally, by passing control from one program to another, there is an increased likelihood of paging.

The LINK command is used to pass control to an application program with an **implied return to the caller.** A data area called a COMMAREA can be passed to the called program. The COMMAREA allows data to be passed between the called and calling programs. When the called program completes processing, it uses the RETURN command to pass control back to CICS Program Control, which returns to the calling module at the next sequential instruction after the LINK command.

8.2.1 LINK Command Format

The format of the LINK command is:

```
EXEC CICS LINK
      PROGRAM (module-name)
      COMMAREA (data-area)
      LENGTH (commarea-length)
```

8.2.2 LINK Command Discussion

The PROGRAM parameter is used to name the LINKed to program which must be defined in the Processing Program Table.

The COMMAREA parameter names a data area to be passed to the LINKed to module. This area is normally within the LINKing module's Working Storage, but COMMAREA can be any data area to which the task has valid addressability, including any Linkage Section area. This is an optional parameter, because there is no requirement that a data area be passed to the LINKed to module. The maximum size of a COMMAREA is 32,767 bytes.

The LENGTH parameter indicates the length of the passed COMM-AREA, and LENGTH is used only in conjunction with the COMM-AREA option. The value specified in the LENGTH option should not be less than the size of the COMMAREA.

8.2.3 Use of the LINK Command

Conventionally, the LINK is used to functionalize a CICS application so that commonly performed functions can be coded in one module rather then redundantly in several programs. Because of the overhead involved with the LINK command, however, the function to be performed should be fairly substantial.

As an example, let's consider a CICS system in which information is to be retrieved from a non-IBM data base. The Data Base Management System executes in another region in the same mainframe with CICS. Application programs access information from the data base. Online update of the data base is not done. Rather, online programs build a "transaction" file containing data base updates. When CICS shuts down, a batch system executes and applies information from the transaction file to the data base.

This technique has its advantages and disadvantages. Recovery subsequent to a CICS system crash is made easier because there is no need to coordinate backout between CICS and the data base system. However, we can't show old information to terminal users. Information from our transaction file and the data base must be combined or merged together so that CICS programs display the latest information. The application code required to access the data base might be fairly substantial. Additionally, data retrieved from the data base must be "updated" in memory by transaction file data. All told, this could be a good sized function.

Each application program could be coded to retrieve and merge information, or a subroutine could be coded to perform just this function. Application programs using the data base interface module would be smaller, and maintenance due to data base changes would require modification in only the one data base interface module. Although there is overhead in using the LINK command, there is also obvious benefit. Application developers are able to create a functionalized system in which redundant routines are not included in multiple programs.

8.2.4 Coding Examples of the LINK Command

The following examples illustrate the use of the LINK command and the use of a COMMAREA to pass information between the LINKing and LINKed to modules. The first example is the LINKing program, and the second is the LINKed to module.

```
IDENTIFICATION DIVISION.
PROGRAM-ID.
    LINKING.
ENVIRONMENT DIVISION.
DATA DIVISION.
WORKING-STORAGE SECTION.
77  COMMAREA-LEN                 PIC S9(4)  COMP.
01  COMMAREA-DATA.
    04  FUNCTION-CODE            PIC X.
    04  RETURN-CODE              PIC X VALUE 'X'.
        88  RECORD-FOUND         VALUE '0'.
        88  RECORD-NOT-FOUND     VALUE '1'.
        88  ERROR-CODE           VALUE '2'.
    04  RECORD-AREA              PIC X(1000).
    .
    .
    .
PROCEDURE DIVISION.
    .
    .
    .
A100-CALL-IORTN.
    MOVE +1002 TO COMMAREA-LEN.
    MOVE '1' TO FUNCTION-CODE.
    EXEC CICS LINK PROGRAM ('IORTN')
        COMMAREA (COMMAREA-DATA) LENGTH(COMMAREA-LEN)
        END-EXEC.
    IF RECORD-FOUND . . . . .
```

Note that the return code passed from the linked to program can be tested directly after the LINK command. This is the point of return from the LINK command.

```
IDENTIFICATION DIVISION.
PROGRAM-ID. LINKTO.
ENVIRONMENT DIVISION.
DATA DIVISION.
WORKING-STORAGE SECTION.
      .
      .
LINKAGE SECTION.
01   DFHCOMMAREA.
      04   REQUEST-CODE    PIC X.
      04   RETURN-CODE     PIC X.
      04   PASS-RECORD     PIC X(1000).
      .
      .
PROCEDURE DIVISION.
*    PROGRAM DOES ITS PROCESSING AND MOVES DATA
*    AND A RETURN CODE INTO THE PASSED COMMAREA. IN
*    ORDER TO PASS CONTROL BACK THIS MODULE USES A
*    PROGRAM CONTROL RETURN COMMAND.
      EXEC CICS RETURN END-EXEC.
*    THE RETURN COMMAND PASSES CONTROL TO CICS
*    WHICH RETURNS CONTROL TO THE LINKING MODULE
*    AT THE NEXT SEQUENTIAL INSTRUCTION AFTER THE
*    LINK COMMAND.
```

8.3   THE XCTL COMMAND

As with the LINK command, the XCTL command enables a CICS program to pass control to another module. There is no implied return to the transferring module, and therefore CICS does not have to obtain a Register Save Area to store the caller's registers. There is in this respect less overhead using XCTL than the LINK command. However, the overhead of going to another storage area is still present. As with the LINK command, a COMMAREA can be passed to the transferred to program.

8.3.1   XCTL Command Format

The format of the XCTL command is:

```
EXEC CICS XCTL
      PROGRAM (module-name)
      COMMAREA (data-area)
      LENGTH (commarea-length)
```

The parameters of the XCTL command are used in the same manner as the LINK command discussed above.

8.3.2 Use of the XCTL Command

The XCTL command is used in a slightly different manner because there is no return. An example of XCTL use is a menu-handling program. The program receives an input menu screen and, based upon the function chosen by the terminal operator, transfers to the appropriate program. An example of a small program that uses the XCTL command is provided after our discussion of the RETURN command.

8.4 THE RETURN COMMAND

The RETURN command passes control from an application program back to CICS. CICS determines if control is to be passed back to another application program or if the task is to be ended. This determination is made based upon whether the task is executing at the highest application logical level.

The concept of execution logical levels is illustrated in Figure 8-1. This depicts the processing of a CICS task in which several application programs execute. Program Control LINK and XCTL commands are used within the application programs to pass control. Program 1 is the first program invoked by CICS, because it is defined in a Program Control Table entry for the entered TRANSID. Program 1 executes at the highest application logical level, meaning that if a RETURN command were issued by Program 1, control would pass back to CICS and the task would be detached or ended.

Program 1, however, uses the LINK command to pass control to Program 2 with an implied return. If Program 2 issued a RETURN, control would pass to CICS and CICS would reinvoke Program 1. Therefore, we say that Program 2 is executing at a lower logical level. In this case Program 2 can be described as executing at the second application logical level. Program 2, however, XCTLs to Program 3. There is no implied return to Program 2, so Program 3 also executes at the second application logical level.

Program 3 utilizes the LINK command to invoke Program 4. Since there is an implied return, Program 4 is executing at the third application logical level. Program 4 issues a RETURN and control passes back one logical level to the next instruction after the LINK in Program 3. Program 3 also RETURNs, and control passes back one logical level to the next instruction after the LINK in Program 1. The LINK command causes control to pass to a module at a lower logical level, because processing control must be retraced on a Last-In-First-Out (LIFO) basis. This illustration is used to explain application logical levels within a CICS task, and is by no means a recommendation that applications be structured in this

Figure 8-1. Task logical levels.

CICS Controls the Region

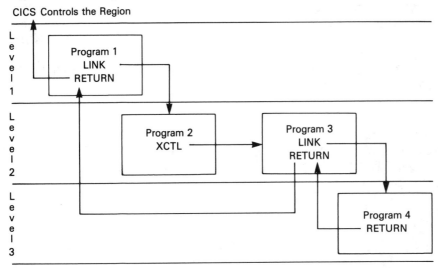

Program 1 receives control from CICS. Program 1 is executing at the highest application logical level. The LINK instruction in Program 1 causes task processing to pass to Program 2. CICS acquires a Register Save Area and saves the registers of Program 1 so that it can return control to Program 1 when there is a RETURN executed in a program executing at application level 2. Program 2 issues an XCTL instruction that does not imply a return to Program 2 and therefore the transferred to module, Program 3 also executes at the second application logical level. Program 3 LINKs to Program 4 and the implied return to Program 3 means that Program 4 executes at the third application logical level. When Program 4 issues a RETURN command, control passes back to Program 3. When Program 3 issues a RETURN command control passes back to Program 1 and a RETURN from Program 1 returns control back to CICS and the task is terminated. The execution of all programs depicted above is within a *single task*. The TRANSID, COMMAREA, and LENGTH options of the RETURN command can only be used by Program 1 because these options are valid only for a module executing at the highest logical level.

manner. There is overhead with both the LINK and XCTL commands, and therefore these commands should only be used for functional reasons.

8.4.1 RETURN Command Format

The format of the RETURN command is:

```
EXEC CICS RETURN
      TRANSID (tran)
      COMMAREA (commarea-name)
      LENGTH (commarea-length)
```

8.4.2 RETURN Command Discussion

RETURN command options can be included only in a program executing at the highest-application logical level. If execution is at a second or lower logical level, the only way that the RETURN command can be coded is:

```
EXEC CICS RETURN END-EXEC.
```

The TRANSID parameter is used to accomplish pseudoconversational processing. CICS saves the TRANSID named in the RETURN command in the terminal's entry in the Terminal Control Table. As soon as there is an input from the terminal, CICS uses the saved TRANSID to initiate a new task to continue transaction processing.

The COMMAREA option can be used only if a next TRANSID is also specified in the RETURN command. The COMMAREA names a data area that is to be saved for the next task. Generally data are passed between pseudoconversational tasks, because the data areas associated with a task are released when the task ends. This means that a task's dynamic Working Storage is released when the RETURN TRANSID is issued. The COMMAREA can thus be used to save information that will be needed in the next task.

The LENGTH option defines the length of the commarea to be saved by CICS and passed to the next task.

8.4.3 Coding Example Using the XCTL and RETURN Commands

The following coding example illustrates a pseudoconversational program that sends a menu screen and then transfers control to a program based upon the terminal operator's selection:

```
IDENTIFICATION DIVISION.
PROGRAM-ID.  ROUTER.
ENVIRONMENT DIVISION.
DATA DIVISION.
WORKING-STORAGE SECTION.
77   TERM-LEN                 PIC S9(4)   COMP VALUE +12.
77   COMM-LEN                 PIC S9(4)   COMP.
77   PROGRAM-NAME             PIC X(8).
01   DFHAID   COPY DFHAID.
01   TERMINAL-INPUT.
     05   INPUT-TRANSID       PIC X(4).
     05   FILLER              PIC X.
     05   NAME-CODE           PIC X(8).
LINKAGE SECTION.
*    Remember that the Execute Interface Block is inserted
*      here by the translator. Since this is automatically
*      available, the program can test the EIB immediately
*      in the Procedure Division.

01   DFHCOMMAREA              PIC X(8).

PROCEDURE DIVISION.
*    The EIBCALEN is used to determine whether this is the
*    first or second time into this program. If the trans-
*    action was just initiated by the terminal operator, then
*    there could be no COMMAREA because there was no prior
```

```
*   pseudoconversational task that RETURNed with a TRANSID
*   and COMMAREA.

    IF EIBCALEN = 0 NEXT SENTENCE
       ELSE GO TO B000-XCTL-FUNCTION.

A100-INITIAL-ENTRY.
    EXEC CICS RECEIVE INTO(TERMINAL-INPUT)
         LENGTH(TERM-LEN)   END-EXEC.

A100-SEND-MAP.
*   Application code to send an output menu to the terminal.
    MOVE +8 TO COMM-LEN.
    EXEC CICS RETURN TRANSID(INPUT-TRANSID)
         COMMAREA(NAME-CODE) LENGTH(COMM-LEN) END-EXEC.
B000-XCTL-FUNCTION.

*   The PF keys are used to determine which program to
*   pass control to. Because DFHAID is copied into the
*   program, the names for the terminal keys defined in
*   DFHAID can be used to test the EIBAID field.

    IF EIBAID = DFHPF15
       MOVE 'APGM15A' TO PROGRAM-NAME
       GO TO B100-XCTL.
    IF EIBAID = DFHPF16
       MOVE 'APGM16A' TO PROGRAM-NAME
       GO TO B100-XCTL.
    IF EIBAID = DFHPF17
       MOVE 'APGM17A' TO PROGRAM-NAME
       GO TO B100-XCTL.
    IF EIBAID = DFHPF18
       MOVE 'APGM18A' TO PROGRAM-NAME
       GO TO B100-XCTL.
    IF EIBAID = DFHCLEAR
       EXEC CICS SEND CONTROL FREEKB END-EXEC
       EXEC CICS RETURN END-EXEC.
    GO TO A100-SEND-MAP.
B100-XCTL.
    MOVE EIBCALEN TO COMM-LEN.
    EXEC CICS XCTL PROGRAM (PROGRAM-NAME)
         COMMAREA (DFHCOMMAREA) LENGTH (COMM-LEN)
         END-EXEC.
```

8.5 THE ABEND COMMAND

The ABEND command is used to abnormally terminate a task because of
an unrecoverable error condition. ABEND passes control directly back to
CICS. CICS sends a transaction abend message to the terminal and writes

a transaction dump to the CICS Dump Data Set. The dump can be printed using the batch Dump Utility Program (DFHDUP). The ABEND command names a four-character abend code that is included in the transaction dump and the terminal message.

8.5.1 ABEND Command Format

The format of the ABEND command is:

```
EXEC CICS ABEND
     ABCODE (code)
```

The ABCODE parameter names the four-character abend code that is to be included in the abend terminal message and the transaction dump. The abend code should *not* begin with the letter "A," as CICS abends begin with this letter. Also, abend codes should be standardized within the application. The same error condition should result in the display of the same abend code regardless of the application program issuing the ABEND. This makes the system much more comprehensible from the user's perspective, and it also facilitates documenting the application. Operations departments usually require documentation on application ABEND codes, and a standardized approach means less to document.

8.6 THE LOAD COMMAND

The LOAD command can be used to obtain the storage address of an application program. It can also be used to request that CICS increment the resident use count in the program's Processing Program Table entry beyond the life of the requesting task. This ensures that a nonresident program will not be released from CICS storage.

8.6.1 LOAD Command Format

The format of the LOAD command is:

```
EXEC CICS LOAD
        PROGRAM (program)
        SET (pointer)
        ENTRY (pointer)
        HOLD
        LENGTH (len-fld)  or  FLENGTH (len-fld)
```

8.6.2 LOAD Command Discussion

The PROGRAM option names the application program that is the target of the LOAD request. The SET option names a Linkage Section pointer that CICS is to set to the **program's load address.** The ENTRY option names a Linkage Section pointer that CICS is to set to the **program's entry point address.**

The HOLD option is used to request that CICS not decrement the program's resident use count when this task terminates. When the LOAD is done, the use count is incremented by one. If HOLD is omitted, CICS decrements the resident use count automatically when the task ends. HOLD tells CICS not to do this. If CICS does not decrement the use count when the task ends, the program is made "resident" until the use count is decremented. The use count can be decremented with the RELEASE command discussed below.

8.7 THE RELEASE COMMAND

The RELEASE command can be used to request that CICS decrement the resident use count subsequent to a LOAD with the HOLD option. The resident use count is decreased by one for each RELEASE command executed.

8.7.1 RELEASE Command Format

The format of the RELEASE command is:

```
EXEC CICS RELEASE
        PROGRAM (program)
```

8.7.2 LOAD and RELEASE Command Use

The LOAD and RELEASE commands are not used very often within CICS application programs. Any loading of nonresident programs because of TRANSIDs entered, LINKs, or XCTLs is done by CICS without an application request to do so. **The usual case in which the LOAD is used is when an application table is defined as an assembler language program to CICS.** LOAD is used to gain addressability to a table of this sort, and HOLD can be used to force CICS to not release the module from storage.

The following sample code is an example of a small table coded as an assembler language program. This "program" contains no instructions, and its only use is as a table for other programs. The module has an entry in the Processing Program Table, and is therefore viewed by CICS as another application program. Following the BAL program is a COBOL module that accesses the table via the LOAD command and uses the data contained in the module.

```
SAMPTBL   CSECT
          DC      CL3'001'
          DC      CL20'NEW YORK'
          DC      CL3'002'
```

```
            DC      CL20'SAN FRANCISCO'
            DC      CL3'003'
            DC      CL20'NEW ORLEANS'
            END

IDENTIFICATION DIVISION.
PROGRAM-ID.  ACCESSIT.
ENVIRONMENT DIVISION.
DATA DIVISION.
WORKING-STORAGE SECTION.
77  TABLE-LENGTH          PIC S9(4)   COMP.
01  CITY-IDS.
    04  CITY-ID-1          PIC X(20).
    04  CITY-ID-2          PIC X(20).
    04  CITY-ID-3          PIC X(20).
LINKAGE-SECTION.
01  BLLS.
    04  FILLER             PIC S9(8)   COMP.
    04  TABLE-PTR          PIC S9(8)   COMP.
01  TABLE-DATA.
    04  LOCATION-CD-1    PIC XXX.
    04  CITY-ID-1        PIC X(20).
    04  LOCATION-CD-2    PIC XXX.
    04  CITY-ID-2        PIC X(20).
    04  LOCATION-CD-3    PIC XXX.
    04  CITY-ID-3        PIC X(20).
PROCEDURE DIVISION.
          .
          .
          .

        EXEC CICS LOAD PROGRAM ('SAMPTBL')
            SET(TABLE-PTR) LENGTH(TABLE-LENGTH)
            END-EXEC.
*   TABLE LENGTH CAN BE VERIFIED BY TESTING THE
*     LENGTH FIELD NAMED IN THE COMMAND.
    IF TABLE-LENGTH = 69 NEXT SENTENCE
    ELSE . . . take error recovery action.

    MOVE CITY-ID-1  TO OUTPUT-CITY1.
    MOVE CITY-ID-2  TO OUTPUT-CITY2.
    MOVE CITY-ID-3  TO OUTPUT-CITY3.
```

Note that the HOLD option is omitted in this example. In this case CICS increments the resident use count for SAMPTBL by one for each task that executes through the program ACCESSIT. Since the HOLD option is not included in the command, CICS will automatically remember to decrement the use count by one as each task completes.

Condition	LINK	XCTL	RETURN	LOAD	RELEASE	ABEND
INVREQ			A			
NOTAUTH	A	A	A	A	A	
PGRMIDERR	A	A		A	A	

Figure 8-2. Matrix of conditions and program control commands.

8.8 CONDITIONS APPLICABLE TO PROGRAM CONTROL COMMANDS

The three conditions that can occur during program control commands are INVREQ, NOTAUTH, and PGRMIDERR. The default course of action for all three conditions is to terminate the task with a unique ABEND code. The INVREQ is applicable only to the RETURN command. This condition can occur if a RETURN command names a TRANSID or COMMAREA in an invalid context. These options of the RETURN can only be used by a program that is executing at the highest-application logical level. Also, the program must be executing on behalf of a task that is associated with a terminal. There are internal means of initiating tasks in CICS, and internal tasks need not be associated with a terminal. If a nonterminal task uses a RETURN with TRANSID, the INVREQ occurs.

The NOTAUTH condition indicates a resource security check failure, and is applicable to all program control commands except ABEND. The PGRMIDERR occurs if there is a request for a program that is not defined in the Processing Program Table or if the program's entry is disabled. This type of PGRMIDERR can occur during LOAD, LINK, or XCTL command processing. In eXtended Architecture (XA) systems which utilize 31-bit addressing, PGRMIDERR also results when a program utilizing 24-bit addressing performs a LOAD request for a program that is placed in extended storage above the 16-megabyte line.

Figure 8-2 breaks out which unusual conditions are applicable to particular commands.

8.9 STORAGE CONTROL COMMANDS

Storage Control commands are used to request a dynamic storage allocation and release a previously acquired storage allocation. The GETMAIN command requests storage, and FREEMAIN releases a storage allocation.

8.9.1 GETMAIN Command Format

The format of the GETMAIN command is:

```
EXEC CICS GETMAIN
    SET (bll-cell)
    LENGTH (length)   or   FLENGTH (length)
    INITIMG (field)
    NOSUSPEND
```

8.9.2 GETMAIN Command Discussion

The SET option names a Linkage Section pointer that CICS sets to the address of the allocated storage.

The LENGTH or FLENGTH options define the length of the storage requested. The LENGTH specifies a 2-byte binary length, and the FLENGTH option specifies a 4-byte binary length. The maximum amount of storage that can be requested by a program running in 24-bit mode cannot exceed 65,505 bytes. Storage for 24-bit mode programs is always obtained below the 16M line. In XA systems, 31-bit mode programs will get storage above the 16M line if both the FLENGTH option is used and the amount of storage exceeds 4095 bytes. For programs obtaining XA storage, the maximum amount is 1 gigabyte (1,073,741,824 bytes).

The INITIMG option names an initialization image that is to be used to initialize the storage area. In COBOL this option must name a 1-byte data field that contains the initialization image. If INITIMG is omitted the storage is not initialized. It is normally more efficient not to request initialization, because storage control must reference the entire storage area in order to initialize it, and the likelihood of paging is thus increased.

The NOSUSPEND option makes the GETMAIN request conditional. If storage is available the allocation is made. However, if there is no storage to satisfy GETMAIN, then control passes back at the next instruction and the situation is handled programmatically. If NOSUSPEND is not included and the NOSTG condition has not been anticipated through HANDLE or IGNORE processing, the GETMAIN is unconditional. If there is no storage available, the requesting task is suspended until the storage request can be satisfied.

8.9.3 FREEMAIN Command Format

The format of the FREEMAIN command is:

```
EXEC CICS FREEMAIN
    DATA (data-area)
```

```
IDENTIFICATION DIVISION.
PROGRAM-ID.
    SAMPLE1.
ENVIRONMENT DIVISION.
DATA DIVISION.

WORKING-STORAGE SECTION.
77  LEN-FIELD            PIC S9(4) COMP VALUE +100.
77  BLANK               PIC X VALUE SPACES.

LINKAGE SECTION.

01  BLL-CELLS.
        04  FILLER       PIC S9(8) COMP.
        04  DYN-BLL      PIC S9(8) COMP.
01  DYNAMIC-AREA         PIC X(100).

PROCEDURE DIVISION.
    .

    .

        EXEC CICS GETMAIN SET (DYN-BLL)
            LENGTH (LEN-FIELD)
            INITIMG (BLANK)   END-EXEC.
*   Application code to use the dynamically acquired storage.

        EXEC CICS FREEMAIN
            DATA (DYNAMIC-AREA)   END-EXEC.
*   Note that the GETMAIN names the BLL-cell, whereas the
*   FREEMAIN names the 01-level data area associated with the
*   BLL-cell.
```

Figure 8-3. Coding example of GETMAIN and FREEMAIN.

8.9.4   FREEMAIN Command Discussion

The DATA option names the data area to be freed. In COBOL this is the
01-level data area associated with the BLL cell used to address the storage
allocation. An example of the GETMAIN and FREEMAIN commands is
provided in Figure 8-3.

8.10   WHEN TO USE GETMAIN

Much of the storage used by a Command Level task is provided automatically and transparently by CICS. Any data area defined in the task's
Working Storage is automatically acquired when CICS initiates the task
and obtains the dynamic copy of the program's Data Division. Therefore,

the most difficult thing to envision about Storage Control commands is not how to code them, but rather when to use them. What this really involves is program structuring. For batch-oriented programmers, CICS programs present a choice that is not relevant to batch COBOL. In a batch COBOL program, the programmer cannot choose to place data areas in either the Linkage Section or the Working-Storage Section. A data area must go in one or the other, and there really is no choice. If a COBOL program is being called by another module and a data area is passed, the passed data must be defined in the Linkage Section. If the data area is not being passed to the program, then it must be defined in Working Storage.

In CICS programs there are many data areas that can be placed in either part of the Data Division, depending on whether MOVE or LO-CATE mode is used in a related CICS command. An example of a data area of this type is a file record. If MOVE mode is used in the READ command, then the area is defined in Working Storage; conversely, the Linkage Section is used if LOCATE mode is chosen. For data areas associated with LOCATE mode commands, CICS acquires storage and sets a pointer to the address of the data. However, even if a data area is not used in a LOCATE mode command, it can still be coded in the Linkage Section.

Let's consider a program that allows a terminal operator in customer service to remove a customer charge. For security reasons, a password field is included on the data screen, and the operator is required to verify his or her identity at the moment that the transaction is being performed. In the event that an operator is unable to provide a valid password after two or three attempts, the program terminates the transaction by abending. However, it is desirable that the invalid attempt be noted. Prior to abending, the program writes a record to a security file. When CICS comes down, this file is printed and any security problems are reported.

Breaches of security are unusual, and a security record is not created during typical execution of the program. The data area could be defined in the Working-Storage Section, or it could be placed in the Linkage Section. If the record is placed in Working Storage, the storage needed for the security record will always be acquired as part of each task's Working Storage. Since this area is used on an exception-only basis, most of the tasks that execute in the program will have an area allocated in their dynamic storage that will not be used. If the record is 150 bytes and this is a heavily used transaction, every task will have 150 bytes of unused area in Working Storage.

If the security record is defined in the Linkage Section, Working Storage will be smaller by 150 bytes and the typical execution of the program will require less storage. If a security breach is detected, there is a problem. In this instance the program is not reading a record, and therefore CICS does not automatically acquire storage for the record area. Yet storage is needed before the program can begin moving data into the

Linkage Section record area. The program can acquire storage with a CICS GETMAIN. Subsequent to the GETMAIN command, the record can be built and written to the security file. The following is an example of using GETMAIN to obtain storage for the Linkage Section security record:

```
DATA DIVISION.
WORKING-STORAGE.
77  STG-AMOUNT              PIC S9(4)   COMP VALUE +150.
01  SEC-ID.
    04  TERMINAL-NAME       PIC X(4).
    04  TIME-OF-ATTEMPT     PIC S9(7)   COMP-3.
    04  DATE-OF-ATTEMPT     PIC S9(7)   COMP-3.
*   SINCE WORKING STORAGE DOES NOT CONTAIN A DEFINITION OF
*   THE SECURITY FILE RECORD, THIS MODULE'S WORKING STORAGE IS
*   SMALLER BY 150 BYTES. WHAT IS MORE SIGNIFICANT IS THAT
*   EACH TASK EXECUTING IN THIS PROGRAM WILL HAVE A SMALLER
*   WORKING STORAGE. IF THIS IS A HEAVILY USED FUNCTION, A
*   SIGNIFICANT AMOUNT OF STORAGE CAN BE SAVED.
LINKAGE SECTION.
01  BLLS.
    04  FILLER              PIC S9(8)   COMP.
    04  SEC-REC-PTR         PIC S9(8)   COMP.
01  SEC-RECORD-AREA.
    .  Fields in the record area.
PROCEDURE DIVISION.
    .
    .
Z100-SECURITY-BREACH.
    EXEC CICS GETMAIN SET(SEC-REC-PTR) LENGTH(STG-AMOUNT)
    END-EXEC.

    .  COBOL code to move data into SEC-RECORD-AREA.

    MOVE EIBTRMID TO   TERMINAL-NAME.
    MOVE EIBDATE  TO   DATE-OF-ATTEMPT.
    MOVE EIBTIME  TO   TIME-OF-ATTEMPT.

    EXEC CICS WRITE DATASET('SECMAST') FROM(SEC-RECORD-AREA)
        RIDFLD(SEC-ID) LENGTH (150) END-EXEC.
    EXEC CICS FREEMAIN DATA(SEC-RECORD-AREA) END-EXEC.
Z100-SECURITY-EXIT.   EXIT.
```

Thus, in CICS programs we can place data areas in the Linkage Section and use a GETMAIN command to acquire actual storage. Therefore, any data area that can go into Working Storage could be placed in the Linkage Section. In deciding where to define a data area, there are several issues that should be considered. First, we should be cognizant of the fact that there is a fair amount of overhead for CICS to do a GETMAIN. The fewer GETMAINs we do, the less overhead there is in terms of Storage Control processing. Additionally, every GETMAIN acquires a separate storage allocation. Allocated areas may be adjacent to each other, or they may be in completely different storage locations. The more storage locations referred to during execution, the greater the likelihood of paging.

Data areas that are defined in Working Storage are acquired by CICS when the task is initiated, and this area is allocated in one executing pass through Storage Control. Furthermore, the storage is contiguous in Virtual Storage, and this means that there is less probability of paging during task execution. What we really have to consider is whether or not a storage area is one which would be used in a typical execution of the program. If the area is utilized in all or most cases, we next have to determine if CICS would automatically provide the storage. For example, CICS provides storage for LOCATE mode commands (such as a file READ). If CICS is going to acquire storage automatically regardless of where we code the data area, then the area should be placed in the Linkage Section.

On the other hand, if CICS would not obtain storage automatically, we must consider if the area is frequently used. If so, Working Storage would be more efficient to use. Remember, the area is going to be used; we are going to need the storage regardless of whether we utilize Working Storage or the Linkage Section. If the data area is placed into Working Storage, we don't save storage but we don't have the overhead of storage control processing (and possibly increasing the task's locality of reference). If we place the data area in the Linkage Section, we don't save storage and we will have the additional overhead of doing a GETMAIN.

Conversely, if the data area is lightly used, as in the case of a work area for exception processing, then the Linkage Section should be utilized. Although a GETMAIN will be required for exceptional case processing, the size of Working Storage will be smaller for the most typical execution of the program. However, one must consider the size of the work area. If there is a message area used for error processing, the Linkage Section is an obvious candidate, but if the area is small, perhaps 20 to 30 bytes, then it hardly pays to have the added overhead of GETMAIN processing.

Let's look at a couple of examples. Program 1 is going to use a file record area in a READ command. CICS will acquire file storage for the task regardless of whether MOVE or LOCATE mode is used. If the record is defined in the Linkage Section, the task's Working Storage will be smaller. For input operations of this sort, the Linkage Section is a more efficient choice.

Program 2 is going to write new records to a file. In the case of a write, CICS does not automatically acquire storage if the record is in the Linkage Section. If the record is placed in Working Storage, the storage is allocated along with dynamic task storage. If the typical execution path through the program involves writing a record, Working Storage is more efficient for record definition.

In our examples we have cut-and-dried cases. However, things are rarely this simple in actual programs. In most cases, if users are allowed to add records to a file, we have to provide them with a record update capability. In a CICS program that interacts with a video terminal, the largest parts of the program are those portions that deal with processing screen data. Because of this, most transactions are functionalized around screen images, with a single program or two pseudoconversational programs that process a single screen. When two programs are used, one program processes the first phase of transaction processing, which involves displaying a data entry screen and returning with a TRANSID naming the second program. The second program is invoked when the operator has completed entering information. The second program receives the data, performs validation, and either updates the file or sends an error message to the operator (based upon whether the entered data is valid or has one or more errors).

Since the largest part of a screen-oriented program involves screen handling, it is a very common practice to combine file functions within a program. Therefore, a file update transaction would commonly have both add and change functions handled within a single CICS program. In this case we are in a bit of a quandry. If the file record is placed in the Linkage Section, our READ UPDATE acquires storage and presents the record in this storage area. We can simply move the updated fields into the record subsequent to the READ UPDATE and REWRITE the record to the file, thus, the most efficient way to handle update processing is to place the data record in the Linkage Section. On the other hand, we have the add function to consider. If the record is in the Linkage Section, then a GETMAIN is required before we can build the file record to be written to the file. This is less efficient for add processing then placing the record in Working Storage.

We have to consider how often the program would be adding as opposed to updating, and place the record in accordance with the most frequent execution path. If in 90% of the cases we will be adding records to the file, then the record area is more efficiently placed in Working Storage. If we will be updating the file 90% of the time, then the placing the record in the Linkage Section results in more efficient execution for 9 out of 10 executions.

The last consideration to bear in mind is the degree to which the program itself will be used. If a program will be used infrequently, it's not necessary to agonize about where to place data areas most efficiently. However, if the program is to be a heavily used module, then efficiency in coding is not only worthwhile but clearly required. Any inefficiency in the program will be compounded by every task that executes in the module.

8.11 UNUSUAL CONDITIONS ASSOCIATED WITH STORAGE REQUESTS

There are no unusual conditions that occur during the execution of the FREEMAIN command. The LENGERR and NOSTG conditions are associated with GETMAIN. LENGERR can occur during the execution of a GETMAIN specifying the FLENGTH option. If the FLENGTH requests an amount of storage in excess of the maximum allowable size, the LENGERR condition is raised. A 24-bit mode program may not request more than 65,505 bytes, and a 31-bit mode module is limited to 1024K bytes. The default course of action for LENGERR is to terminate the task with a unique ABEND code.

NOSTG indicates that no storage is available to satisfy a GETMAIN. This condition is processed in a different way than the other unusual conditions we have examined thus far. If it is not anticipated through unusual condition processing (which includes the use of NOSUSPEND in the GETMAIN), the NOSTG condition results in the requesting task being suspended until storage becomes available. If NOSTG is anticipated through unusual condition processing, the GETMAIN is treated as a conditional request. If storage is available, it is acquired for the task. If there is no storage, the program is reinvoked and appropriate action can be taken. Appropriate action might be for the task to ABEND itself. Running out of storage is serious for the CICS system. Depending on the nature of the transaction, ABENDing might or might not be a viable alternative.

A simple inquiry function can be terminated this way and thereby free storage for the system. However, a complex update program is more problematic. For one thing, a terminal operator has spent time entering data, and the operator's time is wasted if we ABEND. If the transaction is protected by Dynamic Transaction Backout, the situation is worse. In order to ABEND the task, CICS has to perform backout. Storage is required to do this, but the system is short of storage. In the inquiry program we have a programmatic solution to NOSTG, and therefore it makes sense to do conditional GETMAINs. However, there isn't much that we can do to alleviate the situation in the update program. If the program is not going to take some form of action, the GETMAINs might as well be unconditional.

8.12 TASK CONTROL COMMANDS

The commands of task control address functions that are required in a multitasking environment. These commands include: ENQ, DEQ, and

SUSPEND. ENQ and DEQ allow a task to reserve and release a resource respectively. The SUSPEND allows a task to release control back to the CICS task dispatcher.

8.12.1 ENQ Command Format

The format of the ENQ command is:

```
EXEC CICS ENQ
        RESOURCE (name)
        LENGTH (length)
        NOSUSPEND
```

8.12.2 ENQ Command Discussion

The RESOURCE parameter provides the name of the resource to be reserved or enqueued for the task. The name can be a character string of up to 255 bytes that names the resource, or it can be a storage address contained within a pointer such as a BLL cell. The resource name is a "logical" name in that the CICS system does not relate the resource name to an actual physical resource. **ENQ works because the same name is enqueued upon by all application tasks that are seeking to use a resource serially.** Therefore, ENQ is a kind of honor system. The ENQ only works if all tasks perform the ENQ using the same resource name. Issuing an ENQ does not provide access to the resource in question.

As an example of ENQ use, let's consider a system in which audit control totals are kept in a memory table. At periodic intervals a task writes the audit totals to an audit file and then clears the table. We want the table to be used in a serial fashion, because the following chain of events could result in a loss of data from the table: Task 1 accesses the audit table and initiates a write of the audit record. Meanwhile, Task 2 is dispatched, accesses the table, and adds to the audit control fields. Task 1 regains control and clears the table. The information that Task 1 wrote to the audit file did not include the information saved by Task 2, and by clearing the table, Task 1 wipes out the data saved by Task 2. This loss of data can be avoided by making the resource serially reusable.

A name such as "AUDITBL" is assigned to the resource by the system designers. This name is not defined to CICS; the name is a mutually agreed upon standard by the application developers. All programs that use the resource ENQueue on the agreed upon resource name, and CICS gives "ownership" to only one task at a time. Task 1 ENQueues upon the table and begins writing the audit record. Task 2 is dispatched, ENQueues upon "AUDITBL," and is forced to wait until the resource becomes available. Task 1 regains control, clears the table, and DEQueues the "AUDITBL." Task 2 can then obtain "ownership" and safely update the table.

The name "AUDITBL" is nothing more than a character string that all programs ENQueue upon before using the resource. If a program fails to perform the ENQ or uses an incorrect spelling for the resource name, the ENQ does not work. Using the ENQueue has nothing to do with getting to the resource. If the Audit Table were an assembler language program containing only data fields, the LOAD command could be used to gain the module's address. The LOAD command would thus be the mechanism used to get physical access to the resource.

The LENGTH option defines the length of the resource name. If this parameter is omitted, CICS assumes that the RESOURCE parameter points to a 4-byte pointer containing a storage address to be enqueued upon. Therefore, a length of 4 bytes is assumed if the LENGTH option is not explicitly coded.

Most of the ENQueues acquired for a task are done internally by CICS facilities, so ENQ and DEQ commands are not used extensively in application programs. However, there are times when an application controlled resource, such as a memory table, must be made serially reusable, and then the ENQ command is used.

8.12.3 DEQ Command Format

The format of the DEQ command is:

```
EXEC CICS DEQ
       RESOURCE (name)
       LENGTH (length)
```

8.12.4 DEQ Command Discussion

The options of the DEQ command are identical to those of ENQ. If a task performs an ENQ and fails to DEQ the resource, CICS remembers to perform the DEQ when the task ends or a SYNCPOINT is taken.

8.13 UNUSUAL CONDITIONS ASSOCIATED WITH ENQ/DEQ

The ENQBUSY condition is applicable to the ENQ command. Anticipating ENQBUSY makes the subsequent ENQ request conditional. If the resource is not available, the task receives control back and can programmatically deal with the situation. The NOSUSPEND option can be included in the ENQ command to make the request conditional, or standard HANDLE or IGNORE condition processing can be used. An unconditional ENQ results in the requesting task being suspended until the resource becomes available.

8.14 SUSPEND COMMAND FORMAT

The format of the SUSPEND command is:

EXEC CICS SUSPEND

8.14.1 When to Use SUSPEND

The SUSPEND command is used to pass control back to CICS to enable CICS to perform multitasking. If there is a higher priority task ready to process, the higher-priority task is dispatched. If there is no higher-priority task ready, then the task issuing the SUSPEND is given control back again. The purpose behind issuing a SUSPEND appears at first glance to be altruistic, but this is not the case. The SUSPEND is used so that the SUSPENDing task will not be timed out as a runaway task. By returning control back to the task dispatcher, the runaway task interval is refreshed before the task is reinvoked. Most application programs do not need to use this command. However, a process-bound program such as one performing complex processing (insurance rating or bubble sorting) could be subject to a timeout, and would have to use the SUSPEND command.

REVIEW EXERCISE

Provide a short answer to each of the following questions.

1. What is the program resident use count? What purpose does it serve?
2. What is the effect of including the HOLD option in a LOAD command?
3. Why should an application ABEND code never begin with the letter "A?"
4. When may a program use the TRANSID or COMMAREA options of the RETURN command?
5. Functionally, how do the LINK and XCTL commands differ?
6. What is the COMMAREA, and how can it be used?
7. Under what circumstances would a CICS program utilize the SUSPEND command?
8. How does the HANDLE CONDITION ENQBUSY affect a subsequent ENQ command?
9. In some cases the ENQ can be coded with a LENGTH field. What does the LENGTH field define? What is implied if the LENGTH option is omitted?

Each of the following describes a storage area that can be coded in either Working Storage or the Linkage Section. After each description relate where the area should be coded for maximum efficiency, and state the reasons for your choice.

1. An inquiry-only program is to be coded. A file with a 500-byte record is to be read.
2. A general update program is to be coded. Records on the file will be updated and deleted. In 10% of the processing at most, records will be added to the file. The file record area is 250 bytes.
3. During month-end processing, a program is to send a large screen of information to the terminal. During the rest of the month a small message is used. Where should the data area for the month-end screen be placed?
4. For error processing, a 500-byte audit record is to be written to a security file.
5. Subsequent to updating a master file, an audit trail record is to be written to an audit file. The record is 200 bytes in length.
6. A program to add new vendors to a vendor master file is to be written. In the event of a data entry error, the program is also to have the ability to update file records.

CODING EXERCISE

```
1.    IDENTIFICATION DIVISION.
      PROGRAM-ID.  CICSSMP1.
      ENVIRONMENT DIVISION.
      DATA DIVISION.
      WORKING-STORAGE SECTION.
      77  COM-LEN              PIC S9(4)  COMP  VALUE +400.
      01  COM-DATA.
          04  COM-REC-ID       PIC X(8).
          04  COM-FUNC-CD      PIC X.
          04  COM-RET-CD       PIC X   VALUE '0'.
          04  COM-RECORD       PIC X(390).
      PROCEDURE DIVISION.
      *  Code a command to LINK to a program named "IORTN" and
      *  pass COM-DATA.

2.    IDENTIFICATION DIVISION.
      PROGRAM-ID.  CICSSMP3.
      ENVIRONMENT DIVISION.
      DATA DIVISION.
      WORKING-STORAGE SECTION.
      77  TBL-LEN              PIC S9(4)  COMP.
      LINKAGE SECTION.
      01  BLLS.
          04  FILLER           PIC S9(8)  COMP.
          04  PGM-POINTER      PIC S9(8)  COMP.
```

```
      01    ZIP-CODE-TABLE.
                   .
                   .

      PROCEDURE DIVISION.
      *  Code a command to LOAD to a program named 'ZIPTBL.'
```

3.
```
      IDENTIFICATION DIVISION.
      PROGRAM-ID.  CICSSMP3.
      ENVIRONMENT DIVISION.
      DATA DIVISION.
      WORKING-STORAGE SECTION.
      77   COM-LEN               PIC S9(4)   COMP   VALUE +400.
      01   COM-DATA.
           04   COM-REC-ID       PIC X(8)
           04   COM-FUNC-CD      PIC X.
           04   COM-RET-CD       PIC X   VALUE '0'.
           04   COM-RECORD       PIC X(390).
      LINKAGE SECTION.
      01   DFHCOMMAREA.
           04   LS-REC-ID        PIC X(8)
           04   LS-FUNC-CD       PIC X.
           04   LS-RET-CD        PIC X   VALUE '0'.
           04   LS-RECORD        PIC X(390).
      PROCEDURE DIVISION.

      *  Code a COBOL instruction to test if the program is being
      *  entered subsequent to a pseudoconversational output
      *  to the terminal. If this is the case, branch to the
      *  paragraph named B100-SECOND-TIME.


      *  Code a RETURN to CICS and pass the COM-DATA area.
      *  The TRANSID "T002" is to be used.

      B100-SECOND-TIME.
```

4.
```
      IDENTIFICATION DIVISION.
      PROGRAM-ID.  CICSSMP4.
      ENVIRONMENT DIVISION.
      DATA DIVISION.
      WORKING-STORAGE SECTION.
      77   LEN-FIELD             PIC S9(4)   COMP   VALUE +100.
      77   BLANK                 PIC X VALUE SPACES.
      LINKAGE SECTION.
      01   BLL-CELLS.
           04   FILLER           PIC S9(8)   COMP.
           04   DYN-BLL1         PIC S9(8)   COMP.
      01   DYNAMIC-AREA1         PIC X(100).
```

PROCEDURE DIVISION.
* Code a command to acquire the amount of storage contained
* in 'LEN-FIELD.' The 'BLANK' field contains the
* initialization value for the allocation. 'DYN-BLL1' is
* to be used to address the storage area.

* Code a command to free the storage acquired above.

5. Code a command to release control back to CICS so that it can perform multitasking.
6. Code a set of commands to reserve and release a resource named "AUDIT-CONTROL-FILE-33427." Code any Working Storage or Linkage Section fields required for either command.

ANSWERS TO REVIEW EXERCISE

Provide a short answer to each of the following questions.

1. What is the program resident use count? What purpose does it serve?

The program resident use count is a counter of program use kept by CICS in a program's entry in the Processing Program Table. Each time a task uses a program, CICS increments the resident use count by one. When a task is through using a program, CICS decrements the resident use count by one. The resident use count enables CICS to keep track of whether or not a program is in use and must therefore be kept resident. Nonresident CICS programs can be released if CICS needs the storage only if they are not in use. The master terminal transactions CSMT and CEMT can be used to refresh a CICS program only if the program is not in use.

2. What is the effect of including the HOLD option in a LOAD command?

When a task uses a program, CICS increments the program's use count by one. The LOAD command causes this to happen (among other things). When the HOLD option is included, CICS does not decrement the program's use count automatically upon task termination.

3. Why should an application ABEND code never begin with the letter "A?"

CICS abend codes begin with the letter "A," and so most systems support people would assume at a first glance that the abend came from CICS as opposed to being a user abend code.

4. When may a program use the TRANSID or COMMAREA options of the RETURN command?

The TRANSID and COMMAREA options of the RETURN command may be used when returning control back to CICS to terminate a task. Thus, a linked to module issuing a RETURN cannot use these options. The linked to program is returning to the program that called it, and not back to CICS for task termination.

5. Functionally, how do the LINK and XCTL commands differ?

The LINK command implies a return to the calling module, whereas the XCTL does not. The LINK is therefore similar to a PERFORM of another program, and the XCTL is like a GO TO.

6. What is the COMMAREA, and how can it be used?

The COMMAREA is a communication area that can be used to pass data between application programs during LINK or XCTL processing. A COMMAREA can also be named on a RETURN TRANSID command to pass data between two pseudoconversational tasks.

7. Under what circumstances would a CICS program utilize the SUSPEND command?

A program would use the SUSPEND command when performing a very process-bound function, such as a bubble sort. The reason for using the SUSPEND is to prevent a task from timing out.

8. How does the HANDLE CONDITION ENQBUSY affect a subsequent ENQ command?

The ENQ command would be a conditional request. CICS reserves the resource if available, but if the resource is already owned by another task, CICS returns control to the application program making the conditional ENQ request.

9. In some cases the ENQ can be coded with a LENGTH field. What does the LENGTH field define? What is implied if the LENGTH option is omitted?

The LENGTH field in the ENQ command indicates the length of the resource name. If it is omitted, a four-byte length is assumed.

Each of the following describes a storage area that can be coded in either Working Storage or the Linkage Section. After each description relate where the area should be coded for maximum efficiency, and state the reasons for your choice.

1. An inquiry-only program is to be coded. A file with a 500-byte record is to be read.

Linkage Section. Use of LOCATE mode would allow the program to use the data in CICS's work area.

2. A general update program is to be coded. Records on the file will be updated and deleted. In 10% of the processing at most, records will be added to the file. The file record area is 250 bytes.

Linkage Section. In 90% of the cases LOCATE mode would be more efficient.

3. During month-end processing, a program is to send a large screen of information to the terminal. During the rest of the month a small message is used. Where should the data area for the month-end screen be placed?

Linkage Section. Month-end processing will only occur once a month. During the rest of the time, Working Storage would be needlessly large.

4. For error processing, a 500-byte audit record is to be written to a security file.

Linkage Section. Error processing is the exception case; if placed in Working Storage, the program's storage would typically be needlessly large.

5. Subsequent to updating a master file, an audit trail record is to be written to an audit file. The record is 200 bytes in length.

Working Storage. We are not reading the audit file first, and we are always writing this record. By placing the record in Working Storage, we obtain needed storage with one execution through Storage Control. The audit record storage is acquired along with our dynamic Working Storage. Also, the storage references are tighter during execution, because Working Storage is contiguous.

6. A program to add new vendors to a vendor master file is to be written. In the event of a data entry error, the program is also to have the ability to update file records.

Working Storage. The typical execution is going to write a record, and therefore we need storage to build the record.

ANSWERS TO CODING EXERCISE

```
1.    IDENTIFICATION DIVISION.
      PROGRAM-ID.  CICSSMP1.
      ENVIRONMENT DIVISION.
      DATA DIVISION.
      WORKING-STORAGE SECTION.
      77  COM-LEN              PIC S9(4)  COMP  VALUE +400.
      01  COM-DATA.
          04  COM-REC-ID       PIC X(8).
          04  COM-FUNC-CD      PIC X.
```

```
        04  COM-RET-CD      PIC X   VALUE '0'.
        04  COM-RECORD      PIC X(390).
    PROCEDURE DIVISION.
  * Code a command to LINK to a program named 'IORTN' and
  * pass COM-DATA.
        EXEC CICS LINK PROGRAM('IORTN')
            COMMAREA (COM-DATA)   LENGTH(COM-LENGTH)
            END-EXEC.
```

2.  ```
    IDENTIFICATION DIVISION.
    PROGRAM-ID.  CICSSMP3.
    ENVIRONMENT DIVISION.
    DATA DIVISION.
    WORKING-STORAGE SECTION.
    77  TBL-LEN             PIC S9(4)  COMP.
    LINKAGE SECTION.
    01  BLLS.
        04  FILLER          PIC S9(8)  COMP.
        04  PGM-POINTER     PIC S9(8)  COMP.
    01  ZIP-CODE-TABLE.
          .
    PROCEDURE DIVISION.
  * Code a command to LOAD to a program named 'ZIPTBL.'
        EXEC CICS LOAD PROGRAM('ZIPTBL') SET(PGM-POINTER)
            LENGTH(TBL-LEN) END-EXEC.
    ```

3.  ```
    IDENTIFICATION DIVISION.
    PROGRAM-ID.  CICSSMP3.
    ENVIRONMENT DIVISION.
    DATA DIVISION.
    WORKING-STORAGE SECTION.
    77  COM-LEN             PIC S9(4)  COMP  VALUE +400.
    01  COM-DATA.
        04  COM-REC-ID      PIC X(8)
        04  COM-FUNC-CD     PIC X.
        04  COM-RET-CD      PIC X   VALUE '0'.
        04  COM-RECORD      PIC X(390).
    LINKAGE SECTION.
    01  DFHCOMMAREA.
        04  LS-REC-ID       PIC X(8)
        04  LS-FUNC-CD      PIC X.
        04  LS-RET-CD       PIC X   VALUE '0'.
        04  LS-RECORD       PIC X(390).

    PROCEDURE DIVISION.
  * Code a COBOL instruction to test if the program is being
  * entered subsequent to a pseudoconversational output
    ```

```
*   to the terminal. If this is the case, branch to the
*   paragraph named B100-SECOND-TIME.
        IF EIBCALEN = 0 NEXT SENTENCE
        ELSE GO TO B100-SECOND-TIME.

*   Code a RETURN to CICS and pass the COM-DATA area.
*   The TRANSID "T002" is to be used.
        EXEC CICS RETURN TRANSID ('T002')
                COMMAREA(COM-DATA) LENGTH(COM-LEN)
        END-EXEC.
    B100-SECOND-TIME.
```

4.
```
    IDENTIFICATION DIVISION.
    PROGRAM-ID.  CICSSMP4.
    ENVIRONMENT DIVISION.
    DATA DIVISION.
    WORKING-STORAGE SECTION.
    77  LEN-FIELD          PIC S9(4)  COMP  VALUE +100.
    77  BLANK              PIC X VALUE SPACES.
    LINKAGE SECTION.
    01  BLL-CELLS.
        04  FILLER         PIC S9(8)  COMP.
        04  DYN-BLL1       PIC S9(8)  COMP.
    01  DYNAMIC-AREA1      PIC X(100).

    PROCEDURE DIVISION.
    *   Code a command to acquire the amount of storage contained
    *   in 'LEN-FIELD.' The 'BLANK' field contains the
    *   initialization value for the allocation. 'DYN-BLL1' is
    *   to be used to address the storage area.

        EXEC CICS GETMAIN SET(DYN-BLL1) LENGTH(LEN-FIELD)
                INITIMG(BLANK) END-EXEC.
    *   Code a command to free the storage acquired above.

        EXEC CICS FREEMAIN DATA (DYNAMIC-AREA1)
                END-EXEC.
```

5.   Code a command to release control back to CICS so that it can perform multitasking.

```
        EXEC CICS SUSPEND END-EXEC.
```

6.   Code a set of commands to reserve and release a resource named "AUDIT-CONTROL-FILE-33427." Code any Working Storage or Linkage Section fields required for either command.

WORKING-STORAGE SECTION.
77 RES-LENGTH   PIC S9(4)   COMP   VALUE +24.
77 RES-NAME   PIC X(24)   VALUE 'AUDIT-CONTROL-FILE-33427'.

PROCEDURE DIVISION.
     EXEC CICS ENQ RESOURCE(RES-NAME)
          LENGTH(RES-LENGTH) END-EXEC.
     EXEC CICS DEQ RESOURCE(RES-NAME)
          LENGTH(RES-LENGTH) END-EXEC.

chapter *9*

Introduction to Basic Mapping Support

9.1 BASIC MAPPING SUPPORT (BMS)

Basic Mapping Support is a CICS facility that enables application programs and terminals to exchange information without the program being aware of and coding for device-dependent control information. Basic Mapping Support is most useful in the formatting and interrogation of video terminal data streams. In order to understand what BMS does and why it makes online programming considerably easier, it is necessary to discuss the format of data sent to and received from a video terminal. The most frequently used type of terminal equipment in CICS systems is the 3270 or 3270-compatible type of terminal. Consequently, our discussion of BMS deals with this type of device.

9.2 3270 DATA STREAMS

In batch print programs, data are formatted by building output that occupies an entire print line. If a printer has the capacity for 132 characters per line, then the actual data formatted are 132 positions in length. In fact, there may only be a small number of actual data characters, but blanks or spaces (X"40") are used to pad out each line of print and position the locations of data characters. The following COBOL data area might be used to format a report print line for output to a batch printer:

```
01   TITLE-LINE.
     05   FILLER       PIC X(10)     VALUE SPACES.
```

```
05  RPT-DATE    PIC X(8).
05  FILLER      PIC X(30)    VALUE SPACES.
05  RPT-TITLE   PIC X(36).
05  FILLER      PIC X(29)    VALUE SPACES.
05  FILLER      PIC X(5)     VALUE 'PAGE'.
05  PAGE-NM     PIC X(4).
05  FILLER      PIC X(10)    VALUE SPACES.
```

The areas between actual data fields and titles are padded with spaces, and it is these intervening spaces that determine the horizontal positioning of data. In this line of print we are transmitting 53 bytes of actual data and using 79 spaces to position the data fields.

Early video terminals worked in much the same way. The difference was that, instead of sending one line or row at a time, an entire screen of data was formatted at one time and sent in its entirety to the terminal. One of the early video terminals had the capacity to display 1920 character positions on its screen. Therefore, to display a data screen on the terminal, the application program would format a data area of this size. Data were positioned within the work area by padding areas between actual data fields with spaces, just like the approach used in batch print programs today.

Sending 1920 characters of information to position many fewer actual bytes of data, however, is quite wasteful in a communications environment. In most cases multiple terminals are connected to a single control unit. The terminals all share common services provided within the control unit. Because the terminals do not need individually to contain the communications intelligence provided by the control unit, they can be built and sold less expensively. However, there is one physical connection between the computer and the control unit; all data transmitted between the terminals attached to the control unit and the host computer travel over this single path. This means that numerous terminals share one communications path. Nevertheless, only one message at a time can travel on the single path. Therefore, the more information transmitted between each terminal and the host computer, the longer other terminals have to wait to send and receive data.

There are two ways in which a control unit and its attached terminals can be connected to a mainframe computer: local or remote. Figure 9-1 illustrates a network in which there are local and remote terminal connections. In a local connection, the control unit is attached by a high-speed computer channel. Data can travel very rapidly and with very few errors over a computer channel, and local attachment is indeed superior to remote attachment. However, there is a physical limitation to the length of computer channels. Quite often terminals in business offices are located at a distance beyond this length restriction. If the distance to be traversed is beyond local limitations, then it is usually necessary to use the services of a communications carrier.

Figure 9-1. Network with local and remote terminals.

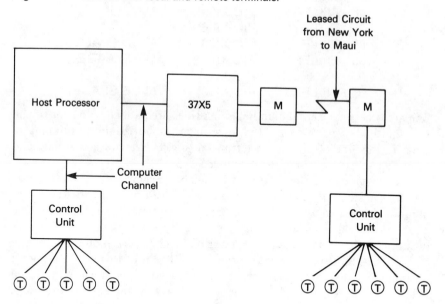

37X5 is a Communication Control Unit. M=modem; T=terminal.

A carrier is a company or group that is given government permission to construct a communications network. Examples of carriers are the local telephone operating companies, AT&T and MCI. There are many carriers and many different communications services allowed to lay cable or construct other types of communications facilities. Most companies that have a need to communicate data beyond their local property boundaries use services provided by a carrier because it is illegal to build long-distance communications facilities without government permission.

Therefore, in order to support data communication networks, it is often necessary to lease a dedicated communications circuit or line from a carrier. The carrier is paid a monthly fee, and the company leasing the circuit can utilize the line to support data communications between an online system and terminals in remote locations. The fees for carrier services can account for a large part of the cost associated with building and maintaining a data communications network. The fewer communications paths or circuits required, the less expensive are network costs. Therefore, one of the goals of online system designers is to attach as many terminals on one communications circuit as possible. The major limitation is the response time that is needed by system users. If we place 32 terminals on one 3274 control unit with only one communications circuit, our circuit costs are half what they would be if we needed two controllers (with 16 terminals attached to each) and two communications circuits.

In planning the network, one of the things that has to be taken into account is the amount of information that is to be exchanged (called "message traffic"). If we are transmitting 1920 characters between each terminal and the mainframe for each input or output, as opposed to an average transmission of 250 characters, then we need more communications circuits to achieve similar response times. Since cost optimization is one of the goals of system design, we choose to send less information and place larger numbers of terminals on each communications circuit.

However, one of the things that cannot be sacrificed is the usability of the system. We want information to be displayed in a formatted manner so that it appears in a way that is user friendly. In other words, we don't want to transmit 250 characters and have the data packed together at the top of the screen. We want the information spaced and formatted as it would be in a batch print report. What is needed is a data-positioning mechanism other than padding with spaces.

The 3270 family of terminals has such a technique for positioning data. **There are certain nonprintable characters that are used to tell the terminal where to position data.** These nonprintable characters are called buffer control orders. Some of the 3270 buffer control orders are listed below.

HEX VALUE	BUFFER ORDER	MEANING
X'11'	SBA	Set buffer address
X'1D'	SF	Start a field
X'13'	IC	Insert cursor

Each position on the terminal screen is given a unique address, and data are preceded with a buffer control order such as the SBA (Set Buffer Address) and an actual terminal buffer address. The SBA tells the terminal that an address follows, and the combination of SBA and address tells the terminal to position data and where to position them. Each data field to be displayed is preceded by this information; what we accomplish is data formatting that is friendly to users without the overhead of transmitting an excessive amount of data.

The only negative aspect of the 3270 data addressing mechanism is that writing application programs to perform this type of data formatting is a time-consuming process. Also, any change in the positioning of data means that the program has to be changed to reflect the new buffer addresses for changed field positions. Basic Mapping Support allows application programmers to construct screen maps which contain the device-dependent information for data formatting. Along with the screen map (called a physical map), a record area called a symbolic map is constructed. The symbolic map is a program data area that is copied into the application program and used for data formatting of terminal input and output. For output display formatting, the application programmer moves data into fields in the symbolic map. The program then invokes the services of BMS. BMS is given the symbolic map data area and the name of the physical map. The symbolic map contains application-oriented information only. The physical map contains the device-oriented information. BMS combines the device-oriented information from the physical map and the application information from the symbolic map, and creates a device-oriented data stream.

On the input side, BMS interrogates the device-oriented data stream sent by the terminal and places data into the program's symbolic map. The program can then refer to input data by field name, as opposed to checking buffer addresses and relating addresses to data fields. BMS is thus an interface between the easiest way for application programmers to handle terminal data and the manner in which 3270-type video terminals are designed to receive and send information.

9.3 BUILDING MAPS

There are two ways to construct the physical and symbolic maps used for application program interaction with BMS. The older one is a batch mechanism. Macro instructions are coded to define screen maps. The macro source code is then assembled to create a physical map and a companion symbolic map. Alternately, maps can be created interactively using the Screen Definition Facility (SDF). SDF runs under CICS, but is a separate program product.

9.4 GENERATING MAPS USING BMS MACROS

There are three macro instructions that are used to generate BMS maps: DFHMSD, DFHMDI, and DFHMDF. The DFHMSD macro is used to define a set of maps (mapset). There can be one or more maps within a mapset, but typically there is only one. The DFHMDI macro defines a map within a mapset. The DFHMDF macro defines a field within a map. The macros are assembler language source code, and therefore must be coded in accordance with assembler language coding rules. The coding rules as they pertain to BMS macros are listed with examples in Fig. 9-2.

The best way to start discussing BMS macros is by looking at a sample mapset definition. An example of a simple set of source code macros to create a BMS map is provided in Fig. 9-3.

The first statement is the DFHMSD macro used to define a mapset. The mapset name is the name provided for the macro—"SMAP01M" in this case. This name is important, because it must be provided in the MAPSET option of the SEND MAP and RECEIVE MAP commands used to request output and input mapping. The TYPE parameter indicates whether a physical map (TYPE=MAP) or symbolic map (TYPE=DSECT) is to be created. In most CICS installations, the JCL procedure used to assemble

Figure 9-2. Assembler language coding rules.

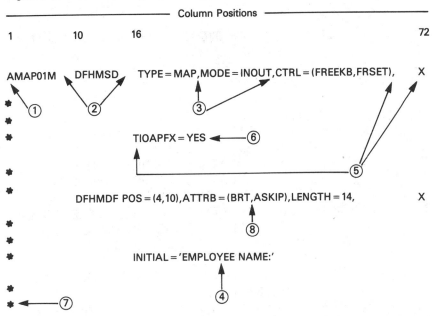

1. The name field must be coded in column 1 and should be 7 characters or less. In some cases the name field is optional and need not be coded. The first character of a name must be alphabetic.
2. The macro call or operation code must be separated from the name field by at least one blank and must be followed by at least one blank.
3. Parameters are all keyword parameters and keywords must be spelled correctly. Parameters are separated from each other by a single comma.
4. Parameter values that include one or more blanks must be enclosed in single quotes.
5. To continue a statement onto another line, follow the last parameter on the line with a comma and place a nonblank character in column 72. The nonblank character in column 72 must be included. The continuation must begin in column 16.
6. To end a statement, do not include a comma after the last parameter.
7. No embedded blank lines may be included. A comment is indicated by an asterisk in column 1.
8. When 2 or more values are to be coded for a single parameter they are enclosed in parentheses and separated by commas.

maps results in two assemblies of the source code, with the value for TYPE being specified by a SYSPARM. When this is the case, the source code just indicates TYPE=MAP and the assembly procedure creates both the physical and symbolic maps. The MODE parameter specifies the way in which the mapset is to be used. In this case the mapset is defined for both input and output mapping.

The LANG parameter defines the source language for the symbolic map. The symbolic map is source code that is brought into an application program via a copy statement. Therefore, the symbolic map must be in the appropriate programming language. Other options for this parameter include assembler, PL/I, or RPG. The specification of COBOL in the

Columns

```
1          10       16                                              7
SMAP01M    DFHMSD   TYPE=MAP, TIOAPFX=YES,MODE=INOUT,
                    LANG=COBOL, TERM=3270, DATA=FIELD,
                    CTRL=(FREEKB,FRSET)
SMAP1MM    DFHMDI   SIZE=(24,80)
           DFHMDF   POS=(1,25),ATTRB=ASKIP,LENGTH=27,
                    INITIAL='EMPLOYEE INFORMATION SCREEN'
           DFHMDF   POS=(4,10),ATTRB=ASKIP,LENGTH=16,
                    INITIAL='EMPLOYEE NUMBER'
EMPNO      DFHMDF   POS=(4,28),ATTRB=ASKIP,LENGTH=9
           DFHMDF   POS=(6,10),ATTRB=ASKIP,LENGTH=14,
                    INITIAL='EMPLOYEE NAME:'
EMPNA      DFHMDF   POS=(6,28),ATTRB=(UNPROT,IC),LENGTH=30
           DFHMDF   POS=(6,59),ATTRB=ASKIP,LENGTH=1
           DFHMDF   POS=(8,10),ATTRB=ASKIP,LENGTH=14,
                    INITIAL='EMPLOYEE ADDR:'
EMPAD1     DFHMDF   POS=(8,28),ATTRB=UNPROT,LENGTH=20
           DFHMDF   POS=(8,49),ATTRB=ASKIP,LENGTH=1
EMPAD2     DFHMDF   POS=(9,28),ATTRB=UNPROT,LENGTH=20
           DFHMDF   POS=(9,49),ATTRB=ASKIP,LENGTH=1
EMPERR     DFHMDF   POS=(24,1),ATTRB=(ASKIP,BRT),LENGTH=78
           DFHMSD   TYPE=FINAL
           END
```

Figure 9-3. Example of source code macros to create a BMS map.

sample under discussion results in the generation of a symbolic map with COBOL source code as illustrated below:

```
C    01   SMAP1MMI.
C         02   FILLER PIC X(12).
C         02   EMPNOL    COMP  PIC S9(4).
C         02   EMPNOF    PICTURE X.
C         02   FILLER REDEFINES EMPNOF.
C           03 EMPNOA     PICTURE X.
C         02   EMPNOI   PIC X(9).
C         02   EMPNAL    COMP PIC S9(4).
C         02   EMPNAF    PICTURE X.
C         02   FILLER REDEFINES EMPNAF.
C           03 EMPNAA     PICTURE X.
```

```
C          02  EMPNAI     PIC X(30).
C          02  EMPAD1L    COMP PIC S9(4).
C          02  EMPAD1F    PICTURE X.
C          02  FILLER REDEFINES EMPAD1F.
C             03 EMPAD1A     PICTURE X.
C          02  EMPAD1I    PIC X(20).
C          02  EMPAD2L    COMP PIC S9(4).
C          02  EMPAD2F    PICTURE X.
C          02  FILLER REDEFINES EMPAD2F.
C             03 EMPAD2A     PICTURE X.
C          02  EMPAD2I    PIC X(20).
C          02  EMPERRL    COMP PIC S9(4).
C          02  EMPERRF    PICTURE X.
C          02  FILLER REDEFINES EMPERRF.
C             03 EMPERRA     PICTURE X.
C          02  EMPERRI    PIC X(78).
C    01  SMAP1MMO REDEFINES SMAP1MMI.
C          02  FILLER PIC X(12).
C          02  FILLER PIC X(3).
C          02  EMPNOO PIC X(9).
C          02  FILLER PIC X(3).
C          02  EMPNAO PIC X(30).
C          02  FILLER PIC X(3).
C          02  EMPAD1O PIC X(20).
C          02  FILLER PIC X(3).
C          02  EMPAD2O PIC X(20).
C          02  FILLER PIC X(3).
C          02  EMPERRO PIC X(78).
```

Don't worry about all of the strange looking data fields contained in the symbolic map. As soon as we have discussed how to generate maps, we will go over each field and discuss its use in depth. At this point it is sufficient to understand that the symbolic map is source code, and that this source code work area is used to exchange information with Basic Mapping Support.

The TERM parameter defines the type of terminal, in this case a 3270. The DATA parameter indicates that there are fields defined in the mapset. The CTRL parameter indicates control options for output mapping. TIOAPFX is required for Command Level programs. Coding TIOAPFX=YES causes a 12-byte filler to be created at the beginning of the symbolic map. This 12-byte filler potentially masks a CICS storage chain. If the map is used from the Linkage Section, care must be taken not to overlay this storage chain or CICS will in all likelihood crash. If the map is copied into Working Storage, the 12 bytes do not mask a storage chain and the area can be overlayed without causing a problem.

The second statement in Fig. 9-3 is the DFHMDI macro, which defines a map within the mapset. In this example there is one map within the mapset, as indicated by the fact that there is only one DFHMDI macro coded. The name of this macro, "SMAP1MM," is the MAP name, and this name must be used in input or output mapping commands in the MAP option. As shown in the sample symbolic map provided above, this name with an "I" or an "O" appended is used in the symbolic map. There are two 01-level names given within the symbolic map. The "I" named area, SMAP1MMI, is intended for input processing, and the "O" named area is intended for output processing. The SIZE parameter of the DFHMDI macro specifies the size of the map with regard to the dimensions of the terminal screen. In this example the map is to encompass 24 lines by 80 columns.

The next 12 statements are DFHMDF macros, which define the fields in the map. Note that seven of these macros are not named. The remaining five are named EMPNO, EMPNA, EMPAD1, EMPAD2, and EMPERR, respectively. Fields for each named DFHMDF macro are contained in the symbolic map. The names in the map, however, have an extra character appended. Unnamed fields do not appear in the symbolic map. For example, the first DFHMDF macro appearing in Fig. 9-3 is unnamed. This field contains an initial value or constant that is needed for the screen display. This screen title field is not going to be changed in the program, and therefore the macro to generate it is unnamed. Only those fields that are actually going to be used in the application program are coded with names in the BMS source code. The reason for not defining names for unused fields is to keep the size of the symbolic map as small as possible. This area requires storage in each CICS task using the map, and it is desirable to keep storage requirements as small as possible. The DFHMDF macro allows a field to be defined with an INITIAL value. This permits screen field titles to be specified in the map definition so that these constant values don't have to be moved to the symbolic map area by the application program. Since the field titles can be defined in the map definition, we normally don't reference the constant fields in the application program, and therefore do not need to name these fields in the map definition.

The POS parameter indicates the positioning of the field. The first DFHMDF macro indicates that the first field is to be positioned at row 1, column 25. The size of a field is defined with the LENGTH parameter. There is a slight inconsistency about the specification of the POS and LENGTH parameters that involves a control field called the attribute byte. Each field on the terminal screen begins with a 1-byte device control field called an attribute byte. The attribute byte describes how each data field is to be treated by the terminal. The attribute controls the display characteristics of the field, the data enterability of the field, the type of field, and whether the field's data are to be transmitted back to the computer. The POS parameter indicates the positioning of the field's attribute byte. Therefore, the first DFHMDF macro in our example indicates that row 1, column 25 is the position of the attribute byte. The actual data for the field begins in column 26. The LENGTH parameter indicates the actual data length *excluding the attribute byte*. This field begins in column 26, and is 27 positions long. Therefore, the total field length including the attribute is 28. If we had wanted to place another field directly after this one, we would calculate the next available position, which would be column 53 (the field begins in column 25, the attribute is 1 byte long, and the data length is 27).

9.5   THE ATTRIBUTE BYTE

The attribute byte determines the characteristics of terminal data fields. For example, there are display options that govern how the field is displayed. The choices include normal intensity (NORM), darkened (DRK) so that the field is not visible, or bright (BRT). These are mutually exclusive options. The data enterability of the field can specify that the field is to be protected, unprotected, or automatically skipped. The PROT characteristic indicates that the field is to be protected. In this case the cursor can be positioned by the field, but the operator cannot enter data. The UNPROT option specifies that the field is unprotected and can have data entered by the operator. ASKIP indicates that the field is to be protected, and that the cursor is to automatically skip over the field when the tab keys are used for cursor positioning. PROT, UNPROT, and ASKIP are mutually exclusive.

The type of field can be alphabetic (by default) or numeric (NUM). Defining a field with the NUM attribute indicates that the keyboard is to be shifted to facilitate the entry of numeric data. However, this does not mean that the field will always contain only numeric data, because nonnumeric information can still be entered by the terminal operator.

One of the bits in the attribute is called the modified data tag (MDT). If the MDT is a "1," the field's data are to be transmitted to the computer when a device interrupt key is pressed. If the MDT is a "0," the terminal does not transmit the data back to the host. The MDT may be set programmatically or by the terminal operator entering data into the field. The MDT is used so that information displayed on the terminal screen but unmodified by the operator is not retransmitted to the host. If, for example, an employee name is read from a file and displayed on the terminal, the terminal transmits the contents of the field back to the computer only if the field is altered by the operator. This keeps data transmission to a minimum, because only those fields actually altered by the operator are transmitted. When one considers that unaltered fields are still on the file, it becomes apparent why it is unnecessary for this data to be retransmitted to the host.

9.6 STOPPER FIELDS

There are three unprotected fields in the map: EMPNA, EMPAD1, and EMPAD2. After each of these three fields with the ATTRB=UNPROT, there is a 1-byte field defined as ATTRB=ASKIP. This 1-byte field occupies the next available position after each unprotected field, and serves as a stopper or delineation for the unprotected field. As an example, the EMPNA field begins in row 6, column 28. The field data length is 30 characters. The starting position of 28, plus the 1-byte attribute plus the 30-byte data length means that the next available space on the screen is 59; therefore the stopper field is positioned in row 6, column 59. The stopper field is exactly what its name implies. **A stopper should be coded after each UNPROT field in a map.** The reason for this is that the length specification in the DFHMDF macro describes how long the field should be within the symbolic map, and does *not* limit how many characters of data an operator can physically enter into the terminal. In fact, the operator can enter data up to the next field on the screen. Therefore, the stopper is not required if two fields are adjacent to each other. However, we normally space fields a little further apart in consideration of the person who is going to be looking at the screen.

   If the stopper were omitted after an unprotected field and there were not another field adjacent to it, the operator could enter more data than defined in the BMS map. In this case, the data would be in the terminal's buffer and visible to the operator. The extra data would be transmitted to the host when a device interrupt occurred, but BMS would discard the data, giving us only the amount of data that can be accommodated in the symbolic map field. If we take the EMPNA field as an example, without the stopper defined at POS=(6,59) the operator could overrun the field's length and enter 35 characters of information. A program using the services of BMS would receive only 30 characters, and the remaining five characters would be truncated. The operator would be looking at a screen with 35 characters, but our program would update a file with 30 characters of data. By including a stopper, the operator is prevented from entering more data than the program is able to receive. The attribute given to the stopper field in the sample map is ASKIP, meaning that as the operator enters the 30th character permissible for the EMPNA field, the cursor advances to the next position. Since that location on the screen is filled with a field that is to be protected and auto-skipped, the cursor jumps to the next unprotected field on the screen or the EMPAD1 field. If the operator enters less than 30 characters, the tab key is used to advance the cursor to the EMPAD1 field.

The stopper field can also be defined as PROT if we want to call the operator's attention to the fact that the field is filled. If the stopper is a protected field but not auto-skipped (PROT as opposed to ASKIP), then the entry of 30 characters in the EMPNA field results in the cursor being positioned at the stopper field. Since the field is defined as protected, the operator is not able to enter information; if he or she continues to key data after the cursor is positioned at the stopper, the keyboard locks and does not accept data into the field. A little figure appears in the lower left corner indicating that the field is protected. The operator is thus aware of the fact that the EMPNA field has been filled. The operator must then press the RESET key and tab to the next unprotected field before continuing data entry. Normally the stopper is not defined as PROT because of the extra keystrokes involved for the operator. However, defining the stopper as PROT does make the operator clearly aware of the end of the data entry field due to the inconvenience of having to reset and tab.

In the sample code the stopper field is not named, because in the programs using the map we do not intend to use the stopper field. Its purpose is merely to limit the number of characters that can be entered by the operator to reflect the field size in the program. However, the stopper field can be useful at times. For example, consider a data entry screen with many fields. When an operator enters information into a screen and presses a device interrupt key, we receive the data into an application program and validate the data. If one or more errors are found, we send an error message to the operator and perhaps cause erroneous fields to be displayed with high intensity. If a single field is in error, we can use a message area defined in the map (EMPERR is such a field). However, as the number of fields in error increases, it becomes more difficult to select an error message that describes the nature of each error.

One approach that can be used is to send a general legend in the error message field, such as:

1=numbers only   2=letters only   3=zip/state   4=no embedded −

If the stopper field is named in the map definition, it can be used for a character code referring to the error legend. In this way there is an indication of the type of error found for each error detected. Normally this is done only with very complex data entry screens in which there are common editing rules for field contents.

9.7 TESTING AND USING MAPS

After creating a map, the CICS transaction "CECI" can be used to display it on a screen. Enter:

CECI SEND MAP(mapname) MAPSET(mapsetname) ERASE

The command is syntax checked and then displayed on the screen. Press the ENTER key; the command is executed and the map is displayed on the screen. It is a good idea at this point to actually test each data entry field in the map. This permits the verification of stopper field placement, as we can count the number of characters that can physically be entered into each UNPROT field.

The final BMS macro coded in the mapset definition is an ending DFHMSD TYPE=FINAL. This is required, since assembly errors result if this statement is omitted. The END statement is an assembler language statement indicating the end of the assembler source code. If this statement is omitted, a level 4 diagnostic is generated by the assembler, but this error is a warning. BMS source code is then assembled first to create a physical map which is actually a load module. The load module name is normally that of the mapset or the name specified for the DFHMSD macro. This load module name must be defined in the CICS Processing Program Table for the mapset to be used during program execution under CICS.

A second assembly generates a symbolic map or copy code that is used in the application program. This copy code is placed in a map library used during the compilation of CICS programs. The map library is typically a partitioned data set in OS systems, and the member name within the map library is the mapset name. Therefore, when coding a CICS program, the following statement can be used to bring in the symbolic map copy code:

01 COPY mapset-name.

Note that the copy statement does not have a data name defined. It is best to code the map copy statement in this way. However, if a name is desired, there is only one name that does not result in a compile error. This is the name defined in the DFHMDI with an "I" concatenated to it. The only named copy that can be coded for our sample map is:

01 SMAP1MMI COPY SMAP01M.

Any other name on the copy statement would result in a compile error. This is because the copy code generated consists of an input symbolic map named after the DFHMDI with an "I" concatenated, and an output symbolic map named after the DFHMDI with an "O" appended. The output map redefines the input map, and the generated code for the map we have been using as an example includes the statement:

01 SMAP1MMO REDEFINES SMAP1MMI.

If the program alters the name "SMAP1MMI" by including a different name on the copy statement, the compiler cannot process the 01-statement of the output map correctly. Consequently, the compile error "OBJECT OF A REDEFINES IS UNDEFINED" results. Once the symbolic map is copied into the source program, it is used as a work area to exchange information with BMS. It is important to remember that the map is not a data area that is sent directly to a terminal.

9.8 FORMATS OF BMS MAP DEFINITION MACROS

Having examined the process of map generation and looked at and analyzed the source code to create a map, we ought to discuss each of the three map generation macros in detail.

9.8.1 Format of the DFHMSD Macro

The format of the DFHMSD macro is:

```
msname DFHMSD TYPE=DSECT  or  MAP,
          TIOAPFX=YES,
          STORAGE=AUTO  or  BASE=name
          MODE=IN  or  OUT  or  INOUT
          LANG=ASM  or  COBOL  or  PL/I  or  RPG
          CTRL=PRINT  or  FREEKB, ALARM, FRSET
          EXTATT=NO  or  MAPONLY  or  YES
          COLOR=DEFAULT  or  color
          VALIDN=MUSTFILL, MUSTENTER, TRIGGER
          HILIGHT=OFF,BLINK,REVERSE,UNDERLINE
          TERM=3270-1  or  3270-2  or  3270
```

9.8.1.1 DFHMSD Macro Discussion Msname is the name of the map-set. **This name is normally used as the load module name for the physical map,** and as such there must be an entry in the Processing Program Table (PPT) for the map to be used during CICS execution. **This is also the name of the symbolic map that is brought into the source module.** The mapset name is also specified in the MAPSET option of the SEND MAP and RECEIVE MAP BMS commands.

DFHMSD is the operand or macro call. TYPE defines the entity to be created. DSECT indicates a symbolic map, and MAP requests a physical map. Most JCL procedures result in both being created in one job.

TIOAPFX=YES must be coded for a map that is to be used in a Command Level program. This option generates a 12-byte filler in the beginning of the symbolic map.

STORAGE=AUTO or BASE=name are mutually exclusive options that describe the treatment of map storage. STORAGE=AUTO specifies that multiple symbolic maps within a mapset are each to have unique storage, as opposed to redefining each other. BASE=name indicates that symbolic maps are to overlay or redefine each other. The BASE=name option is invalid for maps used in an assembler program.

MODE defines how the map is to be used. IN indicates that the map is to be used for input operations only. OUT specifies that only output mapping is to be done. INOUT permits the map to be used for both input and output.

LANG indicates the source code language of the symbolic map.

CTRL defines control options when the map is used for output operations. PRINT is included to start a printer. ALARM sounds the terminal alarm. FREEKB unlocks the keyboard without requiring that the operator press the RESET key. FRSET requests that all field Modified Data Tags (MDTs) be turned off prior to the placement of output data into the terminal buffer.

EXTATT defines support for extended attributes as applicable to specific terminals. Extended attributes include the use of:

1. special display options such as color fields, inverse display, or field underlining or
2. special field editing options like mandatory field entry.

NO means that extended attributes are not used. YES requests a symbolic map that allows extended attributes to be altered programmatically. MAPONLY indicates that the physical map may contain fields with extended attributes, but that the symbolic map need not contain information permitting their modification by the application program.

COLOR specifies the default mapset color. This can be overridden on a map or field basis. The possible colors include blue, green, turquoise, red, pink, yellow, and neutral.

VALIDN defines default field validation for the mapset. This can be overridden for individual maps or fields within maps. MUSTFILL requires the operator to fill the entire field before being able to move the cursor. MUSTENTER requires data to be entered into the field before the cursor can be moved. Field validation applies to the 8775 terminal.

HILIGHT defines default field highlighting within the mapset. The default can be overridden for individual maps or fields. OFF means that no highlighting is requested, BLINK defines blinking fields, REVERSE indicates inverse video, and UNDERLINE requests underlined fields. Before becoming enthusiastic about the use of some of these options, remember that a human being has to look at the screen. Blinking fields, for example, can drive some people to distraction.

TERM indicates the type of terminal the mapset is created for. The terminals supported are listed in the IBM CICS Application Programmer's Reference. This list is quite extensive, and includes devices other than the

3270 type. For the 3270 we can specify: use 3270-1 for a 40-column display, 3270-2 for an 80-column display, or 3270 when it is not necessary to differentiate.

9.8.2 Format of the DFHMDI Macro

The format of the DFHMDI macro is:

```
mapname DFHMDI SIZE=(line,column),
        LINE=line-number,
        COLUMN=column-number,
        CTRL=PRINT  or  FREEKB, ALARM, FRSET
        EXTATT=NO  or  MAPONLY  or  YES
        COLOR=DEFAULT  or  color
        VALIDN=MUSTFILL, MUSTENTER, TRIGGER
        HILIGHT=OFF,BLINK,REVERSE,UNDERLINE
        TERM=3270-1  or  3270-2  or  3270
```

9.8.2.1 DFHMDI Macro Discussion Mapname defines the name of a map within a mapset. The map name must be provided in SEND MAP and RECEIVE MAP commands.

DFHMDI is the operation code or macro call. SIZE defines the size of the map with regard to the terminal screen. LINE indicates the number of vertical lines in the map. COLUMN defines the number of horizontal columns. Valid values for either SIZE option are from 1 through 240, but are limited, of course, by the terminal screen size.

LINE indicates the starting line of the map. The default is line 1.

COLUMN specifies the starting column of the map. The default is column 1.

CTRL, EXTATT, COLOR, VALIDN, HILIGHT, and TERM options are used in the same manner as described in the discussion of the DFHMSD macro, except that they pertain to a map within the mapset when coded in the DFHMDI.

9.8.3 Format of the DFHMDF Macro

The format of the DFHMDF macro is:

```
fldname DFHMDF POS=(line,column),
        LENGTH=data-length,
        INITIAL='initial-field-constant',
        JUSTIFY=(LEFT  or  RIGHT, BLANK  or  ZERO)
        ATTRB=(ASKIP  or  PROT  or  UNPROT,
               NUM, DET, IC, FSET,
               BRT,  or  NORM  or  DRK),
        GRPNAME=name,
```

```
OCCURS=number-of-occurrences,
COLOR=DEFAULT  or  color,
VALIDN=MUSTFILL, MUSTENTER, TRIGGER,
HILIGHT=OFF,BLINK,REVERSE,UNDERLINE,
PICIN='pic-value'
PICOUT='pic-value'
```

9.8.3.1 Discussion of the DFHMDF Macro Fldname is the optional field name. If provided, the fldname must be seven characters or less and begin with an alphabetic character. Only those fields that are actually referenced in an application program are given names.

DFHMDF is the operation code or macro call.

POS provides the positioning of the field. Fields should be defined in ascending sequence across a line, and then on successive lines. The POSitioning of the field actually describes the placement of the field's attribute byte. Therefore, the data begin in the next position.

LENGTH defines the length of the field exclusive of the attribute byte.

INITIAL is used to define a literal value for a field. Usually screen titles are defined in the map source code by using the INITIAL parameter. In that way it is not necessary for the application program to move titles into a work area, and the symbolic map need not contain such fields.

JUSTIFY defines how BMS is to position and pad data within the symbolic map **during input mapping operations.** The default is for alphabetic fields to be left justified and padded with spaces, and for NUMeric fields to be right justified and padded with zeroes. The JUSTIFY parameter can be used to override these defaults.

ATTRB defines the default characteristics of the field as follows:

1. ASKIP/PROT/UNPROT defines whether data can be entered into the field, and if the cursor can be positioned by it. These are mutually exclusive values, so you get to pick only one. ASKIP means that the field is protected, and that the cursor does not advance to the field when the tab keys are used to skip to the next field on the screen. PROT means that the field is protected, but that the cursor does position at the field. UNPROT means that the field is unprotected or can receive data keyed by the operator. These attributes describe the way in which the field is treated by the terminal. An operator cannot enter data into a field unless it is defined as unprotected. However, an application program can move data into any field represented in the symbolic map, regardless of its enterability status at the terminal.

2. NUM defines the field as NUMeric. The keyboard is shifted to facilitate the entry of numeric data.

3. DET specifies that the field is selector pen detectable. Some terminals, most notably those used as system consoles, are equipped with light pens. This allows the console operator to hold the light

pen to a terminal screen and make a selection. This option is rarely utilized in application systems.

4. IC indicates that the cursor is to be positioned at a field. This is specified for only one field in a map, serves as the initial or default cursor position, and is usually the first unprotected field on the screen. However, if the first data entry field is rarely entered, IC can be specified for the most commonly used first field.

5. FSET indicates that the Modified Data Tag for this field is to be set on. This causes the field to be transmitted back to the host regardless of whether the terminal operator has modified the field or not. The use of this option should be avoided whenever possible. In a certain type of TCAM environment (called POOLED TCAM), the TRANSID of the RETURN command cannot be used. Yet we are desirous of writing pseudoconversational programs. In this case the next TRANSID is actually placed on the screen, and the TRANSID field is given the ASKIP, DRK, and FSET characteristics. In this way the TRANSID is always read back from the terminal, and has the same effect as if entered by the user. In most other cases we want to know which fields were in fact changed by the operator, and therefore we do not turn on the MDT with the FSET option.

6. BRT/NORM/DRK are mutually exclusive options that define the display quality of a field. BRT causes the field to be displayed with high intensity. NORM results in normal display. DRK causes the field to be invisible when looking at the screen. DRK is normally used for passwords and the like.

The default attributes NORM and ASKIP occur if the ATTRB parameter is omitted. If multiple options are to be coded, it is required that they be enclosed in parentheses and separated by commas.

GRPNAME is used to group together successive fields within the symbolic map. Fields in a group are part of a higher-level data structure within the symbolic map. The name given to the data structure is that specified in the GRPNAME parameter. Group fields need not be contiguous, but fields within a group must follow one another without any intervening fields. GRPNAME is coded for each field's DFHMDF within the group. The reason for defining a group is so that the application program can reference a collection of fields with a group name.

OCCURS defines multiple occurrences of a single field, both in the symbolic and physical maps. In a COBOL symbolic map, the OCCURS clause is used to define the repeated field, and a subscript can be used to process various occurrences. This parameter cannot be used to define a collection of fields that are repeated as a group, and therefore **OCCURS and GRPNAME are mutually exclusive.**

The use of COLOR, VALIDN, and HILIGHT is described in the discussion of the DFHMSD. On the DFHMDF macro these options can be used to override map/mapset defaults.

PICIN and PICOUT are used to define COBOL editing pictures within the input and output symbolic map areas, respectively. Since the input and output areas redefine each other, both PICIN and PICOUT cannot be used for the same field. PICOUT is particularly useful when displaying dollar amounts on a screen, because standard COBOL editing can be used to float in a dollar sign or otherwise edit numeric data.

9.9 COORDINATING SYMBOLIC AND PHYSICAL MAPS

One of the most important things to understand about the symbolic map is that it is nothing more than a program work area that is used to pass information between BMS and the application program. The map is a parameter area used to talk to BMS, and not a terminal data area as such. The use of the fields in the symbolic map is dictated by the conventions used by Basic Mapping Support, and not by terminal considerations.

There is a direct correspondence between the physical and symbolic maps. This enables BMS to recognize field displacements in the symbolic map and relate them to the physical map. Conceptually, the physical map pairs a displacement of a symbolic map field to an appropriate buffer address for output mapping operations. For input mapping, BMS relates a buffer address sent along with data fields to a displacement in the symbolic map. Therefore, the symbolic map must be coordinated with the physical map. If a screen change results in a change to the source code, new versions of both maps are normally required. Also, programs using the symbolic map should be recompiled to obtain the latest version of the symbolic map.

The recompilation is, however, not always required. If a NAMED DFHMDF field changes in length or a new NAMED DFHMDF macro is added to the source code, then the program recompilation is required, because the new version of the symbolic map contains changes in field displacements. It is the displacement in the symbolic map that BMS uses to identify fields, and if displacements are altered the program needs the new symbolic map so that mapping is done correctly. Normally, we just recompile the program whenever a map is reassembled.

REVIEW EXERCISE

Provide a short answer to each of the following questions.

1. What is Basic Mapping Support? What aspect of online programming is facilitated through the use of BMS?
2. What two methods can be used for generating BMS maps?
3. What is the physical map?
4. What is the symbolic map?

5. What rules must be followed for continuing BMS macro statements onto successive lines?
6. List three limitations on the use of names in BMS macros.
7. Why is it desirable to omit names for some fields defined in a BMS map? What type of field would we want to name? What type of field do we want to avoid naming?
8. Usually, when a change is made to a BMS map, it is necessary to recompile the program(s) using the map. Why is this necessary? Under what circumstances could we omit program recompilation?
9. Why are stopper fields used after UNPROTected fields in a BMS map?
10. Why is it a good idea to omit a name on the copy statement used to bring the symbolic map into a CICS program?

Match each of the following with a definition provided below.

_____ 1. DFHMSD	_____ 11. UNPROT
_____ 2. FSET	_____ 12. FREEKB
_____ 3. DFHMDI	_____ 13. TIOAPFX
_____ 4. MODE	_____ 14. LANG
_____ 5. DFHMDF	_____ 15. SIZE
_____ 6. POS	_____ 16. ATTRB
_____ 7. ASKIP	_____ 17. IC
_____ 8. BRT	_____ 18. JUSTIFY
_____ 9. INITIAL	_____ 19. LENGTH
_____ 10. PROT	_____ 20. FRSET

A. BMS macro used to define a field within a map.
B. Used to make a field protected and not permit the cursor to be positioned at the field.
C. Must be used in maps to be used in a command level program. This parameter requests a 12-byte filler that masks a CICS storage chain.
D. BMS macro used to define a mapset.
E. Used to define a field such that an operator can key data into it.
F. BMS macro used to define a map within a mapset.
G. Used to define a literal value for a field. This is typically done for screen title fields.
H. Used to define the dimensions of a map within a mapset.
I. Used to position the attribute byte and subsequent field within a map.
J. Used to define the size of a data field exclusive of the field attribute.
K. Used to define a field such that the operator cannot enter data into the field.
L. Used to request field data padding and justification.

M. Used to define a field such that the field is always read back from the terminal.

N. Defines how a mapset is to be used.

O. Requests that field MDTs be reset during output operations.

P. Defines the source code language of the symbolic map.

Q. Defines the characteristics of a display field.

R. Requests that the keyboard be unlocked so that the operator does not have to press the RESET key prior to data entry.

S. Defines the initial cursor position within a map.

T. Requests that a field be displayed with high intensity.

ANSWERS TO REVIEW EXERCISE

Provide a short answer to each of the following questions.

1. What is Basic Mapping Support? What aspect of online programming is facilitated through the use of BMS?

Basic Mapping Support is an interface between application programs and the device-oriented data streams that video display terminals require for data display. BMS facilitates programming for video display terminals, because the application builds and receives terminal data in a logical record referred to as a symbolic map.

2. What two methods can be used for generating BMS maps?

Maps can be generated interactively using a product such as the Screen Definition Facility (SDF), or using batch macro instructions.

3. What is the physical map?

The physical map is a load module that is defined to CICS in the Processing Program Table. The physical map is used by BMS during mapping operations. It contains device-oriented information about a particular screen to be displayed on a terminal. It also contains information about application fields that are defined in a symbolic map and used in an application program.

4. What is the symbolic map?

The symbolic map is a copy member that is brought into an application program. It contains source code defining the fields within a map/mapset.

5. What rules must be followed for continuing BMS macro statements onto successive lines?

BMS macro statements can be continued onto successive lines by ending a statement with a comma, placing a nonblank character in column 72, and beginning the continuation in column 16.

6. List three limitations on the use of names in BMS macros.

Macro names should not exceed seven characters, they cannot begin with a numeric character, and they must begin in column 1.

7. Why is it desirable to omit names for some fields defined in a BMS map? What type of field would we want to name? What type of field do we want to avoid naming?

Only fields that are represented in BMS source code by named macros are generated in the symbolic map. We want to name those fields that the program will actually be using so the fields will be available in the symbolic map. We want to omit names for constant fields, such as titles on a screen that we are not going to reference in the application program.

8. Usually, when a change is made to a BMS map, it is necessary to recompile the program(s) using the map. Why is this necessary? Under what circumstances could we omit program recompilation?

If we alter a map such that one or more field displacements are changed in the symbolic map, it is necessary to recompile the program so that the program contains the latest source code for the physical map. We could omit the recompilation if no named fields were added or changed in terms of length.

9. Why are stopper fields used after UNPROTected fields in a BMS map?

Stopper fields are used to terminate data entry in an UN-PROTected field. If omitted, the terminal would permit data to be entered up to the next field attribute. Thus, the operator could enter more data than the field definition allows. By putting a stopper at the end of UNPROTected fields, this is prevented.

10. Why is it a good idea to omit a name on the copy statement used to bring the symbolic map into a CICS program?

In the symbolic map generated for COBOL programs, there are two maps which redefine each other. The symbolic map names are built from the name given to the DFHMDI macro with an "I" and an "O" appended. The output map structure begins with the statement: mapnameO REDEFINES mapnameI. If the copy statement is given a name other than mapnameI, a compile error would result indicating that the object of a redefines is not defined. In order to avoid the possibility of this error, the name is omitted from the copy statement.

Match each of the following with a definition provided below.

D	1. DFHMSD	E	11. UNPROT
M	2. FSET	R	12. FREEKB
F	3. DFHMDI	C	13. TIOAPFX
N	4. MODE	P	14. LANG
A	5. DFHMDF	H	15. SIZE
I	6. POS	Q	16. ATTRB
B	7. ASKIP	S	17. IC
T	8. BRT	L	18. JUSTIFY
G	9. INITIAL	J	19. LENGTH
K	10. PROT	O	20. FRSET

chapter **10**

BMS and Application Programming

10.1 USING THE SYMBOLIC MAP IN AN APPLICATION PROGRAM

The symbolic map contains five field names for each of the named DFHMDF macros defined in map generation. In the map source code we examined in Fig. 9-3, there were five named DFHMDF macros: EMPNO, EMPNA, EMPAD1, EMPAD2, and EMPERR. Note that the companion symbolic map illustrated in Chapter 9 does not contain fields with these exact names. The names in the symbolic map are formed by appending a single character to DFHMDF names. For each named DFHMDF macro there is an "L" field, an "F" field, an "A" field redefining the "F" field, an "I" field, and an "O" field redefining the "I" field.

The "O" field is used as the output data field so that information which is to be displayed on the screen is moved to the appropriate "O" field. Using the symbolic map provided above, we might code the following information to place data read from a file into the symbolic map:

```
MOVE FILE-KEY    TO EMPNOO.
MOVE FILE-NAME   TO EMPNAO.
MOVE FILE-ADDR1 TO EMPAD1O.
MOVE FILE-ADDR2 TO EMPAD2O.
```

After having moved in the information to be displayed, the SEND MAP instruction is used to request that BMS interrogate the data in the symbolic map and build a terminal-oriented data stream. The terminal data are then passed to Terminal Control and transmitted to the terminal.

The format of the SEND MAP instruction is illustrated below.

10.1.1 Format of the SEND MAP Command

The format of the SEND MAP command is:

```
EXEC CICS SEND MAP (DFHMDI-name)
                MAPSET (DFHMSD-name)
                FROM  (data-area-name)
                DATAONLY  or  MAPONLY
                CURSOR
                ERASE   or   ERASEAUP
                FREEKB
                ALARM
                FRSET
```

10.1.2 SEND MAP Command Discussion

MAP provides the name of the map to be sent to the terminal. This is the name given to the DFHMDI macro in the map generation.

MAPSET specifies the name of the mapset to be sent to the terminal. This is the name of the DFHMSD macro.

FROM names the data area, typically the symbolic map that contains output application data to be sent to the terminal.

DATAONLY or MAPONLY is used to qualify the output mapping operation. If neither of these options is coded, then BMS merges data from the symbolic map with information from the physical map. Physical map data with this default include the field titles and device control information.

If MAPONLY is specified, then BMS merges no application data into the output terminal message. This option might be used to send a menu screen to a terminal. For a menu screen there is no application information, only the constants or field titles defined in the mapset by specifying the INITIAL= option of the DFHMDF macro.

DATAONLY, on the other hand, specifies that application data from the symbolic map and device control information from the physical map are to be sent to the terminal. However, field titles are not transmitted to the terminal in this case. It is important to remember that **the terminal has a buffer,** and once data are sent to the terminal they remain there until the program ERASEs during an output or the operator presses the CLEAR key. The first map that we send to the screen within a single transaction is normally sent in the default mode, specifying neither DATAONLY nor MAPONLY. This results in the display of application data and field titles.

Once displayed, these data remain at the terminal until cleared. For any subsequent output using the same map (such as a "TRANSACTION COMPLETE" message), it is not necessary to resend field titles which are already displayed. Therefore, the DATAONLY option would be included in this case.

CURSOR indicates that we want to override the default cursor position defined in the map. The default position is indicated by including a field (DFHMDF macro) attribute of IC. A value may be used with the CURSOR option, or dynamic repositioning may be done by setting an "L" field in the symbolic map to X"FFFF". In a COBOL program this is accomplished by moving a −1 to the appropriate "L" field.

ERASE or ERASEAUP is used to clear screen information. ERASE indicates that the entire terminal screen is to be erased prior to the display of data. ERASEAUP causes only UNPROTected fields to be cleared.

FREEKB causes the keyboard to be freed so that the terminal operator doesn't have to press the RESET key.

ALARM sounds the audible alarm when the map is sent. The ALARM is actually a beeping sound. Since the sound can be irritating, we normally only use the ALARM option when we want to particularly call the operator's attention to something on the screen. The ALARM can be turned off at the terminal, and if this feature is used excessively, operators may do just that.

FRSET requests that modified data tags be reset or turned off prior to placing the output on the screen.

10.1.3 Example of SEND MAP to Send Data to a Video Terminal

An example of this instruction to send our data to the screen is provided below:

```
EXEC CICS SEND MAP('SMAP1MM')
      MAPSET ('SMAP01M') FROM (SMAP1MMO)
      ERASE FREEKB END-EXEC.
```

Note that the MAP option names the mapname defined for the DFHMDI macro. The MAPSET option provides the name given to the DFHMSD macro. The FROM parameter names the output area generated within the symbolic map. ERASE requests that the terminal screen be erased prior to displaying the data. FREEKB frees the keyboard so that the operator can enter data. If this option is omitted, the operator normally has to press the RESET key before the keyboard is freed. This output command displays the field titles defined in the physical map, as well as the application data placed into the symbolic map area prior to output. Therefore, the data screen displayed for the operator would look like Fig. 10-1.

The application program then RETURNs to CICS with a TRANSID option, because video terminal interaction is usually pseudoconversational.

Figure 10-1. Screen displayed at the terminal.

EMPLOYEE INFORMATION SCREEN

EMPLOYEE NUMBER: 999999999
EMPLOYEE NAME: KING KONG SENIOR
EMPLOYEE ADDRESS: EMPIRE STATE BLDG
                     34TH STREET, NYC

Command used to display this screen:
EXEC CICS SEND MAP ('SMAP1MM')
          MAPSET ('SMAP01M') FROM (SMAP1MMO)
          ERASE FREEKB END-EXEC.

Since neither DATAONLY nor MAPONLY is specified, data from the symbolic map and everything from the physical map are combined and sent to the screen. Since ERASE is included in the command, the terminal screen is cleared before data are written to it. The inclusion of the FREEKB option frees the keyboard so that the terminal operator doesn't have to press the RESET key.

The operator enters information into one or more data fields. If the operator enters information into a field, the Modified Data Tag is set on; if the operator tabs passed a field, the MDT is left off. After data entry is completed, the operator presses a device interrupt key such as the ENTER key. The terminal sends back to the host computer only those fields actually modified by the operator, or those fields with the Modified Data Tag set on. Preceding each field in the terminal input data stream is device-dependent information, including the buffer addresses of each modified field.

The data are still displayed on the terminal screen, even though a copy of information contained in the modified fields has been transmitted to the host. These screen data remain in the terminal's buffer until the program issues an output request with the ERASE option or the operator presses the CLEAR key. The data transmitted by the terminal are received into the CICS region, and the saved TRANSID from the prior task's RETURN is used to start a new task to process the data. The application program uses a RECEIVE MAP instruction to request that BMS interrogate the data stream sent by the terminal and place data into the symbolic map.

10.1.4 Format of the RECEIVE MAP Command

The format of the RECEIVE MAP command is:

```
EXEC CICS RECEIVE MAP   (DFHMDI-name)
          MAPSET        (DFHMSD-name)
          INTO (area-name) or   SET (BLL)
          FROM (area-name)
          LENGTH (length)
```

10.1.5   RECEIVE MAP Command Discussion

MAP names the map to be used for input mapping.

MAPSET names the mapset containing the map used for input mapping.

INTO or SET specify the mode of input. INTO names a data area that is normally a symbolic map copied into Working Storage. SET indicates that the map is copied into the Linkage Section. The SET option names a BLL cell used to obtain addressability to the storage obtained and formatted by BMS. In most cases, the symbolic map is placed in Working Storage because all of the task's storage is acquired with one storage request by CICS. If the map is placed into the Linkage Section, BMS must do a GETMAIN for storage to be used for input mapping.

FROM is a rarely used option. This option names a work area that contains data that have already been RECEIVEd in **native mode or terminal format.** We are asking BMS to map input that is contained in a program storage area, as opposed to mapping in the latest Terminal Input/Output Area (TIOA). This probably seems a little odd, because it implies that a terminal control RECEIVE is done first and subsequently we ask BMS to interrogate the RECEIVEd data. As an example of where this might prove useful, let's consider a transaction that involves several screens of input. We want the transaction to be flexible, and permit the operator to dynamically select a next screen to process by using a routing field defined in a fixed position in all maps. The operator enters a one-character code indicating where to go next. Instead of redundantly coding tests in all screen processing programs, we decide to utilize a routing program which serves as a central switch. The router RECEIVEs terminal input into a data area, interrogates the routing code, and transfers control to the appropriate program. The terminal input is received by the router and passed to the transferred to module. If the transferred to module needs to use the services of BMS, it could use the FROM option of the RECEIVE MAP to request that BMS map in FROM the passed data area. One word of caution about this example: A program requesting input mapping has to have some way of determining that the screen data and the map used for input mapping coincide. BMS just interrogates data based upon the mapset/map that is named in an input request.

LENGTH defines the LENGTH of the area named in the FROM option. If the FROM option is omitted from a RECEIVE MAP command, then the LENGTH option cannot be included. Thus, FROM and LENGTH go hand in hand.

10.1.6   Example of the RECEIVE MAP Command

An example of this command as it might be coded in a program receiving our map is provided below:

```
EXEC CICS RECEIVE MAP('SMAP1MM')
    MAPSET('SMAP01M') INTO (SMAP1MMI)
END-EXEC.
```

Fields within the symbolic map are used by BMS to pass data fields received from the terminal and to provide information about the received data. The "L" field is a length field used by BMS to indicate the actual length of data received from the terminal. If no data were entered into the field, then the length is zero. The "F" field is used during input mapping to indicate that a field has been modified to nulls. If an operator positions the cursor at the BEGINNING of a data entry field and then presses the Erase End of Field Key, BMS sets the "F" field to X"80".

The "I" field is where BMS places the actual input data. Data are padded and justified within the "I" field. The padding and justification are based upon the JUSTIFY parameter of the DFHMDF macro. The default value for JUSTIFY, if not coded explicitly, is dependent on the type of field. Alphabetic fields are padded with spaces and left justified. If a field has the NUM attribute, and is therefore considered numeric, the default is to right justify and pad with zeros. Coding other values in the JUSTIFY parameter can alter this, however.

If no data were entered in a particular field, BMS sets the "I" field to low values. However, if an operator presses the space bar across the contents of a field, the terminal transmits the spaces entered into the modified field, and BMS treats spaces as data. In this case the "L" field is the length of the entered spaces, and the "I" field contains spaces. Sometimes this is accepted as a way of clearing a field, but this has its dangers. For example, an operator may inadvertently enter data into a field, realize the mistake, and space out the data. In this case, if we accept spaces as data, we update our file with spaces. Because of the ambiguity of this situation, it is a frequent practice to treat spaces as if no data had been entered on input. If an operator can indeed clear a field, the desire to do so is indicated by entering a predefined value such as "/*" into the field. In this way we definitely know what the operator means to do.

The contents of symbolic map fields subsequent to input mapping are summarized in Fig. 10-2. An application program interrogates the symbolic map to discern which fields have been entered; if a field was entered, validation is performed. The application code to accomplish this is illustrated in Fig. 10-3. In the sample code, a field matrix is used so that the program can set field indicators used at subsequent points in program processing.

After interrogating the symbolic map and performing data validation, we next determine if all data are correct and the file is to be updated, or if one or more fields are invalid and error processing is to be performed. We are able to test the field matrix to determine the validity of entered data.

Field	BMS Use of the Field

L   BMS uses the length field to indicate the length of data received from the terminal. If no data were received, the L field is set to 0. This field is tested to determine if the operator modified the field by keying data.

F   BMS uses the flag field to indicate that the field has been modified to nulls. This is accomplished by placing the cursor at the FIRST position of a field and pressing the ERASE EOF key. In this case the L field equals 0 and the I field is set to low values. Only the F field indicates that the operator has erased the field contents. BMS sets the F field to X"80" in this case. This is the only time that BMS uses this field for input operations. Other than indicating that a field has been cleared, the F field is not used. The F field can be tested in a COBOL program by the following code:

```
WORKING-STORAGE SECTION.
01   FLAG-INDICATOR PIC S9(4) COMP VALUE +128.
01   FILLER REDEFINES FLAG-INDICATOR.
       05   FILLER    PIC X.
       05   HEX-80    PIC X.
PROCEDURE DIVISION.

    IF EMPNAF = HEX-80
```

I   BMS places input data into the I field. Received data are padded and justified based upon the field type and the coding of the JUSTIFY parameter in the DFHMDF macro. If JUSTIFY is omitted for a field, the default justification is for alphabetic fields to be left justified and padded with spaces, and for NUMeric fields to be right justified and padded with zeroes. If no data are received for a field, BMS sets the I field to low values.

Figure 10-2. Symbolic map field use for input mapping.

The following instruction could be used to accomplish this:

```
IF NAME-ERROR PERFORM B200-ERROR-PROCESSING THRU
    B200-ERROR-EXIT
ELSE
    PERFORM B150-UPDATE-FILE THRU B150-UPDATE-EXIT.
```

We will examine COBOL source code that might be contained in the two subroutines named above. However, something that we must remember in coding either subroutine is the fact that the data are still in the terminal buffer.

In the file update routine, we move information from the symbolic map into a file record to update the file. However, we must test each field to make sure that the field was changed before we move the contents of the symbolic map into the file record. If no data had been entered, then the field would contain low values, and we would wipe out file data if we merely coded MOVE instructions without checking this. Therefore, we

```
WORKING-STORAGE SECTION.
01   FIELD-MATRIX.
     05   NAME-FLD          PIC X      VALUE '0'.
          88  NAME-ENTERED             VALUE '1'.
     05   ADDR1-FLD         PIC X      VALUE '0'.
          88  ADDR1-ENTERED           VALUE '1'.
     05   ADDR2-FLD         PIC X      VALUE '0'.
          88  ADDR2-ENTERED           VALUE '1'.
01   FILLER REDEFINES FIELD-MATRIX.
     05   INDICATORS        PIC XXX.
          88  ALL-FIELDS-ENTERED   VALUE '111'.
01   ERROR-MATRIX.
     05   NAME-ERR          PIC X      VALUE '0'.
          88  NAME-ERROR              VALUE '1'.


PROCEDURE DIVISION.
        .
        .

        PERFORM B140-INTERROGATE-SCREEN-INPUT
              THRU B140-INTERROGATE-INPUT-EXIT.

        .
        .
B140-INTERROGATE-SCREEN-INPUT.

*   TEST IF NAME FIELD ENTERED BY TESTING THE "L" FIELD FOR
*      0. IF THE "L" FIELD IS 0 THEN THE "I" FIELD CONTAINS
*      LOW-VALUES AND NOTHING WAS ENTERED INTO THE
*      FIELD. AS A PRECAUTION AGAINST THE OPERATOR INAD-
*      VERTENTLY PRESSING THE SPACE BAR ACROSS A FIELD
*      THE "I" FIELD IS ALSO TESTED FOR SPACES. IF THE "I" FIELD
*      CONTAINS SPACES THE "L" FIELD CONTAINS A VALUE
*      GREATER THAN 0.
*
        IF EMPNAL = 0 OR EMPNAI = SPACES NEXT SENTENCE
             ELSE MOVE '1' TO NAME-FLD
             IF EMPNAI IS ALPHABETIC NEXT SENTENCE
                  ELSE MOVE '1' TO NAME-ERR.

        IF EMPAD1L = 0 OR EMPAD1I = SPACES NEXT SENTENCE
             ELSE MOVE '1' TO ADDR1-FLD.

        IF EMPAD2L = 0 OR EMPAD2I = SPACES NEXT SENTENCE
             ELSE MOVE '1' TO ADDR2-FLD.

B140-INTERROGATE-INPUT-EXIT. EXIT.
```

Figure 10-3. Sample code to interrogate input.

make sure that each field has been entered before updating file record fields. An update routine using the field matrix coded in Fig. 10-3 is illustrated below:

```
B150-UPDATE-FILE.
     EXEC CICS READ UPDATE
          DATASET ('APPFILE')
          SET(FILE-BLL)
          LENGTH (FILE-LEN)
          RIDFLD (COM-KEY)
     END-EXEC.
     IF NAME-ENTERED MOVE EMPNAI TO FILE-NAME.
     IF ADDR1-ENTERED MOVE EMPAD1I TO FILE-ADDR1.
     IF ADDR2-ENTERED MOVE EMPAD2I TO FILE-ADDR2.
     EXEC CICS REWRITE DATASET ('APPFILE')
          FROM(FILE-INPUT-AREA)
          LENGTH (FILE-LEN)
     END-EXEC.
B150-UPDATE-EXIT. EXIT.
```

Having performed the file update, we now send a message to the operator indicating the successful completion of transaction processing. At this point, the symbolic map contains the input data mapped in by BMS. These data are already at the terminal, so there is no need to transmit them back again. **If BMS finds an "O" field containing low values during output mapping, it does not transmit the field to the terminal.** Spaces are transmitted, however, and would effectively erase data on the screen. We want to minimize data transmission, and we therefore avoid the needless transmission of data by clearing "O" fields to low values. If the map is copied into Working Storage, we can clear the entire map in one move by coding:

```
MOVE LOW-VALUES TO SMAP1MMO.
```

This cannot be done if the map is being used in the Linkage Section, because there is a separate storage chain for data defined in the Linkage Section. We coded TIOAPFX=YES in the DFHMSD macro so that there would be a 12-byte filler to mask this chain. If we cleared the entire 01-level the storage chain would be wiped out, and CICS would in all likelihood crash. In the case of a Linkage Section Map, we would code individual statements to clear the symbolic map as follows:

```
MOVE LOW-VALUES TO EMPNAO.
MOVE LOW-VALUES TO EMPAD1O.
MOVE LOW-VALUES TO EMPAD2O.
```

The SEND MAP command can be coded with the DATAONLY option. This causes BMS to omit sending the constants or titles defined in the physical map. The screen titles are already displayed on the screen from the first SEND MAP, which did not include the DATAONLY option. An example of a SEND MAP requesting that only data contained in the symbolic map area be sent to the terminal is provided below.

```
MOVE 'TRANSACTION ACCEPTED' TO EMPERRO.
EXEC CICS SEND MAP ('SMAP1MM')
      MAPSET ('SMAP01M')
      FROM (SMAP1MMO)
      DATAONLY
      FREEKB
      FRSET
END-EXEC.
```

Note that the ERASE option is omitted from this SEND MAP command. We are relying upon the fact that the screen titles and data entered by the operator are still in the terminal's buffer. We are going out of our way to avoid transmitting this information back to the terminal. If the ERASE option were included, the data at the terminal would be erased. The operator would see the screen go blank except for the "TRANSACTION ACCEPTED" message, which we moved to EMPERRO.

10.2 OUTPUT MAPPING SUMMARY

The first output from a transaction utilizes "O" fields for data, and the SEND MAP instruction utilizes a full merge of information. This includes application data contained in the symbolic map and the field titles defined in the physical map, and is accomplished by coding neither MAPONLY nor DATAONLY. If neither of these mutually exclusive options is chosen, BMS does a full merge of symbolic and physical map information. Also, in the first output we include the ERASE option. The terminal screen is used as the medium for information exchange between the terminal operator and the application program. Therefore, it is desirable to initialize the screen when the transaction commences by including ERASE.

Any second or subsequent output involving the same map can take advantage of data already present in the terminal's buffer. The contents of "I/O" fields are displayed on the screen and contained in the terminal's buffer. By clearing the "I/O" fields to low values in the symbolic map, we avoid BMS retransmitting received data back to the terminal. **Nulls are not transmitted.** We also include the DATAONLY option to preclude needless transmission of screen titles. Lastly, we omit the ERASE option of the SEND MAP command, because we are relying on the fact that the titles and data fields are at the terminal, and in this instance we don't want the screen cleared.

10.2.1 Error Processing

Error processing involves highlighting fields in error and positioning the cursor to the first error field. The "A" field is used to dynamically alter a field's attribute value as defined during map creation. The "A" field is thus used to highlight any error fields. Figure 10-4 illustrates the attribute byte and some of the values used to indicate various field characteristics. By following across a line, it is possible to select the field characteristics desired. For example, to highlight a field we could select the character "H"

| ATTRIBUTE | | | | | | Bits | Hex Code | | Graphic Character |
Prot	A/N	High Intens	Sel Pen Det	Non Disp PRT	MDT ON	23 4567	EBCD	ASCII	
U						00 0000	40	20	b
U					Y	00 0001	C1	41	A
U			Y			00 0100	C4	44	D
U			Y		Y	00 0101	C5	45	E
U		H	Y			00 1000	C8	48	H
U		H	Y		Y	00 1001	C9	49	I
U		–	–	Y		00 1100	4C	3C	<
U		–	–	Y	Y	00 1101	4D	28	(
U	N					01 0000	50	26	&
U	N				Y	01 0001	D1	4A	J
U	N		Y			01 0100	D4	4D	M
U	N		Y		Y	01 0101	D5	4E	N
U	N	H	Y			01 1000	D8	51	O
U	N	H	Y		Y	01 1001	D9	52	P
U	N	–	–	Y		01 1100	5C	2A	*
U	N	–	–	Y	Y	01 1101	5D	29	)
P						10 0000	60	2D	–
P					Y	10 0001	61	2F	/
P			Y			10 0100	E4	55	U
P			Y		Y	10 0101	E5	56	V
P		H	Y			10 1000	E8	59	Y
P		H	Y		Y	10 1001	E9	5A	Z
P		–	–	Y		10 1100	6C	25	%
P		–	–	Y	Y	10 1101	6D	5F	–
P	S					11 0000	F0	30	0
P	S				Y	11 0001	F1	31	1
P	S		Y			11 0100	F4	34	4
P	S		Y		Y	11 0101	F5	35	5
P	S	H	Y			11 1000	F8	38	8
P	S	H	Y		Y	11 1001	F9	39	9
P	S	–	–	Y		11 1100	7C	40	@
P	S	–	–	Y	Y	11 1101	7D	27	'

H = High   P = Protected   U = Unprotected
N = Numeric S = Automatic skip Y = Yes

Figure 10-4. Attribute Character Summary.

and move this value to the "A" field for any error fields detected. To highlight the name field, we could code the following:

MOVE 'H' TO EMPNAA.

The symbolic map containing this attribute value is presented to BMS during output mapping. BMS transmits the attribute to the terminal, and the field is dynamically highlighted.

The second aspect of error handling is positioning the cursor at the first field in error. In the map source code, the DFHMDF macro is used to determine the default cursor position. In the map shown earlier in this text, the employee name field was coded as follows:

EMPNA DFHMDF POS=(6,28),ATTRB=(UNPROT,IC), LENGTH=30

The IC contained within the ATTRB parameter indicates this field as the Initial Cursor position. If we do not override the cursor positioning via a SEND MAP command, then BMS positions the cursor at this field by default. Normally IC is specified for the first unprotected field on the screen. IC should be defined for only one DFHMDF macro. If specified for multiple fields, BMS places the cursor at the last field for which IC is defined.

Dynamic cursor positioning can be accomplished in two ways: the hard way and the easy way. In both cases the CURSOR option of the SEND MAP command is used. The hard way involves the CURSOR option, and a hard-coded value indicating where the cursor is to be placed. The presence of the CURSOR option informs BMS that we want the cursor to be dynamically repositioned, and the value indicates the location. Of course, if the locations of fields change, then the hard-coded positioning must also change.

The easy way is called symbolic cursor positioning; as its name suggests, hard-coded values are not used. With symbolic cursor positioning, the CURSOR option is included in the SEND MAP command, but no value is included. A SEND MAP command utilizing symbolic cursor positioning might look like this:

```
EXEC CICS SEND MAP('SMAP1MM') MAPSET ('SMAP01M')
       FROM (SMAP1MMO) CURSOR DATAONLY FREEKB
END-EXEC.
```

With this command we have informed BMS that the cursor positioning is to be dynamically overridden, but we have not specified where the cursor is to go. This is done symbolically by moving X"FFFF" to the "L" field where the cursor is to be positioned. In a symbolic map for a COBOL program, the "L" fields are defined as PIC S9(4) COMP. An "L" field can be set to

X"FFFF" by moving a −1 to it. The following code would set an "L" field to indicate its selection for symbolic cursor positioning:

    MOVE −1 TO EMPAD1L.

If multiple fields are in error, the −1 can be moved to all of the error "L" fields, and BMS positions the cursor at the first field with X"FFFF" in its length. To highlight and dynamically position the cursor for error processing, we might code the following routine (in this sample code we are utilizing the field matrix set to appropriate values in the B140-INTERROGATE-INPUT-SCREEN routine shown above):

```
* MOVE LOW-VALUES TO THE SYMBOLIC MAP TO CLEAR OUT
*    DATA RECEIVED FROM THE TERMINAL.  THERE IS NO
*    POINT IN TRANSMITTING THE DATA BACK TO THE
*    TERMINAL BECAUSE THE DATA ARE ALREADY THERE. LOW
*    VALUES ARE USED AS A CONVENTION TO INFORM BMS
*    THAT THERE ARE NO DATA TO SEND FOR PARTICULAR
*    FIELDS.  THE SYMBOLIC MAP IS COPIED INTO THE
*    WORKING-STORAGE SECTION, AND CONSEQUENTLY THE
*    ENTIRE MAP CAN BE CLEARED WITH A GROUP MOVE.
*    HOWEVER, IF THE MAP WERE PLACED IN THE LINKAGE
*    SECTION, A GROUP MOVE WOULD WIPE OUT THE CICS
*    STORAGE CHAIN MASKED BY THE TERMINAL INPUT
*    OUTPUT AREA PREFIX (TIOAPFX).

     MOVE LOW-VALUES TO SMAP1MMO.

* TEST THE FIELD MATRIX TO DETERMINE IF A FIELD WAS
*    ENTERED AND, IF SO, WHETHER THE FIELD WAS
*    INCORRECT.

     IF NAME-ENTERED AND NAME-ERROR
        MOVE −1 TO EMPNAL
        MOVE 'H' TO EMPNAA.

* REQUEST A BMS OUTPUT OPERATION.  THE CURSOR
*    OPTION TELLS BMS THAT THE DEFAULT CURSOR
*    POSITION IS TO BE ALTERED FROM THE FIELD SPECIFIED
*    IN THE MAP DEFINITION. BMS THEN LOOKS FOR AN 'L'
*    FIELD WITH X'FFFF'. THE DATAONLY OPTION TELLS BMS
*    NOT TO TRANSMIT THE TITLES OR CONSTANTS
*    CONTAINED WITHIN THE PHYSICAL MAP.  ONLY THE
*    APPLICATION DATA CONTAINED IN THE SYMBOLIC MAP
*    ARE TO BE SENT.  SINCE THE TITLES ARE ALREADY AT THE
*    TERMINAL, THERE IS NO POINT IN RETRANSMITTING
*    THEM. THE DATAONLY OPTION IS USED FOR THE DISPLAY
```

```
*    OF ERROR OR TRANSACTION ACCEPTED MESSAGES.
*    NOTE THAT THE ERASE OPTION WHICH WOULD CLEAR
*    THE SCREEN IS OMITTED.

     EXEC CICS SEND MAP ('SMAP1MM') MAPSET ('SMAP01M')
        FROM (SMAP1MMO) CURSOR FREEKB DATAONLY
     END-EXEC.
```

In order to use symbolic cursor positioning, three things must be done. The MAPSET must be defined as MODE=INOUT, the CURSOR option must be included in the SEND MAP command, and at least one "L" field must contain X"FFFF". Unless all three things are done, symbolic cursor positioning doesn't work. If one moves a −1 to an "L" field and neglects to specify CURSOR in the SEND MAP command, the cursor is positioned at the default location. The CURSOR option can be viewed as the program's way of saying to BMS, "I want to override the cursor location defined in the MAPSET."

On the other hand, if the SEND MAP command specifies CURSOR but no "L" fields contain X"FFFF", then BMS recognizes the request for cursor repositioning but doesn't know where to place it. In this case the cursor is positioned in the upper left corner of the screen, so the "L" field defines the override location. The advantage of utilizing Symbolic Cursor Positioning is that it repositions the cursor by using "L" field names, as opposed to hard-coded locations. If the fields within a map are moved around, all we need do is recompile the program. In contrast, a program specifying fixed locations has to be changed to reflect new field locations.

Error processing is probably the most complex part of screen handling in a CICS program, not only because of altering attributes or cursor locations. The trickiest part of dealing with a video terminal is understanding the function and use of the Modified Data Tag. Thus, there is one more facet of video terminal interaction that must be examined and understood in depth in order to successfully write pseudoconversational data entry/update transactions. First we will go over a couple of facts about what data are sent from a video terminal, and then we will illustrate a potentially serious problem that can occur if terminal interaction is not handled correctly. Finally, we will examine three programming techniques for successfully handling the situation.

10.3 DATA SENT FROM A VIDEO TERMINAL

The data transmitted from a 3270-type video terminal are dependent upon the device interrupt key used by the operator and the status of the Modified Data Tags of screen fields. You will recall that the MDT is a bit in the attribute byte that is turned on when the operator alters a field. There are two types of READs that the terminal can perform: a short

READ and a long READ. For a short READ, the Attention IDentifier (AID) or the name of the device interrupt key is the only information transmitted by the terminal, even if fields were modified prior to the device interrupt. A short READ is done for PA keys (PA1, PA2, and PA3) or the CLEAR key. The CLEAR key also erases the screen.

A long READ is performed for the ENTER key or one of the PF keys. A long READ results in the transmission of the following information: (1) the Attention IDentifier, (2) the cursor position at the time of the device interrupt, and (3) information for modified fields. A modified field is one that has the MDT bit on (either the operator modified the field or it was set on programmatically). The information transmitted about each modified field includes the Set Buffer Address device control order (SBA X "11"), the field address (attribute address + 1), and the actual data contained at the field address. A sample 3270 input data stream is illustrated below:

A	CURSOR	S	FIELD	VARIABLE	S	FIELD	VARIABLE
I	ADDR	B	ADDR	LENGTH	B	ADDR	LENGTH
D		A		DATA	A		DATA

The Attention IDentifier is a single byte naming a PF key or the ENTER key. The AID is placed in the Execute Interface Block field "EIBAID", and this field can be tested to determine the device interrupt key used by the terminal operator. The HANDLE AID command can be used, or EIBAID itself can be interrogated. The copy member DFHAID can be copied into a Command Level program so the EIBAID can be tested against a data name as opposed to a hard-coded value. Figure 10-5 is an expansion of DFHAID. The code to test the AID is below. The example assumes that the CLEAR key is used by the operator to request transaction cancellation. It is standard practice to provide some mechanism for allowing the operator to abort the transaction. All interactive programs should make provision for this cancellation feature so that the operator has more flexibility. Consider how you would like TSO if it didn't allow you to exit from EDIT Mode until you had completed entering a program.

```
    WORKING-STORAGE SECTION.
    01  COPY DFHAID.
        .
        .
    PROCEDURE DIVISION.
        IF EIBAID = DFHCLEAR
            EXEC CICS SEND CONTROL FREEKB END-EXEC
            EXEC CICS RETURN END-EXEC.
```

If the CLEAR key is pressed, we want to exit from the transaction and allow the operator to select a different TRANSID, or perhaps sign off

```
00635            01  DFHAID      COPY  DFHAID.
00636 C          01  DFHAID.
00637 C              02  DFHNULL   PIC  X  VALUE IS ' '.
00638 C              02  DFHENTER  PIC  X  VALUE IS QUOTE.
00639 C              02  DFHCLEAR  PIC  X  VALUE IS '_'.
00640 C              02  DFHCLRP   PIC  X  VALUE IS '_'.
00641 C              02  DFHPEN    PIC  X  VALUE IS '='.
00642 C              02  DFHOPID   PIC  X  VALUE IS 'W'.
00643 C              02  DFHMSRE   PIC  X  VALUE IS 'X'.
00644 C              02  DFHSTRF   PIC  X  VALUE IS 'h'.
00645 C              02  DFHTRIG   PIC  X  VALUE IS '"'.
00646 C              02  DFHPA1    PIC  X  VALUE IS '%'.
00647 C              02  DFHPA2    PIC  X  VALUE IS '>'.
00648 C              02  DFHPA3    PIC  X  VALUE IS ','.
00649 C              02  DFHPF1    PIC  X  VALUE IS '1'.
00650 C              02  DFHPF2    PIC  X  VALUE IS '2'.
00651 C              02  DFHPF3    PIC  X  VALUE IS '3'.
00652 C              02  DFHPF4    PIC  X  VALUE IS '4'.
00653 C              02  DFHPF5    PIC  X  VALUE IS '5'.
00654 C              02  DFHPF6    PIC  X  VALUE IS '6'.
00655 C              02  DFHPF7    PIC  X  VALUE IS '7'.
00656 C              02  DFHPF8    PIC  X  VALUE IS '8'.
00657 C              02  DFHPF9    PIC  X  VALUE IS '9'.
00658 C              02  DFHPF10   PIC  X  VALUE IS ':'.
00659 C              02  DFHPF11   PIC  X  VALUE IS '#'.
00660 C              02  DFHPF12   PIC  X  VALUE IS 'ə'.
00661 C              02  DFHPF13   PIC  X  VALUE IS 'A'.
00662 C              02  DFHPF14   PIC  X  VALUE IS 'B'.
00663 C              02  DFHPF15   PIC  X  VALUE IS 'C'.
00664 C              02  DFHPF16   PIC  X  VALUE IS 'D'.
00665 C              02  DFHPF17   PIC  X  VALUE IS 'E'.
00666 C              02  DFHPF18   PIC  X  VALUE IS 'F'.
00667 C              02  DFHPF19   PIC  X  VALUE IS 'G'.
00668 C              02  DFHPF20   PIC  X  VALUE IS 'H'.
00669 C              02  DFHPF21   PIC  X  VALUE IS 'I'.
00670 C              02  DFHPF22   PIC  X  VALUE IS '¢'.
00671 C              02  DFHPF23   PIC  X  VALUE IS '.'.
00672 C              02  DFHPF24   PIC  X  VALUE IS '<'.
```

Figure 10-5. Contents of DFHAID.

from the system. CICS sees the video terminal as a "conversational" type of device, meaning that the operator enters input and the program responds by sending output. If in the sample code we merely RETURNed to CICS to end the task, then there would be no output to the terminal, and the operator would have to press the reset key before the keyboard would unlock. However, we want to facilitate operator use of the system, and therefore we should send an output to the terminal and free the keyboard. This is accomplished in the sample code above by using the BMS SEND CONTROL command. The SEND CONTROL command is used to send control information without a message to the terminal. Since the operator is exiting from the transaction and there is no message to be sent, the SEND CONTROL command is appropriate in this context.

10.4 FORMAT OF THE SEND CONTROL COMMAND

The format of the SEND CONTROL command is:

```
EXEC CICS SEND CONTROL
        ALARM
        CURSOR (value)
        ERASE   or   ERASEAUP
        FREEKB
        FRSET
```

10.4.1   SEND CONTROL Command Discussion

The options of the SEND CONTROL command are similar to those for the SEND MAP command.

10.5   USING SCREEN CURSOR POSITION

The cursor position is placed into the Execute Interface Block. The field EIBCPOSN can be tested to determine the cursor position. Cursor positioning can be an effective way for an operator to make a selection on certain types of screens. For example, consider a customer service system with an alphabetic search transaction. The operator enters information about the customer (such as last name) and the system displays a screen of names and customer numbers. The operator is to select a customer number for customer inquiry purposes. We could require the operator to enter the customer number selected, or simply to position the cursor by the appropriate choice. Positioning the cursor is by far easier, and precludes a miskeyed number.

10.6   EXAMPLE OF A PSEUDOCONVERSATIONAL TRANSACTION

We will now follow through a pseudoconversational transaction in order to understand a major problem that can occur if error processing is not coded correctly. It is extremely important that the following material be completely understood. A slow, thorough reading of this section is advised, and it may be worthwhile to reread this discussion.

Let's return to the sample employee information transaction discussed earlier. The operator initiates the transaction by entering a TRANSID and an employee number. A CICS application program is invoked. The program reads the employee file and displays the screen illustrated in Fig. 10-6. Note that the attribute bytes are depicted in this figure, and that the MDTs are all 0s or off. The program then RETURNs to CICS with a TRANSID of a second program. The operator modifies the three data entry fields by entering the data depicted in Fig. 10-7. Note that the MDTs for the three data entry fields are now 1's, indicating that these fields are to be transmitted back to CICS. The operator presses the ENTER key, data

Figure 10-6.   Displayed screen.

0EMPLOYEE INFORMATION SCREEN

0EMPLOYEE NUMBER: 0999999999
0EMPLOYEE NAME: 0KING KONG SENIOR
0EMPLOYEE ADDRESS: 0EMPIRE STATE BLDG
                           034TH STREET, NYC
0

0 = Modified Data Tag off.

are transmitted back to the CPU, and CICS starts a task executing in the appropriate program.

The program issues a RECEIVE MAP command, and data are received into the task's symbolic map area, as depicted in Fig. 10-8. Program validation detects that the name field is incorrect because it is not alphabetic. Therefore, file updating is bypassed and an error map is formatted. The code below does the error processing of highlighting the fields in error and placing the cursor in the first field in error:

```
B220-ERROR-PROCESSING.
     MOVE LOW-VALUES TO SMAP1MMO.
     IF NAME-ENTERED
      IF NAME-ERROR
        MOVE -1 TO EMPNAL
        MOVE 'H' TO EMPNAA.
     MOVE 'NAME MUST BE ALPHABETIC' TO EMPERRO.
     EXEC  CICS SEND MAP('SMAP1MM') MAPSET('SMAP01M')
         FROM (SMAP1MMO) DATAONLY CURSOR FREEKB FRSET
     END-EXEC.
```

There is no validation for the two address fields, and therefore they do not have cursor positioning or highlighting. This code causes the screen depicted in Fig. 10-9 to be displayed. Note that all three fields have the

Figure 10-7.   Screen after modification by terminal operator.

0EMPLOYEE INFORMATION SCREEN

0EMPLOYEE NUMBER: 0999999999
0EMPLOYEE NAME: 1COUNT DRACULA 1
0EMPLOYEE ADDRESS: 1VAMPIRE STATE BLDG.
                           1TRANSYLVANIA, PA.
0

0 = Modified Data Tag off; 1 = Modified Data Tag on reflecting operator modification.

```
EMPNOL  = 0000
EMPNOF  = 00
EMPNOI  = LOW-VALUES

EMPNAL  = 000F                          (DECIMAL 15)
EMPNAF  = 00
EMPNAI  = COUNT DRACULA 1

EMPAD1L = 0013                          (DECIMAL 19)
EMPAD1F = 00
EMPAD1I = VAMPIRE STATE BLDG.

EMPAD2L = 0011                          (DECIMAL 17)
EMPAD2F = 00
EMPAD2I = TRANSYLVANIA, PA.

EMPERRL = 0000
EMPERRF = 00
EMPERRI = LOW-VALUES
```

Figure 10-8. Symbolic map contents after RECEIVE MAP.

MDTs off. The option FRSET in the SEND MAP command indicates that this was to be done. The program then RETURNs with its own TRANSID named.

Let's consider two possible actions on the part of the operator. First, the operator realizes the nature of the error and corrects the name field. This turns on the MDT for the name field. The operator is not going to change the address fields unless he/she notes an error in them. This is highly unlikely, however, and therefore the MDTs for these fields remain turned off. The current status of the terminal screen is depicted in Fig. 10-10. When the operator presses the ENTER key, only the name field is transmitted back to CICS. These data pass validation, and the name field is updated. This is an update transaction, and there is no requirement that

Figure 10-9. Screen with error message displayed.

0EMPLOYEE INFORMATION SCREEN

0EMPLOYEE NUMBER: 0999999999
0EMPLOYEE NAME: 0COUNT DRACULA 1
0EMPLOYEE ADDRESS: 0VAMPIRE STATE BLDG.
                         0TRANSYLVANIA, PA.

0NAME MUST BE ALPHABETIC

0 = Modified Data Tag off; 1 = Modified Data Tag on reflecting operator modification.
Name field is high intensity.

Figure 10-10. Screen after corrected by terminal operator.

0EMPLOYEE INFORMATION SCREEN

0EMPLOYEE NUMBER: 0999999999
0EMPLOYEE NAME: 1COUNT DRACULA
0EMPLOYEE ADDRESS: 0VAMPIRE STATE BLDG.
                                   0TRANSYLVANIA, PA.

0NAME MUST BE ALPHABETIC

0 = Modified Data Tag off; 1 = Modified Data Tag on reflecting operator modification.

all data fields be changed. After updating the file, the program SENDs a "TRANSACTION ACCEPTED" message to the operator. This screen is shown in Fig. 10-11. The operator, of course, assumes that all three fields have been captured on the file, but the programming in this case resulted in a loss of data integrity because, subsequent to error processing, we detected only the name field and we therefore updated only this field on the file. Obviously, this cannot be allowed to happen.

The second case we should examine is what happens if the operator receives the error screen shown in Fig. 10-9 and does not fix the name field, but rather changes the second address field. In this case only the second address field is transmitted back to CICS. Assuming the second address field is changed to "WILLIMANTIC, CT," Figure 10-12 depicts the symbolic map after execution of the RECEIVE MAP. Our program updates the address field, and does not detect that the operator didn't correct the erroneously entered name field. When the program displays a "TRANSACTION ACCEPTED" message, the operator probably thinks that the name field was also captured, and that the system has been fooled. This is also an unacceptable situation.

We must have assurance that anything entered by the operator is in fact never "forgotten" by the online system. Our problem derived from the

Figure 10-11. Screen with transaction accepted message.

0EMPLOYEE INFORMATION SCREEN

0EMPLOYEE NUMBER: 0999999999
0EMPLOYEE NAME: 0COUNT DRACULA
0EMPLOYEE ADDRESS: 0VAMPIRE STATE BLDG.
                                   0TRANSYLVANIA, PA.

0TRANSACTION ACCEPTED

0 = Modified Data Tag off; 1 = Modified Data Tag on reflecting operator modification.

```
EMPNOL  = 0000
EMPNOF  = 00
EMPNOI  = LOW-VALUES

EMPNAL  = 0000
EMPNAF  = 00
EMPNAI  = LOW-VALUES

EMPAD1L = 0000
EMPAD1F = 00
EMPAD1I = LOW-VALUES

EMPAD2L = 0010                    (DECIMAL 16)
EMPAD2F = 00
EMPAD2I = WILLIMANTIC, CT.

EMPERRL = 0000
EMPERRF = 00
EMPERRI = LOW-VALUES
```

Figure 10-12. Symbolic map contents after RECEIVE MAP (variation 2 of sample operator input).

fact that we said FRSET in the SEND MAP command. Had we omitted FRSET, then the field MDTs would have been left on. This would have been a satisfactory solution for this transaction, but could result in extra data transmission from the terminal if the transaction kept looping back. For example, when the program sends the "TRANSACTION AC-CEPTED" message, it could also request a next employee number and RETURN with the first program's TRANSID. In this case, if the MDTs were never set off, the terminal would transmit all of the entered data fields back to the first program needlessly. This problem could be resolved by including the FRSET option in the SEND MAP command when sending the "TRANSACTION ACCEPTED" message. When using this approach to the MDTs, it is important to make sure that FRSET is used only where appropriate in the program. Furthermore, any dynamic modification of the attributes to highlighted fields, for example, should have the MDT on. Instead of using "H" for highlighting, use of "I" not only includes high intensity but also sets the MDT on. The one potential problem is that, if a programmer doing maintenance improperly adds FRSET to the wrong SEND MAP, the MDTs will be set off and data may be lost.

Another approach is to selectively turn on the MDTs for all fields entered. This approach may be a little less prone to improper cod-ing/mistakes during program maintenance. Even if FRSET were er-roneously added to a SEND MAP command, using the MDTs in this way would prevent data from being lost. Figure 10-13 is a sample error processing routine using this approach. Note that the MDTs are turned on

```
     S220-ERROR-PROCESSING.
 *   CLEAR OUT SYMBOLIC MAP SO DATA RECEIVED FROM THE
 *     TERMINAL WILL NOT BE RETRANSMITTED BACK.
         MOVE LOW-VALUES TO SMAP1MMO.
 *   CHECK NAME FIELD BY TESTING THE FIELD MATRIX

             IF NAME-ENTERED
               IF NAME-ERROR
                 MOVE −1 TO EMPNAL
                 MOVE 'I' TO EMPNAA
               ELSE
                 MOVE 'A' TO EMPNAA
             ELSE
               IF ADD-PROCESSING
                 MOVE −1 TO EMPNAL.

 *   CHECK FIRST ADDRESS FIELD
             IF ADDR1-ENTERED
                 MOVE 'A' TO EMPAD1A

             ELSE
               IF ADD-PROCESSING
                 MOVE −1 TO EMPAD1L.

 *   CHECK SECOND ADDRESS FIELD
             IF ADDR2-ENTERED
                 MOVE 'A' TO EMPAD2A
             ELSE
               IF ADD-PROCESSING
                 MOVE −1 TO EMPAD2L.

             IF CHANGE-PROCESSING OR ALL-FIELDS-ENTERED
                 MOVE 'NAME MUST BE ALPHABETIC' TO EMPERRO
                 GO TO S220-ERROR-PROCESSING-EXIT.
             IF NAME-ERROR
                 MOVE 'NAME MUST BE ALPHABETIC AND ALL FIELDS
                   REQUIRED' TO EMPERRO
             ELSE
                 MOVE 'ALL FIELDS REQUIRED' TO EMPERRO.
     S220-ERROR-PROCESSING-EXIT.
         EXIT.
```

Figure 10-13. Sample Error Routine Turning on MDTS.

only if the field was modified by the operator. Fields in error and correctly entered fields both have the MDTs set on, but fields that were not entered do not have MDTs turned on. We don't want to blindly turn on all MDTs for all possible fields, because this involves extra transmission and it can make some transactions grossly inefficient. Consider a transaction in which screen data come from three or four files. If the program blindly turns on all MDTs during error processing, then we have to update all files because we can't tell exactly what the operator changed and what was transmitted because we turned on MDTs.

The third way of handling error processing is for the program to save entered information in a place which is available for subsequent tasks. This approach is the most efficient in terms of data communications, but does require a little more coding. The logic of performing error handling this way is as follows: Upon detecting an error, the program moves all data entered into the COMMAREA. The symbolic map is cleared to binary zeros, the error message is moved into the message field, symbolic cursor positioning is performed, and error fields are highlighted without turning on the Modified Data Tags. The SEND MAP specifies FRSET. The operator enters new data and presses the ENTER key. The program performs a RECEIVE MAP. However, before validation can be accomplished, the saved data and the newly entered data must be merged. Fields that the operator didn't rekey contain binary zeroes in the symbolic map. For these fields, the saved COMMAREA data are left as is. Fields that the operator reentered are moved from the symbolic map into the COMMAREA. With this approach we have to be concerned with determining if the operator cleared a field by positioning the cursor at its initial position and pressing the Erase End of Field Key. The operator may do this to avoid updating a field, and we would want to clear the saved COMMAREA data for this field. This can only be detected by testing the "F" field for X"80". A sample program that performs error processing in this way is illustrated in Fig. 10-16. The code for merging new terminal input and saved COMMAREA data is contained in the COBOL subroutine S100-INTERROGATE-SCREEN-INPUT. This routine ends with the paragraph labelled S100-INTERROGATE-INPUT-EXIT.

Which approach to use is really a matter of selecting among tradeoffs in each installation. The first approach—omitting FRSET—is probably the easiest to code, but may cause difficulty unless everyone understands the use of MDTs and FRSET. This is especially important for program maintenance. The second approach—a program turns on MDTs for all entered fields—makes the program impervious to improper use of FRSET during program maintenance. The third approach—saving and merging data—results in the least amount of data transmission, but is undoubtedly a little more complex to code. If dealing with a local network or a lightly used system, then ease of coding would recommend the first or second approach. However, a large remote network with heavily used communications facilities would gain improved performance from the data transmission efficiency of the third approach. Regardless of which technique is used for error handling, it is generally best to decide on an approach and make the chosen method a group standard.

The use of the symbolic map is clearly not difficult, but it is a bit detailed. Figure 10-14 summarizes application program and BMS use of the various symbolic map fields.

Field	Input	Output
L	Used by BMS to present the application program with the length of field data received from the terminal. If field not modified by operator, then L field set to 0.	Used by application program for symbolic cursor positioning. Symbolic cursor positioning is achieved by moving −1 to the L field in a COBOL program and including the CURSOR option in the SEND MAP command.
A	Not used.	Used by application program to dynamically override the default attribute defined for the field when the map was created. This is accomplished by moving an attribute value to the A field prior to an output operation.
F	Used by BMS to inform the program that the operator has cleared the contents of a field by pressing Erase End of Field Key at the beginning of the field. Otherwise F field is unused.	Not used.
I	Used by BMS to pass actual field data to the processing program. Data are padded and justified according to the default or coded JUSTIFY parameter. If field not modified, then I field contains low values.	Not used.
O	Not used.	Used by application program to send data to the screen. For example, data read from an online file can be moved to an O field for transmission to the terminal. If a symbolic map is used for input mapping and reused for output, then the O fields should be set to low values to prevent needless transmission of data already at the terminal.

Figure 10-14. Summary of symbolic map field use.

10.7 SAMPLE TRANSACTION

The following two programs are implementations of the employee master inquiry and update transaction. As mentioned above, the technique of saving data in the COMMAREA during error processing is used. The sample map illustrated above, SMAP01M, is utilized. The transaction involves three entities, the map already coded and two application programs. The first program (see Fig. 10-15) is the one activated when the transaction is initiated. The program validates the initial input, displays a map, and RETURNs to CICS with a TRANSID of the second program. The second program (see Fig. 10-16) is activated after the operator has entered update

Figure 10-15. Program 1.

```
LINE       SOURCE LISTING

00001  00001000      IDENTIFICATION DIVISION.
00002  00002000      PROGRAM-ID.
00003  00003000          PROGRAM1.
00004  00004000      AUTHOR.
00005  00005006          ARLENE J WIPFLER.
00006  00006000      INSTALLATION.
00007  00007000          BETADATA, INC.
00008  00008000          SYSTEMS TRAINING DIVISION
00009  00009000
00010  00009100      REMARKS.
00011  00009200          THIS MODULE IS A SOLUTION FOR THE SECOND PROBLEM
00012  00009304          IN THE PROGRAMMING WORKSHOP.
00013  00009400      ENVIRONMENT DIVISION.
00014  00009600   *  N O T E : THERE ARE NO INPUT/OUTPUT SECTION STATEMENTS OR FILE
00015  00009700   *                CONTROL STATEMENTS. CICS HANDLES ALL FILE SERVICES
00016  00009800   *                ALL FILES THAT ARE TO BE ACCESSED ONLINE MUST BE
00017  00009900   *                DEFINED TO CICS IN THE FILE CONTROL TABLE (FCT).
00018  00010000
00019  00011000      DATA DIVISION.
00020  00012000   *  N O T E : NO FILE SECTION OR FDS ARE CODED IN A CICS PROGRAM
00021  00013000   *                SINCE CICS MANAGES AND CONTROLS FILE ACCESS.
00022  00014000   *                FILES ARE DEFINED IN THE CICS FILE CONTROL TABLE.
00023  00015000   *
00024  00016000      WORKING-STORAGE SECTION.
00025  00017000
00026  00018000   *  N O T E : DEFINE VARIABLE DATA FIELDS HERE. EXECUTE INTER-
00027  00019000   *                FACE DYNAMICALLY ACQUIRES A WORKING-STORAGE AREA
00028  00019100   *                FOR EACH TASK. BECAUSE OF THE FACT THAT EACH TASK
00029  00019200   *                HAS ITS OWN UNIQUE WORKING STORAGE, THE COMMAND
00030  00019300   *                LEVEL COBOL PROGRAM IS ALWAYS REENTRANT.
00031  00019400
00032  00019500
00033  00019605      77  TRMNL-LEN          PIC S9(4) COMP VALUE +16.
00034  00019800      77  FILE-LEN           PIC S9(4) COMP.
00035  00020007      77  COMMAREA-LEN       PIC S9(4) COMP VALUE +81.
00036  00023000   *
00037  00023101      01  TERMINAL-INPUT-AREA.
00038  00023201      05  TERM-TRANSID PIC X(4).
```

253

Figure 10-15. Continued

```
00039 00023301        05  FILLER         PIC X.
00040 00023401        05  TERM-FUNC-CD   PIC X.
00041 00023501        05  FILLER         PIC X.
00042 00023601        05  TERM-KEY       PIC X(9).
00043 00023707    01  COMMAREA-DATA.
00044 00023807        05  COM-INDICATOR  PIC X VALUE '1'.
00045 00023907        05  COM-FUNCTION   PIC X(9).
00046 00024007        05  COM-KEY        PIC X(9).
00047 00024107        05  COM-NAME       PIC X(30).
00048 00024207        05  COM-ADDR1      PIC X(20).
00049 00024307        05  COM-ADDR2      PIC X(20).
00050 00025000   **
00051 00028000    01          COPY SMAP01M.
00052 00029001   **
00053 00029900   * LINKAGE SECTION.
00054 00030000   *
00055 00032000   * THE TRANSLATOR WILL AUTOMATICALLY GENERATE A COPY
00056 00033000   * FOR THE EXECUTE INTERFACE BLOCK. CODE AN 01 DFHCOMMAREA
00057 00034000   * IF YOUR PROGRAM IS TO RECEIVE A COMMAREA. OTHERWISE THE
00058 00035000   * THE TRANSLATOR WILL INSERT AN 01 DFHCOMMAREA PIC X.
00059 00036000   *
00060 00037000   *
00061 00038000   * THE COMMAREA IS A DATA AREA THAT CAN BE PASSED TO A
00062 00039000   * COMMAND LEVEL PROGRAM IN ONE OF THREE WAYS:
00063 00039100   *     1.  THE PROGRAM IS INVOKED VIA A LINK FROM
00064 00039200   *         ANOTHER PROGRAM. THE PROGRAM THAT ISSUED
00065 00039300   *         THE LINK SPECIFIED A COMMAREA IN THE LINK
00066 00039400   *         COMMAND.
00067 00039500   *     2.  THE PROGRAM IS INVOKED VIA AN XCTL FROM
00068 00039600   *         ANOTHER PROGRAM. THE PROGRAM THAT ISSUED
00069 00039700   *         THE XCTL SPECIFIED A COMMAREA IN THE XCTL
00070 00039800   *         COMMAND.
00071 00039900   *     3.  THE PROGRAM IS INVOKED SUBSEQUENT TO A RETURN
00072 00040000   *         TO CICS. A TRANSID SPECIFIED IN THE RETURN
00073 00041000   *         COMMAND CAUSES THE INVOCATION OF THIS PROGRAM.
00074 00042004   *         THE RETURN COMMAND SPECIFIED A COMMAREA. WHICH
00075 00043000   *         CICS SAVES FOR THE SUBSEQUENT TASK.
00076 00044000   **************************************************************
```

```cobol
      *
       01  BLL-CELLS.
      *       THE FIRST BLL CELL IS USED BY CICS.
           05  FILLER         PIC S9(8) COMP.
           05  FILE-BLL       PIC S9(8) COMP.
      *
      *   THE DATA AREAS BELOW MUST CORRESPOND IN ORDER TO THE
      *   ORDER OF THE BLL CELLS DEFINED ABOVE.
      *
       01  FILE-INPUT-AREA.
           05  FILE-KEY       PIC X(9).
           05  FILE-NAME      PIC X(30).
           05  FILE-ADDR1     PIC X(20).
           05  FILE-ADDR2     PIC X(20).
           05  FILLER         PIC X.
      *
      *
      *************************************************************
       PROCEDURE DIVISION.
      *
      *
       A100-RECEIVE-FROM-TERMINAL.
      *           RECEIVE INITIAL INPUT FROM TERMINAL
      *           USING MOVE MODE.
      *
           EXEC    CICS    RECEIVE
                           INTO(TERMINAL-INPUT-AREA)
                           LENGTH (TRMNL-LEN)
                   END-EXEC.
      *
       A110-VALIDATE-INITIAL-DATA.
      *           THE LENGTH OF THE INPUT DATA IS CON-
      *           TAINED IN TRMNL-LEN.
      *
           IF TRMNL-LEN = 16 NEXT SENTENCE
           ELSE
                   EXEC CICS ABEND ABCODE('LERR') END-EXEC.
           IF TERM-FUNC-CD = 'A' OR 'I' OR 'C' OR 'D'
                   NEXT SENTENCE
           ELSE
```

Figure 10-15. Continued

```
001100003             MOVE 'INVALID FUNCTION CODE' TO EMPERRO
001100208             GO TO A180-ISSUE-BMS-NOERASE.
001100301         IF TERM-KEY IS NUMERIC
001100401             NEXT SENTENCE
001100501         ELSE
001100603             MOVE 'INPUT KEY NOT NUMERIC' TO EMPERRO
001100708             GO TO A180-ISSUE-BMS-NOERASE.
001100801     A120-MAIN-LINE.
001109000         EXEC    CICS    HANDLE  CONDITION
001109202                 NOTFND  (A155-RECORD-NOT-FOUND)
001109400         END-EXEC.
001109500
001109601 *
001109700     A140-READ-THE-FILE.
001109800 *
001109900 *
001110002         EXEC    CICS    READ
001110206                 DATASET ('APPFILE')
001111002                 RIDFLD  (TERM-KEY)
001119104                 SET     (FILE-BLL)
001119200                 LENGTH  (FILE-LEN)
001119300         END-EXEC.
001119402 *
001119804     A150-RECORD-ON-FILE.
001119903         MOVE FILE-KEY    TO EMPNOO.
001120003         MOVE FILE-NAME   TO EMPNAO.
001120103         MOVE FILE-ADDR1  TO EMPAD10.
001120208         MOVE FILE-ADDR2  TO EMPAD20.
001120408         IF TERM-FUNC-CD = 'A'
001120408             MOVE 'DUPLICATE RECORD ON FILE' TO EMPERRO
001120508             GO TO A180-ISSUE-BMS-NOERASE
001120608         ELSE
001120702             GO TO A160-ISSUE-BMS-SEND.
001120802     A155-RECORD-NOT-FOUND.
001120902         IF TERM-FUNC-CD = 'A'
001121003             NEXT SENTENCE
001121108         ELSE MOVE 'RECORD NOT ON FILE' TO EMPERRO
001121203             GO TO A180-ISSUE-BMS-NOERASE.
001121301         MOVE TERM-KEY TO EMPNOO.
001121400     A160-ISSUE-BMS-SEND.
                  *
```

001121
001123
001124
001125
001126
001127
001128
001129
001130
001131
001132
001133
001134
001135
001136
001137
001138
001139
001140
001141
001142
001143
001144
001145
001146
001147
001148
001149
001150
001151
001152
001153
001154
001155
001156
001157
001158
001159
001160

```
        EXEC    CICS    SEND MAP('SMAP1MM')
                        MAPSET  ('SMAP01M')
                        FROM    (SMAP1MMO)
                        ERASE
                        FREEKB
                END-EXEC.
        IF  TERM-FUNC-CD = 'I'
            EXEC CICS RETURN END-EXEC.
*
*   A170-RETURN-WITH-NXTRNSID.
*
        IF  TERM-FUNC-CD = 'A' NEXT SENTENCE
            ELSE    MOVE FILE-NAME  TO COM-NAME
                    MOVE FILE-ADDR1 TO COM-ADDR1
                    MOVE FILE-ADDR2 TO COM-ADDR2.
        MOVE TERM-KEY      TO COM-KEY.
        MOVE TERM-FUNC-CD  TO COM-FUNCTION.
        EXEC CICS   RETURN
                    TRANSID  ('PPG2')
                    COMMAREA (COMMAREA-DATA)
                    LENGTH   (COMMAREA-LEN)
                END-EXEC.
    A180-ISSUE-BMS-NOERASE.
**  SCREEN IS NOT BEING ERASED HERE SO THAT THE OPERATOR CAN
**  SEE HIS/HER MISTAKE AS WELL AS THE ERROR MESSAGE.
**
        EXEC    CICS    SEND MAP('SMAP1MM')
                        MAPSET  ('SMAP01M')
                        FROM    (SMAP1MMO)
                        FREEKB
                END-EXEC.
*
    A190-RETURN-WITHOUT-TRANS.
*
        EXEC    CICS    RETURN
                        END-EXEC.
**
**
*       GOBACK.

NO MESSAGES PRODUCED BY TRANSLATOR.
```

Figure 10-16. Program 2.

```
LINE         SOURCE LISTING

00001  000010000  IDENTIFICATION DIVISION.
00002  000020000  PROGRAM-ID.
00003  000030000      PROGRAM2.
00004  000040000  AUTHOR.
00005  000050000      ARLENE J WIPFLER / BETADATA, INC.
00006  000060000  INSTALLATION.
00007  000070000      BETADATA, INC.
00008  000080000      SYSTEMS TRAINING DIVISION
00009  000090000
00010  000100000
00011  000110000  REMARKS.
00012  000120003      THIS MODULE IS THE SECOND PROGRAM IN A PSEUDO-CONVERSATIONAL
00013  000130008      TRANSACTION TO UPDATE AN EMPLOYEE MASTER FILE.
00014  000140000  ENVIRONMENT DIVISION.
00015  000150000  * N O T E :  THERE ARE NO INPUT/OUTPUT SECTION STATEMENTS OR FILE
00016  000160000  *             CONTROL STATEMENTS. CICS HANDLES ALL FILE SERVICES
00017  000170000  *             ALL FILES THAT ARE TO BE ACCESSED ONLINE MUST BE
00018  000180000  *             DEFINED TO CICS IN THE FILE CONTROL TABLE (FCT).
00019  000190000
00020  000200000  DATA DIVISION.
00021  000210000  * N O T E :  NO FILE SECTION OR FDS ARE CODED IN A CICS PROGRAM
00022  000220000  *             SINCE CICS MANAGES AND CONTROLS FILE ACCESS.
00023  000230000  *             FILES ARE DEFINED IN THE CICS FILE CONTROL TABLE.
00024  000240000
00025  000250000  WORKING-STORAGE SECTION.
00026  000260000  * N O T E :  DEFINE VARIABLE DATA FIELDS HERE.  EXECUTE INTER-
00027  000270000  *             FACE DYNAMICALLY ACQUIRES A WORKING-STORAGE AREA
00028  000280000  *             FOR EACH TASK.  BECAUSE OF THE FACT THAT EACH TASK
00029  000290000  *             HAS ITS OWN UNIQUE WORKING STORAGE, THE COMMAND
00030  000300000  *             LEVEL COBOL PROGRAM IS ALWAYS REENTRANT.
00031  000310000
00032  000320000
00033  000330003      77  FILE-LEN        PIC S9(4) COMP  VALUE +80.
00034  000340008      77  COMMAREA-LEN    PIC S9(4) COMP  VALUE +81.
00035  000350003      77  WS-INIT         PIC X           VALUE SPACES.
00036  000360000  *
00037  000370000  *
00038  000371010      01  HEX-VALUE       PIC S9(4) COMP  VALUE +128.
```

258

```
01  FILLER REDEFINES HEX-VALUE.
    04  FILLER                    PIC X.
    04  HEX-80                    PIC X.
*
*01     COPY DFHAID.
*
 01  FIELD-MATRIX.
    03  ENTERED-MATRIX.
        05  NAME-FLD              PIC X  VALUE '0'.
            88  NAME-ENTERED             VALUE '1'.
        05  ADDR1-FLD             PIC X  VALUE '0'.
            88  ADDR1-ENTERED            VALUE '1'.
        05  ADDR2-FLD             PIC X  VALUE '0'.
            88  ADDR2-ENTERED            VALUE '1'.
*
    03  ERROR-MATRIX.
        05  NAME-ERR              PIC X  VALUE '0'.
            88  NAME-ERROR               VALUE '1'.
        05  ADDR1-ERR             PIC X  VALUE '0'.
            88  ADDR1-ERROR              VALUE '1'.
        05  ADDR2-ERR             PIC X  VALUE '0'.
            88  ADDR2-ERROR              VALUE '1'.
*
 01  FILLER REDEFINES FIELD-MATRIX.
    05  INDICATORS               PIC X(6).
        88  EVERYTHING-VALID          VALUE '111000'.
        88  NOTHING-ENTERED           VALUE '000000'.
 01  FILLER REDEFINES FIELD-MATRIX.
    05  ENTERED-INDICATOR        PIC X(3).
        88  ALL-FIELDS-ENTERED        VALUE '111'.
    05  ERROR-INDICATOR          PIC X(3).
        88  UPDATE-DATA-GOOD          VALUE '000'.
                COPY SMAP01M.
*
 01
 LINKAGE SECTION.
*
*  THE TRANSLATOR WILL AUTOMATICALLY GENERATE A COPY
*  FOR THE EXECUTE INTERFACE BLOCK.  CODE AN 01 DFHCOMMAREA
*  IF YOUR PROGRAM IS TO RECEIVE A COMMAREA.  OTHERWISE THE
*  THE TRANSLATOR WILL INSERT AN 01 DFHCOMMAREA PIC X.
*
*
```

495

Figure 10-16. Continued

```
00081   *      THE COMMAREA IS A DATA AREA THAT CAN BE PASSED TO A      00740000
00082   *      COMMAND LEVEL PROGRAM IN ONE OF THREE WAYS:              00750000
00083   *         1.  THE PROGRAM IS INVOKED VIA A LINK FROM            00760000
00084   *              ANOTHER PROGRAM. THE PROGRAM THAT ISSUED         00770000
00085   *              THE LINK SPECIFIED A COMMAREA IN THE LINK        00780000
00086   *              COMMAND.                                         00790000
00087   *         2.  THE PROGRAM IS INVOKED VIA AN XCTL FROM           00800000
00088   *              ANOTHER PROGRAM. THE PROGRAM THAT ISSUED         00810000
00089   *              THE XCTL SPECIFIED A COMMAREA IN THE XCTL        00820000
00090   *              COMMAND.                                         00830000
00091   *         3.  THE PROGRAM IS INVOKED SUBSEQUENT TO A RETURN     00840000
00092   *              TO CICS. A TRANSID SPECIFIED IN THE RETURN       00850000
00093   *              COMMAND CAUSES THE INVOCATION OF THIS PROGRAM.   00860000
00094   *              THE RETURN COMMAND SPECIFIED A COMMAREA WHICH    00870000
00095   *              CICS SAVES FOR THE SUBSEQUENT TASK.              00880000
00096   *                                                              00890000
00097   ************************************************************** 00900000
00098    01  DFHCOMMAREA.                                              00901008
00099        05  COM-INDICATOR            PIC X.                       00902008
00100            88  FIRST-TIME-IN                  VALUE '1'.         00903008
00101        05  COM-FUNCTION-CODE        PIC X.                       00904008
00102            88  ADD-PROCESSING                 VALUE 'A'.         00905008
00103            88  CHANGE-PROCESSING              VALUE 'C'.         00906008
00104            88  DELETE-PROCESSING              VALUE 'D'.         00907008
00105        05  COM-PASSED-KEY           PIC X(9).                   00908008
00106        05  COM-NAME                 PIC X(30).                  00909008
00107        05  COM-ADDR1                PIC X(20).                  00909108
00108        05  COM-ADDR2                PIC X(20).                  00909208
00109   *                                                             00910000
00110    01  BLL-CELLS.                                               00920000
00111   *        THE FIRST BLL CELL IS USED BY CICS.                  00930000
00112        05  FILLER        PIC S9(8) COMP.                       00940000
00113        05  FILE-BLL      PIC S9(8) COMP.                       00950000
00114   *                                                             00960000
00115   *   THE DATA AREAS BELOW MUST CORRESPOND IN ORDER TO THE       00970000
00116   *   ORDER OF THE BLL CELLS DEFINED ABOVE.                      00980000
00117   *                                                             00990000
00118   *                                                             01000000
00119    01  FILE-INPUT-AREA.                                         01010000
00120        05  FILE-KEY           PIC X(9).                        01020000
                                                                      01030000
```

260

```
001121  01040000       05  FILE-NAME              PIC X(30).
001122  01050000       05  FILE-ADDR1             PIC X(20).
001123  01060000       05  FILE-ADDR2             PIC X(20).
001124  01070000       05  FILLER                 PIC X.
001125  01080000
001126  01090000  ***********************************************************
001127  01210000
001128  01220000   PROCEDURE DIVISION.
001129  01240008  *     TEST TO DETERMINE IF A COMMAREA IS PRESENT.  IF NOT THEN
001130  01240008  *     THIS INDICATES AN ILLEGAL ENTRY INTO THIS PROGRAM.  NO
001131  01250008  *     COMMAREA MEANS THAT THE FIRST PROGRAM DID NOT RETURN WITH
001132  01260008  *     A TRANSID AND COMMAREA TO THIS SECOND MODULE.  THE ONLY
001133  01261008  *     OTHER WAY FOR THIS MODULE TO BE INVOKED IS IF AN OPERATOR
001134  01262008  *     ENTERS THE TRANSID THAT INVOKES THIS PROGRAM.  THIS IS
001135  01263008  *     NOT THE CORRECT WAY TO BEGIN THE EMPLOYEE INFORMATION
001136  01264008  *     TRANSACTION AND THEREFORE WE WILL ABEND IF THIS IS THE
001137  01265008  *     CASE.
001138  01266008  *
001139  01266111
001140  01267011      IF EIBCALEN = 81 NEXT SENTENCE
001141  01268008         ELSE EXEC CICS ABEND ABCODE ('IENT') END-EXEC.
001142  01268111
001143  01269008  *
001144  01269108  *     THE MAPFAIL CONDITION CAN OCCUR DURING INPUT MAPPING.
001145  01269208  *     THIS OCCURS IF THE OPERATOR ENTERS NO DATA AND THE
001146  01269308  *     PROGRAM DID NOT TURN ON ANY MDTS.  IN THESE CIRCUMSTANCES
001147  01269408  *     THERE IS NO FIELD DATA RECEIVED FROM THE TERMINAL AND BMS
001148  01269508  *     CANNOT PERFORM INPUT MAPPING.  IF NO HANDLE CONDITION
001149  01269608  *     IS USED FOR MAPFAIL THEN THE TASK ABENDS AND CICS SENDS
001150  01269708  *     A MESSAGE TO THE TERMINAL INDICATING THE ABEND CODE OF
001151  01269808  *     AEI9.  IN ORDER TO INTERCEPT THIS THE FOLLOWING HANDLE
001152  01269908  *     CONDITION IS CODED.
001153  01270008  *
001154  01270114      EXEC CICS HANDLE CONDITION
001155  01270214         MAPFAIL (A150-MAPFAIL-ROUTINE)
001156  01270314         END-EXEC.
001157  01270411
001158  01270509  *
001159  01280001   A100-MAIN-LINE.          RECEIVE THE MAP  TO GET THE DATA ENTERED
001160  01290001  *                                BY THE TERMINAL OPERATOR.
001161  01300001  *
001162  01310001      EXEC CICS RECEIVE MAP('SMAPIMM')
```

261

Figure 10-16. Continued

```
001163  01320001              MAPSET('SMAP01M')   INTO (SMAP1MMI)
001164  01330001           END-EXEC.
001165  01341011
001166  01350011   IF DELETE-PROCESSING
001167  01370011      PERFORM    S130-DELETE-PROCESSING    THRU
001168  01380011                 S130-DELETE-PROCESSING-EXIT
001169  01410011
001170  01430000      GO TO A180-SEND-TRAN-GOOD.
001171  01440011
001172  01450011 *
001173  01451011
001174  01460011   PERFORM    S100-INTERROGATE-SCREEN-INPUT      THRU
001175  01470011              S100-INTERROGATE-INPUT-EXIT.
001176  01480011
001177  01490011   IF ADD-PROCESSING
001178  01491011      IF EVERYTHING-VALID
001179  01500011         PERFORM S120-ADD-PROCESSING    THRU
001180  01510011                 S120-ADD-PROCESSING-EXIT
001181  01520011         GO TO A180-SEND-TRAN-GOOD
001182  01630011      ELSE
001183  01631011         PERFORM S220-ERROR-PROCESSING       THRU
001184  01640003                 S220-ERROR-PROCESSING-EXIT
001185  01650011         GO TO A160-SEND-ERROR-SCREEN.
001186  01651009
001187  01652011   IF CHANGE-PROCESSING AND NOTHING-ENTERED
001188  01653011      GO TO A155-FORMAT-NODATA-MESSAGE.
001189  01654011   IF CHANGE-PROCESSING AND UPDATE-DATA-GOOD
001190  01655009      PERFORM S110-CHANGE-PROCESSING      THRU
001191  01656011              S110-CHANGE-PROCESSING-EXIT
001192  01657011      GO TO A180-SEND-TRAN-GOOD
001193  01658011   ELSE
001194  01659011      PERFORM S220-ERROR-PROCESSING       THRU
001195  01840000              S220-ERROR-PROCESSING-EXIT
001196  01841009      GO TO A160-SEND-ERROR-SCREEN.
001197  01842009
001198  01843016 * A150-MAPFAIL-ROUTINE.
001199  01844011      IF EIBAID = DFHCLEAR
001200  01845009         EXEC CICS SEND CONTROL ERASE FREEKB END-EXEC
001201  01846009         EXEC CICS RETURN END-EXEC.
001202  01847009 * A155-FORMAT-NODATA-MESSAGE.
                   MOVE LOW-VALUES TO SMAP1MMO
                   MOVE 'ENTER DATA TO UPDATE FILE OR CLEAR TO CANCEL'
```

```
00203  01848009           MOVE   -1 TO EMPERRO.
00204  01849011           MOVE   -1 TO EMPNAL.
00205  01850003       A160-SEND-ERROR-SCREEN.
00206  01860000           EXEC   CICS   SEND MAP('SMAP1MM')
00207  01870000                         MAPSET   ('SMAP01M')
00208  01880000                         FROM     (SMAP1MMO)
00209  01900001                         DATAONLY
00210  01901018                         FRSET
00211  01910003                         CURSOR
00212  01920000                         FREEKB
00213  01930000           END-EXEC.
00214  01940000       **
00215  01960000           EXEC   CICS   RETURN
00216  01970000                         TRANSID    ('PPG2')
00217  01980000                         COMMAREA   (DFHCOMMAREA)
00218  01981009                         LENGTH     (COMMAREA-LEN)
00219  01982009                         END-EXEC.
00220  01990009       **
00221  02030009       A180-SEND-TRAN-GOOD.
00222  02040000           EXEC   CICS   SEND MAP('SMAP1MM')
00223  02050000                         MAPSET   ('SMAP01M')
00224  02060000                         FRSET
00225  02061018                         FROM     (SMAP1MMO)
00226  02070000                         DATAONLY
00227  02080000                         FREEKB
00228  02090000           END-EXEC.
00229  02100000       **
00230  02110000       **
00231  02130000           EXEC   CICS   RETURN
00232  02140000                         END-EXEC.
00233  02150000       **
00234  02160000       **
00235  02170002           EJECT
00236  02180003       S100-INTERROGATE-SCREEN-INPUT.
00237  02181010       *
00238  02182010           IF FIRST-TIME-IN MOVE LOW-VALUES TO COM-NAME
00239  02183011                                               COM-ADDR1
00240  02183211                                               COM-ADDR2.
00241  02184019       *
00242  02185010           MOVE '2' TO COM-INDICATOR.
00243  02188010           IF EMPNAL = 0 OR EMPNAI = SPACES
00244                        GO TO S100-TEST-ADDR1.
```

263

Figure 10-16. Continued

```
00245  02189110          MOVE EMPNAI TO COM-NAME.
00246  02189510      S100-TEST-ADDR1.
00247  02189610          IF EMPAD1L = 0 OR EMPAD1I = SPACES
00248  02190010              NEXT SENTENCE
00249  02190110          ELSE MOVE EMPAD1I TO COM-ADDR1.
00250  02191010      S100-TEST-ADDR2.
00251  02193010          IF EMPAD2L = 0 OR EMPAD2I = SPACES
00252  02194010              NEXT SENTENCE
00253  02194110          ELSE MOVE EMPAD2I TO COM-ADDR2.
00254  02194210      S100-TEST-FOR-HEX-80.
00255  02194310          IF EMPNAA  = HEX-80 MOVE LOW-VALUES TO COM-NAME.
00256  02194410          IF EMPAD1A = HEX-80 MOVE LOW-VALUES TO COM-ADDR1.
00257  02195010          IF EMPAD2A = HEX-80 MOVE LOW-VALUES TO COM-ADDR2.
00258  02196010      S100-TEST-COM-NAME.
00259  02197010          IF COM-NAME = LOW-VALUES
00260  02197110              NEXT SENTENCE
00261  02197210          ELSE MOVE '1' TO NAME-FLD
00262  02197310               IF COM-NAME IS ALPHABETIC
00263  02197410                   NEXT SENTENCE
00264  02197510               ELSE MOVE '1' TO NAME-ERR.
00265  02197610          IF COM-ADDR1 = LOW-VALUES
00266  02197710              NEXT SENTENCE
00267  02197810          ELSE MOVE '1' TO ADDR1-FLD.
00268  02197910          IF COM-ADDR2 = LOW-VALUES
00269  02198010              NEXT SENTENCE
00270  02198110          ELSE MOVE '1' TO ADDR2-FLD.
00271  02199010      S100-INTERROGATE-INPUT-EXIT.
00272  02199110          EXIT.
00273  02471009          EJECT
00274  02471111      S110-CHANGE-PROCESSING.
00275  02471211          EXEC CICS READ UPDATE
00276  02471311              DATASET('APPFILE') RIDFLD(COM-PASSED-KEY)
00277  02471411              SET(FILE-BLL) LENGTH(FILE-LEN)
00278  02471510          END-EXEC.
00279  02471617          IF NAME-ENTERED
00280  02471710              MOVE COM-NAME  TO FILE-NAME.
00281  02471817          IF ADDR1-ENTERED
00282  02471910              MOVE COM-ADDR1 TO FILE-ADDR1.
00283  02471910          IF ADDR2-ENTERED
00284  02472017              MOVE COM-ADDR2 TO FILE-ADDR2.
```

```
           EXEC CICS REWRITE DATASET('APPFILE')
                     FROM(FILE-INPUT-AREA)
                     LENGTH(FILE-LEN)
           END-EXEC.
           MOVE LOW-VALUES TO SMAP1MMO.
           MOVE 'RECORD UPDATE SUCCESSFUL' TO EMPERRO.
       S110-CHANGE-PROCESSING-EXIT.
           EXIT.
           EJECT.
       S120-ADD-PROCESSING.
           EXEC CICS GETMAIN SET(FILE-BLL)
                     LENGTH(FILE-LEN) INITIMG(WS-INIT)
           END-EXEC.
           MOVE COM-PASSED-KEY TO FILE-KEY.
           MOVE COM-NAME TO FILE-NAME.
           MOVE COM-ADDR1 TO FILE-ADDR1.
           MOVE COM-ADDR2 TO FILE-ADDR2.
           EXEC CICS WRITE DATASET('APPFILE')
                     FROM(FILE-INPUT-AREA) LENGTH(FILE-LEN)
                     RIDFLD(COM-PASSED-KEY)
           END-EXEC.
           MOVE LOW-VALUES TO SMAP1MMO.
           MOVE 'RECORD ADDED TO FILE' TO EMPERRO.
       S120-ADD-PROCESSING-EXIT.
           EXIT.
           EJECT.
       S130-DELETE-PROCESSING.
           IF EMPNAI = 'DELETE'
           EXEC CICS DELETE DATASET ('APPFILE')
                     RIDFLD (COM-PASSED-KEY)
           END-EXEC
           MOVE LOW-VALUES TO SMAP1MMO
           MOVE 'RECORD DELETED' TO EMPERRO
           ELSE
           MOVE LOW-VALUES TO SMAP1MMO
           MOVE 'DELETE CANCELLED' TO EMPERRO.
       S130-DELETE-PROCESSING-EXIT.
           EXIT.
           EJECT.
       S220-ERROR-PROCESSING.
           MOVE LOW-VALUES TO SMAP1MMO.
```

Figure 10-16. Continued

```
00327                    IF NAME-ENTERED AND NAME-ERROR
00328                        MOVE -1 TO EMPNAL
00329                        MOVE 'H' TO EMPNAA
00330                    ELSE
00331                        IF ADD-PROCESSING AND NOT NAME-ENTERED
00332                            MOVE -1 TO EMPNAL
00333                        ELSE NEXT SENTENCE.
00334   *
00335                    IF ADDR1-ENTERED NEXT SENTENCE
00336                    ELSE
00337                        IF ADD-PROCESSING
00338                            MOVE -1 TO EMPAD1L.
00339   *
00340                    IF ADDR2-ENTERED NEXT SENTENCE
00341                    ELSE
00342                        IF ADD-PROCESSING
00343                            MOVE -1 TO EMPAD2L.
00344                    IF CHANGE-PROCESSING OR ALL-FIELDS-ENTERED
00345                        MOVE 'NAME MUST BE ALPHABETIC' TO EMPERRO
00346                        GO TO S220-ERROR-PROCESSING-EXIT.
00347                    IF NAME-ERROR
00348                        MOVE 'NAME MUST BE ALPHABETIC AND ALL FIELDS REQUIRED'
00349                            TO EMPERRO
00350                    ELSE
00351                        MOVE 'ALL FIELDS REQUIRED' TO EMPERRO.
00352   S220-ERROR-PROCESSING-EXIT.
00353                    EXIT.
00354                    EJECT
00355   Z999-END-OF-PROGRAM.
00356   *
00357                    GOBACK.
00358   *
00359
```

NO MESSAGES PRODUCED BY TRANSLATOR.

TRANSLATION TIME:- 0.00 MINS.

```
02879410
02879603
02879711
02880003
02880115
02880203
02880303
02881000
02882011
02888011
02889003
02889111
02889211
02889311
02889903
02890003
02890111
02890303
02890403
02890512
02890610
02890703
02890803
02891203
02891303
02891411
02891504
02891604
02891705
02891804
02892000
02900000
02910000
```

information. This module validates entered information and, if it is correct, updates the file. If data are incorrect, an appropriate error message is displayed.

10.8 CICS TABLE DEFINITIONS

In support of this transaction, CICS table definitions have to be made. Both programs and the BMS mapset must be defined in the Processing Program Table so that CICS can manage the use of these load modules. Additionally, the TRANSID used by the terminal operator to invoke the first program must be defined in the Program Control Table, along with the internally generated TRANSID for the second program named in the RETURN command issued by the first program. Our PPT and PCT table entries might look like Fig. 10-17. The file used must also be defined in the File Control Table.

10.9 THE SYMBOLIC MAP IN PERSPECTIVE

The symbolic map is merely a program work area (like any data structure defined in an application program). The benefit of using the BMS symbolic map is that we don't have to code the work area and risk misdefining

```
Processing Program Table (PPT)
DFHPPT TYPE=INITIAL,SUFFIX=PA
.
DFHPPT TYPE=ENTRY,PROGRAM=SMAPO1M,
   PGMLANG=ASSEMBLER
DFHPPT TYPE=ENTRY,PROGRAM=PROGRAM1,
   PGMLANG=COBOL
DFHPPT TYPE=ENTRY,PROGRAM=PROGRAM2,
   PGMLANG=COBOL
.
DFHPPT TYPE=FINAL

Program Control Table (PCT)
DFHPCT TYPE=INITIAL,SUFFIX=PA
.
DFHPCT TYPE=ENTRY,TRANSID=PPG1,PROGRAM=PROGRAM1,
   TRNPRTY=2
DFHPCT TYPE=ENTRY,TRANSID=PPG2,PROGRAM=PROGRAM2,
   TRNPRTY=3
.
DFHPCT TYPE=FINAL
```

Figure 10-17. Sample table entries.

EMPLOYEE INFORMATION BROWSE

NUMBER	NAME	ADDRESS	
999999999	XXXXXXXXXXXXXXXXXXXX	XXXXXXXXXX	XXXXXXXX
999999999	XXXXXXXXXXXXXXXXXXXX	XXXXXXXXXX	XXXXXXXX
999999999	XXXXXXXXXXXXXXXXXXXX	XXXXXXXXXX	XXXXXXXX
999999999	XXXXXXXXXXXXXXXXXXXX	XXXXXXXXXX	XXXXXXXX
999999999	XXXXXXXXXXXXXXXXXXXX	XXXXXXXXXX	XXXXXXXX
999999999	XXXXXXXXXXXXXXXXXXXX	XXXXXXXXXX	XXXXXXXX
999999999	XXXXXXXXXXXXXXXXXXXX	XXXXXXXXXX	XXXXXXXX
999999999	XXXXXXXXXXXXXXXXXXXX	XXXXXXXXXX	XXXXXXXX
999999999	XXXXXXXXXXXXXXXXXXXX	XXXXXXXXXX	XXXXXXXX
999999999	XXXXXXXXXXXXXXXXXXXX	XXXXXXXXXX	XXXXXXXX
999999999	XXXXXXXXXXXXXXXXXXXX	XXXXXXXXXX	XXXXXXXX
999999999	XXXXXXXXXXXXXXXXXXXX	XXXXXXXXXX	XXXXXXXX
999999999	XXXXXXXXXXXXXXXXXXXX	XXXXXXXXXX	XXXXXXXX
999999999	XXXXXXXXXXXXXXXXXXXX	XXXXXXXXXX	XXXXXXXX
999999999	XXXXXXXXXXXXXXXXXXXX	XXXXXXXXXX	XXXXXXXX
999999999	XXXXXXXXXXXXXXXXXXXX	XXXXXXXXXX	XXXXXXXX
999999999	XXXXXXXXXXXXXXXXXXXX	XXXXXXXXXX	XXXXXXXX
999999999	XXXXXXXXXXXXXXXXXXXX	XXXXXXXXXX	XXXXXXXX
999999999	XXXXXXXXXXXXXXXXXXXX	XXXXXXXXXX	XXXXXXXX
999999999	XXXXXXXXXXXXXXXXXXXX	XXXXXXXXXX	XXXXXXXX

CLEAR KEY TO END   PF19-PAGE BACK   PF20-PAGE FORWARD

Figure 10-18.   Sample screen with field groups.

one or more fields. Since field displacements within the symbolic map are extremely significant to BMS during mapping operations, any miscoded fields could throw off BMS, and we could wind up with some strange looking screens. Therefore, we normally use the symbolic map just as it is created. However, there may be circumstances in which using the symbolic map created by assembling BMS macros may not facilitate programming.

The OCCURS clause that can be coded in the DFHMDF macro allows the definition of a single field which is repeated for multiple occurrences. However, we may have a map in which we need to process groups of fields that occur multiple times. Such a screen is depicted in Fig. 10-18. In this screen we have 20 lines that are identical, but each line contains four fields. The OCCURS parameter can be used only for individual fields that repeat, so we must define DFHMDF macros for all four fields across all 20 lines. Each of the 80 fields (4 per line × 20 lines) must be given a unique name if we want to use the field in the program and don't want assembly/compile errors. Our BMS source code might look something like this:

```
SETNAM    DFHMSD TYPE=MAP,TIOAPFX=YES, . . .
APNAM     DFHMDI SIZE=(24,80), . . .
          DFHMDF POS=(1,18),LENGTH=27,                              X
                INITIAL='EMPLOYEE INFORMATION BROWSE'
          DFHMDF POS=(2,5),LENGTH=6,INITIAL='NUMBER'
          DFHMDF POS=(2,13),LENGTH=4,INITIAL='NAME'
          DFHMDF POS=(2,44),LENGTH=7,INITIAL='ADDRESS'
    START OF NAMED DFHMDF MACROS USED TO OUTPUT BROWSE INFO
    TO THE SCREEN. SINCE THIS IS BROWSE MODE THE DEFAULT
    ATTRIBUTE OF (NORM,ASKIP) IS USED.
1NUM      DFHMDF POS=(3,4),LENGTH=9
1NAM      DFHMDF POS=(3,15),LENGTH=20
1AD1      DFHMDF POS=(3,37),LENGTH=10
1AD2      DFHMDF POS=(3,49),LENGTH=10
    19 MORE SETS OF THE 4 FIELDS ABOVE WITH DIFFERENT NAMES
          DFHMDF POS=(24,1),LENGTH=55,                              X
                INITIAL='CLEAR KEY TO END PF19 PAGE BACKWARDX
                PF20 PAGE FORWARD'
          DFHMSD TYPE=FINAL
```

The symbolic map generated from this source can be expected to have a
12-byte filler for the TIOAPFX, followed by 20 collections of fields
representing the 20 repeated lines. If we use this symbolic map as is in a
COBOL program, the program must have 20 sets of MOVE instructions to
move file data to each of the 20 lines. Therefore, in this example it is not
convenient to use the generated symbolic map.

Since the symbolic map is nothing more than a data structure, there
is no reason that it cannot be redefined within our program. We can use a
standard COBOL data structure to redefine the map. The benefit of
redefining the map is that the data structure can make use of the COBOL
OCCURS clause to define occurrences of lines. The following code could
be used to accomplish this end:

```
01    COPY MSETNAM.
01    MAP-TABLE REDEFINES MAPNAMI.
      03    TIOAPFX-FILLER    PIC X(12).
      03    GROUP-LINE OCCURS 20 TIMES.
            04    NUML              PIC XX.
            04    NUMA              PIC X.
            04    NUMBER            PIC X(9).
            04    NAML              PIC XX.
            04    NAMA              PIC X.
            04    NAME              PIC X(20).
            04    AD1L              PIC XX.
            04    AD1A              PIC X.
            04    ADDRESS1          PIC X(10).
```

```
04   AD2L                    PIC XX.
04   AD2A                    PIC X.
04   ADDRESS2                PIC X(10).
```

In the COBOL program, MAP-TABLE field names can be used to actually reference the data areas in the symbolic map. By utilizing a subscript, it is possible to code the following instructions to format data in the symbolic map:

```
PERFORM FORMAT-SCREEN THRU FORMAT-SCREEN-EXIT
VARYING I FROM 1 BY 1 UNTIL I > 20.
            .
            .
            .
FORMAT-SCREEN.
       MOVE EMP-NUM TO NUMBER (I).
       MOVE EMP-NAM TO NAME (I).
       MOVE EMP-AD1  TO ADDRESS1 (I).
       MOVE EMP-AD2  TO ADDRESS2 (I).
FORMAT-SCREEN-EXIT.      EXIT.
```

When using this technique, it is important to remember a couple of points. Don't forget to include the filler for the TIOAPFX. Each named DFHMDF macro must be included in terms of storage definition, and the L and A fields must be accounted for. If fields don't align properly when the program sends the map to a terminal, check the redefined area and make sure you have accounted for all fields in the symbolic map.

CODING AND REVIEW EXERCISE

The coding exercise that follows references the following source code:

```
SAMPLE     DFHMSD TYPE=MAP,MODE=INOUT,LANG=COBOL,          X
                  TIOAPFX=YES, TERM=3270,                  X
                  DATA=FIELD,CTRL=(FREEKB,FRSET)
SMAP       DFHMDI SIZE=(24,80)
           DFHMDF POS=(1,34),LENGTH=11,INITIAL='DATA SCREEN'
           DFHMDF POS=(3,20),LENGTH=9,INITIAL='CUSTOMER:'
CUSTNAM    DFHMDF POS=(3,30),LENGTH=30,ATTRB=(UNPROT,IC)
           DFHMDF POS=(3,61),LENGTH=1
           DFHMDF POS=(5,20),LENGTH=8,INITIAL='ADDRESS:'
ADDRESS    DFHMDF POS=(5,30),LENGTH=30,ATTRB=UNPROT
           DFHMDF POS=(5,61),LENGTH=1
ERRMSG     DFHMDF POS=(24,1),LENGTH=78,ATTRB=(BRT,ASKIP)
           DFHMSD TYPE=FINAL
           END
```

1. Name two objects that will be created as a result of assembling the above source code.

2. List the data fields that will be generated in the copy statement or symbolic map for the source code listed above.
3. Code a statement to copy the above symbolic map into a CICS COBOL program.
4. Code a CICS command to send the above map to a terminal. Titles in the physical map and application data from the symbolic map are to be sent.
5. Code a CICS command to send the map to a terminal if only the application data from the symbolic map are to be sent.
6. Describe when a full merge of data would be useful for output mapping, DATAONLY option, or MAPONLY option.
7. How does BMS use the L field during input mapping?
8. How is symbolic cursor positioning accomplished? Cite three things that must be done.
9. How does BMS use the F field during input mapping?
10. How does an application programmer dynamically change a field attribute? Cite one example when this would be useful.
11. We have read a file record that contains two fields that are to be sent to a terminal using a map generated from the source code above. The fields in the file area are named NAME and ADDR. Code the instructions to move the data into the symbolic map and send the map to the screen using a full merge of data from the symbolic and physical maps.
12. We have sent the map described above to a terminal in a pseudo-conversational task. The operator has entered data and pressed the ENTER key, and a task has been initiated by CICS. Code a command to receive the input into the symbolic map.
13. Code the instructions to interrogate the data fields to determine if they have been modified by the terminal operator. The following field matrix and status field may be used to keep track of fields. The name field is to be alphabetic only, and there is no validation for address.

```
01  FLDS-ENTERED.
    04  NAM-1    PIC X VALUE '0'.
        88       NAME-ENTERED   VALUE '1'.
    04  ADD-1    PIC X VALUE '0'.
        88       ADDRESS-ENTERED   VALUE '1'.

01  NAME-STATUS       PIC X VALUE '0'.
        88       NAME-ERROR    VALUE '1'.
```

14. Code an error processing routine in which MDTs are to be turned on for those fields entered by the operator. The symbolic map is assumed to be copied into Working Storage. Fields that were entered incorrectly are to be highlighted, and MDT set on. The cursor is to be positioned at the first error field. Fields that were entered correctly are just to have the MDT on. An error message "PLEASE CORRECT

BRIGHT FIELDS" is to be displayed on the screen.

15. Code a SEND MAP to send the output described in #14. Make sure that the SEND MAP command includes options that are correct in the context of error processing.

ANSWERS TO CODING AND REVIEW EXERCISE

The coding exercise that follows references the following source code:

```
SAMPLE      DFHMSD TYPE=MAP,MODE=INOUT,LANG=COBOL,            X
                   TIOAPFX=YES, TERM=3270,                    X
                   DATA=FIELD,CTRL=(FREEKB,FRSET)
SMAP        DFHMDI SIZE=(24,80)
            DFHMDF POS=(1,34),LENGTH=11,INITIAL='DATA SCREEN'
            DFHMDF POS=(3,20),LENGTH=9,INITIAL='CUSTOMER:'
CUSTNAM     DFHMDF POS=(3,30),LENGTH=30,ATTRB=(UNPROT,IC)
            DFHMDF POS=(3,61),LENGTH=1
            DFHMDF POS=(5,20),LENGTH=8,INITIAL='ADDRESS:'
ADDRESS     DFHMDF POS=(5,30),LENGTH=30,ATTRB=UNPROT
            DFHMDF POS=(5,61),LENGTH=1
ERRMSG      DFHMDF POS=(24,1),LENGTH=78,ATTRB=(BRT,ASKIP)
            DFHMSD TYPE=FINAL
            END
```

1. Name two objects that will be created as a result of assembling the above source code.

   Symbolic and physical maps are created.

2. List the data fields that will be generated in the copy statement or symbolic map for the source code listed above.

   CUSTNAML, CUSTNAMA, CUSTNAMF, CUSTNAMI, CUSTNAMO
   ADDRESSL, ADDRESSA, ADDRESSF, ADDRESSI, ADDRESSO
   ERRMSGL, ERRMSGA, ERRMSGF, ERRMSGI, and ERRMSGO.

3. Code a statement to copy the above symbolic map into a CICS COBOL program.

   01 COPY SAMPLE.

4. Code a CICS command to send the above map to a terminal. Titles in both the physical map and application data from the symbolic map are to be sent.

   EXEC CICS SEND MAP('SMAP') MAPSET('SAMPLE') ERASE
   FROM (SMAPO) FREEKB END-EXEC.

5. Code a CICS command to send the map to a terminal if only the application data from the symbolic map are to be sent.

EXEC CICS SEND MAP('SMAP') MAPSET('SAMPLE')
FROM (SMAPO) FREEKB DATAONLY END-EXEC.

6. Describe when a full merge of data would be useful for output mapping, DATAONLY option, or MAPONLY option.

A full merge of symbolic map data and physical map titles is used as the first output from a CICS transaction. Normally, the ERASE option is also included to clear the screen for the new display.

The DATAONLY option is used for second or subsequent outputs from a transaction once the screen has been displayed. The titles are displayed at the terminal, and are contained in the terminal's buffer. Therefore, there is no need to retransmit them. We also omit the ERASE option because we are relying upon the fact that the screen contains information that we want preserved.

MAPONLY may be used to send a menu screen or a data entry screen when there are no application data to send along with screen titles and constants.

7. How does BMS use the L field during input mapping?

BMS places the length of data received back from the terminal into each field's L field. The operator may have entered 10 bytes of information into a field with a capacity of 20 bytes. In this case the L field would be set to 10 and the data would be placed into the I field. Data placed into the I field are padded and justified according to the field's specification in the JUSTIFY parameter in the DFHMDF macro.

8. How is symbolic cursor positioning accomplished? Cite three things that must be done.

The mapset must be defined as MODE=INOUT, the SEND MAP command must include the CURSOR option without any value specified, and a -1 must be moved to the appropriate L field.

9. How does BMS use the F field during input mapping?

The F field is used as a flag to indicate that the operator pressed Erase End of Field to erase the entire contents of the field. The field has been modified, but there are no data. BMS sets the F field to X"80", the L field to zero, and the I field to low values.

10. How does an application programmer dynamically change a field attribute? Cite one example when this would be useful.

A field attribute can be dynamically altered by moving a new attribute value to the A field in the symbolic map. This is very useful for highlighting error fields.

11. We have read a file record that contains two fields that are to be sent to a terminal using a map generated from the source code above. The fields in the file area are named NAME and ADDR. Code the instructions to move the data into the symbolic map and send the map to the screen using a full merge of data from the symbolic and physical maps.

```
MOVE NAME TO CUSTNAMO.
MOVE ADDR TO ADDRESSO.
EXEC CICS SEND MAP ('SMAP') MAPSET('SAMPLE') ERASE
    FROM(SMAPO) FREEKB  END-EXEC.
```

12. We have sent the map described above to a terminal in a pseudo-conversational task. The operator has entered data and pressed the ENTER key and a task has been initiated by CICS. Code a command to receive the input into the symbolic map.

```
EXEC CICS RECEIVE MAP('SMAP') MAPSET ('SAMPLE')
    INTO(SMAPI) END-EXEC.
```

13. Code the instructions to interrogate the data fields to determine if they have been modified by the terminal operator. The following field matrix and status field may be used to keep track of fields. The name field is to be alphabetic only, and there is no validation for address.

```
01  FLDS-ENTERED.
      04  NAM-1    PIC X VALUE '0'.
          88       NAME-ENTERED   VALUE '1'.
      04  ADD-1    PIC X VALUE '0'.
          88       ADDRESS-ENTERED   VALUE '1'.

01  NAME-STATUS        PIC X VALUE '0'.
          88       NAME-ERROR    VALUE '1'.
PROCEDURE DIVISION.
      .
B100-INTERROGATE-SCREEN.
      IF CUSTNAML = 0 or CUSTNAMI = SPACES NEXT SENTENCE
      ELSE
          MOVE '1' TO NAM-1
          IF CUSTNAMI IS ALPHABETIC NEXT SENTENCE
          ELSE
              MOVE '1' TO NAME-STATUS.
```

```
    IF ADDRESSL = 0 OR ADDRESSI = SPACES NEXT SENTENCE
    ELSE
        MOVE '1' TO ADD-1.
B100-INTERROGATE-EXIT.   EXIT.
```

14. Code an error processing routine in which MDTs are to be turned on for those fields entered by the operator. The symbolic map is assumed to be copied into Working Storage. Fields that were entered incorrectly are to be highlighted, and MDT set on. The cursor is to be positioned at the first error field. Fields that were entered correctly are just to have the MDT on. An error message "PLEASE CORRECT BRIGHT FIELDS" is to be displayed on the screen.

```
D100-ERROR-PROCESSING.
    MOVE LOW-VALUES TO SMAPO.
    IF NAME-ENTERED
        IF NAME-ERROR
            MOVE -1 TO CUSTNAML
            MOVE 'I' TO CUSTNAMA
        ELSE
            MOVE 'A' TO CUSTNAMA.
    IF ADDRESS-ENTERED
        MOVE 'A' TO ADDRESSA.
    MOVE 'PLEASE CORRECT BRIGHT FIELDS' TO ERRMSGO.
```

15. Code a SEND MAP to send the output described in # 14. Make sure that the SEND MAP command includes options that are correct in the context of error processing.

```
    EXEC CICS SEND MAP('SMAP') MAPSET('SAMPLE')
        FROM(SMAPO) FREEKB DATAONLY CURSOR FRSET
    END-EXEC.
```

chapter *11*

Program Debugging

11.1 GETTING STARTED

In the previous chapters we examined the basics of writing a CICS application program. In this chapter we are going to discuss the techniques and methodology of program debugging. Most programs are initiated from a CICS terminal, and therefore we enter information that invokes the program to be tested. In menu-driven systems we select a menu option that leads to the appropriate program or, if the program is invoked by a unique transaction identifier, we enter the TRANSID and any optional data. In this manner we try out all of the functions that the program is supposed to perform.

Program testing online can be a very heady experience because of the instantaneous nature of interactive processing. This is especially true if the programmer is used to working on batch systems. Online, one invokes a program and the results are immediately apparent on the screen. As a result, it is quite possible to become lulled by the apparent ease of testing, and enter transaction after transaction to try out the different program functions. However, interactive testing can be compared to listening to music. The experience, no matter how pleasurable, is fleeting. Because of this, it is important to be particularly organized.

Before even approaching a CICS terminal, it is wise to develop a script or test log of what is to be tested. The program should be analyzed, and each different function or error condition should be listed. After this, one can plan test data so that all of the logical paths of the program can be

276

tested. What is important is not how many transactions are entered, but what is tested with each entry. As an example of test log development, let's consider the program represented in Fig. 10-15. There are numerous things to be tested in this program. For example, the operator is to enter a function code. Valid functions are "I" for inquiry only, "C" for change or record update, "D" for record deletion, and "A" for record addition. The operator is also supposed to enter a 9-byte numeric key of the record to be operated upon. A script for testing this module is illustrated in Fig. 11-1. Note that the various logical combinations are represented in the script, as is the test data that is to be entered at a CICS terminal. In the RESULT column we can record what happens when the appropriate conditions are tested. As you can imagine, without the test log as a record of each test, it can become quite difficult to remember exactly what happened at the beginning of the testing session. In the sample script we are assuming that a record with the key of "999999999" is on the file, and that record "000000000" is not. In real life, however, one cannot make such assumptions. The CICS transaction CECI can be used to verify exactly which records are in fact on the file. For example, prior to creating the script one could use CECI and browse the file. This could be accomplished by signing on to CICS and entering the following:

CECI STARTBR

CICS then displays the format of the STARTBR command. For file browsing it is necessary to define fields or variables for use within the browse. This can be done by pressing PF5 once in conversation with CECI. Variable names begin with the ampersand (&). Let's say we define two variables for our CECI session. &KEY is defined as a 9-byte field, and &REC as an 80-byte field. The variables are defined by entering the variable names and sizes into the CECI variable screen and pressing ENTER. After the variables are defined, the starting key can be placed into the &KEY field by entering a value in the area to the right of the field

Condition	Data	Result
Invalid function code	PPG1 X,999999999	
Nonnumeric file key	PPG1 I,A99999999	
Function "I" and record not on file	PPG1 I,000000000	
Function "I" and record on file	PPG1 I,999999999	
Function "A" and record on file	PPG1 A,999999999	
Function "A" and record not on file	PPG1 A,000000000	
Function "C" and record on file	PPG1 C,999999999	
Function "C" and record not on file	PPG1 C,000000000	
Function "D" and record on file	PPG1 D,999999999	
Function "D" and record not on file	PPG1 D,000000000	

Figure 11-1. Sample test log.

size. To return to the command format screen, press ENTER again. We then type the command:

STARTBR DATASET(ddname) RIDFLD(&KEY)

along the top or command line and press the ENTER key. CECI syntax checks and displays the command, with a message indicating that pressing ENTER executes the command. After the command is executed, the response from the command is displayed on the lower part of the screen. If the response is normal, we are ready to begin retrieving records. Returning the cursor to the command line, enter:

READNEXT DATASET (ddname) RIDFLD (&KEY) INTO (&REC)

By continuing to press the ENTER key, we are able to browse through the file and ascertain the information needed to create the test log. The browse is ended by entering:

ENDBR DATASET (ddname)

on the command line. After ending the browse, we can exit from CECI. To end the CECI session, it is necessary to press PF3/PF15 and then the CLEAR key. When the session terminates, the variables are deleted.

Having developed a script for all of the conditions to be tested, we are now ready to begin testing the program online. Before entering a test TRANSID, however, we want to be certain that the latest version of the program is the one we are testing. If CICS was brought up after the module was compiled and linked, then CICS has the latest version. **However, if the compilation took place after CICS was initialized, we need to use CEMT to obtain the latest copy of the program.** This can be accomplished by entering:

CEMT SET PR(program-name) NEW

In order to exit from CEMT, it is necessary to press PF3/PF15 and then the CLEAR key. We can now proceed to enter the transactions listed in the test script and record the results of each entry.

There is another CICS system transaction that is very useful in debugging command level programs—CEDF. CEDF is the CICS Execute Diagnostic Facility, and it is exactly what it sounds like, an invaluable debugging aid. It is also extremely easy to use. As a matter of fact, the only problem with CEDF is that it takes the adventure out of debugging because it is so effective and easy to use. There are other CICS debugging packages that are more powerful in some ways, but with a little practice CEDF can be used to debug most programs. Also, CEDF comes as part of CICS.

All you do to use CEDF is to enter CEDF into the terminal and press the ENTER key. CEDF responds that the terminal is in EDF mode. Clear the screen and enter your TRANSID and any optional data. CEDF halts program execution at key points, including task initiation and command execution. For each CICS command there is a stop taken before and after execution. PF5/PF15 can be used to display the contents of Working Storage subsequent to task initiation. Data in Working Storage can be modified, and execution continued. At each break point involving a command, the command is displayed. Literal values within commands can be overwritten, so some coding errors can be temporarily patched before a command is executed. After command execution, the response code is displayed. By pressing ENTER after a stop is taken, task execution is continued. In this manner one can interactively trace the command processing through an application program as it executes. At task termination, after a program executes a RETURN with or without TRANSID, CEDF displays a message asking if you wish to continue the use of EDF beyond the task. This message is positioned in the lower right portion of the screen, and the default response "NO" is provided. If testing a pseudoconversational transaction, you must replace "NO" with "YES" so that EDF will take stops in the next task.

CEDF is the good news. Now comes the bad news. When first testing an online module, it is very common to encounter task abends. Task abends can occur for a variety of reasons, including program errors that result in a program check, unusual conditions happening during command execution, and various other things. In our meanderings through CICS debugging we will discuss the various abend codes; for now let's examine how CICS traps program checks and task abends.

11.2 CAPTURING ONLINE ERRORS

During CICS system initialization processing, error capture macros are issued. The System Recovery Program (DFHSRP) is named as an exit address for error capture. As a result, any abnormal task terminations that occur during CICS processing are intercepted (and potentially processed) by the System Recovery Program. The operating system is invoked when a CICS task abends. The operating system then passes control to DFHSRP, which attempts recovery action.

In order to take recovery action, DFHSRP must first understand the type of error that has occurred. To this end, the System Recovery Program recognizes three categories of errors: errors within an application task, storage violation errors, and errors that occur during the execution of a CICS system subtask. The System Recovery Program responds to each of these three types of errors in a different manner.

11.2.1 Application Task Errors

The case of the application task error is the simplest one to handle, since the offending task can be purged. The application task is not, after all, an integral part of CICS, and purging it does not affect the viability of the system as a whole. Therefore, DFHSRP recovers from application task failures by purging the abending task and requesting that an abend dump be written to the Dump Data Set. A message is also sent to the appropriate terminal informing the operator of the task abend. Application program failures are indicated by an abnormal termination code of ASRA. ASRA signals a program check, such as a data exception (0C7), an addressing exception (0C5), an operation exception (0C1), or a protection exception (0C4). Common causes of online program checks are uninitialized program fields, improper use of BLL cells, or overrun subscripts.

11.2.2 Storage Violation Errors

The storage within the CICS region is allocated on an as needed basis to each task that executes under CICS. When a task completes processing and RETURNs control to CICS, CICS releases the storage allocated to the task. Task storage is returned to the dynamic storage area so that the storage may be used by future tasks. It is necessary that CICS keep track of all of the storage that is allocated to the various tasks within the region on a task-by-task basis. In order to do this, Storage Control creates storage accounting areas or address chains between the separate storage allocations given to each task. The head of a task's storage chain can be found in the Task Control Area. Additionally, free storage areas within the CICS region are frequently kept on Free Area Queue Element (FAQE) chains. A FAQE indicates a free piece of storage. The Storage Accounting Area and Free Area Queue Element are control areas that are important in maintaining accounting of storage by Storage Control. If one of these control areas is corrupted, CICS recognizes a storage violation.

When a storage violation is detected, storage recovery is attempted. Free areas have forward pointers to the next free area and backward pointers to the previous free area. One of the things that CICS can do is attempt to follow such chains from both directions, and in this way isolate and recover overlayed information. User storage or storage given to an application task has duplicate storage accounting areas at the beginning and end of a storage allocation. Because the information is duplicated, it is possible to verify Storage Control operations. If Storage Recovery can recover lost information, or at least contain the extent of the damage, the CICS region does not terminate. However, if storage recovery cannot be accomplished, the online system terminates in a crash.

During application program testing, this type of system termination is not uncommon. A storage violation of this sort normally results from improper use of a BLL cell, oversubscripting a memory table, or overrunning a storage area. If the program is using the Linkage Section, it is a good idea to review where and how you are gaining addressability to referenced data areas. Remember, you must first get addressability to a real piece of storage before you can start moving data to fields defined in the Linkage Section. If the program is building a memory table, be certain that you are handling the index or subscript properly. If the program is utilizing the GETMAIN command to acquire dynamic storage, verify that the length requested in the command is actually the number of bytes that you are using.

11.2.3 System Task Abend

The most serious online error is an abend that occurs in a CICS system subtask. Each task in the CICS system, be it an application task or a system subtask, is represented to CICS via a Task Control Area. The TCA is the functional equivalent of the OS Task Control Block (TCB), and as such it is used by CICS to control task execution. A task in CICS is said to execute under a TCA. This means that the TCA internally represents an executing entity to CICS. When an application task is executing, the application Task Control Area is considered the executing entity, and any programs that process on behalf of the task run or execute under that TCA. This is true even if the application task passes control to a CICS management module for a CICS service. If, for example, the File Control Program is invoked to provide access to a file record, File Control runs under the application TCA.

There are, however, system functions that are done in support of the entire CICS system. These system functions are done on behalf of all tasks, and not to provide a single application task with a resource or other service. For example, Task Control is the effective supervisor of the CICS region. As such, Task Control runs as a CICS dispatcher and performs the task switches that comprise multitasking. When Task Control runs as the CICS dispatcher, it runs under its own Task Control Area. This system subtask—the dispatcher—is an integral part of CICS. Without the dispatcher to perform task switches, there would be no CICS system. There are three CICS functions that run as system subtasks: *dynamic multitasking, terminal network management,* and *journal management.* As pointed out above, an application task (TCA) that fails can be purged from the system. However, a system task (TCA) failure indicates the inability of CICS to continue online processing. Therefore, a failure or abend that occurs in a system subtask brings down the entire CICS region. An error of this sort is usually caused by an application program error that overlayed a CICS internal work area. The most likely causes include those discussed under storage violations. Sometimes application programmers are unwilling to believe that they could actually do something so significant as to crash the system, and they waste a great deal of time trying to implicate CICS itself. If your installation has recently gone to a new release of CICS, it is certainly possible that the software is at fault. However, this would really be the exceptional case. The best policy is to take a good look at the application program and verify the use of BLL cells and the Linkage Section.

The first time you bring the system down, it seems very embarrassing. Very frequently, several people are attempting to test CICS programs concurrently, so the fact that the system crashes is a sort of communal affair. However, it might be worthwhile to reflect upon the fact that not everyone can kill CICS. It takes genius, albeit misguided genius, to make an error that is serious enough to cause a crash. Therefore, one might take a kind of perverse pride in bringing CICS to its knees, rather than assuming a defeatist attitude and being afraid to continue testing.

11.3 COMMON CICS ABEND CODES

When the processing of a task results in an error condition the task is abended, and a unique abend error code is typically provided by CICS. The abend code is recorded in three places. First, an abend message is written to the terminal associated with the task. Second, an abend message containing task information is written to a CICS queue so that a record of the abend can be recorded in the CICS statistics printed when the system is shut down. Third, the abend code is included in a transaction dump that is written to the Dump Data Set. The Dump Data Set is a disk data set provided for the purpose of recording abend dumps. Dumps can be printed using a CICS batch program provided for this purpose. The name of this module is the *Dump Utility Program* (DFHDUP).

There are two major categories of abend codes: those that are applicable to Command Level tasks only, and those that are general CICS abend codes. The ones that are applicable for Command Level are a result of Execute Interface Processing, and normally result from unusual conditions that occur during command execution. These abends can be avoided by using the HANDLE or IGNORE CONDITION statements, or otherwise trapping unusual conditions. The general CICS abend codes are provided by the various management facilities beyond the Execute Interface. First we will discuss the more general CICS abend codes and relate these to program errors, and then we'll deal with the Execute Interface abend codes.

There are numerous abend codes used by the various CICS facilities. However, contained in the abend code is an indicator of the facility requesting the abend. The first character of all CICS abend codes is the letter "A." The second two characters represent the facility detecting the task's problem. For example, abends requested by Task Control begin with the three characters "AKC," Storage Control abends begin with "ASC," and System Recovery abends being with "ASR." In our discussion we are going to examine only the abend codes which occur most frequently during program testing and debugging, since an all-inclusive list would be extremely lengthy. However, a definitive list of abend codes and general

CICS messages can be found in the "CICS MESSAGES AND CODES" manual, which can be ordered from IBM.

11.3.1 ABMA

The ABMA abend is a BMS abend code indicating that a request to BMS specified a data length that is invalid. In the event of this abend, check the initialization of any length field used in a BMS request. Normally, the LENGTH option is omitted from SEND MAP commands because we want the entire symbolic map to be scanned for output and this is the default if LENGTH information is not provided. In the RECEIVE MAP, the LENGTH option is permitted only in conjunction with the FROM option naming a storage area containing a terminal-oriented data stream to be mapped.

There are several things to look for whenever an invalid length is the cause of an abend. First, make sure that the length field itself is properly defined. Unless the FLENGTH option is used, all length fields are 2-byte binary fields. In COBOL this would be coded as a PIC S9(4) COMP field. If the length field is defined as PIC 99, for example, this may well be the problem. If we move 16 to a 2-byte binary field, the actual value contained in storage is X"0010". On the other hand, if 16 were moved to a PIC 99 field, the field's contents would be X"F1F6". That's quite a difference. The second thing to check is that either the field is initialized with a VALUE clause, or you are moving a correct value to the field prior to command execution.

11.3.2 ABMB

The ABMB occurs if a BMS output operation requests that the cursor be positioned beyond the actual size capacity of the terminal. This abend can generally be avoided by using symbolic cursor positioning as opposed to specifying a hard-coded value.

11.3.3 ABMI

This abend indicates that a RECEIVE MAP names a mapset defined as an output only map (MODE=OUT in the DFHMSD macro). If you want to use the map for input operations, change the MODE parameter to INOUT.

11.3.4 ABMO

This abend is the reverse of ABMI. In this case, a SEND MAP names a mapset defined solely as an input map (MODE=IN). Proceed as for ABMI.

11.3.5 ABM0

ABM0 indicates that a map named in a BMS mapping request is not contained in the named mapset. Check to ensure that the map name is the name of the DFHMDI macro. This abend normally indicates a spelling error in the specification of the MAP option of a command.

11.3.6 AFCA

This abend indicates that a file operation was requested but the file is disabled. This is not usually a coding error, although a misspelled file name could erroneously reference a disabled data set. However, the likelihood of this happening is very small. The master terminal transaction CEMT can be used to inquire about the file in question, and possibly enable it. Just enter: CEMT I DA(ddname). CEMT then displays a line of file information including the file's status with regard to being open/closed and enabled/disabled. To attempt to change the status of the file, overtype the appropriate indicator. For example, if the file is listed as DIS (meaning that it is disabled), overtype this with ENA (for enabled). The condition DISABLED can also be handled to capture a disabled file condition.

11.3.7 AICA

This is the runaway task abend in CICS. In an earlier chapter we discussed the fact that the task dispatcher sets a time limit called the runaway task interval before it dispatches a task. This limits the amount of time that the task can process without returning back to CICS with a request that permits CICS to perform a task switch. A single task may be dispatched many times, but each separate dispatch is of limited duration. This is intended to capture and purge a looping task. Normally, the AICA means that there is a program loop between CICS service requests. However, this is not always the case. The task could be doing a very process-bound function (such as a bubble sort) and thereby overrun the CICS runaway interval. To cure the problem, use a SUSPEND command in the application program to periodically pass control back to CICS. If the program is not performing a process-bound function, use CEDF to trace the execution path and narrow down the area containing the loop.

Not all task loops are trapped by the runaway interval. If, for example, a program loop includes a call to CICS which allows a task switch, the looping task does not time out. Many CICS commands result in a return to CICS and an ensuing task switch. A task in this type of loop never times out, because every time the program is reentered it is with a refreshed runaway task interval. The symptom of this is that you enter the TRANSID and get no response; the terminal just remains locked. At this point our old friend CEMT can be used again. Proceed to another terminal and enter CEMT I TAS to inquire about the tasks in the system. If your task is listed, position the cursor after the task's information and type PUR for purge. Occasionally this has to be done two or three times. After purging the task, use CEDF to trace command execution to determine the location of the loop.

If your transaction is not listed in the task list displayed by CEMT, this indicates another problem. Video terminals are defined to CICS as being conversational devices. This means that the operator enters data, there is an output response from CICS, and then the operator is permitted to enter again. Chances are that the program did not SEND or SEND MAP to the terminal. Just press the RESET key and use CEDF to verify program command execution.

11.3.8 AKCP

AKCP indicates that the task has been purged during a system stall. CICS keeps track of how long it has been since an application task has processed, and after a stall limit it recognizes that the system is going nowhere. This is usually caused by the system being short of storage or tasks being deadlocked. At any rate, there are a lot of waiting tasks in the system tying up resources. In an attempt to end the system deadlock, CICS performs triage and purges tasks that are defined as stall purgeable. Normally this does not indicate an application program error per se, but if task deadlocks are the cause, there may be a dark cloud hanging over your application. If the AKCP occurs once in a while, you don't have to get out the umbrella, but if it occurs frequently during testing perhaps resource utilization within and across application programs being tested ought to be reviewed. The systems programming staff can aid in the effort to ascertain the identity of deadlocked resources. A full system dump taken when the stall occurs reveals which tasks were in the system and what resources caused task deadlock.

11.3.9 AKCS

AKCS indicates a deadlock timeout purge. This means that the task was waiting for a CICS controlled resource for an amount of time defined as the deadlock timeout. This value is specified in the Program Control Table entry of each TRANSID to which it pertains. This abend does not indicate a program bug per se, but some deadlock situations can be prevented by programming standards. If all programs that use common resources do so in a prescribed sequence, the incidence of task deadlocks is dramatically reduced.

11.3.10 APCN

This abend indicates that the resident use count of a module in the Processing Program Table is already zero and an attempt has been made to decrement the count. The resident use count indicates the number of tasks currently using a module. When CICS starts a task to execute in a module, it increments the resident use count so that the program cannot be released from storage while in use. When a task completes using a module, CICS decrements the resident use count to reflect that there is one less task utilizing it. The resident use count can also be decremented by the Program Control RELEASE command. APCN may reflect a program executing too many RELEASE commands, perhaps because of a loop.

11.3.11 APCT

This abend indicates one of two possible problems has occurred: (1) a called for module is not defined in the Processing Program Table, or (2) the program's entry is disabled. Enter CEMT I PR(name) to ascertain which case has occurred. Either the module cannot be located, or its entry is displayed with the DIS characteristic. If the module is disabled, just overtype DIS with ENA and the module can be enabled. A module can become disabled if its resident use count is greater than zero (meaning that it is in use) and a request is made for a new copy [CEMT SET PR(name) NEW]. The resident use count must be zero before a new copy can be obtained. **If the resident use count is greater than zero, enable the program with CEMT and then use CECI to RELEASE the program.** When the resident use count is equal to zero, CEMT cooperates with NEW requests.

The most common cause of APCT is misspelling. A LINK or XCTL may have a misspelled PROGRAM name or, more commonly, a BMS SEND or RECEIVE MAP has a misspelled MAPSET name. Remember that the physical map is a load module defined as such to CICS in the Processing Program Table. The MAPSET option provides the load module name.

11.3.12 ASCF

ASCF indicates an invalid FREEMAIN request. Each piece of dynamically acquired storage has a storage accounting area. CICS does not trust application programs to provide a length specification in a FREEMAIN request. Rather, it consults the storage accounting area and determines how much storage is to be freed. Therefore, as part of FREEMAIN processing, Storage Control looks at the storage accounting area. This abend indicates that the area specified to be freed does not contain a recognizable storage accounting area. Check any FREEMAINs used in the program, and verify that the task has valid addressability to the FREEMAIN area.

11.3.13 ASCR

This abend indicates an invalid storage GETMAIN request. This normally occurs because of an invalid LENGTH specification in a GETMAIN command. Check the length field to be certain that it contains a value greater than zero and that the field is defined properly as a binary field.

11.3.14 ASRA

ASRA is a trusty (although not always welcome) companion of the CICS programmer. This abend indicates that a program check has occurred. In order to ascertain the type of abend (0C7, 0C4, etc.) and the general location, test the program with CEDF. The most common causes of ASRA are invalid or uninitialized data fields and improper use of the Linkage Section.

11.4 EXECUTE INTERFACE ABENDS

Most of the unusual conditions associated with CICS commands have unique 4-character abend codes that will ensue if the condition occurs during processing and is left to default. Since these conditions have been discussed in the context of various commands, we will not go over them again in this chapter. However, a list of abend codes and the related conditions can be found in Appendix B. One condition (MAPFAIL, which results in an abend of AEI9) is discussed below.

11.4.1 AEI9

If a BMS map is sent to the screen with all modified data tags (MDTs) off (as would be the normal case for the first output from a transaction) and the operator fails to enter data before pressing a device interrupt key, then there are no data to be sent back to CICS. The terminal sends back the identity of the device interrupt key, but no data fields. In this case BMS raises the MAPFAIL condition and, if left to default, the AEI9 abend occurs. It is normally desirable to prevent this abend because the user may have mistakenly hit the device interrupt key. Time has already been spent invoking the transaction, and to allow it to terminate would force a user who meant to enter data to begin the transaction again. Therefore, we would normally HANDLE or IGNORE the condition MAPFAIL. In the MAPFAIL error routine, we might send a message requesting that the user enter data or cancel the transaction and then RETURN with TRANSID.

11.4.2 Conclusion

With a little patience and practice, you will find it quite easy to debug CICS programs. Just remember that, after you find a bug and recompile the program, it is necessary to use CEMT to get the latest version into CICS.

11.5 OTHER DEBUGGING FACILITIES

With the use of CEDF or other interactive debugging aids, most program bugs can be found without utilizing the other debugging aids that come with CICS. However, occasionally it is necessary to use either the Trace Control or Dump Control facilities to troubleshoot a program or system problem. Therefore, we will briefly discuss the use of these facilities.

11.6 TRACE CONTROL FACILITY

CICS Trace Control is a debugging aid that permits system and program trace information to be saved in a main storage trace table and an auxiliary storage trace data set (the Aux Trace data set). The memory trace table is used to save trace information regarding the processing of all tasks within the CICS system. The size or number of entries in the trace table is defined by the systems programmer in the System Initialization Table (SIT). Even if a large trace table is defined, it is finite. When all of the entries in the trace table have been utilized, wrap around occurs and older trace information is replaced with new trace data.

Trace information is often utilized to debug problems that occur because of the task mix within CICS or the interaction of two or more tasks. In the debugging of these types of problems, we generally need to see what has been happening during the execution of multiple tasks. Trace table wrap around may therefore overlay needed information. To this end, the Aux Trace data set can be used to collect trace information over a longer period of time. The use of Aux Trace means that trace data is saved both in the memory trace table and in the Aux Trace data set. Since there is a fair amount of overhead involved with writing trace information to Aux Trace, we want to be fairly selective about when and for how long auxiliary tracing is done. Auxiliary tracing is initiated by using the master terminal transaction CEMT to turn on Aux Trace. We then perform the testing for which traces are to be collected. After the test is concluded, the master terminal transaction can be used to turn off Aux Trace and close the trace data set. The contents of Aux Trace can be printed using the Trace Utility Program (DFHTUP).

11.6.1 The Memory Trace Table

The trace table is pointed to by the main CICS system control block, the Common System Area (CSA). The CSA field CSATRTBA contains the address of a trace table header. The trace table header contains the address of the last used trace table entry and the beginning and ending address of the entire table. Thus, the first 12 bytes of the trace table header are in the format delineated here:

Trace Table Header—Pointed to by CSATRTBA		
Bytes 0-3	Bytes 4-7	Bytes 8-11
Address of the Last Used Entry	Address of the Beginning of the Trace Table	Address of the End of the Trace Table

To make sense of trace information, it is necessary to understand a couple of things. Trace entries are created on a system basis, so entries for all executing tasks are interleaved. Therefore, in examining trace information it is necessary to look for entries that pertain to the task or tasks of concern. Each task that enters the CICS system is given a unique task number. This unique identifier is saved in each trace entry.

Trace information is contained in each CICS transaction abend dump in an interpreted format. A sample of trace information contained in a transaction dump is provided in Fig. 11-2. As you can see, the task number is provided for each horizontal entry under the heading Task. Also, under the area labeled Trace Type there is a description of which CICS module created the trace and the service that was being processed. When examining trace information in a transaction dump, first ascertain the task number(s) of interest. Then, start at the end of the table and trace backwards to determine what has happened.

A little earlier we discussed the fact that an application task error could crash the CICS system. Suppose that several programs are being tested when the system crashes. In this case, a CICS system dump is normally produced, and the trace table is included. In order to determine what caused the abend, examine the trace table information. In this case, it is necessary to locate the trace table and interpret the information contained therein. Locating the table is fairly easy, as the Common System Area address is contained in register 13 of the dump. Just go through the Register Save Areas provided in the beginning of the listing until you locate one that has register 13 pointing to the CSA. The CSA is recognizable in storage because IBM copyright information precedes it. Also, the constant "WORKAREA" is contained within the CSA. The field CSATRTBA is located at X"11C" from the beginning of the CSA. Using the information contained in the trace table header, it is possible to mark off the last used entry and the beginning and end of the table. Then you scan backward to see who was executing and what they were doing. The general format of trace entries is contained in Fig. 11–3.

As an alternative, you could bring CICS back up again, turn on Aux Trace, recreate the system crash, and print the information contained

Figure 11-2. Sample trace table listing.

TIME OF DAY	ID	REG 14	REQD	TASK	FIELD A	FIELD B	CHARS	RESOURCE	TRACE TYPE
16:48:18.161728	EA	40568576	0003	02211	01000100	00091228	....	CEDF	TMP PCT LOCATE
16:48:18.161792	EA	405388B8	0005	02211	01000100	004F4B08	....		TMP RETN NORMAL
16:48:18.161824	F1	40568812	EA04	02211	00000C48	010934F4	4		SCP GETMAIN CONDITIONAL INITIMG
16:48:18.162112	C8	50523866	0004	02211	00099000	8A040C48	....		SCP ACQUIRED TCA STORAGE
16:48:18.162240	D0	5056965C	0604	02220	00000000	C3C5C4C6	....CEDF		KCP CREATE
16:48:18.162336	EA	40568CA2	0003	02211	0C000100	004F4B08	....	CEDF	TMP PCT TRANSFER
16:48:18.162400	EA	405388B8	0005	02211	0C000100	00000000	....		TMP RETN NORMAL
16:48:18.162496	F0	40238654	0404	02211	10000000	00000000	....		KCP SUSPEND NON-DISPATCHABLE
16:48:18.162528	D0	5056965C	0A04	02211	00000000	00000000	....		KCP SUSPEND
16:48:18.162656	D0	5056AD06	0504	02220	00000000	00000000	....		KCP DISPATCH
16:48:18.162688	FC	055595E0	0503	02220	00200001	000934F4	4		ZCP ZSUP START UP TASK
16:48:18.162752	E5	50559754	0C03	02220	00099738	00000000	....	CEDF	XSP SECURITY CHECK
16:48:18.162816	E5	40560322	0005	02220	00000000	00000000	....		XSP SECURITY RETN

```
16:48:18.162848  E7 0055A7EC 0004 02220 00000000 00000000 ........           ERM ENTRY
16:48:18.162880  E7 0055A7EC 0004 02220 00000000 000000FF ........           ERM RESPONSE
16:48:18.162912  F2 4055A864 8804 02220 00000000 00000000 ........  DFHEDFP  PCP XCTL-CONDITIONAL
16:48:18.162944  EA 404EEF8A 0003 02220 01000300 00099214 ........  DFHEDFP  TMP PPT LOCATE
16:48:18.163008  EA 405388B8 0005 02220 01000300 004BD480 ......M.           TMP RETN NORMAL
16:48:18.163072  E5 5023B0FE 0C03 02220 0009976C 00000000 ........  CEDF     XSP SECURITY CHECK
16:48:18.163104  E5 40560322 0025 02220 00000000 00000000 ........           XSP SECURITY RETN
16:48:18.163136  E5 5023B14C 0C03 02220 0009976C 00000000 ........  A02H     XSP SECURITY CHECK
16:48:18.163168  E5 40560322 0025 02220 00000000 00000000 ........           XSP SECURITY RETN
16:48:18.163232  F2 4023B270 0104 02220 00000000 00000000 ........  DFHEDFD  PCP LINK
16:48:18.163264  EA 404EEF8A 0003 02220 01000300 00099214 ........  DFHEDFD  TMP PPT LOCATE
16:48:18.163296  EA 405388B8 0005 02220 01000300 004BD4D0 ......M.           TMP RETN NORMAL
16:48:18.163328  F1 404EEB86 8904 02220 00000050 010934F4 ...E...4           SCP GETMAIN
16:48:18.163392  C8 50523866 0004 02220 00099C50 89000058 ...E....           SCP ACQUIRED RSA STORAGE
16:48:18.163456  F1 8056BEEE CC04 02220 00001CCC 010934F4 .......4           SCP GETMAIN INITIMG
```

291

Trace Table Entry	
Byte 0	Trace ID that indicates the facility causing the trace entry
Bytes 1–2	Type of request field
Bytes 3–4	Reserved
Bytes 5–7	Unique task number that is used to isolate task-unique trace entries
Bytes 8–15	Additional facility dependent information
Bytes 16–23	Resource name
Bytes 24–27	Contents of register 14, which is the return address of caller
Bytes 28–31	Time of day

Figure 11-3.   General format of Trace Table Entry.

in the Aux Trace data set. As mentioned above, the Trace Utility Program can be used to print the contents of the Aux Trace data set. Figure 11–4 illustrates the JCL used to run the Trace Utility Program. The STEPLIB names the CICS module load library containing DFHTUP. The DFHAUXTR DD statement names the trace data set to be printed. If you do not know the DSNAME of this data set, the CICS execution JCL procedure should be examined to see the DSNAME of the DD statement named DFHAUXTR. The DFHAXPRT DD provides the SYSOUT class for the listed output. DFHAXPRM provides information about the type of listing desired. This is a PARM data set that defines criteria for selecting trace entries to be printed. One or more PARM statements can be placed in the DFHAXPRM data set.

```
//CSTZC01A    JOB  1724,ARLENE,CLASS=N,MSGCLASS=A
//STEP1       EXEC PGM=DFHTUP
//STEPLIB     DD   DSN=CICSV17.LOADLIB1,DISP=SHR
//DFHAUXTR    DD   DSN=CICSV17.TEST.TRACE,DISP=SHR
//DFHAXPRT    DD   SYSOUT=A
//DFHAXPRM    DD   *
    ALL
    TERMID=(T001,T002,T003)
    TRANID=(A01A,A01B)
    TIMERG-(072200,080000)
    TYPETR=(000,255)     SPECIFIED IN DECIMAL
    TYPETR=(00,FF)       SPECIFIED IN HEXADECIMAL
/*
//
```

Figure 11-4.   JCL to run the Trace Utility Program.

The parameter ALL requests the printing of all entries. TERMID can be used to name one or more terminals for which trace entries are to be printed. TRANID can name one or more transaction identifiers, TIMERG can request traces within a given time range, and TYPETR can specify only certain types of traces. Therefore, if we know what information interests us, we can print only that data. Otherwise, we can print the entire data set. A sample of the printed output from DFHTUP is shown in Fig. 11-5.

In addition to system trace information, the ENTER command can be used to create a user trace entry. The format of the ENTER command is:

```
EXEC CICS ENTER
            TRACEID     (id)
            FROM        (area-name)
            RESOURCE    (name)
```

The TRACEID option defines a unique trace ID for the trace table entry. This is a 2-byte binary value in the range of 0 to 199 (so that there is no conflict with trace IDs used by CICS modules).

The FROM option names a data area containing 8 bytes of information to be placed into the trace entry. This information occupies bytes 8 to 15 of the trace entry, as indicated in Figure 11-3.

The RESOURCE option provides an 8-byte resource name to be included in bytes 16 to 23 of the trace entry.

11.7 DUMP CONTROL FACILITY

The Dump Control facility processes dump requests from application programs or system modules. If an invalid storage request is received by Storage Control, it requests a task abend with an ensuing dump (ASCR); if the System Recovery Program intercepts a program check, it requests a task termination with a dump (ASRA). Storage dumps are written to a sequential data set called the Dump Data Set. Most installations use two Dump Data Sets named DFHDMPA and DFHDMPB in the CICS execution JCL. These two data sets can be used alternately (if one becomes full, the alternate can be used). The Dump Utility Program can be used to print the contents of the dump data set, but the data set to be printed must not be active at the time. Thus, if the Dump Data Set has to be printed during CICS execution, it is possible to switch to the alternate. Switches can be accomplished using the master terminal transaction CEMT. CICS calls one data set Dump "A" and the other Dump "B." In response to a request to switch data sets, CICS issues a response defining which data set is currently active.

An application program may initiate a transaction dump by using either the Program Control ABEND command or the Dump Control

Figure 11-5. Sample output from the Aux Trace data set.

TIME OF DAY	ID	REG 14	REQD	TASK	FIELD A	FIELD B	CHARS	RESOURCE	TRACE TYPE
16:47:32.054208	EA	405388B8	0005	02178	01000300	004BD4A8	·:··		TMP RETN NORMAL.
16:47:32.054240	F1	404EEB86	8904	02178	00090050	010934F4	·ε·4		SCP GETMAIN
16:47:32.054304	C8	50523866	0005	02178	00091C30	89090058	···4		SCP ACQUIRED RSA STORAGE
16:47:32.054368	FC	502380AC	0103	02178	00040000	010934F4	···4		ZCP ZARQ APPL REQ WAIT
16:47:32.054464	F0	505573CC	4004	02178	00000000	00000000	····		KCP WAIT DCI=DISP
16:47:32.054528	D0	5056AD06	0504	02178	00000000	00000000	····		KCP DISPATCH
16:47:32.054592	FC	502380C0	2804	02178	00000000	00000000	····		ZCP RETN ZARQ APPL REQ
16:47:32.054656	F0	405680BA	0003	02178	01000100	00091228	····		KCP LOCATE
16:47:32.054720	EA	405388B8	0003	02178	01000100	004F4B08	····	CEDF	TMP PCT LOCATE
16:47:32.054752	EA	402380FC	1204	02178	01000100	C3C5C4C6	·CEDF	CEDF	TMP RETN NORMAL.
16:47:32.054784	F0	402380FC	0003	02178	01000100	00091228	····		KCP ATTACH
16:47:32.054816	EA	405388B8	0005	02178	01000100	004F4B08	····	CEDF	TMP PCT LOCATE
16:47:32.054848	EA	40568576	0003	02178	01000100	010934F4	·CEDF	CEDF	TMP RETN NORMAL.
16:47:32.055168	F1	40568812	EA04	02178	00000C48	00000C48	···4		SCP GETMAIN CONDITIONAL INITIMG
16:47:32.055328	C8	50523866	0604	02178	00099000	8A040C44	····		SCP ACQUIRED TCA STORAGE
16:47:32.055424	D0	5056965C	0604	02178	0C000100	C3C5C4C6	·CEDF	CEDF	KCP CREATE
16:47:32.055584	EA	40568CA2	0003	02178	0C000100	004F4B08	····		TMP PCT TRANSFER
16:47:32.055616	F0	40238654	0404	02178	10000000	00000000	····		TMP RETN NORMAL.
16:47:32.055744	D0	5056965C	0A04	02201	00000000	00000000	····		KCP SUSPEND NON-DISPATCHABLE
16:47:32.055772	EA	5056AD06	0504	02201	00000000	00000000	····		KCP SUSPEND
16:47:32.055872	FC	505595E0	0503	02201	00000001	00000001	····		KCP DISPATCH
16:47:32.055904	E5	50559754	0005	02201	00099738	00099738	···4	CEDF	ZCP ZSUP START UP TASK
16:47:32.055968	E5	40560322	0005	02201	00000000	00000000	····		XSP SECURITY CHECK
16:47:32.056000	E7	0055A7EC	0004	02201	00000000	00000000	····		XSP SECURITY RETN
16:47:32.056096	E7	0055A7EC	0004	02201	00000000	0000000F	····		ERM ENTRY
16:47:32.056160	F2	4055A864	8804	02201	00000300	00000000	····		ERM RESPONSE
16:47:32.056192	EA	404EEF8A	8003	02201	01000300	00099214	····	DFHEDFP	PCP XCTL-CONDITIONAL
16:47:32.056256	E5	405388B8	0005	02201	01000300	004BD480	····	DFHEDFP	TMP PPT-LOCATE
16:47:32.057088	E5	5023B0FE	0CO3	02201	0009776C	00000000	···M		TMP RETN NORMAL.
16:47:32.057376	E5	40560322	0025	02201	00000000	00000000	····	CEDF	XSP SECURITY CHECK
16:47:32.057440	E5	5023B14C	0C03	02201	0009776C	00000000	····		XSP SECURITY RETN
16:47:32.057536	F2	40560322	0104	02201	00000000	00000000	····		XSP SECURITY CHECK
16:47:32.057568	EA	4023B270	0003	02201	01000300	00000000	····		XSP SECURITY RETN
16:47:32.057632	F1	405388B8	0005	02201	01000300	00099214	····	A02H	PCP LINK
16:47:32.057728	C8	404EEF8A	8904	02201	00090050	04BD4D0	···M	DFHEDFD	TMP PPT LOCATE
16:47:32.058112	F1	405388B8	CC04	02201	00001CCC	010934F4	·ε·4	DFHEDFD	TMP RETN NORMAL.
16:47:32.058240	C8	50523866	0004	02201	00001CD8	010934F4	···4		SCP GETMAIN
16:47:32.058272	E1	8056BEEE	2024	02201	0009B010	89000058	···Q		SCP ACQUIRED RSA STORAGE
16:47:32.058336	F2	8022A13A	0004	02201	8022AD14	8C001CD8	····		SCP GETMAIN INITIMG
16:47:32.058368	E1	8056CC3E	00F4	02201	0009B010	00000E0E	····		SCP ACQUIRED USER STORAGE
16:47:32.058400	E1	8022A158	0004	02201	0009B010	00000E0E	····		EIP HANDLE-ABEND ENTRY
16:47:32.058432	E1	8022A158	00F4	02201	0009B010	00000202	····		PCP SETXIT,ROUTINE
16:47:32.058464	E1	8022A176	0004	02201	0009B010	00000202	····		EIP HANDLE-ABEND RESPONSE
16:47:32.058560	E1	8022A1AA	0004	02201	0009B010	00000208	····		EIP ADDRESS ENTRY
16:47:32.058592	E1	8022A1E4	0004	02201	0009B010	00000208	····		EIP ADDRESS RESPONSE

DUMP command. The ABEND command terminates the task, whereas the DUMP command produces a storage dump and allows the task to continue execution. The format of an ABEND dump is fixed, while the DUMP command has options regarding what is to be recorded. The ABEND command was examined in the chapter dealing with Program Control commands. The format of the DUMP command is as follows:

```
EXEC CICS DUMP
          DUMPCODE (code)
          FROM       (area-name)
          LENGTH     (size)  or  FLENGTH (size)
          TASK
          STORAGE
          PROGRAM
          TERMINAL
          TABLES
          PCT
          PPT
          FCT
          SIT
          TCT
          DCT
          COMPLETE
```

DUMPCODE permits the specification of a unique dump code. This dump "name" is included in the dump, and is useful for keeping track of multiple dumps requested from several places in a program. The dump code is limited to four characters.

FROM names a user data area that is to be included in the storage dump. Additionally, the TCA/TWA, CSA/CWA, trace table, registers, and TCTTE are included.

LENGTH or FLENGTH define the length of the area specified in the FROM option. These options are mutually exclusive.

TASK, STORAGE, PROGRAM, TERMINAL, TABLES, and the specification of various CICS tables are optional parameters used to request that different areas be included in the storage dump. These options can be used in conjunction with each other in a single command. However, only one copy of any data area is dumped. Figure 11-6 illustrates the areas dumped using these options.

COMPLETE, as its name implies, requests a complete dump of all storage related to the requesting task as well as the system tables.

By default (i.e., if no options are specified in a DUMP command), the data areas associated with the TASK option are included. The only difference between TASK and the default is that the TASK option includes DL/I areas where applicable.

Dump Options

	TASK	STORAGE	PROGRAM	TERMINAL	TABLES	COMPLETE	PPT	PCT	TCT	FCT	SIT	DCT
TCA/TWA	Y	Y	Y	Y		Y						
CSA/CWA	Y	Y	Y	Y		Y						
PROGRAMS USED BY THE TASK	Y		Y			Y						
TRACE TABLE	Y	Y	Y	Y		Y						
REGISTER SAVE AREAS	Y		Y			Y						
TRANSACTION STORAGE	Y	Y				Y						
TCTTE OR DCT ENTRY	Y	Y	Y	Y		Y						
REGISTERS	Y	Y	Y	Y		Y						
TERMINAL INPUT/OUTPUT AREAS	Y			Y		Y						
PPT						Y	Y					
PCT						Y		Y				
DCT						Y						Y
FCT						Y				Y		
TCT						Y			Y			
SIT						Y					Y	

Y = yes, the area is included.

TCA/TWA = Task Control Area or the main control block used to control a task. The Transaction Work Area (TWA) is an optional user extension of the TCA. If the TWA is used, its size is defined in a transaction's Program Control Table (PCT) entry.

CSA/CWA = Common System Area or main control block of the entire CICS region. The Common Work Area (CWA) is an optional user extension of the CSA. If utilized, its size is defined in the System Initialization Table (SIT).

Register Save Area = data area used to save a program's registers, as when a LINK command is executed. This allows CICS to restore the registers and return to the next sequential instruction after the LINK in the linking program.

Transaction Storage = all of the separate pieces of storage allocated to the task and chained from the task's TCA storage chain.

Program Storage = storage containing application programs used by the task.

TCTTE = Terminal Control Table Terminal Entry for the terminal associated with the task. When this area is dumped, the TCTUA or terminal's user area is included.

TIOAs = all of the Terminal Input/Output Areas pointed to by the terminal's entry in the Terminal Control Table. This would encompass any terminal-associated input/output areas for the task.

PPT = Processing Program Table, which defines all programs.

PCT = Program Control Table in which all TRANSIDs must be defined.

FCT = File Control Table that contains a definition of the online files.

DCT = Destination Control Table defining Transient Data queues.

SIT = System Initialization Table defining system initialization and many of the control parameters that drive CICS processing.

TCT = Terminal Control Table defining CICS's terminal environment.

In OS systems, DL/I control areas are included when TASK or COMPLETE is specified.

Figure 11-6. Dump options.

11.7.1 Printing the Dump Data Set

Once a dump has been requested or a transaction abend has occurred, the next step is to obtain the storage dump by printing the contents of the Dump Data Set. A sample job stream to accomplish this is shown below:

```
//PRTDUMP   JOB  1725,ARLENE,CLASS=N,MSGCLASS=A
//STEP1     EXEC PGM=DFHDUP,PARM=DOUBLE
//STEPLIB   DD   DSN=CICS.LOADLIB1,DISP=SHR
//DFHDMPDS  DD   DSN=TEST.CICS.DUMPA,DISP=SHR
//DFHPRINT  DD   SYSOUT=A
```

PARM=DOUBLE indicates that the printout is to be double-spaced. STEPLIB DD names the CICS load library containing the Dump Utility Program. DFHDMPDS DD names the CICS Dump Data Set that is to be printed. The DSNAME of this data set can be obtained from the CICS execution JCL (DDNAMEs DFHDMPA or DFHDMPB). The output class is defined with the DFHPRINT DD statement. Note that there is no PARM data set defined for DFHDUP. There is, in fact, no mechanism for selectively printing certain dumps. This can be a bit cumbersome if the data set contains many dumps and only one is actually needed. In this case, switch data sets using the master terminal transaction and then cause the dump again. Then switch a second time and print the Dump Data Set with the single dump. There is one danger with this approach. When the second switch is performed, the former data set is opened for output and any dumps on it are lost. Therefore, one ought to ascertain that other CICS programmers do not need any of these dumps before performing this maneuver.

11.8 USING A TRANSACTION ABEND DUMP

Often the reason that a transaction dump is requested by CICS is most easily resolved by just looking up the CICS-provided ABEND code. In this case, however, the ASRA ABEND code tells us that there has been a program check, and knowing that this caused the abnormal termination does not shed a great deal of light on why the problem occurred. Most of the time program checks are best found interactively using CEDF or another debugging facility, although there are instances when being able to read a formatted transaction dump can be quite helpful. Basically it is important to know which instruction caused the program check and how to locate the data areas utilized by the task.

Figure 11-7 is the first page of a CICS transaction dump. The ABEND code is on the top line of the printout. As you can see, this is an ASRA dump. The TRANSID is right next to the ABEND code. The fourth line of the listing shows the contents of the Program Status Word

Figure 11-7. Beginning of CICS transaction dump.

```
CICSTST7      --- CICS TRANSACTION DUMP ---      CODE=ASRA      TASK=D31C                DATE=11/18/86      TIME=16:47:40

SYMPTOMS- AB/UASRA PIDS/5740XX100 FLDS/F000KC RIDS/DEBUG1C

CICS/VS LEVEL = 0170        1          2          3          4

PSW            078D0000   001F6AF8   00060007   00000000
REGS 14-4      504EE0B2   001F6E68   00060007   001F6AD2   001F6AE2   001F6728   0009B3DC
REGS 5-11      FF000000   0009C1EC   00000000   0009C7C3   0009C7C4   001F6DFC   001F6050   001F6050

TASK CONTROL AREA (USER AREA)              ADDRESS 0009B190 TO 0009C19F    LENGTH 00001010

00000000  0009B000 0047C8FC 01093934 0056EBC0 0009B5F0 0000644C 00000100 40310DA0  *................H..........0.*
00000020  504BB1DC 004B9DB0 00000000 0009CA38 0009B8F4 504BAFAA 00000050 004B4B48  *..............................4.*
00000040  404EDEB8 C1E2D9C1 00000000 004B4AC8 0009CB30 0009CA30 504EE0B2 0009CA30  *..+.ASRA.......H......-H..*
00000060  FE000000 C1D7D7C6 C9D3C540 00006000 004EEA70 047FCD00 0047FCD0 004EDA84  *....APPFILE ....+....+..*
00000080  504EE0B2 001F6E68 C1E2D9C1 001F6AD2 001F6AE2 001F6728 00000007 00000000  *+...>.ASRA.......+.ASRA..+.*
000000A0  504EE0B2 001F6E68 0009C7C3 0009C7C4 001F6050 001F6DFC FF090900 01090900  *+...>....GC..GD..-......K..S.*
000000C0  00000000 001F6AE2 00000000 24000000 00000000 06020000 00000000 00000000  *.....A...............*
000000E0  00000000 00000000 00000000 00000000 00000000 00000000 00000000 00000000  *....................*
00000100  00000000 00000000 00000000 00000000 00000000 00000000 00000000 00000000  *....................*
00000120  LINES TO  00000140  SAME AS ABOVE
00000160  00000000 00000028 0009B2F8 0009B5BC 0000025C 0009B328 0000025C C5C9C240  *................8...........*
00000180  0009B490 00000000 00000000 404040040 00093934 0009B3E0 02810000 028100000  *...............H....H....*
000001A0  0009B490 000C8000 004B4AC8 004B4AC8 00000000 00000000 00000000 00000000  *...........h...H...H.*
000001E0  0047C088 0009C8F0 A05CCCDE 904BCCFE 00000000 00000000 0009B4E8 00093934  *...h...HO..GM....H..*
00000200  00000000 0009A000 0D000000 A05CCCDE 904BCCFE 00000000 0009C1EC 00000004  *...........HO.GM....*
00000220  00000000 00000000 804BC7D4 0009C820 0009B490 0009B490 00000000 00000000  *...........G..H.........*
00000240  0047FCE8 0009C5BC 56B8FC 001F6050 0047FCE8 0009C5BC 0009C1B0 0009B328  *...Y.E.......Y.E...Y.-.E*
00000260  001F6098 004EFA60 0009B000 0056E7C0 0056B694 001F6882 004CBCB0 8009B3E0  *-q.+-......m..-...*
00000280  0009B190 00000000 00000000 00000000 00000000 0009C948 0009C948 00000000  *.....................I..I*
000002A0  0009B490 0009C7E8 C4F3F1C3 00022205C D5F0F7D4 FF000010 40C4C6C8 C5C9C240  *....GY.f.D31C.*N07M..*
000002C0  0164740C 0086322F D7D7C6C9 D3C54000 000000C1 D7D7C6C9 D7D7C6C9 D3C54000  *.f.D31C..APPFILE..APPF*
000002E0  000000C1 D7D7C6C9 D3C54000 00000000 00000000 00000000 00000000 00000000  *.APPFILE..APPF*
00000300  LINES TO  00000380  SAME AS ABOVE
000003E0  0005D8DC 00000001 00000000 00000000 00000000 00000000 00000000 00000000  *...Q...*
00000400  LINES TO  00000420  SAME AS ABOVE
00000440  42000068 00000000 FF09B658 004BCC12 0009C981 D3C9C6D6 E2E3D6D9 004B4B48  *...................Em..ia.E*
00000460  0009C948 0009C7DC 0009C594 0009CA30 004BC5D3 0009C7E8 0009C59C 004B4AC8  *...G...Em....*
00000480  0009B328 0009B190 0056E7C0 FE09B658 004BCD03 00568D04 004BC5E0 004B4AC8  *..I...0.KC.*
000004A0  00000000 48000020 FE09B5F4 F0000023 00568D04 00000000 004B9780 00000000  *.....0....*
000004E0  0009B804 504BB756 0009B756 0009B5F4 0009C594 004B9D80 004BADB0 004B7DD0  *.......Em.*
00000500  004BC5E0 00093934 0009B328 504BB756 0056E7C0 FE09B658 F500C6C3 A04B7F1C  *..E.....-.4.Em..X.*
00000520  01000000 00000000 904B7EC4 904B8844 B04B7EDC 904B7EEC A04B7F2C 00000000  *.........X..=D.=H..=..*
00000540  904B7F64 00000000 804B8844
```

(PSW). The PSW contains two important pieces of information, and consists of four full words of storage which have been marked off as 1, 2, 3, and 4. The second full word contains the address of the next sequential instruction which would have executed had the program check not occurred. This address is X"001F6AF8". The last byte of the third full word indicates the type of program check. This area, which is underlined in Fig. 11-7, contains X"07", indicating that the abend 0C7 or data exception has occurred. Following the PSW is a display of the general registers. Register 6, which is underlined, contains the address of the task's dynamic copy of Working Storage. This address is X"0009C1EC". Remember that the load module's Working Storage is not used as task storage. Therefore, if we want to locate the task's data areas, we must examine its dynamic copy of Working Storage. Following this is a listing of the Task Control Area. The TCA contains two separate areas. The user portion of the TCA displayed in Fig. 11-7 is used as a communications area between CICS modules executing on behalf of the task.

Figure 11-8 is the second page of the storage dump. The user part of the TCA is continued on this page. This is followed by the system TCA, which contains the important CICS task pointers and information. At a displacement of X"11" is the unique task number. This 3-byte field is underlined and contains X"02205C". Knowing the task number, we are able to select trace table information relevant to the task. Figure 11-9 is the third page of the dump. The first item in this figure is the Last In First Out stack of Task Control. LIFO stacks are used by CICS management facilities as register save areas or other task-unique work areas pertinent to the task. After the LIFO stack, a Register Save Area is displayed. Register 6 is underlined in the register display. If the contents of register 6 on the first page of the dump do not contain the task's Working Storage address, use the address in register 6 of the Register Save Area. After the Register Save Area comes the Common System Area.

Figure 11-10 is the fourth page of the dump, and contains the start of the Trace Table. The first entry shown in the table is for a task the ID of which is TCP. This is the terminal control subtask. KCP appears as the task in the sixth trace entry, and is the task dispatcher's task. Another system subtask that may appear in traces (although not in evidence here) is JJJ. JJJ is a journal subtask that manages a CICS journal.

Figure 11-11 is the thirteenth page of the dump. Here we see the end of the Trace Table. Note that the last entry in the table is for Task 02205, the abending task. After the Trace Table is user storage. User storage consists of all of the separate pieces of storage given to the task by CICS during the task's execution. Consequently, the storage designated as "USER" storage can contain a variety of information, depending on what the task was doing. Among the things of interest in user storage areas is the task's dynamic copy of the Data Division. The piece of storage directly after the Trace Table in Fig. 11-11 is the Transaction Abend Control Block, which

Figure 11-8. Second page of storage dump.

```
TASK CONTROL AREA (USER AREA)          ADDRESS 0009B190 TO 0009C19F     LENGTH 00001010

000005C0  00000000 00000000 00000000 904B9F52 00539C18 0005D8E8 804B98D8   *................*
000005E0  904B9A76 0009B214 00000000 804BAA94 804B8E1E 00045AD8 00000000   *.........m......*
00000600  0000007E 0009CA30 00000000 804CBCB0 0009CB40 00800000 0009A004   *....=.D.Q.......*
00000620  8009B7C4 0005D8DC 0009CA30 0009B7B0 40000000 00800000 00000000   *....x...........*
00000640  0055A7EC 004B8DB0 00EC0900 00550001 504B8B24 0055A62A 00500AA8   *..o.MF.4........*
00000660  50559628 0000A6C6 0009B658 0009B7F4 F1000000 0009B214 004B4AC8   *.......l........*
00000680  0009B658 00000000 00000000 00000000 00000000 00000000 00000000   *................*
000006A0  00000000 00000000 00000000 00000000 00000000 00000000 00000000   *................*
000006C0  00000000 00000000 00000000 FE09BA28 E500E7E2 0055F8A0 00000000   *.....V.XS.8.....*
000006E0  00000000 00000000 00000000 00000000 00000008 00000000 00000000   *................*
00000700  00000000 00000000 0009B6F8 00000000 00000008 00000000 00000000   *................*
00000720  00000000 00000000 00000000 00010DC9 00000000 00000000 0009B658   *........8.......*
00000740  00000000 004B8DB0 604BA382 80000000 48000000 0009B658             *.......I..tb....*
00000760  00000000 504B7DB0 504B7DB0 00000000 00000000 0009B658             *................*
00000780  00000000 00000000 00000000 00000000 00000190 00000000             *................*
000007A0  00000000 00000000 00000000 00000000 00000000 00000000             *................*
000007C0  00000000 00000000 00000000 805377A4 00000000 00000000             *................*
000007E0  FE09BAB8 EA00E3D4 0053376FC 805377924 00539C18 00000000           *.......TM.......*
00000800  00000000 805377876 00000000 805377924 00000000 00000000           *................*
00000820  00083718 0009BA58 00000000 00000000 00000000 00000000             *................*
00000840  LINES TO SAME AS ABOVE
00000860  00000880 00083718 0009BA58 00000000 00000007 00000000             *.....h..........*
000008A0  805388DA 00539C18 00045AD8 00000000 0009B214 00000000             *................*
000008C0  0047FE70 0009B804 00044E54 00000000 0008370C 00000000             *.....H..........*
000008E0  004B4AC8 00000000 00000000 00000000 00045AD8 00000000             *................*
00000900  00000000 00000000 00000000 00000000 00000000 00000000             *.....Q...+......*
00000920  00000000 00000F20 SAME AS ABOVE 00000505 00000000 00000000        *................*
00000940  LINES TO SAME AS ABOVE
00000F40  00000000 0000FE0 SAME AS ABOVE 00000000 00000000 00000000          *............q...*
00000F60  LINES TO SAME AS ABOVE
00001000  00000000 8A041198 0009CA30 00000000 00000000 00000000             *.......q........*


TASK CONTROL AREA (SYSTEM AREA)         ADDRESS 0009B000 TO 0009B18F     LENGTH 00000190

00000000  8A041198 0009CA30 0009CAE0 8022205C 00500AA8 00045A80 00000000    *.......q......**
00000020  0009C1A0 00044970 00000000 00000000 FE4CBCB0 0009C5BC 00000000    *..A....8......A.*
00000040  0009C1A0 0009B2F8 00000000 00000000 00000000 0009B328 00000000    *..ASRA..........*
00000060  FE09BAB8 00000000 80000000 FE09B5E0 0009B5F0 00000000 00000000    *........Aq......*
00000080  0009393934 00000000 FE09C198 00570E28 00000000 00000000 00000000  *.......D3lC.....*
000000A0  C1E2D9C1 00000000 0009CA30 C4F3F1C3 00000000 00000000 00000000    *ASRA............*
000000C0  00000000 001F6008 00000000 00000000 0009B214 004CBCB0 00000000    *...I...I........*
000000E0  00000000 106000000 10600000 01000300 004CBCB0 021CD5E6 00000000   *................*
00000100  00000000 0009B580 00000000 1108C1F0 E3F7D910 00000000 00000000    *.............A003T*
00000160  00010000 00000000 00000000 F0F3E3E2                               *.0l5l6..........*
00000180  05F0F1F5 F1F64040                                                 *................*
```

300

LIFO STACK ENTRY OWNED BY DFHKCP

```
00000000   42000000  00000000  FF09B658  004BCC12  0009C981  0009CA11  0009C7E8  0009C59C   *.......I....G....Em.....Ia...E*
00000020   0009C948  0009C7DC  0009C594  0009CA30  0009CD03  0056C538  004BC5E0  004BC4C8   *....................X....0.KC...*
00000040   0009B328  0009B190  0056E7C0  004BC658  F000D2C3  00568D04  F000F000  00000000   *................*
00000060   00000000
```

           REGS 0 THRU 15   ADDRESS 0047C960 TO 0047C99F   LENGTH 00000040

```
00000000   00000000  0009C7C4  001F6AE2  001F6728  0009B3DC  FF090000  0009C1EC  0009C59C   *....GD.....K...S....-...-....E*
00000020   0009C7C4  001F6DFC  001F6050  001F6050  0009C5BC  0009B490  001F6E68  00000000   *.GD.....-...-...E*
```

COMMON SYSTEM AREA   ADDRESS 0056E7C0 TO 0056EBBF   LENGTH 00000400

```
00000000   00000000  00005FA8  00036C38  5056AD06  4049692A  00A56858  00000FE3   *.......y.....Y.....$....H...*
00000020   00000000  0047CAFC  00495826  90495B3E  0047C8E0  00A56874  0047CBE7  0009B000   *.......*....28.l...*
00000040   00000000  0047CB78  00496826  0010020C  0009B190  1647407F  07D00100  07D00100   *.....l...*
00000060   00000000  005C4179  00FF2F8   0000DCF1  00570180  00000000  0057D030  0086322F   *.*.......Y.......*
00000080   00000000  00570130  E8FFFFFE  0000001E  00570180  0000001B  03FD0030  E738E717   *.....*
000000A0   00000000  00047170  0004D000  00004D2A  00005F8   00000000  00000000  C500FF00   *...........0...*
000000C0   00000000  000A0002  0000A400  0056EBC0  0056EFC8  00000000  006FF2F8  004AB738   *....u....+....H...*
000000E0   00000000  40567B44  00523090  004EEA70  0055DC70  004957EC  00526558  006F2F8   *.iD........iD..H*
00000100   00000000  004AF1C4  00048778  0047C8B8  00551550  01556F00  0047FB90  00000000   *..1D......H...+...H..*
00000120   00000000  00000000  00522000  004B42D0  004AAF98  00043000  00570C28  00000000   *...........q...A*
00000140   00000000  0047C8E0  00522726C  00052226C  0047C110  00571798  00000000  00000000   *....H......R.2..*
00000160   00000000  00000000  00000000  D9017BF2  0102EB49  00000000  00000000  00000000   *......R.2..*
00000180   00000000  00000000  00070F2F  00007140  00000000  00000000  0056E758  00000000   *.......D..D6....*
000001A0   00000000  D19C07FF  0114C46C  0114C4F6  00000000  00025800  E6D6D9D2  C1D9C5C1   *.J....D...D6...*
000001C0   00000000  001C008C  02205C00  00667B00  00648500  00000000  00000000  00000000   *........*....e*
000001E0   00000000  00C00000  0C000000  0C000000  00000000  00000000  00000000  00000000   *...............*
00000200   00000000  07002200  00000000  00000000  00000000  00000000  00000000  00000000   *...............*
00000220   00000000  000003E0  SAME AS ABOVE
           LINES TO     0056EBC0    SAME AS ABOVE
```

CSA OPTIONAL FEATURE LIST   ADDRESS 0056EBC0 TO 0056EEE7   LENGTH 00000328

```
00000000   00000000  00000000  0049AAB0  0047B470  004A379A  00520344  00520344  00520344   *.............U*
00000020   00494224  00493B30  00000000  00000000  0051FE00  00520344  00570D48  00570D48   *...d.4iS.....0....b.R...E*
00000040   00000000  01F4F15B  00000000  0000FE04  0048AAEC  0086322F  00570D48  00570D48   *.+....M....0...b.R...E*
00000060   80570D84  00522BF0  80200460  00049710  0049A640  00000000  004BC5E0  0056E7C0   *.....+.....wO..A....*
00000080   00570E28  0056B694  0056D910  0056C5E0  0055C5E0  004BC5E0  004AEF10  004B3C80   *....wO..A...X..T..*
000000A0   00524EB0  004ED430  0055EAE0  0055224B  0055645C0  004A5DE0  0056EE68  00487240   *....wO..A..X..T..5..*
000000C0   00497110  0049A6F0  0049C1A0  0055970   00000000  00000000  0056569A4  0056607B0   *.+...wO..A....5..l*
000000E0   00522A20  00522710  0055597   0049E34A  004A7E3A  00000000  004A69F0  004A2A2A   *...=..r*
00000100   005477C0  00541A0C  0049DC00  0049DC00  004A17FA  00499990  004EDA84  00076DC0   *...k...D......7m.r*
00000120   004A926A  004A4528  0049DC00  005647C0  00000000  005660C0  005660C0  00490FE4   *...D...x....u...B*
00000140   0053576C4  0002AA7C  004F0080  0053A780  0049C264  004C9C264  00492544  00490FE4   *...u....x.u...x.*
00000160   0053BAC0  00000000  0053EE768 0053A780  00000000  00534C4D8  0047C070  0056EEE8   *...D..B..u...D*
00000180   0047FB80  00014000  00187420  00000000  00000000  00000000  0056EEE8  0004DA80   *...D.*
000001A0   00000000  00000000  00005818  00005818  40000000  00000000  D9404040  00480E60   *.*
000001C0   0AE40AFE  80800000  00000000  00000000  E0000000  C3C9C3E2  00480E60  00481000   *.U.............CIC*
```

Figure 11-10. Fourth page of storage dump.

CSA OPTIONAL FEATURE LIST   ADDRESS 0056EBC0 TO 0056EEE7   LENGTH 00000328

```
00000240  9BD9016E 58323400 9BD9016E 58323400  00000000 00000000 00006018 00000000  *.R......R.......*
00000260  00000000 00000000 00000000 00000000  00000000 00000000 00000000 00000000  *................*
00000280  00000000 00000000 00000000 00000000  00000000 00000000 00000000 00000000  *................*
000002A0  00000000 00000000 00000000 00539E00  00000000 00000000 00000000 00000000  *................*
000002C0  00000000 00000000 LINES TO
000002E0  00000000 00000000 00000300 SAME AS ABOVE                                   *................*
00000320  00000000 00000300
```

TRACE TABLE

TRACE HDR   02000B80   02000020   02003FE0 80000IFF 005C4163 17633C01 00000000 000000

ADDRESS 02000020 TO 02003FFF   LENGTH 00003FE0

TIME OF DAY	ID	REG 14	REQD	TASK	FIELD A	FIELD B	CHARS	RESOURCE	TRACE TYPE
16:47:33.627296	C9	505238A2	0004	TCP	0009E000	85090898	....		SCP RELEASED TERMINAL STORAGE
16:47:33.627552	FC	70555CEC	1604	TCP	01090001	000934F4	4		ZCP ZRVS RECEIVE SPECIFIC
16:47:33.627616	F1	60552AA4	E304	TCP	000489E0	000934F4	4		SCP GETMAIN CONDITIONAL INITIMG
16:47:33.627648	C8	50523866	4004	TCP	400489E0	85000218	4		SCP ACQUIRED TERMINAL STORAGE
16:47:33.628352	F0	40556B58	0904	TCP	40010000	D90FFB8A	....		KCP WAIT DCI=LIST
16:47:33.725920	D0	5056AD06	0504	TCP	00000000	00000000	....		KCP SYSTEM RESUME
16:47:33.726560	F0	5056AD06	0504	TCP	40000000	00000000	....		KCP DISPATCH
16:47:33.726744	F0	5056AD06	0904	KCP	40010000	0047B320	....R...		KCP WAIT DCI=LIST
16:47:34.727744	D0	5056AD06	0904	KCP	D90FFBA2	D90FFBA2	....		KCP SYSTEM RESUME
16:47:34.727968	F0	5056AD06	0504	TCP	40000000	00000000	....R...		KCP DISPATCH
16:47:34.728160	F0	40556B58	0904	TCP	40010000	0047B320	....		KCP WAIT DCI=LIST
16:47:35.640480	D0	5056AD06	0904	TCP	00010000	D90FFC97	....R...		KCP SYSTEM RESUME
16:47:35.640576	FC	40556ABE	1404	TCP	016D0001	00076BF4	4		ZCP ZRAC RECEIVE ANY
16:47:35.640640	FC	5051192E	1304	TCP	016D01A0	01076BF4	4		ZGET GETMAIN
16:47:35.640704	EE	705509C8	2314	TCP	00137D40	5081F0F1	'...E.01	0DB10C11	VIO RECEIVE OIC DATA
16:47:35.640736	EE	705509C8	0024	TCP	00042C00	01076BF4	4	0DB10C11	VIO DATA
16:47:35.640800	F1	50550D42	A504	TCP	00048C00	85040218	4		SCP GETMAIN CONDITIONAL
16:47:35.640864	C8	50523866	1103	TCP	00200001	00076BF4	4		SCP ACQUIRED TERMINAL STORAGE
16:47:35.641408	F0	50558D4E	9304	TCP	D5F0F7F0	C1F0F1C1	N070A01A		ZCP ZATT ATTACH
16:47:35.641440	EA	50568576	0003	TCP	01040100	0056F2D0	....2...		ZCP ATTACH-CONDITIONAL
16:47:35.641504	EA	40538BB8	0025	TCP	01040100	004FF188	....1...		TMP PCT LOCATE
16:47:35.641568	EA	40558CA2	0003	TCP	0C000100	004FF188	....1...	A01A	TMP RETN NORMAL
16:47:35.641632	EA	40538BB8	0025	TCP	0C000100	00000000	....		TMP PCT TRANSFER
16:47:35.641664	FC	40558E3E	1125	TCP	40000000	0047B320	....	A01A	TMP RETN NORMAL
16:47:35.641824	F1	40556B58	4004	TCP	40010000	0047B320	....		ZCP RETN ZATT ATTACH
16:47:35.641952	C8	40569F46	EA04	KCP	00000B08	8A040B08	....		KCP WAIT DCI=LIST
16:47:35.642304	D0	50523866	0604	TCP	D5F0F7F0	C1F0F1C1	N070A01A		SCP GETMAIN CONDITIONAL INITIMG
16:47:35.642464	D0	5056A22E	0504	TCP	C1F0F1C1	C1F0F1C1	....	A01A	SCP ACQUIRED TCA STORAGE
16:47:35.642528	FC	5056AD06	0503	TCP	00000001	00076BF4	4		KCP DISPATCH
16:47:35.642560	E5	50559754	0C03	TCP	0009E6F8	00076BF4	..W8....4		ZCP ZSUP START UP TASK
16:47:35.642656	E5	40560322	0005	02203	00000000	00000000	....		XSP SECURITY CHECK
16:47:35.642688	E7	0055A7EC	0004	02203	00000000	00000000	....		XSP SECURITY RETN
16:47:35.642752	E7	0055A7EC	8804	02203	00000000	000000FF	....		ERM ENTRY
16:47:35.642784	F2	0055A864	0003	02203	01000300	0009E214	....		ERM RESPONSE
16:47:35.642848	EA	404EEF8A	8004	02203	01000300	004CAB7C	....S...	APGM01A	TMP XCTL-CONDITIONAL
16:47:35.642880	EA	404EEF8A	0003	02203	01000300	004CAB7C	....S...	APGM01A	TMP PPT LOCATE
16:47:35.642944	EA	504EFEAA	8C04	02203	00000694	01076BF4	4		TMP RETN NORMAL
16:47:35.643008	F1	504EFEAA	8C05	02203	00000694		4		SCP GETMAIN

Figure 11-11. Thirteenth page of storage dump.

TIME OF DAY	ID	REG 14	REQD	TASK	FIELD A	FIELD B	CHARS	RESOURCE	TRACE TYPE
16:47:40.689824	C8	50523866	0004	02205	0009C820	8C0000C8	.H....H		SCP ACQUIRED USER STORAGE
16:47:40.689888	F1	0056C8DA	CC04	02205	0009C7C4	01093934	.H....		SCP GETMAIN INITIMG
16:47:40.689920	C8	50523866	0004	02205	0009C8F0	8C000048	.HO...		SCP ACQUIRED USER STORAGE
16:47:40.689984	E1	501F6A04	00F4	02205	00000000	00000204	.A...		EIP HANDLE-CONDITION RESPONSE
16:47:40.690016	E1	501F6A9C	0004	02205	0009C1EC	00000602	.A...		EIP READ ENTRY
16:47:40.690048	F5	004BC646	F103	02205	00000500	00000000			FCP CTYPE LOCATE
16:47:40.690080	EA	404BB79E	0003	02205	01000500	0009B214		APPFILE	TMP FCT LOCATE
16:47:40.690176	EA	40538BB8	0045	02205	00000000	004B4AC8	...H	APPFILE	TMP RETN NORMAL
16:47:40.690208	F5	404B8DEC	0004	02205	000000A4	01093934			FCP RETN NORMAL
16:47:40.690240	F1	0056C8DA	CC04	02205	0009C940	8C0000B8			SCP GETMAIN INITIMG
16:47:40.690272	C8	50523866	0004	02205	00090012	01093934	I....		SCP ACQUIRED USER STORAGE
16:47:40.690336	F1	0056C8DA	CC04	02205	0009CA00	8C090028			SCP GETMAIN INITIMG
16:47:40.690400	C8	50523866	0004	02205	00090000	00000000		APPFILE	SCP ACQUIRED USER STORAGE
16:47:40.690432	C8	004BCADE	8003	02205	0009090EC	01093934			FCP GET
16:47:40.690496	F5	504B978A	8F04	02205	0009CA30	8F0900F8	.8		SCP ACQUIRED FILE STORAGE
16:47:40.690528	C8	50523866	0004	02205	0009CA30	01093934			SCP GETMAIN
16:47:40.690592	F1	604B9AF8	8F04	02205	00090058	8F090000			SCP ACQUIRED FILE STORAGE
16:47:40.690624	C8	50523866	0004	02205	0009CB30	8F090000			SCP GETMAIN
16:47:40.691008	F0	5056AD06	0504	02205	00000000	0000064C			KCP WAIT DCI-DISP
16:47:40.691072	D0	5056AD06	0504	02205	0009CB30	01093934			KCP DISPATCH
16:47:40.691136	F1	604B9B2A	4004	02205	00000000	8F090068			SCP FREEMAIN
16:47:40.691168	C9	505238A2	8105	02205	93080010	40840000			SCP RELEASED FILE STORAGE
16:47:40.691232	F5	404B8DEC	6004	02205	1009CA30	01093934			FCP RETN NOTFND
16:47:40.691264	F1	304BCC12	1003	02205	0009CA30	8F0900F8			FCP RELEASE
16:47:40.691360	F1	404B9B2A	4004	02205	0009CA30	01093934			SCP FREEMAIN
16:47:40.691392	C9	505238A2	0004	02205	0009CA30	8F0900F8	.8		SCP RELEASED FILE STORAGE
16:47:40.691424	F5	404B8DEC	02F4	02205	00000000	00000602			FCP RETN NORMAL
16:47:40.691488	E1	501F6A04	6004	02205	C1E2D9C1	01093934	ASRA.	ASRA	EIP READ RESPONSE
16:47:40.691968	F2	80495086	CC04	02205	0009CA30	C1E2D9C1			PCP ABEND
16:47:40.692032	F1	404EDEB8	0004	02205	0009CA30	8C0000A8			SCP GETMAIN INITIMG
16:47:40.692064	C8	504EE0B2	FE04	02205	00000000	0047CAFC	.ASRA	ASRA	SCP ACQUIRED USER STORAGE
16:47:40.692128	F4	504EE0B2	4004	02205	80010001	D9100247	.R...		DCP TRANSACTION
16:47:40.692800	F0	40496908	0904	KCP	80000000	00000000			KCP WAIT DCI=SINGLE
16:47:40.739392	D0	5056AD06	0504	02205	00000000	00000000			KCP SYSTEM RESUME
16:47:40.739904	D0	5056AD06	0504	02205	00000000	00000000			KCP DISPATCH

```
TRANSACTION STORAGE -USER    ADDRESS 0009CA30 TO 0009CADF    LENGTH 000000B0

00000000  8C0000A8 0009CA00 00001840 C4C6C8E3 C1C3C240 80600010 C1E2D9C1  *....y.......DFHTACB*
00000020  C4C5C2E4 C7F1C340 00000000 00000000 50D7E2E6 80600000 00000000  *DEBUGIC....REGS.PSW*
00000040  0009B3DC FF000000 D9C5C7E2 0009C1EC 001F6AD2 001F6AE2 001F6728  *.......A...GC..GD*
00000060  0009B190 0056E7C0 0009B490 001F6E68 001F6DFC 001F6050 001F6050  *...X*
00000080  00000000 8C0000A8 0009CA00 00000000 078D0000 00060000 00060007  *...y*
000000A0  00000000


TRANSACTION STORAGE -USER    ADDRESS 0009CA00 TO 0009CA2F    LENGTH 00000030

00000000  8C090028 0009C940 F3F3F3F2 F2F2F6F5 F4F3F3F3 F2F2F2F6 F5F40909  *....I 3332226543332222*
00000020  09090909 8C090028 0009C940                                      *.......I*
```

is created by CICS when a task terminates abnormally. This control block contains the ABEND code at a displacement of X"1C", the program name at a displacement of X"20", the general registers (0 to 15) at the abend at a displacement of X"50", and the Program Status Word at a displacement of X"90". As we have seen, this information is available and labeled in other parts of the dump.

Figure 11-12 is page 14 of the dump. Based upon the contents of register 6, we established that the task's Working Storage begins at address X"0009C1EC". The last piece of user transaction storage shown in Fig. 11-12 is storage at the address X"0009C1A0" to X"0009C81F". This area contains the task's unique storage. When looking for the task's unique storage, it is necessary to look at the addresses of the different pieces of user storage and determine which area contains the dynamic Working Storage. By subtracting the starting address of the storage area from the address of dynamic Working Storage, we can obtain the offset into the user storage area at which Working Storage begins.

> 0009C1EC   Working Storage address
> 0009C1A0   Start of user storage area
> ─────────
>
> 4C   Displacement

Thus, Working Storage unique to this task is at an offset of X"4C" from the beginning of the transaction storage area. The first full word of Working Storage is underlined in the figure.

Figure 11-13 is page 15 of the dump. The transaction storage containing dynamic Working Storage is continued on this page. The next data area holds the contents of the TCTUA, the user area associated with the terminal. This is followed by the Terminal Control Table Terminal Entry. After this is a pseudo-Sign on Table Entry, and then a piece of terminal input/output storage titled TERMINAL STORAGE. This area contains the input data entered to initiate the task. The last area in Fig. 11-13 is Program Storage, which contains the storage for a load module used on behalf of the task. In a CICS dump there is Program Storage for each of the load modules used by the task, including programs and BMS maps.

Note that the Program Storage address begins at X"001F6008" and ends at X"001F7707". You will recall that the PSW shown in Fig. 11-7 contains the address of the next instruction to be executed after the instruction that bombed. This address is contained in the second full word of the PSW. By looking at Fig. 11-7, we find that this address is X"001F6AF8". The address of the next instruction is contained within this Program Storage area. Therefore, we know that this is the program that abended, and we know that the program's load address is X"001F6008", the start of this Program Storage area.

Figure 11-12. Fourteenth page of storage dump.

```
TRANSACTION STORAGE -USER          ADDRESS 0009C940 TO 0009C9FF     LENGTH 000000C0

00000000   8C0000B8 0009C8F0 C1D7D7C6 C9D3C540 00000000 084B4AC8 0009CA08 00090009   *.....: HOAPPFILE .......*
00000020   8009C1F2 004B7478 00000000 00000000 00000000 00000000 00000000 00000000   *..A2................*
00000040   00000000 00000080   SAME AS ABOVE
00000060   LINES TO
000000A0   00000000 00000000 00000000 FF000000 00000000 8C0000B8 0009C8F0            *....*


TRANSACTION STORAGE -USER          ADDRESS 0009C8F0 TO 0009C93F     LENGTH 00000050

00000000   8C000048 0009C820 501F6A04 00000000 00000000 0009C7E8 001F69B8 000000FF   *.......H....A...GC..GD...G*
00000020   0009B3DC FF000000 0009C1EC 0009C7C3 00000000 0009C7C4 001F6050            *......E.......H.*
00000040   001F6718 0009C5BC 8C000048                                               *.....H.A.*


TRANSACTION STORAGE -USER          ADDRESS 0009C820 TO 0009C8EF     LENGTH 000000D0

00000000   8C0000C8 0009C1A0 00B60301 00000000 00000000 00000000 00000002 00000000   *.....H...A...Hi*
00000020   00000000 00000000 00000000 00000000 00000000 00000000 00000000 00000000   *................*
00000040   00000000 00000000 00000000 00000000 00000000 00010400 0009C8 0009C5       *.......HO..E...*
00000080   BC020400 00000000 00000000 00000000 00000000 00FF0000                     *......H..A.*
000000C0   00000000 0009C1A0


TRANSACTION STORAGE -USER          ADDRESS 0009C1A0 TO 0009C81F     LENGTH 00000680

00000000   8C1F0678 0009B000 00000000 501F6E44 A04EFBF2 0056EBC0                     *......................*
00000020   001F6D7C 501F6E28 001F66C8 001F6DFC F6F5F4C1 001F6050                     *.....-.....G..H...*
00000040   001F6718 001F64C0 00FFF3F3 F3F2F2F2 F6F5F4C1 00000000                     *......+....33322*
00000060   00000000 004EFE54 00100000 001F00F1 F3F3F2F2 FFFF0000                     *...........13332*
00000080   00000000 00000000 SAME AS ABOVE  00000100
000000A0   LINES TO
000000C0   00000000 00000000 00000000 00000000 00000000 00000000
000000E0   00000000 00000000 00000000 00000000 00000000 00000000
00000120   00000000 00000000 00000000 00000000 00000000 C9D5E5C1   *.....LID FUNCTION CODE*
00000140   00000000 00000000 00000000 40404040 C1E3C540 D9C5C340   *.....ADD FUNCTION—DUPLI*
00000160   D3C9C440 C6E4D5C3 E3C9D6D5 D7D3C9C3 C1E3C540 40404040   *.....C, D, OR I/O*
00000180   40404040 C1C4C440 C6E4D5C3 D9C5C3D6 D9C5C340 40404040
000001A0   40404040 6B40D6D9 40C96D40 C5D9D9D6 D9C5C340 40404040   *.....OT FOUND*
000001E0   D6E34D5C4 D940C6C9 C961D640 F04B0000 00280000 40404040  *.....CURED FOR FILE*
00000200   C3E4D9C5 C440C6D6 D940C6C9 C240F1F7 F04B0000 40404040  *.....LD TABLE DFHEITAB 1*
00000220   00000000 D3C440E3 C1C2D3C5 C2401F7 F04B0000 00000000
00000240   40404040 C5C9E3C1 C2401 00000000 00000000
00000260   00000000 SAME AS ABOVE  00000280
000002C0   00000000 00000000 00000000 C1D7D7C6 C9D3C540 00000000   *.....APP*
000002E0   00000000 00000000 00000000 C9D3C540 00000000 00000000
00000300   00000000 00000000 40404040 40404040 4000000 00000000
00000320   LINES TO  00F0F0F1 F2F54040 40404040 40404040 00300000
00000360   05010080 F2F54A9C 00000000 0009C7E8 501F6A26 001F6728   *.....00125*
00000400   0009B3EC 0009C1EC 0009B3DC FF000000 001F6DFC 001F6050   *......A..GC..GD..G*
00000460   001F6718 001F6718 2002A04B 0009C7C3 00000000 00000000
00000480   00000000 00000000 0056B874 00000000 00000000
000004A0   LINES TO  000005A0   SAME AS ABOVE
```

Figure 11-13. Fifteenth page of storage dump.

```
TRANSACTION STORAGE -USER              ADDRESS 0009C1A0 TO 0009C81F    LENGTH 00000680
000005C0  00000000 00000000 00000000 001F6050  E2E8E2D6 E4E34040  *..........&SYSOUT *
000005E0  E3000000 001F60D8 00000000 00000000  001F6E68 0009C1EC  *T.....-Q..........*
00000600  00000000 00000000 00000000 00000000  FF000000 0009C1EC  *..................*
00000620  00000000 00000000 0009B490 0009C7D4  000489EC 00000000  *..........GM......*
00000640  00093AF4 00000000 0009C59C 0009C594  8009C1F2 00000000  *...4....E..Dm..G.E*
00000660  00000000 00000000 00000000 00000000  00000000 0009B000  *..................*

TERMINAL CONTROL TBL USER AREA         ADDRESS 00093AF4 TO 00093BF2    LENGTH 000000FF
00000000  00000000 00000000 00000000 00000000  00000000 00000000  *..................*
00000020  00000000 00000000 00000000 00000000  40404040 40000000  *..................*
00000040  00000000 00000000  SAME AS ABOVE
00000060  LINES TO 000000C0
000000E0  00000000 00000000 00000000  00000000 000000             *..............*

TERMINAL CONTROL TABLE                 ADDRESS 00093934 TO 00093AEB    LENGTH 000001B8
00000000  D5F0F7D4 99F20006 000489E0 00000910  0009B190 00093AF4 FF000000  *N07Mr2.i........i.*
00000020  00000000 0CF0F1F5 20000080 00002B00  00107D14 0001A002 000476B4  *...015............*
00000040  00000000 20000080 07801850 0D702B50  8001A002 01B80000 0008AF24  *..................*
00000060  00000000 08000000 00000001 0008AE74  00049A04 00000000 0008AF24  *..................*
00000080  00000000 00000000 00000000 000445A4  00000000 01000000 00001100  *.........u........*
000000A0  00000000 00000000 08000000 00840000  24000000 26000000 00008400  *.......d..........*
000000C0  08240089E 00000000 00000000 000C0000  08000000 02000000 00000200  *.i................*
000000E0  00240026 00000000 00000000 00000000  FFFF5040 00000000 00000200  *..................*
00000100  00000000 00000000 0DD90C11 00000000  00000000 00250000 00000000  *.....R............*
00000120  00000000 00000000 00000000 00000000  00250000 00260000 00000000  *..................*
00000140  00000000 00000000 00000000 00000000  20A00002 01002010 00000000  *..................*
00000160  00000000 00000000 000000E0 00000000  00000000 0000AEC 1000C000   *..................*
00000180  00000000 00000000 000768C4 0008AED5  00000000 0008AED5 10000014   *.....D..N.........*
000001A0  00000000 00000000 00000000 00000000  00000000 00000000            *..............*

PSEUDO SIGN-ON TABLE ENTRY             ADDRESS 000476B4 TO 000476E1    LENGTH 0000002E
00000000  00000000 00000000 002E4000 00000000  00000000 0000002B 00002BF0  *.................0*
00000020  F1F50005 F0F1F5F1 F6404040 0000                                  *15.0151 6...*

TERMINAL STORAGE                       ADDRESS 000489E0 TO 00048BFF    LENGTH 00000220
00000000  85040218 00093938 0010D040 C4F3F1C3  40C16BF3 F3F3F2F2 F2F6F5F4  *e........ D31C A,3332*
00000020  00000000 00000000 00000000 00000000  00000000 00000000           *..............*
00000040  00000000 001001E0  SAME AS ABOVE
00000200  00000000 00000000 00000000 00000000  00000000 85040218 00093938  *.........e........*

PROGRAM STORAGE                        ADDRESS 001F6008 TO 001F7707    LENGTH 00001700
00000000  C4C6C8E8 C3F1F7F0 58F00010 58F0F000  58F0F004 58F0F0D0 58F0F00C  *DFHYC170.0..00..00..00*
00000020  58FF000C 07FF58F0 001058F0 F0058F0   F0D058F0 F01458F0 F00858FF  *.H..d....)..0..DEB*
00000040  00C858FF 018407FF 90ECD00C C4C5C2E4  4580F010 C7F1C340 E5E2D9F1  *.q..o....o.......*
00000060  0700989F F02407FF 96021034 00010 7FE  001F6DFC 001F6050           *..................*
```

We have now found enough information in the transaction dump to begin debugging the program check. Below is a summary of helpful information that we have determined from the dump:

TASK WORKING STORAGE ADDRESS: X"0009C1EC"

PSW TYPE OF ABEND INDICATOR: 0C7 OR DATA EXCEPTION

PROGRAM LOAD ADDRESS: X"001F6008"

PSW NEXT INSTRUCTION: X"001F6AF8"

Now all we need to do is relate this information to the COBOL program so we can determine the instruction that caused the ABEND. In order to do this, we need a compiled listing of the exact load module that executed and caused the ABEND. Figure 11-14 is the first page of the compiled program listing.

Figure 11-15 is the Linkage Editor map of the load module. Note that under the heading CONTROL SECTION is a list of all of the control sections (CSECTs) contained in this load module. In batch our application program is normally the first CSECT in the LOAD module, and therefore we can locate the ABEND instruction by merely subtracting the module's load address from the next instruction address contained in the PSW. This yields a displacement into the application program, which can be related to a COBOL instruction by utilizing COBOL's Procedure Division map (PMAP) or a condensed version called the CLIST.

Things are a little different for a CICS Command Level program, because a Command Level CSECT is placed before the application program CSECT. Looking at the Linkage Editor map, we can see that this CSECT is DFHECI, and that it is X"48" bytes in length. This means that at the module's load address we do not have the beginning of the application program, but rather the beginning of DFHECI. The next instruction address in the PSW is within the application CSECT. We need to relate this address to a program displacement so we can find the erroneous instruction. However, the load module address can't be used without adjustment, because it is not the load address of the application program CSECT. In order to use the load address found in the storage dump, we need to add X"48" to compensate for the presence of DFHECI.

Therefore, we do the following calculation:

LOAD ADDRESS IN HEX: 001F6008
+ LENGTH OF DFHECI: 48
———————

ADJUSTED LOAD ADDRESS: 001F6050

Do not assume that DFHECI is always going to be the same size and blithely add X"48" to the load module address; DFHECI can change with each new release of CICS. As a matter of fact, in release 1.5 DFHECI was

Figure 11-14. Beginning of compiled program listing.

```
     1                        16.39.34           NOV 18,1986

00001          IDENTIFICATION DIVISION.
00002          PROGRAM-ID.
00003              DEBUGIC.
00004          AUTHOR.
00005              ARLENE J WIPFLER / BETADATA, INC.
00006          INSTALLATION.
00007              BETADATA, INC.
00008              SYSTEMS TRAINING DIVISION
00009
00010
00011          REMARKS.
00012              THIS MODULE IS A SAMPLE DEBUGGING MODULE WITH A PROGRAM
00013              BUG.  IT IS INTENDED TO BE USED IN CONJUNCTION WITH
00014              A COURSE IN CICS PROGRAMMING/DEBUGGING.
00015          ENVIRONMENT DIVISION.
00016      *
00017          DATA DIVISION.
00018      *
00019          WORKING-STORAGE SECTION.
00020      *
00021          77   TRMNL-LEN          PIC S9(4) COMP.
00022          77   FILE-LEN           PIC S9(4) COMP.
00023          77   TCTUA-LEN          PIC S9(4) COMP.
```

```
00010000
00020000
00030000
00040000
00050000
00060000
00070002
00080002
00090002
00100002
00110000
00120002
00130002
00140002
00150000
00160000
00170000
00180000
00190000
00200000
00210000
00220000
00230000
```

```
                                                                              00240001
                                                                              00250001
                                                                              00260001
                                                                              00270000
                                                                              00280000
                                                                              00290000
                                                                              00300000

000024      77  WS-KEY-FIELD          PIC X(9).
000025      77  WS-FUNCTION-CODE      PIC X.
000026      77  WS-COUNT              PIC S9 COMP-3.
000027     *
000028     *
000029     ***********************************************************************
000030     ***********************************************************************
000031  C  01  SMAPIMMI    COPY SMAP01M.
000032  C  01  SMAPIMMI.
000033  C  02  FILLER PIC X(12).
000034  C  02  EMPNOL    COMP PIC S9(4).
000035  C  02  EMPNOF         PICTURE X.
000036  C  02  FILLER REDEFINES EMPNOF.
000037  C  03  EMPNOA     PICTURE X.
000038  C  02  EMPNOI    PIC X(9).
000039  C  02  EMPNAL    COMP PIC S9(4).
000040  C  02  EMPNAF         PICTURE X.
000041  C  02  FILLER REDEFINES EMPNAF.
000042  C  03  EMPNAA    PICTURE X.
000043  C  02  EMPNAI    PIC X(30).
000044  C  02  EMPADIL   COMP PIC S9(4).
000045  C  02  EMPADIF        PICTURE X.
000046  C  02  FILLER REDEFINES EMPAD1F.
000047  C  03  EMPAD1A    PICTURE X.
000048  C  02  EMPAD1I    PIC X(20).
000049  C  02  EMPAD2L    COMP PIC S9(4).
000050  C  02  EMPAD2F        PICTURE X.
000051  C  02  FILLER REDEFINES EMPAD2F.
           03  EMPAD2A     PICTURE X.
```

309

Figure 11-15. Linkage Editor map of the load module.

CROSS REFERENCE TABLE

CONTROL SECTION

NAME	ORIGIN	LENGTH
DFHECI	00	48
DEBUGIC	48	E12
ILBOCOM0*	E60	16D
ILBOSRV *	FD0	4A4
ILBOBEG *	1478	188
ILBOMSG *	1600	100

ENTRY

NAME	LOCATION	NAME	LOCATION	NAME	LOCATION	NAME	L
DFHEI1	8	DLZEI01		DLZEI02	8	DLZEI03	
DLZEI04	8	DFHCBLI	26				
ILBOCOM	E60						
ILBOSRV0	FDA	ILBOSR5	FDA	ILBOSR3	FDA	ILBOSR	
ILBOSRV1	FDE	ILBOSTP1	FDE	ILBOST	FE2	ILBOSTP0	
ILBOBEG0	147A						
ILBOMSG0	1602						

LOCATION	REFERS TO SYMBOL	IN CONTROL SECTION
710	ILBOSRV0	ILBOSRV
718	DFHEI1	DFHECI
670	ILBOCOM0	ILBOCOM0
1370	ILBOSTT0	$UNRESOLVED(W)
1364	ILBOBEG0	ILBOBEG
136C	ILBOSND2	$UNRESOLVED(W)

LOCATION	REFERS TO SYMBOL	IN CONTROL SECTION
714	ILBOSR5	ILBOSRV
71C	ILBOSRV1	ILBOSRV
135C	ILBOCOM	ILBOCOM0
1360	ILBOCMM0	$UNRESOLVED(W)
1368	ILBOMSG0	ILBOMSG
15B8	ILBOPRM0	$UNRESOLVED(W)

ENTRY ADDRESS 48

TOTAL LENGTH 1700
***DEBUGIC NOW REPLACED IN DATA SET AMODE 24
RMODE IS 24
AUTHORIZATION CODE IS 0.

X"18" in length. Therefore, if a new release is installed, check the linkage editor map to be certain of the appropriate length.

The next thing to do is to determine the program displacement at which the abend occurred. This is accomplished by subtracting the adjusted load address from the PSW next instruction address, as in the following calculation:

PSW NEXT INSTRUCTION ADDRESS: X"001F6AF8"
− ADJUSTED LOAD ADDRESS: 001F6050
                                                               _____

DISPLACEMENT OF INSTRUCTION AFTER THE ABEND: X"AA8"

Figure 11-16 is a *Procedure Division Map* (PMAP). In the PMAP there is some critical information. COBOL instruction numbers are related to load module displacements. The first three columns in Fig. 11-16 have been marked off with the letters A, B, and C. Column A contains COBOL instruction numbers, column B indicates the COBOL verb of each instruction, and column C provides the hexadecimal displacement or offset into the COBOL program of each instruction. Column C allows us to relate a next instruction offset to an actual COBOL instruction. We are looking for displacement X"AA8". This offset is underlined within column C. This is the instruction that would have executed next had the previous machine language instruction not bombed. Therefore, we go back one machine language instruction to find the abending statement. This instruction location is pointed to by the arrow in Fig. 11-16. By glancing over to column A, we ascertain that the COBOL statement 289 is the one that bombed. Column B tells us that this is an ADD instruction. All we need do is look at the compiled source code listing and locate statement 289.

Figure 11-17 is a listing of the program's Procedure Division that contains 289. Instruction 289 is underlined, and an arrow points to the COBOL statement. The instruction is ADDing 1 to a field named WS-COUNT. Referring back to Figure 11-14, we find that WS-COUNT is a 77-level item, and that this field is not initialized with a VALUE clause. WS-COUNT is underlined in Fig. 11-14. Now all we have to do is find this 1-byte field in the task's dynamic copy of Working Storage to determine the field contents and verify our debugging.

Accordingly, we must consult the Data Division Map to obtain the displacement of WS-COUNT into the program's Working Storage. We know the starting address of the task's dynamic Working Storage; armed with WS-COUNT's offset, we can go to the dump and examine the contents of the field. Figure 11-18 is the page of the DMAP that contains information about WS-COUNT. Information about this field is underlined. We note that WS-COUNT is BASEd from Base Locator 1, the first base address of working storage. Furthermore, the field's displacement is X"010" from the starting address contained in Base Locator 1. Figure

Figure 11-16. Procedure Division Map.

```
A    B                          Loc       Object code         Op    Operand               Operand refs
284  *A100-TEST-ADD
                                 000A7C    58 10 C 020         L     1,020(0,12)           PN=05          DNM=1-461
                                 000A80    07 F1               BCR   15,1

285  IF             PN=03
                                 000A82                        EQU   *
                                 000A86    58 20 C 04C         L     2,04C(0,12)           GN=05          DNM=1-483
                                 000A8A    95 C1 07 82         CLI   00F(6),X'C1'
                                                               BCR   8,2
285  GO
                                 000A8C    58 10 C 01C         L     1,01C(0,12)           PN=04
                                 000A90    07 F1               BCR   15,1

286  MOVE           GN=05
                                 000A92    D2 08 6 027 6 006   MVC   027(9,6),006(6)       DNM=3-14       DNM=1-461
287  MOVE
                                 000A98    92 F1 6 026 C 062   MVI   026(6),X'F1'          DNM=2-99       LIT+2
288  MOVE
                                 000A9C    D2 06 6 030 C 064   MVC   030(2,6),062(12)      DNM=2-131      LIT+4
289  ADD
                                 000AA2    FA 00 6 010 6 024   AP    010(1,6),064(1,12)    DNM=2-0
290  GO
                                 000AA8    58 10 C 024         L     1,024(0,12)           PN=06
                              ↑  000AAC    07 F1               BCR   15,1

291  *A100-ADD-ERROR
292  MOVE           PN=04
                                 000AAE                        EQU   *
                                 000AB4    D2 27 6 082 6 180   MVC   082(40,6),180(6)      DNM=3-136      DNM=3-402
                                 000AB8    92 04 6 0AA         MVI   0AA(6),X'40'          DNM=3-136+40
                                 000ABE    D2 24 6 0AB 6 0AA   MVC   0AB(37,6),0AA(6)      DNM=3-136+41   DNM=3-136+
293  GO
                                 000AC2    58 10 C 030         L     1,030(0,12)           PN=09
                                           07 F1               BCR   15,1

295  *A100-FORMAT-OUTPUT-SCREEN
298  MOVE           PN=05
                                 000AC4                        EQU   *
                                 000AC4    D2 08 6 027 6 006   MVC   027(9,6),006(6)       DNM=3-14       DNM=1-461
299  MOVE
                                 000ACE    92 F1 6 026 C 062   MVI   026(6),X'F1'          DNM=2-99       LIT+2
300  MOVE
                                 000AD4    58 E0 D 220         L     14,220(0,13)          BLL=7
301  MOVE
                                 000AD8    D2 1D 6 033 E 009   MVC   033(30,6),009(14)     DNM=3-44       DNM=7-96
302  MOVE
                                 000ADE    D2 13 6 054 E 027   MVC   054(20,6),027(14)     DNM=3-74       DNM=7-118
303  MOVE
                                 000AE4    D2 13 6 06B E 03B   MVC   06B(20,6),03B(14)     DNM=3-105      DNM=7-138

305  *A100-ISSUE-BMS-SEND
315  MOVE           PN=06
                                 000AEA                        EQU   *
                                 000AEA    D2 16 6 3B0 C 0F2   MVC   3B0(23,6),0F2(12)     DNM=5-230+23   LIT+146
                                 000AF4    92 40 6 3C7         MVI   3C7(6),X'40'          DNM=5-230+24   DNM=5-230+
316  MOVE
                                 000AFA    D2 06 6 338 6 3C7   MVC   338(7,6),3C7(6)       DNM=5-140      LIT+169
317  MOVE
                                 000B06    D2 06 6 250 6 109   MVC   250(7,6),109(6)       DNM=4-182      LIT+5
318  MOVE
                                 000B0C    D2 06 6 340 6 110   MVC   340(7,6),110(6)       DNM=4-200      LIT+176
319  MOVE
                                 000B12    D2 01 6 258 C 062   MVC   258(2,6),062(12)      DNM=5-230      LIT+2
320  CALL
                                 000B16    41 10 5 23C         LA    1,23C(0,5)            PRM=1
                                 000B1A    50 10 D 22C         ST    1,22C(0,13)           DNM=5-140
                                 000B1E    41 10 5 338         LA    1,338(0,5)            PRM=2
                                 000B22    50 10 D 230         ST    1,230(0,13)           DNM=2-18
                                 000B26    41 10 5 018         LA    1,018(0,5)            PRM=3
                                 000B2A    41 10 D 234         LA    1,234(0,13)           DNM=4-182
                                 000B2E    50 10 5 250         ST    1,250(0,5)            PRM=4
                                 000B32    41 10 6 340         LA    1,340(0,6)            DNM=5-158
                                 000B36    50 10 5 23C         ST    1,23C(0,5)            PRM=5
                                 000B3A    41 10 6 3A8         LA    1,3A8(0,6)            DNM=5-212
                                 000B3E    41 10 D 240         LA    1,240(0,13)           PRM=6
                                 000B42    50 10 6 3A8         ST    1,3A8(0,6)            DNM=5-212
```

Figure 11-17. Procedure Division listing (indicating instruction that bombed).

```
00268    *          USED.                                                   01240000
00269    *EXEC      CICS      READ      ('APPFILE')
00270    *                    DATASET   (WS-KEY-FIELD)
00271    *                    RIDFLD    (FILE-BLL)
00272    *                    SET
00273               END-EXEC.                                               01250000
00274               MOVE '                00125    ' TO DFHEIV0
00275               MOVE 'APPFILE' TO DFHEIV1
00276               CALL 'DFHEI1' USING DFHEIV0 DFHEIV1 FILE-BLL DFHDUMMY
00277               WS-KEY-FIELD.
00278                                                                       01300000
00279               IF WS-FUNCTION-CODE = 'A'                               01310000
00280                   MOVE ERRMSG2 TO EMPERRO                             01320000
00281                   GO TO A100-SEND-ERR-MAP.                            01330000
00282               GO TO A100-FORMAT-OUTPUT-SCREEN.                        01340000
00283                                                                       01350000
00284    *      A100-TEST-ADD.                                              01360000
00285               IF WS-FUNCTION-CODE NOT = 'A' GO TO A100-ADD-ERROR.     01370000
00286                   MOVE WS-KEY-FIELD TO EMPNOO.                        01380000
00287                   MOVE '1' TO EMPNOA.                                 01390000
00288                   MOVE -1 TO EMPNAL.                                  01400000
00289                   ADD 1 TO WS-COUNT.                                  01410001
00290                   GO TO A100-ISSUE-BMS-SEND.                          01420000
00291           A100-ADD-ERROR.
00292               MOVE ERRMSG3 TO EMPERRO.                                01430000
00293               GO TO A100-SEND-ERR-MAP.                                01440000
```

313

Figure 11-17. Continued

```
00294   *
00295   *   A100-FORMAT-OUTPUT-SCREEN.                                      01450000
00296   *       MOVE DATA FROM THE FILE RECORD TO MAP FIELDS WITH           01460000
00297   *       THE 'O' ENDING.                                            01470000
00298           MOVE WS-KEY-FIELD TO EMPNOO.                              01480000
00299           MOVE '1' TO EMPNOA.                                       01490000
00300           MOVE -1 TO EMPNAL.                                        01500000
00301           MOVE F-EMPNAME    TO      EMPNAO.                         01510000
00302           MOVE F-EMPADDR1   TO      EMPADIO.                        01520000
00303           MOVE F-EMPADDR2   TO      EMPAD2O.                        01530000
00304   *                                                                  01540000
00305       A100-ISSUE-BMS-SEND.                                          01550000
00306   *                                                                  01560000
00307   *EXEC    CICS    SEND MAP ('SMAP1MM')                             01570000
00308   *                MAPSET ('SMAP01M')
00309   *                CURSOR
00310   *                FREEKB
00311   *                ERASE
00312   *                FROM    (SMAP1MMI)
00313   *                LENGTH  (172)
00314   *       END-EXEC.
00315           MOVE ' I  B   S   00158  ' TO DFHEIV0                      01580000
00316           MOVE 'SMAP1MM' TO DFHC0070
00317           MOVE 172 TO DFHEIV11
00318           MOVE 'SMAP01M' TO DFHC0071
00319           MOVE -1 TO DFHEIV12
00320           CALL 'DFHEI1' USING DFHEIV0 DFHC0070 SMAP1MMI DFHEIV11
00321   DFHC0071 DFHDUMMY DFHDUMMY DFHEIV12.
```

Figure 11-18. Page from DMAP containing WS-COUNT information.

INTRNL NAME	LVL	SOURCE NAME	BASE	DISPL	INTRNL NAME	DEFINITION	USAGE
DNM=1-405	77	TRMNL-LEN	BL=1	000	DNM=1-405	DS 2C	COMP
DNM=1-424	77	FILE-LEN	BL=1	002	DNM=1-424	DS 2C	COMP
DNM=1-442	77	TCTUA-LEN	BL=1	004	DNM=1-442	DS 2C	COMP
DNM=1-461	77	WS-KEY-FIELD	BL=1	006	DNM=1-461	DS 9C	DISP
DNM=1-483	77	WS-FUNCTION-CODE	BL=1	00F	DNM=1-483	DS 1P	COMP-3
DNM=2-000	01	SMAP1MMI	BL=1	010	DNM=2-000	DS 0CL184	GROUP
DNM=2-018	02	FILLER	BL=1	018	DNM=2-018	DS 12C	DISP
DNM=2-039	02	EMPNOL	BL=1	024	DNM=2-039	DS 2C	COMP
DNM=2-050	02	EMPNOF	BL=1	026	DNM=2-050	DS 1C	DISP
DNM=2-066	02	FILLER	BL=1	026	DNM=2-066	DS 0CL1	GROUP
DNM=2-082	03	EMPNOA	BL=1	026	DNM=2-082	DS 1C	DISP
DNM=2-099	02	EMPNOI	BL=1	027	DNM=2-099	DS 9C	DISP
DNM=2-115	02	EMPNAL	BL=1	030	DNM=2-115	DS 2C	COMP
DNM=2-131	02	EMPNAF	BL=1	032	DNM=2-131	DS 1C	DISP
DNM=2-150	02	FILLER	BL=1	032	DNM=2-150	DS 0CL1	GROUP
DNM=2-166	03	EMPNAA	BL=1	032	DNM=2-166	DS 1C	DISP
DNM=2-183	02	EMPNAI	BL=1	033	DNM=2-183	DS 30C	DISP
DNM=2-199	02	EMPADIL	BL=1	051	DNM=2-199	DS 2C	COMP
DNM=2-215	02	EMPADIF	BL=1	053	DNM=2-215	DS 1C	DISP
DNM=2-232	02	FILLER	BL=1	053	DNM=2-232	DS 0CL1	GROUP
DNM=2-249	03	EMPADIA	BL=1	053	DNM=2-249	DS 1C	DISP
DNM=2-266	02	EMPADII	BL=1	054	DNM=2-266	DS 20C	DISP
DNM=2-283	02	EMPAD2L	BL=1	068	DNM=2-283	DS 2C	COMP
DNM=2-300	02	EMPAD2F	BL=1	06A	DNM=2-300	DS 1C	DISP
DNM=2-317	02	FILLER	BL=1	06A	DNM=2-317	DS 0CL1	GROUP
DNM=2-334	03	EMPAD2A	BL=1	06A	DNM=2-334	DS 1C	DISP
DNM=2-351	02	EMPAD2I	BL=1	06B	DNM=2-351	DS 20C	DISP
DNM=2-368	02	EMPERRL	BL=1	07F	DNM=2-368	DS 2C	COMP
DNM=2-385	02	EMPERRF	BL=1	081	DNM=2-385	DS 1C	DISP
DNM=2-402	02	FILLER	BL=1	081	DNM=2-402	DS 0CL1	GROUP
DNM=2-419	03	EMPERRA	BL=1	081	DNM=2-419	DS 1C	DISP
DNM=2-436	02	EMPERRI	BL=1	082	DNM=2-436	DS 78C	DISP
DNM=2-456	01	SMAP1MMO	BL=1	018	DNM=2-456	DS 0CL184	GROUP
DNM=2-473	02	FILLER	BL=1	018	DNM=2-473	DS 12C	DISP
DNM=2-494	02	FILLER	BL=1	024	DNM=2-494	DS 3C	DISP
DNM=3-014	02	EMPNOO	BL=1	027	DNM=3-014	DS 9C	DISP
DNM=3-030	02	FILLER	BL=1	030	DNM=3-030	DS 3C	DISP
DNM=3-044	02	EMPNAO	BL=1	033	DNM=3-044	DS 30C	DISP
DNM=3-060	02	FILLER	BL=1	051	DNM=3-060	DS 3C	DISP
DNM=3-074	02	EMPADIO	BL=1	054	DNM=3-074	DS 20C	DISP
DNM=3-091	02	FILLER	BL=1	068	DNM=3-091	DS 3C	DISP
DNM=3-105	02	EMPAD2O	BL=1	06B	DNM=3-105	DS 20C	DISP
DNM=3-122	02	FILLER	BL=1	07F	DNM=3-122	DS 3C	DISP
DNM=3-136	02	EMPERRO	BL=1	082	DNM=3-136	DS 78C	DISP
DNM=3-156	01	ERRM1MMI	BL=1	0D0	DNM=3-156	DS 0CL93	GROUP
DNM=3-177	02	FILLER	BL=1	0D0	DNM=3-177	DS 12C	DISP
DNM=3-191	02	ERRMSGL	BL=1	0DC	DNM=3-191	DS 2C	COMP
DNM=3-208	02	ERRMSGF	BL=1	0DE	DNM=3-208	DS 1C	DISP
DNM=3-225	02	FILLER	BL=1	0DE	DNM=3-225	DS 0CL1	GROUP
DNM=3-242	03	ERRMSGA	BL=1	0DE	DNM=3-242	DS 1C	DISP
DNM=3-259	02	ERRMSGI	BL=1	0DF	DNM=3-259	DS 78C	DISP

11-19 is a page from the end of the DMAP. This page defines which registers are used for Base Locators. This information, which appears under the heading REGISTER ASSIGNMENT toward the bottom of the page, is underlined. Our Working Storage is under 4096, and therefore we require only one Base Locator or register. However, each additional 4096 bytes (or part thereof) of storage requires an additional Base Locator. We see that register 6 is used as Base Locator 1. Had we required more than one Base Locator, the register(s) assigned would likewise have appeared here.

We found the contents of register 6 in the transaction dump. This register contained the storage address X"0009C1EC". By adding the displacement of WS-COUNT to this address, we derive the storage address of this 1-byte field. WS-COUNT is located at X"0009C1FC".

Figure 11-12 contains the task's dynamic Data Division in the TRANSACTION STORAGE–USER area, starting at address X"0009C1A0". Earlier we noted that the first byte of the task's Working Storage began at

```
            SBL CELLS              0069C
            INDEX CELLS            0069C
            SUBADR CELLS           0069C
            ONCTL CELLS            0069C
            PFMCTL CELLS           0069C
            PFMSAV CELLS           0069C
            VN CELLS               0069C
            SAVE AREA =2           0069C
            SAVE AREA =3           0069C
            XSASW CELLS            0069C
            XSA CELLS              0069C
            PARAM CELLS            0069C
            RPTSAV AREA            006C0
            CHECKPT CTR            006C0

LITERAL POOL (HEX)

00728 (LIT+0)     00FAFFFF  1C00AC02  08800005  03000000  00000000  00000000
00740 (LIT+24)    00000000  00F0F0F0  F7F74040  40020280  00050400  00000000
00758 (LIT+48)    00000000  00000000  000000F0  F0F0F8F2  40404004  02C00005
00770 (LIT+72)    01000014  00004000  0000F0F0  F0F9F140  40400204  C0000501
00788 (LIT+96)    0D000000  00000000  00000000  F0F0F1F1  F0F0F1F1  F7404040
007A0 (LIT+120)   00020602  D0000501  008000F0  F0F1F2F5  404040C1  D7D7C6C9
007B8 (LIT+144)   D3C51804  F1000500  C200001D  E2040000  20F0F0F1  F5F84040
007D0 (LIT+168)   40E2D4C1  D7F1D4D4  E2D4C1D7  F0F1D40E  08800005  00001000
007E8 (LIT+192)   F0F0F1F7  F7404040  D7D7C7F2  1804F000  05000000  00052004
00800 (LIT+216)   000020F0  F0F1F9F2  4040400E  08000005  00001000  F0F0F2F0
00818 (LIT+240)   F7404040  0E0C8000  05000060  00F0F0F2  F1F84040  40D5E3C3
00830 (LIT+264)   E3

            PGT                    006C8

            OVERFLOW CELLS         006C8
            VIRTUAL CELLS          006C8
            PROCEDURE NAME CELLS   006D8
            GENERATED NAME CELLS   00704
            DCB ADDRESS CELLS      00724
            VNI CELLS              00724
            LITERALS               00728
            DISPLAY LITERALS       00831

REGISTER ASSIGNMENT

    REG 6    BL =1

WORKING-STORAGE STARTS AT LOCATION 000A0 FOR A LENGTH OF 003D0.
```

Figure 11-19. Page from DMAP containing Base Locator information.

an offset of X"4C" within this area. The first full word of Working Storage is underlined. By adding WS-COUNT's displacement into Working Storage to the starting point of Working Storage, we can locate this 1-byte field. WS-COUNT is underlined, and an arrow in the margin points to it. WS-COUNT is equal to X"00". The fact that WS-COUNT does not contain a valid packed decimal sign is the reason for the data exception that resulted in the ASRA dump. This error can be rectified by initializing WS-COUNT with a VALUE of 0, or by adding an instruction to MOVE 0 TO WS-COUNT before attempting to ADD to the field.

In debugging this ASRA dump, it was not necessary to locate the Linkage Section Base Locators for Linkage or BLL cells. However, had we been dealing with another type of program check (such as an 0C4) this might have been necessary. Remember that an 0C4 is also a CICS ASRA, and therefore we must consult the PSW to determine the type of program check. In order to find the Linkage Section, we must return to the compile listing. Figure 11-20 is the COBOL Task Global Table Memory Map. The displacement of the Linkage Section BLL cells can be found in this map on the second line from the bottom. Looking at the map, we find that the BLL cell displacement is X"00678". This represents the BLL cell offset from the beginning of the COBOL module. However, in CICS we are using a dynamic copy of the Data Division, and so we must relate this back to the address of the start of Working Storage, or the contents of register 6. A COBOL program does not begin with Working Storage. Rather, COBOL places a prolog before Working Storage. The purpose of the prolog is to save registers and branch into the executable code of the Procedure Division. The BLL cell displacement is calculated from the beginning of the COBOL module, including the prolog, whereas our dynamic Working Storage address begins after the prolog, with the first byte of Working Storage.

Therefore, we must discover the length of the prolog, and subtract its size from the BLL cell displacement in the COBOL listing. Figure 11-19 tells us the size of the prolog. The last line indicates that Working Storage starts at location 000A0. This means that the prolog is A0 in length. This length is not carved in stone, however, and if your installation gets a new version of the COBOL compiler, this size should be verified. The following calculation is used to adjust the BLL cell displacement.

BLL CELL DISPLACEMENT IN HEX: 00678
− LENGTH OF PROLOG IN HEX: A0
                                 ‾‾‾‾‾‾‾‾

BLL CELL DISPLACEMENT WITHIN
CICS DYNAMIC DATA DIVISION: 005D8

This displacement is then added to the start of Working Storage (or the address contained in register 6) and we have the address of the first BLL cell.

```
                 MEMORY MAP

        TGT                        00470

SAVE AREA                          00470
SWITCH                             004B8
TALLY                              004BC
SORT SAVE                          004C0
ENTRY-SAVE                         004C4
SORT CORE SIZE                     004C8
RET CODE                           004CC
SORT RET                           004CE
WORKING CELLS                      004D0
SORT FILE SIZE                     00600
SORT MODE SIZE                     00604
PGT-VN TBL                         00608
TGT-VN TBL                         0060C
RESERVED                           00610
LENGTH OF VN TBL                   00614
LABEL RET                          00616
RESERVED                           00617
DBG R14SAVE                        00618
COBOL INDICATOR                    0061C
A(INIT1)                           00620
DEBUG TABLE PTR                    00624
SUBCOM PTR                         00628
SORT-MESSAGE                       0062C
SYSOUT DDNAME                      00634
RESERVED                           00635
COBOL ID                           00636
COMPILED POINTER                   00638
COUNT TABLE ADDRESS                0063C
RESERVED                           00640
DBG R11SAVE                        00648
COUNT CHAIN ADDRESS                0064C
PRBL1 CELL PTR                     00650
RESERVED                           00654
TA LENGTH                          00659
RESERVED                           0065C
PCS LIT PTR                        00664
DEBUGGING                          00668
CD FOR INITIAL INPUT               0066C
OVERFLOW CELLS                     00670
BL CELLS                           00670
DECBADR CELLS                      00674
FIB CELLS                          00674
TEMP STORAGE                       00678
TEMP STORAGE-2                     00678
TEMP STORAGE-3                     00678
TEMP STORAGE-4                     00678
BLL CELLS                          00678
VLC CELLS                          0069C
```

Figure 11-20. COBOL Task Global Table Memory Map.

WORKING STORAGE ADDRESS IN HEX: 0009C1EC
+ADJUSTED BLL DISPLACEMENT: 5D8
                                   _____

STORAGE ADDRESS OF BLL CELL 1:   0009C7C4

This BLL address is shown in Fig. 11-13. This figure includes the continuation of the storage area that encompasses the dynamic Data Division. To obtain the displacement of the first BLL cell into this storage area, add

Figure 11-21. Page from DMAP containing Linkage Section information.

		Name		BLL	Offset		DS	Usage
DNM=5-230	01	DFHEIV0		BLL=1	3B0	DNM=5-230	DS 29C	DISP
DNM=5-247	01	DFHEIBLK		BLL=3	000	DNM=5-247	DS 0CL85	GROUP
DNM=5-271	02	EIBTIME		BLL=3	000	DNM=5-271	DS 4P	COMP-3
DNM=5-288	02	EIBDATE		BLL=3	004	DNM=5-288	DS 4P	COMP-3
DNM=5-305	02	EIBTRNID		BLL=3	008	DNM=5-305	DS 4C	DISP
DNM=5-323	02	EIBTASKN		BLL=3	00C	DNM=5-323	DS 4P	COMP-3
DNM=5-344	02	EIBTRMID		BLL=3	010	DNM=5-344	DS 4C	DISP
DNM=5-362	02	DFHEIGDI		BLL=3	014	DNM=5-362	DS 2C	COMP
DNM=5-380	02	EIBCPOSN		BLL=3	016	DNM=5-380	DS 2C	COMP
DNM=5-398	02	EIBCALEN		BLL=3	018	DNM=5-398	DS 2C	COMP
DNM=5-416	02	EIBAID		BLL=3	01A	DNM=5-416	DS 1C	DISP
DNM=5-432	02	EIBFN		BLL=3	01B	DNM=5-432	DS 2C	DISP
DNM=5-450	02	EIBRCODE		BLL=3	01D	DNM=5-450	DS 6C	DISP
DNM=5-468	02	EIBDS		BLL=3	023	DNM=5-468	DS 8C	DISP
DNM=5-483	02	EIBREQID		BLL=3	02B	DNM=5-483	DS 8C	DISP
DNM=6-000	02	EIBRSRCE		BLL=3	033	DNM=6-000	DS 8C	DISP
DNM=6-018	02	EIBRSYNC		BLL=3	03B	DNM=6-018	DS 1C	DISP
DNM=6-035	02	EIBFREE		BLL=3	03C	DNM=6-035	DS 1C	DISP
DNM=6-055	02	EIBRECV		BLL=3	03D	DNM=6-055	DS 1C	DISP
DNM=6-075	02	EIBFIL01		BLL=3	03E	DNM=6-075	DS 1C	DISP
DNM=6-093	02	EIBATT		BLL=3	03F	DNM=6-093	DS 1C	DISP
DNM=6-109	02	EIBEOC		BLL=3	040	DNM=6-109	DS 1C	DISP
DNM=6-125	02	EIBFMH		BLL=3	041	DNM=6-125	DS 1C	DISP
DNM=6-141	02	EIBCOMPL		BLL=3	042	DNM=6-141	DS 1C	DISP
DNM=6-162	02	EIBSIG		BLL=3	043	DNM=6-162	DS 1C	DISP
DNM=6-178	02	EIBCONF		BLL=3	044	DNM=6-178	DS 1C	DISP
DNM=6-195	02	EIBERR		BLL=3	045	DNM=6-195	DS 1C	DISP
DNM=6-211	02	EIBERRCD		BLL=3	046	DNM=6-211	DS 4C	DISP
DNM=6-232	02	EIBSYNRB		BLL=3	04A	DNM=6-232	DS 1C	DISP
DNM=6-253	02	EIBNODAT		BLL=3	04B	DNM=6-253	DS 1C	DISP
DNM=6-274	02	EIBRESP		BLL=3	04C	DNM=6-274	DS 4C	COMP
DNM=6-291	02	EIBRESP2		BLL=3	050	DNM=6-291	DS 4C	COMP
DNM=6-309	02	EIBRLDBK		BLL=3	054	DNM=6-309	DS 1C	DISP
DNM=6-327	01	DFHCOMMAREA		BLL=4	000	DNM=6-327	DS 0CL16	GROUP
DNM=6-348	01	BLL-CELLS		BLL=5	000	DNM=6-348	DS 4C	COMP
DNM=6-370	02	FILLER		BLL=5	004	DNM=6-370	DS 4C	COMP
DNM=6-384	02	TERMINAL-BLL		BLL=5	008	DNM=6-384	DS 4C	COMP
DNM=6-406	02	FILE-BLL		BLL=5	00C	DNM=6-406	DS 4C	COMP
DNM=6-424	02	TCTUA-BLL		BLL=6	000	DNM=6-424	DS 0CL16	GROUP
DNM=6-446	01	TERMINAL-INPUT-AREA		BLL=6	000	DNM=6-446	DS 4C	COMP
DNM=6-478	02	T-TRANSID		BLL=6	004	DNM=6-478	DS 4C	DISP
DNM=6-497	02	FILLER		BLL=6	005	DNM=6-497	DS 1C	DISP
DNM=7-000	02	T-FUNCTION		BLL=6	006	DNM=7-000	DS 1C	DISP
DNM=7-034	02	FILLER		BLL=6	007	DNM=7-034	DS 9C	DISP
DNM=7-051	02	T-EMPNO	←	BLL=7	000	DNM=7-051	DS 9C	DISP
DNM=7-079	01	FILE-INPUT-AREA	←	BLL=7	000	DNM=7-079	DS 0CL80	GROUP
DNM=7-096	02	F-EMPNO		BLL=7	009	DNM=7-096	DS 30C	DISP
DNM=7-118	02	F-EMPNAME		BLL=7	027	DNM=7-118	DS 30C	DISP
DNM=7-138	02	F-EMPADDR1		BLL=7	03B	DNM=7-138	DS 20C	DISP
DNM=7-158	02	F-EMPADDR2		BLL=7	04F	DNM=7-158	DS 20C	DISP
DNM=7-172	01	TCTUA-DATA-AREA		BLL=8	000	DNM=7-172	DS 0CL61	GROUP
DNM=7-200	02	FILLER		BLL=8	000	DNM=7-200	DS 50C	DISP
DNM=7-214	02	FIRST-TIME-SWITCH		BLL=8	032	DNM=7-214	DS 1C	DISP

together the displacement to the start of Working Storage within the storage area and the adjusted BLL cell displacement. The displacement to the start of Working Storage within the TRANSACTION STORAGE–USER area was calculated above as +4C.

WORKING STORAGE DISPLACEMENT IN HEX: 4C
ADJUSTED BLL CELL DISPLACEMENT IN HEX: 5D8
                                         ─────

DISPLACEMENT INTO TRANSACTION
STORAGE FOR FIRST BLL CELL IN HEX: 624

The first BLL cell is underlined in Fig. 11-13. The BLL cells are 4-byte address pointers, so by counting over we can locate any BLL cell. **The first two BLL cells are not used in CICS programs.** The third BLL cell is used to address the Execute Interface Block. This BLL cell contains the storage address X"0009B490". The fourth BLL cell addresses the COMMAREA if one is present. The COMMAREA BLL contains X"FF000000", which indicates that there is no COMMAREA. The fifth BLL cell is the FILLER BLL cell that is defined as the CICS BLL in the Linkage Section. This BLL always contains its own address (it points to itself). After the filler BLL are the user BLL cells in the order in which they were defined in the Linkage Section.

Figure 11-21 contains the part of the DMAP in which the Linkage Section fields are defined. Suppose that we wanted to find the FILE-INPUT-AREA which is defined in the Linkage Section. All that has to be done is to find the area in the DMAP. From Fig. 11-21 we can ascertain that this area is addressed by BLL 7. In the Linkage Section storage that we have located in Fig. 11-13, we count over from BLL 1 to BLL 7; this area is the address of the FILE-INPUT-AREA. An arrow points to the full word that is BLL 7. In Fig. 11-13, BLL 7 contains binary, zeros so we hadn't read the file record yet when the task abended.

REVIEW EXERCISE

Mark each of the following True (T) or False (F).

_____ 1. The CECI transaction permits the entry and execution of CICS commands directly from a CICS terminal.

_____ 2. Errors detected during the execution of CICS system sub-tasks (such as the Task Control dispatcher) are the most serious errors that can occur during CICS execution, because they always result in a system crash.

_____ 3. If an abend occurs in an application task, DFHSRP can recover from the failure by purging the faulty application task.

_____ 4. If the System Recovery Program can recover an online task failure by purging the faulty task from the region, a dump is written to the CICS Dump Data Set and a message is written to the terminal operator indicating that an abend has taken place.

_____ 5. The Linkage Section is just like Working Storage, so it is not necessary to ensure that proper addressability is acquired before using a data area defined therein.

_____ 6. As soon as a CICS application program is completely coded and compiled, it is best to dash to the nearest terminal and start testing immediately.

_____ 7. CECI and CEMT are conversational transactions. This means that, once you have entered the TRANSID, it is necessary to explicitly terminate the session by pressing PF3/PF15 and then the CLEAR key.

_____ 8. Variables defined in CECI last only for the execution of a single command, and must be redefined on a command-by-command basis within each CECI session.

_____ 9. The System Recovery Program categorizes abends based upon three criterion. If the abend is an application task, SRP purges the faulty task. If a storage violation is detected, SRP passes control to the Storage Recovery Program so that storage recovery can be attempted. If the failure is within a system subtask, SRP allows the system to crash.

_____ 10. The most difficult thing to remember about using CEDF is to enter the CEDF TRANSID before initiating the program being tested.

_____ 11. When using CEDF to debug an application program, it is not possible to modify the contents of Working Storage.

_____ 12. An "ASRA" indicates that a program check has occurred. A batch equivalent to an ASRA could be a data exception, an addressing exception, an operation exception, or a protection exception.

_____ 13. A storage violation might be caused by an application program that misuses a BLL cell, oversubscripts a storage table, or otherwise overruns a storage area.

_____ 14. The CEMT transaction can be used to obtain the latest version of a program being tested. This means that, if a module is tested and then recompiled while CICS is up, we can get the new load module into the CICS region by using CEMT and requesting a NEW program copy.

_____ 15. The Dump Utility Program (DFHDUP), which prints the CICS Dump Data set, is parameter driven, and we can therefore select one or more dumps that we want printed.

_____ 16. The Program Status Word (PSW) is provided in a CICS ASRA dump. This area contains a code indicating the type of program check (0C7, 0C4, etc.), and provides the address of the next sequential instruction.

_____ 17. When relating the next sequential instruction of the PSW to an application program, it is not necessary to have a PMAP or CLIST available.

_____ 18. In order to relate a storage next instruction address to a COBOL listing, it is necessary to adjust the program's load address to take into account the length of the DFHECI.

_____ 19. The length of DFHECI can be found in the Linkage Editor map. The stub size can change with new releases of CICS, and it is therefore a good idea to verify its length by looking at the Linkage Editor map, particularly when using a new release of CICS.

_____ 20. To examine the contents of Working Storage fields in a CICS transaction dump, it is merely necessary to locate the load module in storage. Working Storage is, after all, a part of the load module.

ANSWERS TO REVIEW EXERCISE

Mark each of the following True (T) or False (F).

___T___ 1. The CECI transaction permits the entry and execution of CICS commands directly from a CICS terminal.

___T___ 2. Errors detected during the execution of CICS system subtasks (such as the Task Control dispatcher) are the most serious errors that can occur during CICS execution, because they always result in a system crash.

___T___ 3. If an abend occurs in an application task, DFHSRP can recover from the failure by purging the faulty application task.

___T___ 4. If the System Recovery Program can recover an online task failure by purging the faulty task from the region, a dump is written to the CICS Dump Data Set and a message is written to the terminal operator indicating that an abend has taken place.

___F___ 5. The Linkage Section is just like Working Storage, so it is not necessary to ensure that proper addressability is acquired before using a data area defined therein.

___F___ 6. As soon as a CICS application program is completely coded and compiled, it is best to dash to the nearest terminal and start testing immediately.

___T___ 7. CECI and CEMT are conversational transactions. This means that, once you have entered the TRANSID, it is necessary to explicitly terminate the session by pressing PF3/PF15 and then the CLEAR key.

___F___ 8. Variables defined in CECI last only for the execution of a single command, and must be redefined on a command-by-command basis within each CECI session.

___T___ 9. The System Recovery Program categorizes abends based upon three criterion. If the abend is an application task, SRP purges the faulty task. If a storage violation is detected, SRP passes control to the Storage Recovery Program so that storage recovery can be attempted. If the failure is within a system subtask, SRP allows the system to crash.

___T___ 10. The most difficult thing to remember about using CEDF is to enter the CEDF TRANSID before initiating the program being tested.

___F___ 11. When using CEDF to debug an application program, it is not possible to modify the contents of Working Storage.

___T___ 12. An "ASRA" indicates that a program check has occurred. A batch equivalent to an ASRA could be a data exception, an addressing exception, an operation exception, or a protection exception.

___T___ 13. A storage violation might be caused by an application program that misuses a BLL cell, oversubscripts a storage table, or otherwise overruns a storage area.

___T___ 14. The CEMT transaction can be used to obtain the latest version of a program being tested. This means that, if a module is tested and then recompiled while CICS is up, we can get the new load module into the CICS region by using CEMT and requesting a NEW program copy.

___F___ 15. The Dump Utility Program (DFHDUP), which prints the CICS Dump Data Set, is parameter driven, and we can therefore select one or more dumps that we want printed.

___T___ 16. The Program Status Word (PSW) is provided in a CICS ASRA dump. This area contains a code indicating the type of program check (0C7, 0C4, etc.), and provides the address of the next sequential instruction.

___F___ 17. When relating the next sequential instruction of the PSW to an application program, it is not necessary to have a PMAP or CLIST available.

___T___ 18. In order to relate a storage next instruction address to a COBOL listing, it is necessary to adjust the program's load address to take into account the length of the DFHECI.

___T___ 19. The length of DFHECI can be found in the linkage editor map. The stub size can change with new releases of CICS, and it is therefore a good idea to verify its length by looking at the Linkage Editor map, particularly when using a new release of CICS.

_____F_____ 20. To examine the contents of Working Storage fields in a CICS transaction dump, it is merely necessary to locate the load module in storage. Working Storage is, after all, a part of the load module.

chapter *12*

Application Design Facilities

In this chapter we address the use of CICS in order to design online systems. We begin with a discussion of three facilities that are quite useful from a design standpoint: Transient Data, Temporary Storage, and Interval Control. Our examination will include a discussion of the command coding and unusual conditions associated with each command. However, we also focus upon the general design use of each facility within an application. The aspects of CICS that we have dealt with up to now are relatively easy to understand in terms of online utilization. However, in the case of the facilities mentioned above it requires in-depth knowledge to envision how they might be used. Therefore, we will also relate examples pertaining to the application of these features.

12.1 TRANSIENT DATA

Transient Data is a general queueing facility within CICS. There are two types of Transient Data queues that can be built; both of these must be defined in a CICS table called the Destination Control Table (DCT). The Destination Control Table defines the type of queue and specifies special features (such as queue recoverability where applicable). From the vantage point of program coding, the differences between the two types of queues—Extrapartition and Intrapartition—are unremarkable. The same commands are used to write to or read from either type of queue. **However, in designing a CICS system, the differences between the uses of these two types of Transient Data are enormous.**

12.1.1 Extrapartition Transient Data

Extrapartition Transient Data provides the ability to read from or write to a standard sequential file. Normally, Extrapartition Transient Data is used as a shared DASD mechanism between a CICS region and another region, either a batch job or another online system. Outside of CICS, the Extrapartition Transient Data queue is, in fact, a standard sequential data set built on any QSAM supported device. Extrapartition queues can be either an input to or an output from CICS—**a single queue may not be both.** Normally, Extrapartition Transient Data queues are used sparingly, if at all.

The reason for this derives from the overhead incurred with its heavy utilization. The access method support for *Extrapartition Transient Data* is provided by the *Queued Sequential Access Method* (QSAM). To understand the significance of this fact, remember some basic facts about CICS multitasking. First, good performance is achieved through the concurrent processing of application tasks. CICS overlaps task processing with input or output operations. When one task is forced to wait for the completion of I/O, CICS allows another task to execute. However, CICS can retain control of the central processor (and thereby perform multitasking subsequent to an input or output request) only when using the Basic Access technique. Normally, CICS uses the basic technique and can therefore multitask while I/O operations are going on. However, the queued technique is used with Extrapartition Transient Data, and the entire CICS region waits for I/O operations. No internal CICS multitasking is done during Extrapartition Transient Data I/O operations. If used a great deal, this can affect response time.

As an example of how Extrapartition Transient Data can be used, let's consider a user who desires to have occasional ad hoc reports printed online. The user never knows in advance of CICS processing which reports are going to be needed, and many of the possible reports involve sorting information and reading and summarizing multiple files. Furthermore, there is no predictable sequence as to which reports are needed. If we knew in advance that specific reports would be desired, then we could run a batch job before CICS comes up and save reports in an online file. Printing them online would then be a simple matter. However, to create all possible reports every evening when none might be desired would be a waste of computer time.

On the other hand, to include all of the reporting programs in the CICS system and perform extensive processing in the online region is equally undesirable. What we need is a way to share DASD between CICS and a batch region. An output Extrapartition Transient Data queue to CICS could be defined as an internal reader to the operating system. When the user in our example selects a particular report from a report menu, our online program could write a few JCL statements to this output queue, thereby submitting a job to run the appropriate reporting system in batch.

The output report is written to a sequential disk data set, and this data set becomes an input Extrapartition Transient Data queue to CICS. When the report is complete, a CICS application program reads and prints the data online. Although the I/O using Extrapartition Transient Data does not allow CICS to multitask, the benefit of off loading heavy processing away from the online region is evident.

12.1.2 Intrapartition Transient Data

Intrapartition Transient Data queues are internal to CICS, that is, they can be created and read only within the CICS region. Conceptually, Intrapartition queues are separate sequential groups of data records. Physically, however, all intrapartition data are stored in one physical data set with the DDNAME of DFHINTRA. DFHINTRA is a VSAM data set that is dynamically carved up to accommodate logical record queues. Transient Data saves next input and next output pointers for each queue in the queue's Destination Control Table entry, and a space map is used to allocate control intervals within DFHINTRA. Since VSAM is used, the CICS wait associated with Extrapartition Transient Data queues is not applicable to Intrapartition queues.

Transactions can be initiated automatically in association with Intrapartition queues. When such a queue is defined in the Destination Control Table, a trigger level, TRANSID, and destination factor can be defined. The trigger level specifies a record count within each queue; when reached, it causes CICS to internally initiate or trigger a task. The TRANSID of the automatic task is defined in the queue's Destination Control Table entry, and the task can be associated with a CICS terminal or it can be an internal task (one that is not attached to a terminal). The following is an example of a Destination Control Table entry for an Intrapartition Transient Data queue:

```
DFHDCT TYPE=INTRA,DESTID=T001,DESTFAC=TERMINAL,
       TRIGLEV=1,TRANSID=ROUT
```

The DESTID parameter is the logical name of the queue used when records are to be saved or retrieved using CICS commands. The Transient Data program monitors the number of records written to the queue, and when the TRIGLEV is reached the TRANSID "ROUT" is used to initiate an internal task. ROUT must be defined in the Program Control Table, and the program associated with this transaction must also be represented in the Processing Program Table. The DESTination FACtor of the terminal implies that there is a terminal required for the automatic task. A terminal name (TERMID) can be defined in the queue's Destination Control Table entry. **If a terminal ID is not explicitly defined, CICS assumes that the required terminal has the same name (TERMID) as the queue (DESTID).** When the ROUT transaction is to be triggered, CICS schedules the use of the terminal associated with the queue. The ROUT transaction is initiated, and attached to the terminal T001. The DESTFAC of FILE can also be used, in which case the initiated task is strictly an internal task, and not associated with a terminal.

As an example of how this facility could be used, let's examine a hospital information system. Patient laboratory test results are entered and stored in a patient data base. However, in addition, it is also desirable to note patients with abnormal test results and automatically schedule the display of information regarding these individuals at appropriate terminals. The attending medical staff can thus be alerted immediately and take appropriate action. In this case, the data entry program detecting an abnormality could write a queue record containing the patient number to the intrapartition queue defined above. As soon as a single item is written to the destination T001, the ROUT transaction is initiated at the terminal with the same name. The application program associated with the ROUT transaction reads the queue and retrieves and displays the patient information from the patient data base. In this application it is necessary to respond to the presence of a data record by initiating a CICS transaction. Utilizing Intrapartition Transient Data, this capability is exactly what is provided. Automatic transaction initiation is not available for Extrapartition Transient Data. Intrapartition Transient Data queues can be recoverable by CICS, whereas Extrapartition queues cannot. Thus, the two types of Transient Data are really quite different. From the perspective of program coding, however, the same commands are used to store and retrieve data records.

12.2 THE WRITEQ TD COMMAND

The WRITEQ TD command is used to store a record in a Transient Data queue defined in the Destination Control Table. The format of the command is as follows:

```
EXEC CICS WRITEQ TD QUEUE    (destid)
                    FROM     (record-name)
                    LENGTH   (length)
                    SYSID    (system-name)
```

12.2.1 WRITEQ TD Command Discussion

The QUEUE option is used to name the Transient Data queue or DESTination IDentifier as defined in the Destination Control Table.

The name of the data record is supplied in the FROM option, and the length of the record is provided in the LENGTH option.

SYSID is included if the queue is to be built in another CICS system. In this case, the name of the other system is provided with this option.

12.3 THE READQ TD COMMAND

The READQ TD command is used to retrieve a record from a Transient Data queue. The format is as follows:

```
EXEC CICS READQ TD QUEUE    (destid)
                   INTO     (area)  or    SET    (BLL-cell)
                   LENGTH   (area)
                   SYSID    (system-id)
                   NOSUSPEND
```

The NOSUSPEND option is used in lieu of HANDLE, IGNORE, or other unusual condition processing for the QBUSY condition. See the explanation of QBUSY below.

12.4 THE DELETEQ TD COMMAND

The DELETEQ TD command is used to delete an Intrapartition queue. Usually Transient Data queues are readable only once. As records are read the pointers to them are deleted, and thus such a queue is self-deleting. However, the information in the Destination Control Table can define a queue that is not deleted as read, and in this case the DELETEQ TD is used when the queue is no longer needed. Likewise, if a queue is built and then no longer needed, it could be deleted. Deleting queues when appropriate is important, because space within DFHINTRA is not limitless.

The format of the command is:

```
EXEC CICS DELETEQ TD QUEUE (destid)
                     SYSID (system-name)
```

12.5 UNUSUAL CONDITIONS ASSOCIATED WITH TRANSIENT DATA

The unusual conditions that can occur during the processing of Transient Data commands are listed and described below.

IOERR (Input/Output ERRor) can occur during READQ TD or WRITEQ TD execution. Unless HANDLEd or IGNOREd, the task is terminated.

ISCINVREQ indicates that an error passed from a remote system cannot be classified as one of the other conditions. This is pertinent to WRITEQ TD, READQ TD, and DELETEQ TD. The default course of action is for CICS to terminate the task.

LENGERR can occur in several situations. For READQ TD in MOVE mode, the LENGTH option is either omitted when accessing a queue with variable length records, or indicates a size smaller than the actual record retrieved. For WRITEQ TD, either the LENGTH option is not specified for a queue with variable length records, or it specifies a size that is larger than the maximum record size defined for a queue in the Destination Control Table entry. This condition can also occur if an incorrect record length is defined for a queue with fixed length records. This last instance is applicable to either input or output. If the condition is left to default, the task is terminated.

NOSPACE can occur during an attempt to WRITEQ TD to an Intrapartition queue. This indicates that DFHINTRA has run out of space, and the default course of action is task termination.

The NOTAUTH condition indicates that CICS security has detected a failure during an attempt to use a Transient Data queue. NOTAUTH is applicable to READQ TD, WRITEQ TD, and DELETEQ TD.

The NOTOPEN condition can occur for READQ TD or WRITEQ TD when an Extrapartition queue is closed. By default the task is terminated when the condition occurs.

In OS systems the QBUSY condition can occur during the processing of a READQ TD against an Intrapartition queue that is being deleted or written to by another task. Unless the condition is HANDLEd or IGNOREd, the reading task waits until the queue is no longer busy. The NOSUSPEND option of the READQ TD can be used to prevent task suspension.

QIDERR (Queue IDentification ERRor) occurs when a command is issued for a queue or DESTID that is not defined in the Destination Control Table. This is most commonly due to a spelling error, and can occur during WRITEQ TD, READQ TD, or DELETEQ TD processing. Unless HANDLEd or IGNOREd, the task is terminated by default.

QZERO indicates an attempt to READQ TD against an empty queue. A task reading a queue would detect end of queue data or 'End of File' when CICS raises QZERO. By default the task is terminated.

The SYSID condition occurs when the SYSID option names a system not defined to CICS; it is germane to all three Transient Data commands.

12.6 SUMMARY

Transient Data actually involves two facilities: *Extrapartition* is a mechanism to pass data between CICS and other regions; and *Intrapartition* permits batching of data and subsequent automatic task initiation within the CICS region. Data may be input or output to either type of queue, but Transient Data does not permit record updates. Only Intrapartition queues can be defined as recoverable to CICS.

12.7 THE TEMPORARY STORAGE FACILITY

The Temporary Storage Facility is another queueing mechanism in CICS. Temporary Storage queue functions as a scratch pad or storage facility for temporary data. These data can be stored and used within a single task, or a Temporary Storage queue can be used to pass data between different tasks. Temporary Storage differs from Intrapartition Transient Data in several ways. No automatic transaction initiation facility is associated with building a Temporary Storage queue; the Temporary Storage queue is built dynamically by providing a queue name or DATAID in a WRITEQ TS command. The queue need not be defined in a CICS table before it is built. There is a Temporary Storage Table (TST), but only queues with special requirements (such as recoverability) are defined therein.

Temporary Storage queues may be built in memory (MAIN), or they may be built in a VSAM data set that is dynamically carved up and managed by the Temporary Storage Program (TSP). Normally, only small amounts of data which are to be saved for short duration would be candidates for MAIN Temporary Storage. Most often, Temporary Storage queues are saved in AUXiliary Temporary Storage in the VSAM data set. This data set has the DDNAME of DFHTEMP in the CICS job stream. Data that are saved in Temporary Storage can be retrieved numerous times, and when a queue is no longer needed it must be deleted via an application program command (DELETEQ TS). Failure to explicitly delete queues may result in the system running out of space in DFHTEMP. Unlike Transient Data records, data elements in Temporary Storage can be rewritten or updated.

Let's look at an example of how Temporary Storage can be used. Consider a system in which a non-IBM data base product (such as IDMS, TOTAL, or ADABAS) is used as a data base management system. The data base runs in another region in the same machine as a CICS system. CICS is used as a communications management front end; the data base management system is used to manage data. CICS application programs must retrieve data from the data base for subsequent display and potential update. The interface from CICS application programs is accomplished via data base calls across the CICS/data base regions. This is achieved by an interregion supervisor call (interregion SVC). This type of request is synchronous, meaning that while the data base management system is processing the data access, the CICS region waits. An application transaction involves displaying three screens of data, each of which is obtained from several different data base segments or records. When the transaction is initiated, all of the data base records are retrieved. The information needed for the first display screen is selected and formatted. Being pseudo-conversational, the program will send the screen and return control to CICS. The data areas used during task execution are released when the RETURN is issued; this includes the areas containing data base information. However, the data base information is still needed for subsequent screens. We could retrieve this information from the data base management system each time it is needed, or we could save data in CICS Temporary Storage. In terms of efficient operation, it is best to save the data base information needed using the latter method because Temporary Storage reads are asynchronous and allow CICS to multitask.

Temporary Storage is appropriate because we only require the data temporarily until the screens have all been displayed (and perhaps redisplayed). Much like notes on a scratch pad, the data are saved in Temporary Storage, and they can be reread as many times as needed. When the operator indicates the conclusion of the transaction, we simply delete the TS queue. One consideration is that the name of the queue must allow for reusability. The queue name must be constructed in such a way that multiple operators using the same TRANSID and program have separate queues built for each set of data base records retrieved. A literal value as a queue name does not accomplish this. For example, three terminal operators could enter the same transaction and request different customer account numbers. Let's say the program contains this command:

EXEC CICS WRITEQ TS QUEUE ('TEMP001') FROM (DB-REC)
LENGTH (DB-LEN) END-EXEC.

The queue name in the command is a literal, and regardless of the number of tasks executing within the program, only one queue named 'TEMP001' is built. The problems associated with this should be obvious at this point. The data for our three tasks are mixed within one queue, as opposed to having three queues which each contain a specific customer's information. Furthermore, whenever a task deletes the queue, all of the data are deleted. Obviously, the queue name should be constructed from a unique value associated with each task. The TRANSID and the program name are not unique. While the customer number is unique, using this value would require saving the customer number/queue name across tasks. This can be accomplished, but in this case it is unnecessary. Different operators use different CICS terminals, each of which has a unique terminal name passed as the EIBTRMID in the Execute Interface Block. If the EIBTRMID were used in the construction of the queue name, there would be a unique Temporary Storage queue built for each task. Therefore, the program code might look something like this:

```
DATA DIVISION.
WORKING-STORAGE SECTION.
77  DB-LEN              PIC S9(4)  COMP  VALUE  +52.
01  TS-QUEUE-NAME.
    05  TS-TERMID       PIC X(4).
    05  TS-TRANID       PIC X(4) VALUE 'RET1'.
01  DB-REC              PIC X(52).
    .

PROCEDURE DIVISION.
    .

    MOVE EIBTRMID TO TS-TERMID.
```

EXEC CICS WRITE QUEUE (TS-QUEUE-NAME) FROM (DB-REC)
LENGTH (DB-LEN) END-EXEC.

The use of the CICS terminal name assumes that we are not using pooled TCAM as the telecommunications access method. In the case where pooled TCAM is used, the pooled terminals are used on a next available basis, and therefore there is no one-for-one relationship between the CICS terminal name and an actual terminal. Two pseudoconversational tasks from the same physical terminal may be attached to different pooled terminal entries in the CICS Terminal Control Table. Different terminal entries would have different terminal names, and therefore this use of EIBTRMID simply would not work in a pooled TCAM environment.

In the example discussed above, separate queues were needed for each task. This may not always be the case. A Temporary Storage queue can also be used as a central collection point for information across different tasks. Consider an application in which audit control information is to be saved and at periodic intervals summarized and saved in an audit file. A queue could be built by all of the tasks needing to save audit control information, and at appropriate intervals the queue could be read and the information summarized and permanently recorded. The queue could then be deleted, and the cycle would begin again. In this example, all of the programs saving audit information would use the same queue name, and the queue would serve as a collection point.

There are several things that one should consider when using Temporary Storage. The first is whether or not the queue name should be a literal, resulting in multiple tasks building a single queue. The second is that, when building a queue, we ought to know when it is going to be deleted. In our first example, the queue would be deleted when it was indicated that the operator was through viewing the information and wanted to get on to the next customer or function. In the second case, the program that reads and summarizes the audit queue should delete it. The same program(s) that builds the queue need not delete it, but this must be done or the system will run out of room in DFHTEMP or MAIN storage. Lastly, we should consider if the queue should be recoverable (and therefore so defined in the Temporary Storage Table). In our first example, if the system crashes the operator would initiate the transaction again and the queue would be rebuilt. Therefore, no recoverability is needed. However, in the latter example we do not want to lose audit control information following a system crash, so a recoverable queue is indeed desired.

12.8 TEMPORARY STORAGE COMMANDS

The commands that can be used to build, read, and delete Temporary Storage queues are WRITEQ TS, READQ TS, and DELETEQ TS, respectively.

12.9 THE WRITEQ TS COMMAND

The format of the WRITEQ TS command is:

```
EXEC CICS WRITEQ TS
                    QUEUE      (qname)
                    FROM       (area-name)
                    LENGTH     (length)
                    SYSID      (system-name)
                    MAIN   or  AUXILIARY
                    REWRITE
                    ITEM       (area-name)
                    NOSUSPEND
```

12.9.1   WRITEQ TS Command Discussion

The QUEUE option is used to provide a name for the Temporary Storage queue being written. The name is limited to a maximum size of eight characters.

The FROM option names the data area containing the actual data to be written to Temporary Storage, and the LENGTH option describes the size of the data record.

SYSID provides the name of another CICS system in which the Temporary Storage queue is to be written. The other system must be properly defined to the local CICS system. Use of SYSID is optional.

Either MAIN or AUXILIARY storage may be used for Temporary Storage. AUXILIARY is the default, and causes the data to be saved within the DFHTEMP data set. MAIN should only be used for very small amounts of data that are needed for short duration (for example, during the life of a single task).

REWRITE and ITEM are used together to indicate that an existing Temporary Storage queue element is being updated. This means that an additional record is not being added to the queue. Rather, one of the queue's records is being replaced by the record being written. ITEM names the data area containing the element number. The ITEM option names a 2-byte binary field, and the value indicating an item number is relative to one. The ITEM option may also be used with a WRITEQ TS that does not include REWRITE. In this case, CICS returns the ITEM number of the element written to the queue. The first record written to a new queue is ITEM 1, and so forth.

The NOSUSPEND option is used to indicate that the writing task is to receive control back if the NOSPACE condition occurs.

12.10   THE READQ TS COMMAND

The format of the READQ TS command is:

EXEC CICS READQ TS

QUEUE	(qname)
INTO	(area-name) or SET (BLLcell)
LENGTH	(area-name)
ITEM	(item-number) or NEXT
NUMITEMS	(area-name)
SYSID	(system-name)

12.10.1 READQ TS Command Discussion

The QUEUE option names the Temporary Storage queue to be read.

The INTO or SET option is used to indicate either MOVE or LO-CATE mode input. INTO names an area in Working Storage, and SET names a BLL cell defined in the Linkage Section.

The LENGTH option is used in accordance with the input mode. In MOVE mode (INTO), the application program defines the size of the Working Storage data area which is to receive the input record. In LOCATE mode (SET), CICS returns the length in the field named in the LENGTH option.

ITEM is used to request the input of a particular ITEM number. This option gives us a random access capability within a Temporary Storage queue. If an item number is not specified, then CICS assumes that the next sequential record is to be input.

With the NEXT option, CICS returns the NEXT record in the queue. **It is important to remember that CICS keeps track of each queue on a system basis, rather than on a task-by-task basis.** There is one NEXT pointer per queue. Each successive READQ TS retrieves the NEXT record and causes the pointer to be updated. Unless a specific ITEM number is specified, the queue appears as a sequential data set in which each record is read once in sequence. When the last record has been read, the ITEMERR indicates an end of the queue. Records may subsequently be read indicating a specific ITEM number to be retrieved. The ITEM field is a 2-byte binary field.

The NUMITEMS option allows the application program to determine the number of items in a Temporary Storage queue. When a NUMITEMS field is included in a READQ TS command, CICS returns the number of items contained in the queue. The NUMITEMS field is a 2-byte binary field.

12.11 THE DELETEQ TS COMMAND

The DELETEQ TS command must be used to delete a Temporary Storage queue that is no longer needed. In many cases, CICS is very forgiving of application programming omissions. If we ENQ upon a resource, or obtain storage and do not take appropriate action to DEQ or FREEMAIN, CICS remembers and releases things. However, since Temporary Storage queues are supposed to outlive a task, CICS has absolutely no way of knowing when we no longer need a queue. Unlike Transient Data queues (which are normally deleted as they are being read), Temporary Storage queues *must* be explicitly purged. The format of the DELETEQ TS command is as follows:

EXEC CICS DELETEQ TS QUEUE (qname) SYSID (system-name)

The QUEUE and SYSID options are used in the same manner as described above for other Temporary Storage commands.

12.12   UNUSUAL CONDITIONS ASSOCIATED WITH TEMPORARY STORAGE

There are a number of unusual conditions that can occur during the execution of Temporary Storage commands. In most cases, the default course of action is to terminate the task when one of these conditions occurs. However, the NOSPACE condition is an exception to this. NOSPACE indicates that there is no room in Temporary Storage for the item being saved. If this condition is not HANDLEd or IGNOREd, then the requesting task is suspended within the CICS region until space becomes available. On the other hand, if the NOSPACE condition is HANDLEd or IGNOREd, then the task is not suspended, and control returns to the program based upon the rules for HANDLE or IGNORE condition processing. Essentially, then, the NOSPACE condition can be used to do a conditional write to Temporary Storage, and it is advisable for tasks to HANDLE or IGNORE the NOSPACE condition. Otherwise, when CICS runs out of Temporary Storage space, the system can potentially become overburdened with suspended tasks. The NOSUSPEND option of the WRITEQ TS command can also be used to make the command a conditional request. Figure 12-1 describes the nature of all Temporary Storage unusual conditions, indicating which commands are pertinent.

12.13   INTERVAL CONTROL FACILITY

The Interval Control facility manages the time services of CICS. These include support for time-based automatic transaction initiation, time-related task delay, and task event synchronization. The Interval Control START command can be used to initiate a transaction at a particular time of day, or after a given interval of time.

Since time services can be in either the near or distant future, CICS needs a way of keeping track of each Interval Control request and the information needed to perform the service. In order to accomplish the storage of time service information until the request expires, a small control block called an Interval Control Element (ICE) is created. The

Condition	* * * Explanation * * *
INVREQ	INVREQ indicates something invalid about the request. For example, a WRITEQ TS command may include a length indication of 0. In Macro Level, an application program can save a single data element in Temporary Storage or build a queue of elements. In Command Level, only the building of queues is supported. If a Temporary Storage command seeks to operate upon a single element built via the macro DFHTS TYPE=PUT, this condition occurs. In this case, the command could be either READQ or DELETEQ. INVREQ also occurs when there is an attempt to write to a queue that is locked by CICS for recovery purposes. The condition is applicable to the WRITEQ, READQ, and DELETEQ commands.
IOERR	IOERR indicates an input/output error against the DFHTEMP data set. This condition is applicable to the WRITEQ and READQ commands.
ISCINVREQ	This condition is returned by CICS when an error has occurred accessing a queue on a remote system. ISCINVREQ indicates an error that is not indicative of any of the other conditions. The condition is applicable to the DELETEQ, WRITEQ, and READQ commands.
ITEMERR	ITEMERR indicates that the program is attempting to access an item that is beyond the current size of the queue. This is applicable to the READQ specifying an ITEM number or a READQ NEXT when the end of the queue has been reached. For WRITEQ, this can occur when attempting to update an element with the REWRITE option. The condition is applicable to the WRITEQ and READQ commands.
LENGERR	LENGERR indicates that a MOVE mode READQ specifies an area length with the LENGTH option which is not large enough to accommodate the record being read from Temporary Storage. The condition is applicable to the READQ command.
NOTAUTH	The NOTAUTH condition indicates that resource security level checking has detected a security failure.
NOSPACE	The NOSPACE condition indicates that there is no space within the Temporary Storage data set for a record being written. This condition enables the application program to make the WRITEQ a conditional operation. If the condition is neither IGNOREd nor HANDLEd, and the NOSUSPEND option is omitted, then the WRITEQ is unconditional and the requesting task is suspended within the CICS region until space is released. The condition is applicable to the WRITEQ command.
QIDERR	The QIDERR condition indicates that a queue named in a Temporary Storage command cannot be found. This can occur during any READQ or DELETEQ command specifying a nonexistent queue name, or during a WRITEQ with the REWRITE option. If WRITEQ without the REWRITE option indicates an unknown queue name, CICS assumes that a new queue is being built. The condition is applicable to the DELETEQ, WRITEQ, and READQ commands.
SYSIDERR	This condition indicates a reference to a system that is either not defined or not currently connected to the local CICS system. The condition is applicable to the DELETEQ, WRITEQ, and READQ commands.

Figure 12-1. Unusual Temporary Storage conditions.

Interval Control Element contains all of the information needed to perform the time-related service when the ICE melts.

In order to handle time services in an efficient manner, CICS maintains a chain of Interval Control Elements pointed to by the Common System Area (CSA). The ICE chain is ordered in expiration time sequence, with the first element being the next one to expire. When the task dispatcher executes to perform a task switch or multitasking, the ICE expiration interval is checked. If in fact there is an expired Interval Control request, the task dispatcher invokes Interval Control to handle the time service. The most commonly used Interval Control request is the START command, which is used to request that a task be initiated automatically.

12.14   THE START COMMAND

The START command names a TRANSID that is to be initiated by Interval Control. This internal task can be requested for a particular CICS terminal by including the terminal's name in the TERMID command option, or the task can be an internal task that is not attached to a terminal. If a terminal is requested, then CICS schedules the use of the terminal and acquires this resource before the task is actually attached. For example, a requested terminal is in use; the interval control task will not begin until the task executing at the terminal has ended. Additionally, data can be passed in the START command. Such data are saved until the Interval Control task is initiated and requests the retrieval of its data. Let's examine the format of the START command and then discuss several examples of how this facility can be utilized effectively.

The format of the START command is:

```
EXEC CICS START
                TRANSID      (transid)
                TERMID       (terminal)
                INTERVAL     (hhmmss)  or  TIME (hhmmss)
                FROM         (area-name)
                LENGTH       (data-length)
                RTRANSID     (transid)
                RTERMID      (terminal)
                QUEUE        (dataid)
                REQID        (request-name)
                NOCHECK
                PROTECT
```

12.14.1   START Command Discussion

The TRANSID option names a transaction identifier that must be defined in the Program Control Table (PCT). This is the transaction that is to be automatically initiated.

The TERMID option names a CICS terminal that is to be acquired for the task. The task is not initiated until both the appropriate time arrives and the terminal is available for its use. The terminal must be defined in the CICS Terminal Control Table. If this option is omitted, then the STARTed task is an internal task, one that is not attached to a terminal.

The INTERVAL or TIME option specifies when the task is to be started. TIME specifies the expiration time, whereas INTERVAL specifies an interval of time which is added to the current time of day to arrive at the expiration time. The default value is an INTERVAL (0), meaning that the task is to be initiated immediately. Otherwise, the TIME or INTERVAL is specified as military time in the format of HHMMSS. HH represents the number of hours (which can be up to 99 for an INTERVAL). MM and SS specify the minutes and seconds, respectively (both values can be from 00 to 59).

The FROM option names a data area that contains data to be saved for the time-dependent task. Interval Control saves this data in Temporary Storage, and the DATAID or Temporary Storage name of the data is saved in the Interval Control Element. The data in the FROM area are free form and must, of course, be agreed upon by the STARTing and STARTed tasks. When the Interval Control-started task is initiated, the RETRIEVE command is used to ask for saved data.

The LENGTH option defines the length of the data contained in the FROM area. This is expressed as a 2-byte binary field.

The RTRANSID option is used to pass an additional data element to the STARTed task. The RTRANSID option can be used to pass up to four bytes of data (which ostensibly would be a TRANSID to be subsequently STARTed for the purpose of task piggybacking). As with the FROM data, the STARTed task uses the RETRIEVE command to obtain the RTRANSID data. This task could then do a START for the transaction named in the RTRANSID data.

The RTERMID option is used to pass yet another data element to the STARTed task. The RTERMID option is similar to the RTRANSID option, except that RTERMID is used to contain a terminal name for a subsequent START.

The QUEUE option is used to pass the name of a data queue to the STARTed task. The queue name can be up to eight characters in length.

The REQID option is used to provide a name for the Interval Control request. This is useful if it is anticipated that the request may have to be canceled using the Interval Control CANCEL command. If the REQID option is not specified, then Interval Control usually generates a name for the request, and the name is passed back to the application task in the EIBREQID field of the Execute Interface Block. If the NOCHECK option described below is included for a START command, then the request name is not passed back in the EIBREQID field of the Execute Interface Block.

NOCHECK can be used for a request made for a remote system.

NOCHECK means that there is less error checking provided, so the execution of the START is optimized.

PROTECT indicates that the Interval Control STARTed task is not to be initiated until the requesting task has completed a Logical Unit of Work (LUW). Completing a Logical Unit of Work indicates that the task is committing its modifications to protected resources. Once such work is committed, it is not backed out by CICS if there is a task or system failure. A task indicates completion of an LUW by RETURNing to CICS or by explicitly using the SYNCPOINT command. If the task terminates abnormally before completing an LUW, the START PROTECT requested is cancelled.

12.14.2 Use of the START Command

The START command can be used to be certain that a specific transaction is executed at a given time or at particular intervals, to reschedule activities, or to acquire a particular terminal for a CICS task.

Suppose that a Temporary Storage queue is built with audit control information which is to be read and processed at 15-minute intervals. We wish to be certain that this process takes place without any manual intervention, whether or not new data have been saved to the queue. The problem of "bootstrapping" this function into the CICS system is quite easily resolved. Any programs that are named in a Program List Table for Program Initialization (PLTPI) are executed automatically following CICS system initialization. Such a program could use the START command to name a TRANSID that is to execute in 15 minutes. When the time comes, the transaction is initiated, reads and processes the Temporary Storage queue, does a START for its own TRANSID naming an interval of 15 minutes, and RETURNs to CICS. Thus, the desired function occurs automatically at 15-minute intervals.

As another example, let's consider a credit collection system. A collection file, built by a batch system, is input to an online system that displays information about customers who are delinquent with installment loan payments. The collection file is ordered based upon the degree of delinquency, and the file is to be processed based upon this prioritization. The CICS application programs automatically display customer information in this sequence. When a customer's information is displayed, the terminal operator in the collection department telephones the customer and requests payment. The system allows the collector to record information about the customer's response. However, some customers are not available when the collector telephones. The collector may be told to telephone again in 15 minutes or at 12:00. We want to have some way of rescheduling the display of this account at the appropriate time. Therefore, one of the services available in the transaction is a reschedule request. The application program involved can use the Interval Control START to reschedule. Since the rescheduled request requires the account number to be reprocessed, this information can be passed with the FROM option.

Finally, let's discuss a use of the START to dynamically acquire a terminal. There is a data set containing reports which are to be printed online. The user wants to be able to dynamically request that a particular report be printed, and to this end one or more online printers are available in each user location. Based upon printer availability and health, it is desired for the user to select the equipment dynamically. What is needed is a report menu facility listing the reports available and allowing printer selection. The user invokes the report menu transaction from a video terminal, and the appropriate information is displayed. The user enters the desired selections. Using the Interval Control START, it is a simple matter for the application program to initiate a print transaction at the terminal selected. The print program may be a generalized program capable of printing any report in the file, in which case the identity of the report and any other pertinent information can be passed with the FROM option of the START command. After the START has been issued, the task at the video terminal can inform the user that the report has been scheduled and then RETURN control to CICS. This frees the video terminal while the report is being printed.

12.15   THE DELAY COMMAND

The DELAY command allows a task to request that its execution be delayed until a specific time, or until an interval of time has elapsed. The task requesting a DELAY is kept in the system, and is suspended by CICS until the time arrives. The DELAY is very handy if we are dealing with a small interval of time, but as the amount of time increases, so does the overhead. If we want something to happen at hourly intervals, for example, the expense of keeping a task dormant in the system for an hour has to be considered. The Interval Control request itself does not involve a great deal of overhead, because of the way in which Interval Control Elements are sequenced and checked by CICS. However, the task has resources allocated to it, and these resources (such as storage) are kept during the task's dormant phase. With a large interval, a better approach is for the program to do a START to initiate itself again. The task could then return control to CICS and free its resources. Admittedly, there is a certain amount of overhead involved for CICS to initiate a new task. Therefore, if the interval is small, using DELAY would minimize overhead. The format of the DELAY command is:

```
EXEC CICS DELAY
          INTERVAL (hhmmss)   or   TIME (hhmmss)
          REQID    (request-name)
```

The options of the DELAY command are used in the same manner as in the START command. The only additional note here is that the default time value is an INTERVAL (0). **The effect of a DELAY with the default interval is the same as the Task Control SUSPEND command.**

12.16   THE RETRIEVE COMMAND

The RETRIEVE command is used by an Interval Control-initiated task to request data passed to it by the STARTing task. The format of the RETRIEVE command is:

```
EXEC CICS RETRIEVE
          INTO   (area-name)  or  SET (BLLcell)
          LENGTH  (area-name)
          RTRANSID   (name of 4-byte area)
          RTERMID    (name of 4-byte area)
          QUEUE      (name of 8-byte area)
          WAIT
```

12.16.1   RETRIEVE Command Discussion

Either MOVE mode (INTO) or LOCATE mode (SET) can be used to obtain data passed from the STARTing task with the FROM option. The LENGTH option is used in accordance with the input mode selected.

The RTRANSID, RTERMID, and QUEUE options allow the retrieving task to obtain data passed in the START command.

There may be multiple requests to START a particular TRANSID within the CICS system. If the TRANSID and TERMID are the same for multiple expired START requests, then the task initiated to process the first expired START request can do successive RETRIEVES and obtain all data saved for the identical combination of TRANSID and TERMID. This makes sense, as one program is executing at a particular terminal with different passed data. It is therefore common for a program written in such an application to perform successive RETRIEVE requests and process multiple data elements if such data are available. If the WAIT option is not included in the RETRIEVE command, then CICS raises the ENDDATA condition as an indication that there are no more expired Interval Control STARTs for the same TRANSID and TERMID. If the WAIT option is coded, then the task is suspended to await further data from the expiration of another START request for the same terminal and transaction.

12.17   THE ASKTIME COMMAND

The ASKTIME command allows the Command Level task to request that the EIBTIME and EIBDATE fields in the Execute Interface Block be updated to reflect the current time and date. If ASKTIME is not used, then the EIBTIME and EIBDATE fields reflect the task startup time and date. The ASKTIME command is coded as follows:

```
EXEC CICS ASKTIME
```

The ASKTIME command can also be used to request that CICS place the time into a data field. The data field is a double word length (8 bytes). The format of the ASKTIME command used in this manner is:

EXEC CICS ASKTIME
    ABSTIME (double word-field)

The field named in the ABSTIME option is set to equal the number of milliseconds since January 1, 1900. Subsequent to the ASKTIME with the ABSTIME option, the FORMATTIME command can be used to request that the time and date be formatted. There are several different formatting options that can be requested. The options of the FORMATTIME command are:

EXEC CICS FORMATTIME
    ABSTIME   (field-named-in-ASKTIME)
    YYDDD   (date-field)
    YYMMDD   (date-field)
    YYDDMM   (date-field)
    DDMMYY   (date-field)
    DATE   (date-field)
    DATEFORM   (date-field)
    DATESEP   (date-separator)
    DAYCOUNT   (field)
    DAYOFWEEK   (field)
    DAYOFMONTH (field)
    MONTHOFYEAR (field)
    YEAR   (field)
    TIME   (field)
    TIMESEP   (time-separator)

By and large, the date formatting options are fairly self-explanatory. The DATESEP and TIMESEP parameters allow separator characters to be selected for the components of the date and time, respectively. If omitted, no separator characters are used in the formatted date or time. If the options are coded without specifying values, the defaults are "/" for date and ":" for time.

The DATE and DATEFORM options return the CICS date in the format defined in the Systems Initialization Table. DATEFORM returns a 6-byte field without separators between the components of the date. DATE returns an 8-byte field, and DATESEP can be used to request separators.

DAYCOUNT provides the number of days since January 1, 1900. The format of the field named in the DAYCOUNT option is a 4-byte binary field.

DAYOFWEEK, DAYOFMONTH, and MONTHOFYEAR each provide a 4-byte binary number. With DAYOFWEEK, the number is from

0 (Sunday) to 6 (Saturday). MONTHOFYEAR provides a number from 1 (January) to 12 (December). DAYOFMONTH is the number of the day in the month.

12.18 THE POST COMMAND

The POST command is used to request that CICS inform a task when a defined time has elapsed. POST causes CICS to acquire a 4-byte timer event control area, set the timer area to X"00", and pass the address of this 4-byte area to the requesting task. At the appropriate time, CICS posts the timer event control area by setting the first byte to X"40" and the third byte to X"80". The format of POST is:

```
EXEC CICS POST
          INTERVAL   (hhmmss)  or  TIME (hhmmss)
          SET        (bllcell)
          REQID      (request-name)
```

The INTERVAL, TIME, and REQID options are used as in the Interval Control commands discussed above.

The SET option names the BLL cell that CICS is to set to address the 4-byte event control area. The program can then interrogate an 01-level data area associated with the BLL cell to determine if the timer area has been posted or is no longer binary zeros. It is important to realize that the event control area can be posted only when CICS is given the opportunity to execute. Therefore, the event control area should be checked after returning from CICS command processing.

12.19 THE WAIT EVENT COMMAND

The WAIT EVENT command is used to request that a task be suspended until an event control area has been posted. For example, a task issues a POST command and receives addressability to an event control area. The task can test the area subsequent to CICS commands. Let's say that the task completes whatever processing can be accomplished until the timer has elapsed. The task wants to have its execution suspended until the timer elapses. The WAIT EVENT is used for this purpose. The format of the WAIT EVENT command is:

```
EXEC CICS WAIT EVENT ECADDR (BLL cell)
```

The ECADDR option names a BLL cell that contains the address of the event control area.

12.20 THE CANCEL COMMAND

The CANCEL command is used to cancel an unexpired DELAY, START, or POST request. When a prior DELAY command is to be canceled, the canceling task must use the REQID given when the DELAY request was issued. The task that initially requested the DELAY is suspended in the CICS system awaiting the expiration of the delay time, and therefore the CANCEL must be done by another task in the system. The effect of a CANCEL of this sort is identical to the expiration of the DELAY, in that the delayed task is no longer suspended and is therefore dispatchable.

A CANCEL of a POST request can be performed by the task that requested the POST, or by another task. If the same task that issued the POST is requesting its cancellation, the REQID option should be omitted; otherwise REQID must be used. The format of this command is:

```
EXEC CICS CANCEL
          REQID      (request-name)
          TRANSID    (transid)
          SYSID      (system-name)
```

12.21 UNUSUAL INTERVAL CONTROL CONDITIONS

Figure 12-2 lists the unusual conditions associated with Interval Control commands, explains what the conditions mean, and indicates which commands can result in the occurrence of the condition.

Condition	* * * Explanation * * *
ENDDATA	The ENDDATA condition indicates that there are no data for a task performing a RETRIEVE. This condition can occur if there are no more data waiting for a particular combination of TRANSID and TERMID. As such, this is similar to an END OF FILE condition. ENDDATA can also occur if a non-Interval Control-initiated task issues a RETRIEVE command, or if an Interval Control STARTed task has no data passed with the initiating START command. The task is abended unless the condition is HANDLEd or IGNOREd. Use of the WAIT option with the RETRIEVE command results in the task waiting for more data, rather than causing the ENDDATA condition.
ENVDEFERR	ENVDEFERR indicates that a RETRIEVE command names a data option not used in the initiating START command. For example, the START does not name a QUEUE option, but the RETRIEVE command does. The data options of both a START and an ensuing RETRIEVE must agree.
EXPIRED	The EXPIRED condition indicates that the time requested in an Interval Control command has already expired. This condition is applicable to the DELAY and POST commands.
INVTSREQ	The INVTSREQ condition occurs during a RETRIEVE command if the appropriate Temporary Storage support has not been included in the CICS system. If this occurs, the systems programmer should be notified so that the CICS system can be altered to provide Temporary Storage support.

Figure 12-2. Unusual Interval Control conditions.

Condition	* * * Explanation * * *
INVREQ	The INVREQ condition indicates that there is something invalid about an Interval Control request. Therefore, the coding of the appropriate command should be checked. INVREQ in response to a WAIT EVENT may be caused by an event control area that is above the 16-megabyte line. INVREQ can result from a CANCEL, DELAY, POST, RETRIEVE, START, or WAIT EVENT.
ISCINVREQ	The ISCINVREQ condition indicates a failure from a remote system which does not belong in the other known categories. This condition is pertinent to the CANCEL and START commands.
IOERR	IOERR can occur during I/O operations to Temporary Storage. This condition can occur during a START or RETRIEVE command.
LENGERR	The LENGERR can occur during MOVE mode input RETRIEVE commands. LENGERR indicates that saved data are larger than the input area size specified with the RETRIEVE LENGTH option.
NOTFND	The NOTFND condition can be raised during CANCEL or RETRIEVE commands. For the CANCEL command, this indicates that a named REQID does not correspond to an unexpired Interval Control request. For a RETRIEVE, the NOTFND condition indicates that the data stored for the task were retrieved and released already, possibly using a direct Temporary Storage request.
SYSIDERR	SYSIDERR indicates that the system named with the SYSID option names an undefined remote system. This condition can occur during a START or CANCEL command.
TERMIDERR	TERMIDERR occurs during START command processing if a terminal not named in the Terminal Control Table is requested with the TERMID option.
TRANSIDERR	TRANSIDERR occurs during START command processing if a transaction identifier not defined in the Program Control Table is requested with the TRANSID option.

If the above conditions are neither HANDLEd nor IGNOREd the default action is an abnormal termination of the requesting task. The only exception to this is with the EXPIRED condition; in this case the condition is ignored if not HANDLEd.

Figure 12-2. Continued

REVIEW EXERCISE

Provide a short answer for each of the questions below.

1. Extrapartition and Intrapartition queues are both supported by the Transient Data facility. How does CICS recovery support relate to each type of queue?
2. Do both types of Transient data queues require a CICS table entry before the queue can be used in an application program? If so, provide the table name.

3. Cite the differences in READQ TD and WRITEQ TD command formats for both types of queues. Are there any coding differences for Transient Data queues?

4. What exactly is an Extrapartition Transient Data queue from the operating system's perspective? How does the access method support of Extrapartition Transient Data potentially impact on online performance?

5. Can CICS automatically trigger or initiate a task based upon the number of records in a Transient Data queue? Is this capability associated with both types of Transient Data queues? If not, name the type for which automatic task initiation is supported.

6. Can a task initiated by Transient Data be associated with a CICS terminal? If so, how is this accomplished?

7. What are the special considerations that we have to keep in mind when determining the name of a Temporary Storage queue?

8. Must a Temporary Storage queue be defined in the Temporary Storage Table before being referenced in a CICS application program?

9. A Transient Data queue is normally self-deleting. As a record is read, its pointer is deleted. Is this true for Temporary Storage queues?

10. A Transient Data queue cannot be updated. Is this limitation applicable to Temporary Storage?

11. There are two places where Temporary Storage data can be saved. Name them, and indicate which one is used most typically.

12. How is a Temporary Storage queue made recoverable? Do we always want recoverable queues?

13. What happens if Temporary Storage queues are not deleted?

14. How can a WRITEQ TS be made conditional? Why is it desirable to do this?

15. A Temporary Storage queue is a logically sequential collection of records. If we read the queue without specifying an ITEM number, we receive the next sequential record. Is this next sequential pointer kept on a task-by-task basis or on a system-wide basis?

16. How can we ensure that a Temporary Storage queue name will create a unique queue for each task executing in the same application program?

17. What is the difference between the TIME and INTERVAL options in Interval Control commands?

18. The START command is used to programmatically request task initiation within a CICS system. A TRANSID is named in this command. Must the transaction identifier be named in a CICS table? If so, which one? What about the TERMID option?

19. What happens to data saved as a result of a START command? How does the STARTed task get its data?

20. The ASKTIME command can be used to request that the EIBTIME and EIBDATE fields be updated with the current date and time. If a

task has not performed an ASKTIME, what is contained in these fields?

21. There are four data options that can be specified in the START command. Is there any sort of coordination needed between the program issuing the START and a subsequent program that issues a RETRIEVE for the passed data?

CODING EXERCISE

1. Given the following program work areas, code a CICS command to write a record of 75 bytes to a Transient Data queue named "Q001". Q001 is defined in the Destination Control Table within our local CICS system.

```
DATA DIVISION.
WORKING-STORAGE SECTION.
77  QUEUE-LENGTH           PIC S9(4)  COMP  VALUE +75.
01  QUEUE-DATA-RECORD      PIC X(75).
PROCEDURE DIVISION.
```

2. Given the following program work areas, code a CICS command to read a record of 75 bytes from queue "Q001".

```
77  QUEUE-LENGTH           PIC S9(4)   COMP.
LINKAGE SECTION.
01  BLL-CELLS.
    04  FILLER             PIC S9(8)   COMP.
    04  TD-BLL             PIC S9(8)   COMP.
01  QUEUE-DATA-RECORD      PIC X(75).
PROCEDURE DIVISION.
```

3. Given the following program areas, code a command to save TS-DATA-RECORD in a task-unique Temporary Storage queue.

```
WORKING-STORAGE SECTION.
77  TS-LEN                 PIC S9(4) COMP VALUE +65.
01  TS-DATA-RECORD         PIC X(65).
01  QUEUE-NAME.
    04  TERMID             PIC X(4).
    04  FILLER             PIC X(4)           VALUE 'PGM1'.
PROCEDURE DIVISION.
```

4. Given the following program areas, code a command to read a record from a task-unique Temporary Storage queue. The record desired is the fourth item in the queue.

```
WORKING-STORAGE SECTION.
77  TS-LEN              PIC S9(4) COMP VALUE +65.
77  ITEM-NUM            PIC S9(4) COMP.
01  TS-DATA-RECORD      PIC X(65).
01  QUEUE-NAME.
    04  TERMID          PIC X(4).
    04  FILLER          PIC X(4)        VALUE 'PGM1'.
PROCEDURE DIVISION.
```

5. Given the following program areas, code a command to initiate a task and pass it the data contained in the data area named IC-PASS-DATA. The TRANSID to be used is PRT1. The task is to be attached to a terminal named T001 and is to be started immediately.

```
WORKING-STORAGE SECTION.
77  IC-DATA-LENGTH      PIC S9(4)  VALUE +50.
01  IC-PASS-DATA        PIC X(50).
PROCEDURE DIVISION.
```

ANSWERS TO REVIEW EXERCISE

Provide a short answer for each of the questions below.

1. Extrapartition and Intrapartition queues are both supported by the Transient Data facility. How does CICS recovery support relate to each type of queue?

    Intrapartition queues may be made protected resources, and CICS provides recovery for these queues. Extrapartition queues cannot be made recoverable.

2. Do both types of Transient Data queues require a CICS table entry before the queue can be used in an application program? If so, provide the table name.

    Yes, both types of Transient Data queues must be defined in the Destination Control Table (DCT).

3. Cite the differences in READQ TD and WRITEQ TD command formats for both types of queues. Are there any coding differences for Transient Data queues?

    There are no coding differences for the two types of Transient Data queues.

4. What exactly is an Extrapartition Transient Data queue from the operating system's perspective? How does the access method support

of Extrapartition Transient Data potentially impact on online performance?

Extrapartition Transient Data queues are QSAM files from the operating system's perspective. Because the queued access technique is used for their support, the CICS region waits during physical input/output operations. During this region wait, CICS is unable to perform its internal multitasking, and therefore excessive use can result in slower response times.

5. Can CICS automatically trigger or initiate a task based upon the number of records in a Transient Data queue? Is this capability associated with both types of Transient Data queues? If not, name the type for which automatic task initiation is supported.

The ability to trigger or initiate a task is limited to Intrapartition Transient Data queues.

6. Can a task initiated by Transient Data be associated with a CICS terminal? If so, how is this accomplished?

Yes, the queue is given a destination factor of TERMINAL, and the terminal is named in the queue's DCT entry.

7. What are the special considerations that we have to keep in mind when determining the name of a Temporary Storage queue?

If a literal value is used as a TS queue name, then one queue will be built regardless of the number of tasks executing in programs using the literal value name. This is fine if we want the queue to be a central collecting place for information. However, TS queues are frequently used to save task-unique information, and in this case the queue name must be such that each task will use a different name and therefore build a different queue. This can be accomplished by incorporating the terminal name (EIBTRMID) into the queue name. Each task will be executing at a different terminal, and each will have a unique EIBTRMID.

8. Must a Temporary Storage queue be defined in the Temporary Storage Table before being referenced in a CICS application program?

No, TS queues are intended for use as scratch pads. The only time that a queue is defined in the Temporary Storage Table is when the queue has special requirements (such as recoverability or security checking). Queues that are to be built in a remote CICS system are also defined in the TST.

9. A Transient Data queue is normally self-deleting. As a record is read its pointer is deleted. Is this true for Temporary Storage queues?

No, Temporary Storage queues must be explicitly deleted.

10. A Transient Data queue cannot be updated. Is this limitation applicable to Temporary Storage?

No, by using the REWRITE and ITEM options, we can replace an individual item or record in a TS queue.

11. There are two places where Temporary Storage data can be saved. Name them, and indicate which one is used most typically.

TS queues can be saved in MAIN storage and in the AUX data set (DFHTEMP). Most typically, TS AUX would be used to avoid using memory for long periods of time.

12. How is a Temporary Storage queue made recoverable? Do we always want recoverable queues?

Temporary Storage queues can be made recoverable by defining them as such in the Temporary Storage Table. If a queue is being used to save information between pseudoconversational tasks, then we would not want it to be recoverable, since subsequent to a system crash the user would begin the transaction again and the queue would be rebuilt. A queue that is being used as a central collection place may very well require recoverability.

13. What happens if Temporary Storage queues are not deleted?

The space is not reused. The Temporary Storage data set (DFHTEMP) would eventually run out of space, and tasks seeking to save data would encounter the NOSPACE condition.

14. How can a WRITEQ TS be made conditional? Why is it desirable to do this?

A WRITEQ TS can be made conditional by making provisions for the condition NOSPACE (i.e., HANDLE or IGNORE) or by including the NOSUSPEND option in the command itself. This is desirable because otherwise CICS suspends the task to wait until space becomes available. Generally, NOSPACE means that tasks have neglected to DELETEQ TS when queues are no longer needed. The likelihood of space freeing up is not great if NOSPACE has indeed been caused by such tasks. Therefore, tasks would become suspended waiting for space, and such tasks could accumulate in the system. Not only would we have problems with transactions that use Temporary Storage, but we could also develop problems with the CICS region as a whole as the number of suspended tasks increase.

15. A Temporary Storage queue is a logically sequential collection of records. If we read the queue without specifying an ITEM number, we receive the next sequential record. Is this next sequential pointer kept on a task-by-task basis or on a system-wide basis?

The pointer to each queue is maintained on a system-wide basis.

16. How can we ensure that a Temporary Storage queue name will create a unique queue for each task executing in the same application program?

    Use the terminal ID (EIBTRMID) in constructing a queue name.

17. What is the difference between the TIME and INTERVAL options in Interval Control commands?

    The INTERVAL option specifies an interval of time which is added to the current time to determine expiration time. The TIME option defines the actual expiration time.

18. The START command is used to programmatically request task initiation within a CICS system. A TRANSID is named in this command. Must the transaction identifier be named in a CICS table? If so, which one? What about the TERMID option?

    Yes, the TRANSID must be defined in the Program Control Table and the TERMID must be defined in the Terminal Control Table.

19. What happens to data saved as a result of a START command? How does the STARTed task get its data?

    Interval Control saves data for tasks to be STARTed in Temporary Storage. When a task is initiated, it issues a RETRIEVE command to obtain the data.

20. The ASKTIME command can be used to request that the EIBTIME and EIBDATE fields be updated with the current date and time. If a task has not performed an ASKTIME, what is contained in these fields?

    In lieu of using the ASKTIME command to update EIBTIME and EIBDATE, these fields contain the task startup time and date respectively.

21. There are four data options that can be specified in the START command. Is there any sort of coordination needed between the program issuing the START and a subsequent program that issues a RETRIEVE for the passed data?

    Yes, the same options must be specified on the RETRIEVE command as were named on the START.

ANSWERS TO CODING EXERCISE

1. Given the following program work areas, code a CICS command to write a record of 75 bytes to a Transient Data queue named "Q001". Q001 is defined in the Destination Control Table within our local CICS system.

```
DATA DIVISION.
WORKING-STORAGE SECTION.
77  QUEUE-LENGTH              PIC S9(4)  COMP  VALUE +75.
01  QUEUE-DATA-RECORD         PIC X(75).
PROCEDURE DIVISION.
    EXEC CICS WRITEQ TD QUEUE('Q001')
              FROM(QUEUE-DATA-RECORD)  LENGTH(QUEUE-LENGTH)
              END-EXEC.
```

2. Given the following program work areas, code a CICS command to read a record of 75 bytes from queue "Q001".

```
    WORKING-STORAGE SECTION.
    77  QUEUE-LENGTH              PIC S9(4)  COMP.
    LINKAGE SECTION.
    01  BLL-CELLS.
        04  FILLER                PIC S9(8)  COMP.
        04  TD-BLL                PIC S9(8)  COMP.
    01  QUEUE-DATA-RECORD         PIC X(75).
    PROCEDURE DIVISION.
        EXEC CICS READQ TD QUEUE('Q001') SET(TD-BLL)
              LENGTH(QUEUE-LENGTH)  END-EXEC.
```

3. Given the following program areas, code a command to save TS-DATA-RECORD in a task-unique temporary storage queue.

```
WORKING-STORAGE SECTION.
77  TS-LEN                  PIC S9(4)  COMP  VALUE +65.
01  TS-DATA-RECORD          PIC X(65).
01  QUEUE-NAME.
    04  TERMID              PIC X(4).
    04  FILLER              PIC X(4)            VALUE 'PGM1'.
PROCEDURE DIVISION.
    MOVE EIBTRMID TO TERMID.
    EXEC CICS WRITEQ TS QUEUE(QUEUE-NAME)  LENGTH(TS-LEN)
          FROM(TS-DATA-RECORD)  NOSUSPEND END-EXEC.
```

4. Given the following program areas, code a command to read a record from a task-unique Temporary Storage queue. The record desired is the fourth item in the queue.

```
WORKING-STORAGE SECTION.
77  TS-LEN                  PIC S9(4)  COMP  VALUE +65.
77  ITEM-NUM                PIC S9(4)  COMP.
01  TS-DATA-RECORD          PIC X(65).
01  QUEUE-NAME.
    04  TERMID              PIC X(4).
```

```
    04  FILLER              PIC X(4)              VALUE 'PGM1'.
PROCEDURE DIVISION.
        MOVE EIBTRMID TO TERMID.
        MOVE +4 TO ITEM-NUM.
        EXEC CICS READQ TS QUEUE(QUEUE-NAME)
            INTO(TS-DATA-RECORD)  LENGTH(TS-LEN)  END-EXEC.
```

5. Given the following program areas, code a command to initiate a task and pass it the data contained in the data area named IC-PASS-DATA. The TRANSID to be used is PRT1. The task is to be attached to a terminal named T001, and is to be started immediately.

```
WORKING-STORAGE SECTION.
77  IC-DATA-LENGTH     PIC S9(4)  VALUE +50.
01  IC-PASS-DATA       PIC X(50).
PROCEDURE DIVISION.
        EXEC CICS START TRANSID('PRT1') TERMID('T001')
            FROM(IC-PASS-DATA)  LENGTH(IC-DATA-LENGTH)
            INTERVAL(0)  END-EXEC.
```

chapter *13*

Sample System Design

13.1 OVERVIEW

In order to understand the integration of various CICS facilities in designing an online system, we will briefly discuss a sample application and describe how the system could be planned. Because we assume that the reader is familiar with applying for consumer credit, this application has been selected. A credit system of this type could be used in the processing of home mortgages, installment loans, car loans, department store charge cards, or bank credit cards. The consumer fills out a form detailing financial and credit information, and submits the form for processing. Our online system supports data entry of credit applications, credit analysis, and customer service functions.

As with the design of any system, it is critical to first understand what has to be done from a business perspective. To this end, we must either know the application or interview and observe the user on the job. We should ultimately know exactly what the user does, what information is needed in the performance of the job, and any special requirements. Under the category of special requirements, legal, security, and recovery/restart considerations would be pertinent to the application. Our credit system is going to allow data entry personnel to key data from application forms into the system. When data entry is complete, the system will display pertinent information to credit analysts, who will determine whether the credit request is to be approved or declined.

In addition to the information included in the application form, however, the credit analyst is going to require credit bureau information to verify the credit history of applicants. To this end, arrangements have been made for a communications connection to a credit bureau. The credit bureau provides a record format for inquiries, and the data entry function not only saves data entered by the operator, but also formats a valid credit bureau request record and obtains credit information. Therefore, credit bureau information will also be available for credit analysis. After reviewing the information for each applicant, the credit analyst will enter the disposition of the application and, if applicable, define a credit limit for approved requests. As the final aspect of credit analysis, we must notify the customer of the disposition of the credit application. Therefore, we must include an automated correspondence to print approval or decline letters.

Finally, the system will allow customer service personnel to view and update the customer master data base. In this way the customer service department will be able to answer customer queries and resolve potential problems.

Not all aspects of this system need to be handled during real time CICS processing. For example, there is no benefit to having automated correspondence letters printed in CICS. We can just as well build a batch system to read information collected online and print appropriate letters. By performing this function beyond CICS execution, system performance will not be taxed. As a general rule of thumb, we offload to batch those things that are not real time in nature, and certainly the printing of form letters can be accomplished after the online system has come down for the day.

Another thing that we can analyze in terms of batch processing is the actual updating of our customer master data base. We could perform real-time updates; this would mean that, after a credit approval has been made, customer data would be directly added to the customer master data base. Customer service updates to reflect such things as customer change of address would likewise result in real-time updates. However, if we are updating our data base online, then we potentially need to construct a fairly sophisticated Recovery/Restart system. We would not want incomplete updating done to our customer master data base, and therefore would probably have need for backout capability. CICS Recovery/Restart automatically handles inflight backout of modifications to protected resources by incomplete logical units of work. However, in order to accomplish this, CICS must save backout information on the system log. If we can avoid the need for logging of backout information, then we also avoid the associated overhead.

In some cases, real-time updates must be performed. Consider a worldwide airline reservation system which, by dint of executing across different time zones, is a 24-hour-a-day system. For this type of system, if we don't update online, we don't update. The system is not brought down at the end of 8 or 10 hours. The credit system, on the other hand, is centered in one time zone, and is brought down every evening at the close of the business day. Therefore, from this perspective we have plenty of time to update the data base during the evening and night. We have already determined that the automated correspondence is to be handled within a batch system, and updating the customer master file could be incorporated as a part of this batch system. The information collected online can be saved within a "transaction" file reflecting online transaction execution. This file can be used to update the customer master during execution of the batch system. In terms of recovery, all we need to do is to have a copy of the records written to the transaction file. Any duplicate or incomplete information saved in the transaction file can be weeded out in the batch system. If we planned to update real time, we would need to save both backout and forward recovery information. However, with batch updating of information collected online, it is merely necessary to save forward recovery information. Then if we sustain physical damage to any of the volumes containing the transaction file, we can use forward recovery information to recreate the file. This means the journaling of a single record, as opposed to journaling both before and after image data.

The one hitch with this technique is that the system must appear as if it were real time to the user. For example, if an operator in customer service enters a change of address for a customer, subsequent displays of that customer's information should reflect the latest data for the rest of the processing day. Therefore, we must potentially read information from the customer master data base, as well as data collected in the transaction file, and merge this information together in memory. This means that file access is slightly more complex.

Furthermore, there may be updates to updates. A customer service operator may alter customer address information 10 times during the course of a single day. The likelihood of this happening is not great, but we cannot dismiss the possibility. If we update the transaction file real time, then we may need backout capability. We could, however, simply add new information to the transaction file, giving each new data record a modification level that is part of the prime key. This means that reading transaction file records requires locating the record with the latest modification level. During customer service processing, for example, it is necessary to read the transaction file to find the most recent modification for a customer's information. If no modification exists, then we read the customer master data base. The customer's data is displayed on the terminal screen, and the terminal operator updates one or more fields. The file processing within the CICS application program uses the most current customer information in the system, and then updates this information to reflect the valid changes made by the terminal operator. This updated information is then written to the transaction file. If two or more updates were processed for a single customer, there would be multiple records for the customer on the transaction file. The customer number would be the same for all of the records, but the modification level included as part of the transaction file key could be used to determine which one is the most current record. Let's say that the modification level is a 2-byte binary field and the customer number is a 12-byte field. The transaction file key, in this case, is a 14-byte field, with the last 2 bytes reflecting the change level.

In processing a transaction against a particular customer number, we need to find the latest record. The modification level could be a numeric field, with each change level being reflected as an increment in the 2-byte field. To find the latest record, we would use the STARTBR command to initiate a browse for a customer number. Successive READNEXT commands could then be used until we reach a new customer number. File processing would be as follows: A STARTBR for the customer number is executed, followed by a READNEXT. The program then checks to determine if READNEXT retrieved a record with the appropriate customer number. If not, then the customer master file is read. If the READNEXT results in a record with the desired customer number, then the retrieved record is saved. Another READNEXT is performed. As long as records with the same customer number are retrieved, subsequent READNEXTs are performed.

Although this logic works, this processing is cumbersome, and potentially involves many READNEXTs. It would be far more effective if we could zip right in and locate the latest record, if one exists, with a single operation. This can be accomplished by changing slightly the treatment of the modification level field in the transaction file key. Suppose that the modification level started at the maximum value, and was decremented for each new record. Our modification field is a 2-byte binary field. The first record for a particular customer number would contain a modification level of high values, or X"FFFF". The second record for the same customer number would have its modification level field decremented by one, or be equal to X"FFFE". If the file is a VSAM key sequenced data set, we can use the GTEQ option of the READ command and not have to utilize the STARTBR and subsequent READNEXT. When the READ GTEQ is performed, the key used is customer number and a modification level of low values, or X"0000". GTEQ results in the retrieval of a record with an equal key or the next greater key. Therefore, we retrieve the record which contains the lowest modification level value (or the latest record) in one READ.

13.2 SYSTEM IMPLEMENTATION

The credit system is obviously not a huge system; nonetheless, it is easier to implement the system in small steps. Therefore, one of the approaches that we might take in implementing this system is to divide it into different steps or phases. From this perspective, we have to take into account how pressing business needs are. Is there more of a need for online credit analysis or customer service? The data entry part of the system is actually not a separate entity, because data entry is really done in support of credit analysis. Another consideration is whether or not there is an existing customer data base, or if this is a new aspect of business.

In our example, a customer data base exists, but there is a push to greatly expand the customer base. Therefore, for business reasons it is desired to implement the credit analysis function first. This means that data entry and credit analysis are the primary objectives; we can delay the customer service portion of the system. Therefore, phase I involves the implementation of data entry and credit analysis, and phase II consists of adding the customer service portion. By subdividing the entire system into two phases, the first part of the system should be ready and usable at an earlier data. The decision as to what is to be implemented in the first phase derives from business needs and plans.

There are several advantages to dividing the system into two separately implemented phases. The first benefit is that we can have earlier implementation of the more important portion of the system. Second, if there are design flaws or unknown problems, they will come to light before the entire system is built. We can correct any shortcomings before we continue with the development of the phase II. Last, we may be able to build the system in such a way that the implementation of the second phase is facilitated.

13.2.1 Screen Design

In the case of the credit system, there are existing forms that are used currently. Therefore, the way to start is by examining these documents. To design data entry screens without looking at the forms would be very questionable, since the data entry people will be keying information directly from the forms. If at all feasible, we are going to design the screens to follow the format of the user documents. The credit analysts currently use these forms when making credit determinations, and they are accustomed to the way in which information is presented. Also, in the event that the system is unavailable for long periods of time, the continuity between screen image and form makes manual fallback easier.

The information on the credit application form is fairly extensive. There is information about the applicant, which we will call indicative information. This includes name, address, telephone number, and personal references. There is employment information, which would typically include the name and address of the employer, number of years employed at the position, and salary information. Also, there is information about prior employment. If there is a coapplicant or cosigner for a loan, then there would be similar coapplicant information.

We also can expect there to be financial information about both the applicant and coapplicant (for example, the name of any banks where the applicant and coapplicant have accounts, and the types of accounts).

Information about other assets (such as real estate, bonds, stock securities, or life insurance) would also be elicited on the credit application. Likewise, the form would request liability information, such as other charge accounts, credit cards, or loans.

Based upon the size of the terminal display screen, we can fit varying amounts of information, but it is highly unlikely that all of the data can be contained on one screen. Therefore, we are dealing with a system in which multiple screens of information are to be entered and perused. The application form is divided into five different areas, as follows: applicant current information, coapplicant current information, applicant financial information, coapplicant financial information, and liability information for both the applicant and coapplicant. Based upon the size of the terminals being used and the organization of information on the credit application form, five data entry screens are planned. Figures 13-1, 13-2, 13-3, 13-4, and 13-5 illustrate the five different screens.

13.2.2 File Design

The old customer master file is a multireel tape file, and is therefore inappropriate for online system use. Therefore, we have the opportunity to

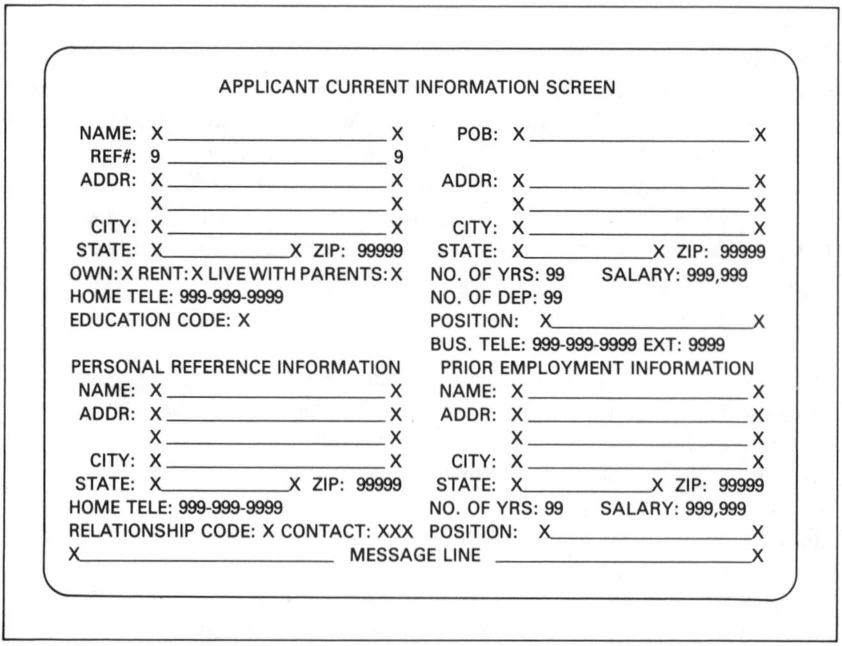

Figure 13-1. Applicant current information screen.

```
              COAPPLICANT CURRENT INFORMATION SCREEN

NAME:  X _____ X    POB:  X _____ X
REF#:  9 _____ 9
ADDR:  X _____ X    ADDR:  X _____ X
       X _____ X           X _____ X
CITY:  X _____ X    CITY:  X _____ X
STATE: X_____X ZIP: 99999    STATE: X_____X ZIP: 99999
OWN: X RENT: X LIVE WITH PARENTS: X   NO. OF YRS: 99   SALARY: 999,999
HOME TELE: 999-999-9999           NO. OF DEP: 99
EDUCATION CODE: X                 POSITION:  X_____X
                                  BUS. TELE: 999-999-9999 EXT: 9999
PERSONAL REFERENCE INFORMATION    PRIOR EMPLOYMENT INFORMATION
NAME:  X _____ X    NAME:  X _____ X
ADDR:  X _____ X    ADDR:  X _____ X
       X _____ X           X _____ X
CITY:  X _____ X    CITY:  X _____ X
STATE: X_____X ZIP: 99999    STATE: X_____X ZIP: 99999
HOME TELE: 999-999-9999           NO. OF YRS: 99    SALARY: 999,999
RELATIONSHIP CODE: X CONTACT: XXX  POSITION:  X_____X
X_____ MESSAGE LINE _____X
```

Figure 13-2. Coapplicant current information screen.

```
              APPLICANT FINANCIAL INFORMATION SCREEN

NAME:          X_____X   INCOME OTHER THAN SALARY: 9,999,999
BANKING REFERENCE INFORMATION          REAL ESTATE
     CHECKING ACCOUNT         PROPERTY:  X _____ X
BANK:      X_____X        CITY:  X _____ X
BRANCH:    X_____X        STATE: X_____ ZIP: 99999
ACCT NUM:  9 _____ 9        SHARE OWNED: 999%
TYPE CODE: XX CREDIT LIM: 999,999  EST. VALUE: 9,999,999.99
     SAVINGS ACCOUNTS         MORTGAGE: 9,999,999.99
BANK:      X_____X                 SECURITIES
BRANCH:    X_____X        NO. OF SHARES:           9,999,999
ACCT NUM:  9 _____ 9        NET WORTH:               9,999,999
CUR BAL:   9,999,999.99       TOTAL MARGIN: 9,999,999
                                   OTHER FINANCIAL ASSETS
BANK:      X_____X        LIFE INS. EQUITY: 9,999,999
BRANCH:    X_____X        COMPANY:   X_____ X
ACCT NUM:  9 _____ 9        POLICY:    9 _____ 9
CUR BAL:   9,999,999.99       OTHER:     X_____ X
X_____ MESSAGE LINE _____X
```

Figure 13-3. Applicant financial information screen.

```
            COAPPLICANT FINANCIAL INFORMATION SCREEN

NAME:        X_____X   INCOME OTHER THAN SALARY: 9,999,999
BANKING REFERENCE INFORMATION          REAL ESTATE
      CHECKING ACCOUNT         PROPERTY: X_____ X
BANK:        X_____X       CITY: X_____ X
BRANCH:      X_____X      STATE:  X_____ ZIP: 99999
ACCT NUM:  9_____ 9        SHARE OWNED: 999%
TYPE CODE: XX CREDIT LIM: 999,999   EST. VALUE: 9,999,999.99
      SAVINGS ACCOUNTS        MORTGAGE: 9,999,999.99
BANK:        X_____X            SECURITIES
BRANCH:      X_____X   NO. OF SHARES:           9,999,999
ACCT NUM:  9_____ 9        NET WORTH:               9,999,999
CUR BAL:   9,999,999.99       TOTAL MARGIN: 9,999,999
                                  OTHER FINANCIAL ASSETS
BANK:        X_____X   LIFE INS. EQUITY: 9,999,999
BRANCH:      X_____X   COMPANY:  X_____ X
ACCT NUM:  9_____ 9        POLICY:   9_____ 9
CUR BAL:   9,999,999.99       OTHER:    X_____ X
X_____         MESSAGE LINE _____X
```

Figure 13-4. Coapplicant financial information screen.

```
                   OTHER CREDIT ACCOUNTS

            APPLICANT                      COAPPLICANT
STORE CARDS:  X_____ X       STORE CARDS:  X_____ X
              X_____ X                     X_____ X
              X_____ X                     X_____ X
              X_____ X                     X_____ X
CREDIT CARDS: X_____ X       CREDIT CARDS: X_____ X
              X_____ X                     X_____ X
              X_____ X                     X_____ X
              X_____ X                     X_____ X
GASOLINE                        GASOLINE
CREDIT CARDS: X_____ X       CREDIT CARDS: X_____ X
              X_____ X                     X_____ X
              X_____ X                     X_____ X
              X_____ X                     X_____ X
OTHER LOANS:      9,999,999     OTHER LOANS:      9,999,999

TOTAL INDEBTEDNESS: 9,999,999   TOTAL INDEBTEDNESS: 9,999,999
X_____         MESSAGE LINE _____X
```

Figure 13-5. Current liability information screen.

design a new DASD data base. We are going to need to perform random retrieval of information from our new customer master file based upon the customer number. In order to have prime key retrieval, we choose a VSAM *Key Sequenced Data Set* (KSDS). CICS Recovery/Restart and Dynamic Transaction Backout (which delete records as part of reversing insertions) do not require any installation enhancements in order to work with the KSDS. If the data set organization did not support record deletion (which is the case with a VSAM *Entry Sequenced Data Set* (ESDS), we would potentially have to implement user exits in DTB and the Recovery/Restart subsystem. The user exit receives control when it is necessary to reverse an addition to an ESDS and logically deletes the record by setting on a record delete flag. Recovery and backout are not a consideration for this system, because we are not performing customer master updates in real time. However, if we were updating online, we would have to evaluate the extra effort to support ESDS use.

Where possible, files that are to be used online should be designed around the processing requirements of the online system. The first step in designing online files is to carefully analyze the data requirements of online screens. Data records should be planned so that the groupings of fields conform to the processing needs of the most frequently used screens. After data grouping requirements have been planned, the ways in which the files are to be processed must be analyzed. Will all data be accessed randomly? Will browse operations be done? How will the frequency of random access compare to the frequency of sequential access? Response time is one of the key factors used to measure the success of an online system. Response time can be optimized by designing files so that a minimum number of accesses are required to obtain or update information. Therefore, the format and structure of online files must be based on processing requirements.

13.2.2.1 Size Considerations The first size consideration is the physical record or VSAM control interval size. For sequential retrieval, as in file browsing, larger physical record or control interval size reads more information into storage in one physical read. However, for random access, larger physical record or control interval size means that much unused information is being read into memory. With random retrieval, only one record from a physical record or control interval is desired, and any other logical records brought into memory are not going to be processed. Larger physical records or control intervals mean larger amounts of storage being used for I/O buffers. If updating is to be done, then larger physical records or control intervals mean that more information is held under exclusive control. VSAM exclusive control is based upon a control interval. This means that, during update processing, no other tasks in the system are allowed update access to the reserved control interval. Obviously, the larger the control interval, the greater the likelihood of other tasks having to wait for update access to other logical records in a control interval undergoing update. The physical record or control interval size is determined on the basis of the type of access required, the type of DASD volume, and the logical record size.

Another consideration is the design of logical records themselves. One can design a single, large, encompassing record which contains most or all of the information about a particular item. Such a record requires only one disk read to bring into storage all of the information about the customer in our case. However, such a record may contain many fields that are not going to be used in the processing of a single screen. These data fields are transferred needlessly into storage, and require a larger work area space. If we are dealing with fixed format records, there may be many empty fields. For example, there may be no cosigner or coapplicant. In this case, a number of fields in the logical record would not contain meaningful data. Not only is memory wasted for buffers and work areas, but disk space may also be wasted.

Large "all encompassing" records can be broken into portions containing logically related fields. Such portions are called segments or segmented records. Segmented records that are designed around the needs of online screens usually result in data transfer optimization, increased efficiency of disk utilization, and smaller storage work area sizes for online tasks. If segments are designed properly, only the data items required for screen formatting are retrieved from disk; particular segments are read by particular screen-processing programs. Commonly used data fields that transcend a single screen can be grouped together to form a root or main segment. Since unrequired fields are not read by programs, the size of file buffers and program work areas is optimized by segmented records. The ideal situation is for a record to correspond to the data requirements of a particular data screen. This results in one read, as opposed to multiple reads for screen processing. The more frequently used the screen, the more beneficial is such an approach in terms of system performance. We will therefore develop our customer master file as a VSAM KSDS with segmented records such that the information needed for each screen will be a separate segmented record. The key of the customer master will be 14 bytes in length. The first 11 bytes form the customer number, and the next 3 bytes form a segment number. The customer master file is to be updated via a batch system which applies customer information collected online. Therefore, we need a "transaction file" in which the online information is collected. The key to the transaction file is to be 16 bytes in length, and will include a 2-byte modification level to allow multiple records to be added to the file to "change" the same segment multiple times. The batch system will select the latest update record per segment, and update the customer master. The format of the logical records on the transaction file is to be similar to record segments on the customer master data base.

13.3 SYSTEM DESIGN PHASE I

Phase I consists of online data entry and credit analysis. However, in addition to the data entered from credit application forms, the credit analyst needs credit bureau reports about each applicant. Therefore, credit bureau request processing is also included in phase I. The automated correspondence function is to be handled in batch, based upon an approval/decline code. Figure 13-6 diagrams the I/O processing of phase I.

13.3.1 Data Entry

The data entry function encompasses five terminal screens, but note that two of the coapplicant screens are identical to applicant screens except for the screen title. Therefore, if the screen title is treated as a data field to be filled in by a processing program, the same BMS maps can be used for applicant or coapplicant current information and financial information. Thus, three screens generated using Basic Mapping Support are required for data entry. Additionally, there are five Command Level application programs. There is a program to process each of the three BMS maps. One program is used to allow the entry of applicant or coapplicant current information. Another program processes applicant or coapplicant financial information. The third screen-oriented program is for the entry of other credit account information. Obviously, the data fields and editing rules vary for each program, but the programs are functionally similar. The data entry function will take the operator through the series of screens, edit entered data, and (when all data have been collected) place the data on the transaction file until the credit determination has been made.

One of the user requirements is that data entry operators be able to hop from screen to screen. We do not want a fixed series in the data entry programs, because in some cases there may be no need to enter certain information. For example, if there is no coapplicant, then two of the screens will have no data to be entered. Therefore, any of the screens must be able to lead to any other screen. The terminal operator can determine the next screen by using PF keys. Another advantage of being able to progress from one screen to any other is that an operator may need to go back to fix something entered incorrectly. The intelligence to go to different programs can be built into each of the screen programs. However, if another screen were to be added at a later time, we would have to go back and perform maintenance on each of the screen-processing programs because each program would contain this redundant code to perform routing.

In this system, we elect to develop a separate routing program that simply acts as a switch to determine which program processes next. The routing program is the fourth data entry program. When the transaction is

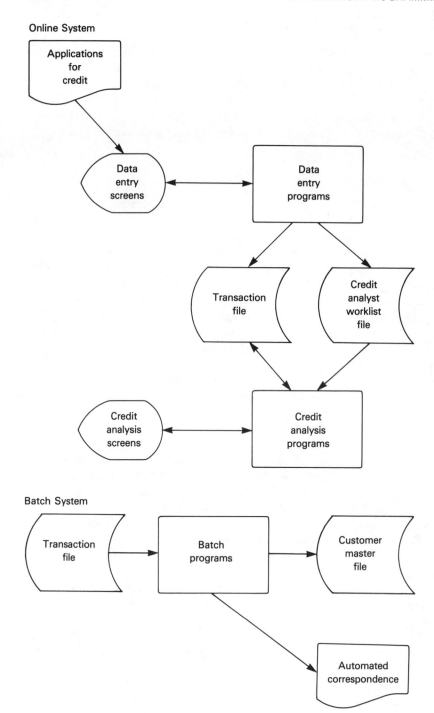

Figure 13-6. I/O diagram of phase I of the credit system.

initiated, we go to the router program, which determines that the applicant current information program is to execute by default. The router transfers control to this program. The applicant current information program displays the appropriate data entry screen, and returns to CICS with its own transaction identifier. The operator enters data and presses a PF key, and we return to the screen-processing program. The program validates the data entered. If incorrect fields are located, the program sends an error message and returns again with its own TRANSID. If the data are correct, then they are saved in a COMMAREA. Control is then passed via a CICS transfer of control back to the router. A COMMAREA is used between pseudoconversational tasks and for passing information between programs during task execution. By interrogating a COMMAREA indicator, the router determines that the mode of entry is from a program within data entry. The program transferring to the router has saved the EIBAID field within the COMMAREA. The router interrogates this passed information, and relates it to the next program. The router uses a CICS transfer of control to invoke the requested program, and this processing continues until all of the data entry information has been collected.

When data entry is complete, the terminal operator uses a PF key to request a final edit of all data across the various data entry screens. The router relates this PF key to a program, and transfers to the appropriate module. This program is the fifth data entry processor. The function of this module is to "cross-foot" all entered data. "Cross-footing" refers to cross-validating the data entered for all data entry screens to make sure that they make sense when taken together. If, for example, the presence of a coapplicant is indicated, we would expect certain information to be present. If there are errors at this time, the cross-footing program sends a message and returns with the TRANSID of the router. The screen that has to be changed must be determined by the terminal operator. The PF key selected causes the router to invoke the selected screen handling program. If the cross-footer finds that all data are correct, it saves data entry information on the transaction file. Then it prepares a credit bureau request and writes the request to an Intrapartition Transient Data queue defined in the Destination Control Table. This queue is defined with a TRANSID, a trigger level of 1, and a destination factor of terminal. The "terminal" in this case is the credit bureau system. When the data record created by the cross-footer is written to the queue, CICS enables the terminal connection and starts a task which is attached to the terminal (the credit bureau). Figure 13-7 gives an overview of the data entry function.

13.3.2 Credit Bureau Processing

Credit bureau processing is accomplished by two programs. Program 1 is initiated when a data record is written to the Intrapartition Transient Data queue associated with the credit bureau. When the program receives

Figure 13-7. Data entry transaction.

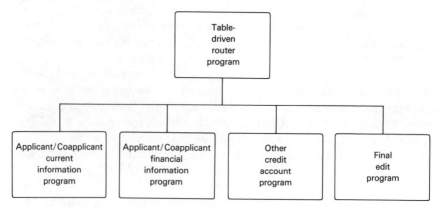

Table-driven router program drives the transaction.

PF1=applicant current information; PF2=coapplicant current information; PF3=applicant financial information; PF4=coapplicant financial information; PF5=other credit accounts; PF6=final edit; PA1=cancel transaction.

control, it is already connected to the credit bureau, as CICS has enabled the connection as a part of transaction initiation. This module merely SENDs and RECEIVEs data to and from the credit bureau. The module reads a record from the queue. The record is in the format defined by the credit bureau, so the program merely issues a CONVERSE command. We are not writing data to a video terminal, and therefore this module is, in fact, conversational. When data has been received back, the program is again given control.

During active periods of data entry, having one task to process all credit bureau requests could bottleneck the system. Therefore, we want this module to do as little processing as possible. Instead of having the credit bureau data interrogated, formatted, and saved on a permanent basis within this module, we want to break out the processing of credit bureau reports into another task. If the processing were done within this task, then such processing would be synchronous with credit bureau conversation. The SEND/RECEIVE program could not be processing while transmitting or waiting for data. Therefore, no transmission would occur while data formatting was taking place. To avoid this, the module writes data received back from the credit bureau to a second Intrapartition Transient Data queue. When data arrive in this second queue, the second program of credit bureau processing is triggered.

Program 2 reads data records from the second Intrapartition Transient Data queue, and formats these records into a data record, which is then written to the transaction file. This module also updates a credit analyst work list file with a reference number of the credit application. Figure 13-8 illustrates credit bureau processing.

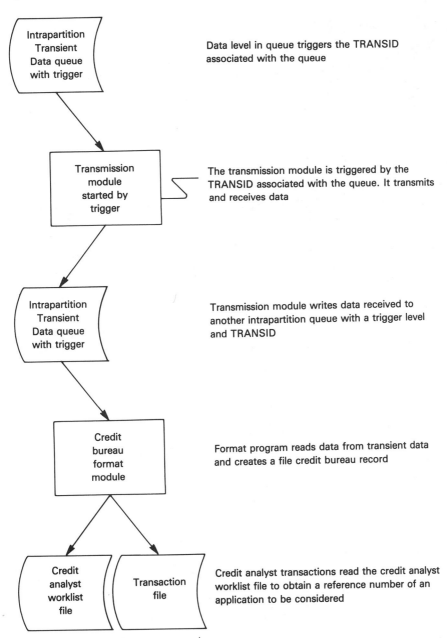

Figure 13-8. Credit bureau processing.

13.3.3 Credit Analyst Function

The credit analyst function is performed by using four BMS screens and six programs. The BMS screens are: the applicant/coapplicant current information screen; the applicant/coapplicant financial information screen; the other credit accounts screen; and the credit bureau information screen. The programs are: a table-driven router program to switch to the various screen-handling programs, as needed by the credit analyst; a program to process either applicant or coapplicant current information screens; a program to process either applicant or coapplicant financial information screens; a program to process the other credit accounts screen; a program to display credit bureau information; and a program to accept a final credit determination and save this status on the transaction file. This module also updates the credit analyst work list file to indicate that the credit application is complete.

The BMS screens used for data entry can also be used for credit analysis. The programs that perform screen handling can be built to allow for use within both data entry and credit analysis. The data entry router can be copied and altered, with a different table to handle the routing of the credit analysis transaction, or two routing tables could be included in one router program, with additional logic to differentiate between the functions. For the credit analysis function, we actually need two new programs and two new BMS screens. The two screens are for the display of credit bureau information and the entry of the final credit determination. The new programs are the credit bureau information display program and the module to accept the credit disposition. Figure 13-9 illustrates the functional relationship between the modules of the credit analysis function.

Figure 13-9.   Credit analysis transaction.

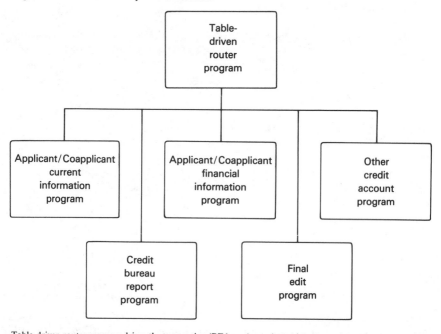

Table-driven router program drives the transaction (PF keys determine which screen viewed / processed next).

13.4 SYSTEM DESIGN PHASE II

Phase II consists of the customer service processing. Figure 13-10 is an I/O diagram of this function. In customer service the most commonly sought information is normally data regarding payments and charges. Therefore, the billing master file is to be available for online inquiries. Figure 13-11 illustrates the BMS screen used for displaying billing information. Provision is also included for saving and displaying general comments that document the customer's inquiries or problems, so a history can be kept of a customer's queries or difficulties. The BMS screen for general comments is illustrated in Fig. 13-12.

Information from the customer master file may also be required. The customer service terminal operators may occasionally need to update customer information (such as change of address) and, therefore, records may be written to the transaction file. Any customer data contained on the transaction file are to be merged with customer master information in memory. In this way, data displayed about customers are always the most current.

The screens and programs developed in phase I can be cannibalized to facilitate the development of phase II. In total there are five screens of information used within phase II. However, only two of these screens are additions to the system. Phase II requires two new programs to handle the displaying of billing and comments screens. The remaining programs are similar to existing programs developed for phase I. We could consider incorporating the logic to process the customer master into the existing

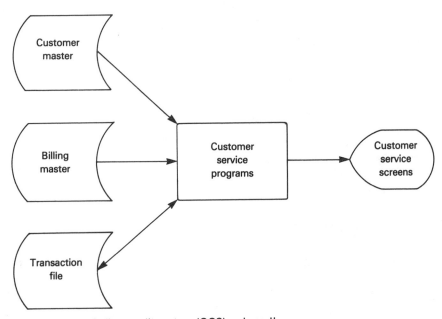

Figure 13-10. Online credit system (OCS)—phase II.

CUSTOMER INFORMATION				DATE: 99/99/99	

NAME: _____ ACCOUNT: 999-99-999

REFERENCE	CHARGES	CREDITS	TRANSACTION DESCRIPTION	DATE	RECEIPT
999999999	9999.99	9999.99	_____	XXX 99	9999999
999999999	9999.99	9999.99	_____	XXX 99	9999999
999999999	9999.99	9999.99	_____	XXX 99	9999999
999999999	9999.99	9999.99	_____	XXX 99	9999999
999999999	9999.99	9999.99	_____	XXX 99	9999999
999999999	9999.99	9999.99	_____	XXX 99	9999999
999999999	9999.99	9999.99	_____	XXX 99	9999999
999999999	9999.99	9999.99	_____	XXX 99	9999999
999999999	9999.99	9999.99	_____	XXX 99	9999999
999999999	9999.99	9999.99	_____	XXX 99	9999999
999999999	9999.99	9999.99	_____	XXX 99	9999999
999999999	9999.99	9999.99	_____	XXX 99	9999999

PREVIOUS BALANCE	TOTAL ADDED	TOTAL CREDITS	NO.DAYS IN BILL CYC.	FINANCE BALANCE	FINANCE CHARGE	NEW BALANCE	AMOUNT NOW DUE
9999.99	9999.99	9999.99	99	9999.99	9999.99	9999.99	9999.99

Figure 13-11. Billing information screen.

NAME: _____ ACCOUNT: 999-99-999

DATE	OPERATOR	COMMENTS
99/99/99	----------------	_____
		_____
		_____
99/99/99	----------------	_____
		_____
		_____
99/99/99	----------------	_____
		_____
		_____
99/99/99	----------------	_____
		_____
		_____
99/99/99	----------------	_____
		_____
		_____

Figure 13-12. General comments screen.

Figure 13-13. Phase II processing.

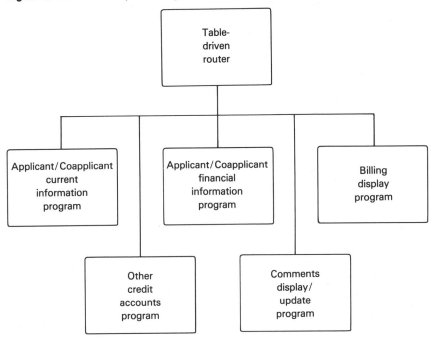

Table-driven router program used to drive the customer service transaction. PF keys determine the next function.

programs, but this might prove cumbersome and make the programs needlessly complex. Therefore, this approach would have to be considered carefully. If we choose not to incorporate the additional logic into the existing programs, they could serve as a basis for developing similar programs for phase II. The bulk of the logic is already coded and tested. Figure 13-13 gives an overview of the processing of phase II. Since this transaction also requires that we provide the operator with the ability to view data in any order, we again make use of a routing program.

APPENDICES

appendix A

VSAM Files

VSAM, the Virtual Storage Access Method, is more encompassing than other IBM file access methods, because there are three different types of VSAM files. The processing that can be done with each type varies a little. Therefore, we will examine each type independently.

A.1 THE KEY SEQUENCED DATA SET (KSDS)

The *Key Sequenced Data Set* is a keyed file, and as such is the VSAM equivalent of an Index Sequential Access Method (ISAM) file. A VSAM KSDS consists of an index component and a data component. During file loading, data records are inserted in collating sequence based upon a prime key. The index is built so that pointers to data records can be used to retrieve records on a random basis for particular prime key values. The index pairs prime key values and data locations within the file. The data location is the *Relative Byte Address* of a control interval (within the data portion of the file) that contains the data record with the prime key value. A Relative Byte Address is a relative position. The RBA of zero starts in the beginning of the data component and is incremented by one for each successive byte.

The KSDS facilitates file updating by allowing both record insertions and record deletions. Let's contrast how record insertions and deletions are handled for the KSDS as compared to an ISAM file. First, we'll look at record insertions.

ISAM additions are not added directly into the prime data area of the file. Rather, they are added into an overflow area. Records in overflow

377

are unblocked and chained to one another, so the access method must retrieve successive records from an overflow area until it arrives at the record being sought. If the desired record is the 21st record in an overflow area, all 20 of its predecessors are retrieved first. This means that excessive I/O and processing time are expended looking for the record.

ISAM deletions are handled on a programmatic level by using the first position in the record as a delete flag. By moving high values (X "FF") to this first byte and rewriting the record, we "logically" delete. When the file is reorganized using a processing program or an appropriate utility program (such as IEBISAM), the logically deleted records are not copied over to the newly reorganized file. This means that disk space is wasted if an ISAM file contains numerous records that are logically deleted. VSAM addresses both of these deficiencies of the ISAM file in the Key Sequenced Data Set. When defining a VSAM KSDS using the VSAM utility program IDCAMS, we can specify that we want embedded free space in the file. This embedded freespace is used for record enlargements or additions.

The VSAM equivalent of the ISAM block is called the control interval. The control interval contains data records and control information, and is the unit of data transferred between DASD and Virtual Storage. However, unlike the block, the control interval is not always the physical record. VSAM uses only certain sizes for physical records, and a control interval that does not correspond to one of these sizes is divided into one or more physical records. However, if a control interval contains more than one physical record, all physical records within the control interval are brought into memory during processing. Chained scheduling is utilized, so overhead is minimized. Control intervals are organized into a larger logical unit called the control area. The control area has no non-VSAM equivalent. The control area has an integral number of control intervals within it. The specification of the control area is useful in defining freespace for a KSDS.

When defining a KSDS, we can define free space on either the control interval level, the control area level, or both. Control interval free space results in a percentage of each control interval being left empty when the file is loaded. The amount of free space, as well as where it begins within the control interval, is kept in control information at the end of each control interval. Additional control information relates the sizes of data records occupying the control interval. Free space specification at the control area level results in a percentage of control intervals within the control area being left empty. Figure A-1 depicts the addition of a record into a VSAM KSDS. The first record is added within existing freespace in the appropriate control interval. Note that VSAM reorganizes records within the control interval so that insertions are done in collating sequence.

Suppose that a heavily updated file runs out of free space in one or more control intervals. In this case, a record addition causes VSAM to perform a control interval split by moving approximately half of the

Figure A-1. Addition of a record to a VSAM Key Sequenced Data Set (KSDS).

```
                                    R   R   R   R   C
A     E     G     H                 D   D   D   D   I
                                    F   F   F   F   D
                                                    F
```

Control Interval Before Addition of Record "C"

```
                                    R   R   R   R   R   C
A     C     E     G     H           D   D   D   D   D   I
                                    F   F   F   F   F   D
                                                        F
```

Control Interval After Insertion of Record "C"

RDF = Record Definition Field with length information about the variable length records in the control interval. If two adjacent records have the same length, then they do not require separate RDF information. Since there is RDF information for each of the records in the control interval, we can assume that the records are of variable length.

CIDF = Control Interval Definition Field with information about the free space in the control interval. This includes the starting point of free space and the length of the free area.

Note that VSAM maintains the control interval in collating sequence by shifting records to accommodate the insertion.

records from a full control interval into an empty one in the same control area. The existence of an empty control interval would derive from control area free space specified when the file was defined and subsequently loaded. As a result of the control interval split, there are now two control intervals with room for records to be added or enlarged.

In the event that no control intervals in the control area are empty, VSAM performs a control area split. VSAM obtains more space for the file, and formats a new control area in the newly acquired space. Then approximately half of the control intervals from the full control area are moved to the newly formatted one. This provides new free space within both control areas.

For sequential access, control area splits may result in disk access arm repositioning and some overhead. However, if free space is used properly and file reorganizations are done when needed, control interval and control area splits can be avoided or minimized. As a matter of fact, we would prefer to avoid such splits online for a couple of reasons. Splitting control intervals and updating the file's index accordingly are time-consuming operations, and frequent control interval splits can cause response time degradation. Control area splits are even more problematic, because they entail even more processing. Also, if the system crashes during a control area split, we could conceivably lose data in control intervals that had been moved into the new control area.

One word of warning about freespace; it is applicable to the VSAM KSDS only. Freespace cannot be specified for an Entry Sequenced Data Set or a Relative Record Data Set. Free space should be specified for a KSDS, taking into account the amount of file growth anticipated. Excessive free space can waste disk space. The activity against a VSAM file, including the number of control interval and control area splits, can be monitored by obtaining a listing of VSAM catalog information. The Access Method Services utility IDCAMS LISTCAT function is used for this purpose. By observing file activity over a period of time, it is fairly easy to optimize freespace.

The Key Sequenced Data Set also permits record deletion. Records are literally removed from the file, and the space occupied by a deleted record is reclaimed as freespace. Figure A-2 illustrates the deletion of a record from a KSDS. Because of physical insertion and deletion, the Key Sequenced Data Set can be called a realtime data set. CICS Recovery/Restart and Dynamic Transaction Backout use the File Control DELETE function to attempt to reverse record insertions. This works with the KSDS.

Figures A-1 and A-2, which depict how VSAM handles record insertion and record deletion within the KSDS, illustrate that the control interval itself is reorganized to accommodate these processes. The KSDS can also accommodate variable length records, and records can be enlarged or made smaller. In all of these cases, VSAM shifts records within the Control Interval on a dynamic basis. That means that a record's Relative

Figure A-2. Deletion of a record from a VSAM Key Sequenced Data Set (KSDS).

```
                                              R   C
  A     C     E     G     H                   D   I
                                              F   D
                                                  F
```

Control Interval Before Deletion of Record "A"

```
                                              R   C
  C     E     G     H                         D   I
                                              F   D
                                                  F
```

Control Interval After Deletion of Record "A"

RDF = Record Definition Field with length information about the variable length records in the control interval. If two adjacent records have the same length, then they do not require separate RDF information. Since there is only one RDF in the control interval, we can assume that the records are of fixed length.

CIDF = Control Interval Definition Field with information about the free space in the control interval. This includes the starting point of free space and the length of the free area.

Note that VSAM maintains the control interval in collating sequence by shifting records to occupy the space emptied by the deleted record. The free space indicator (CIDF) in the control interval is updated to reflect the additional free space reclaimed by the deletion.

Byte Address can change. In CICS commands we are permitted RBA or KEYed access to KSDS data records. However, since RBAs can change, this is a very dangerous practice.

A.2 THE RELATIVE RECORD DATA SET (RRDS)

The Relative Record Data Set is a VSAM direct file, and is always a fixed length file. The file consists of a series of fixed length slots, each of which may or may not contain a data record. The status of each slot within an RRDS control interval is kept as part of the information stored at the end of the control interval. Slots can be updated. Records may be inserted within empty slots, and record deletion results in a slot being made empty. The slot, however, remains in the file, and can be used to contain a new record. The records in a Relative Record Data Set can be retrieved sequentially or randomly, based on a slot number or Relative Record Number. The first slot is Relative Record 1, and so forth.

A.3 THE ENTRY SEQUENCED DATA SET (ESDS)

The Entry Sequenced Data Set is a VSAM sequential file. Records can be retrieved in sequential order or randomly based on a Relative Byte Address. Records cannot be deleted from an ESDS, although they can be updated as long as the record size does not change. Records cannot be inserted within an ESDS, but they can be added at the end of file. Relative Byte Addresses, therefore, remain constant in an ESDS. The advantage of using an ESDS over a KSDS is that finding a particular record does not involve searching an index component and then retrieving a data control interval. With an ESDS, the RBA takes us right to the appropriate data control interval. Of course, we must have some way of "remembering" RBAs or dynamically calculating them.

There is, however, a potential problem that must be addressed if an ESDS is to be modified online and we are using standard CICS recovery. If file modifications consist solely of ESDS record updates, all is well. However, if we are adding records to an ESDS, normal CICS recovery will not work. Backout processing involves reversing any modification. A record that was added to a file is deleted. However, VSAM does not support delete processing against the ESDS. Therefore, CICS Recovery/Restart and Dynamic Transaction Backout processing do not work for the Entry Sequenced Data Set. In order to handle this situation, user code must be added at appropriate exit points in both Dynamic Transaction Backout and CICS Recovery/Restart. This installation-specific code updates ESDS records to indicate that they are logically deleted. Application programs would then have to be coded to test retrieved records for the delete flag, and to treat logically deleted records as if they were not found on the file. The location and setting of the delete flag would be determined in the installation.

A.4 ALTERNATE INDEXES (AIX)

The VSAM *Alternate Index* is an alternate access path for a VSAM KSDS or ESDS. VSAM does not support AIX use with Relative Record Data Sets. Let's look at an example in which it might be very handy to have an alternate access path for data. Suppose an employee master file is built as a KSDS. The prime key is the employee number. It may be desirable to access records from this file based upon some other data field in file records. For example, we may want to retrieve employee information based upon a location code or a skills code.

An alternate index permits this. It is possible to build an alternate index over the base KSDS, and to define a contiguous area within the record that is to serve as an alternate key field. The alternate key can overlap the prime key, but the alternate key must be contiguous. Alternate keys, unlike prime keys, need not be unique; that is, there can be multiple records in the target file with the same value in the alternate key field. VSAM and CICS will inform us when there are duplicates of the alternate keys.

The alternate index is physically a separate file, and must be connected to the base file using a logical connector called a PATH. CICS supports the definition of a PATH entry in the File Control Table. Using standard file access commands which name the PATH DDNAME, File Control supports file operations against a base file using one or more alternate indexes. When accessing data via an alternate index, it is important to remember what is happening. First, the alternate index itself is searched for the alternate key value. A pointer to the data record in the base file is obtained from the alternate index. Then the data from the target file is retrieved.

Because we are really reading two files to retrieve a single record overhead is involved. This is transparent to the application program, but not to the processing that must be done within the system. For this reason, the use of alternate indexes under CICS should be avoided unless there is a clear need for alternate access. VSAM allows multiple alternate indexes to be defined for a single file. However, use of multiple alternate indexes increases overhead. A useful alternate access path must be kept in sync with the data set over which it is built. If a record is added or deleted, the alternate index should also be updated. If changing a data field within the base file modifies an alternate key value, the alternate index must also reflect this change. VSAM will automatically take care of this processing if the alternate index is defined as part of the base data set's upgrade set. This is normally requested when an alternate index is created, so typically no application code is needed. However, inserting a record means that all members of the upgrade set have to be updated, so what we see as one file change will internally snowball into multiple modifications.

appendix B

Common Execute Interface Abends

Execute Interface abends can be intercepted in the application program by using CICS condition handling instructions. If such instructions are not used, then task termination ·results. The following is a list of the more common abend codes. For a complete list, consult the CICS/VS Messages and Codes IBM manual. A list of CICS manual numbers is contained in Appendix C.

Abend code	Associated condition
AEIA	General Error Condition
AEIK	TERMIDERR
AEIL	DSIDERR
AEIM	NOTFND
AIEN	DUPREC
AIEO	DUPKEY
AEIP	INVREQ
AEIQ	IOERR
AEIR	NOSPACE
AEIS	NOTOPEN
AEIT	ENDFILE
AEIU	ILLOGIC
AEIV	LENGERR
AEIW	QZERO

AEIZ	ITEMERR
AEI0	PGMIDERR
AEI1	TRANSIDERR
AEI2	ENDDATA
AEI9	MAPFAIL
AEYH	QIDERR

appendix **C**

Bibliography of IBM Manuals

CICS/OS/VS VERSION 1 RELEASE 7 MANUALS:

Title	Number
General Information	GC33-0155
Release Guide	GC33-0132
Library Guide	GC33-0356
Application Programming Primer	SC33-0139
Application Programmer's Reference Command Level	SC33-0241
Application Programmer's Reference Macro Level	SC33-0079
Messages and Codes	SC33-0226
CICS-Supplied Transactions	SC33-0240
Resource Definition (Online)	SC33-0168
Resource Definition (Macro)	SC33-0237
Customization Guide	SC33-0239
Installation and Operations Guide	SC33-0071
Facilities and Planning Guide	SC33-0202
Intercommunicaton Facilities Guide	SC33-0230
Recovery/Restart Guide	SC33-0230
Performance Guide	SC33-0229
Performance Data	SC33-0212
Data Areas	LY33-6035
Diagnosis Reference	LC33-0243

CICS/OS/VS VERSION 1 RELEASE 7 REFERENCE CARDS:

Title	Number
Application Programmer's Reference Summary Command Level	GX33-6047
Program Debugging Reference Summary	SX33-6048

Glossary

AID Attention IDentifier; key pressed by a terminal operator to cause a device interrupt. The AID can be tested in the application program, as it is presented in the Execute Interface Block in the EIBAID field.

ATI Automatic Transaction Initiation; the process of using an internal facility in CICS to start up a transaction. Interval Control can be used to start transactions on the basis of time, and Intrapartition Transient Data queues can have trigger levels defined such that writing a predefined number of records causes transaction initiation.

BDAM Basic Direct Access Method. Also, a type of file which allows direct access.

BMS Basic Mapping Support; a facility in CICS that serves as an interface between device-dependent data formatting and application programs. Using the services of BMS, application programmers format and receive data in a logical record called a symbolic map. BMS appends any device-dependent control information which may be required.

BTAM Basic Telecommunications Access Method; a low-level access method which requires that CICS have complete network knowledge. In BTAM systems, CICS performs network management functions, and the network is owned by the CICS region.

CECI A CICS-supplied transaction which can be used to enter and execute CICS commands directly from a terminal. Using CECI, the application programmer can try out CICS commands before coding them in an application program. This transaction is also useful in creating test data, as it can be used to update CICS files online.

CEDF A CICS-supplied transaction which can be used during program debugging. Prior to entering the TRANSID to be tested, the programmer enters

CEDF into a terminal. After CEDF has been initiated in this way, the user TRANSID is entered, along with any appropriate data. CEDF causes stops in execution at program initiation, termination, and before and after each command.

CEMT A CICS-supplied transaction intended for use by a master terminal operator. CEMT permits CICS resources inquiry and modification. CEMT is useful for the application developer, because it permits new copies of programs to be loaded, files to be opened/closed, and looping tasks to be purged.

COMMAREA A COMMunications AREA which can be passed between application programs during LINK or XCTL processing. The COMMAREA can also be used to pass data between pseudoconversational tasks.

CSA Common System Area; main control block of CICS. Many of CICS's data values are kept in the CSA, and pointers to system tables and management modules are also stored in this area.

CSMT A CICS-supplied transaction. CSMT is an older and far less friendly master terminal transaction.

DASD Direct Access Storage Device; A device type which permits direct access (such as disk), as opposed to a sequential medium (such as tape).

DBP Dynamic Backout Program; performs dynamic transaction backout for failing application tasks. Dynamic backout works for tasks that are defined as requiring it in the PCT. However, DTB works only for protected resources.

DCP Dump Control Program; services dump requests from CICS and application programs. Dumps are written to the Dump Data Set.

DCT Destination Control Table; all Transient Data queues are defined herein.

DTB Dynamic Transaction Backout; reverses modifications to protected resources by failing application tasks. DTB must be requested for appropriate transaction identifiers in the PCT.

DUP Dump Utility Program; used in batch to print the contents of the CICS Dump Data Set.

EIB Execute Interface Block; contains read-only information that is helpful to CICS Command Level programs. The data structure for the EIB is inserted into the application program by the CICS preprocessor or translator, and CICS automatically passes the EIB to Command Level tasks.

ESDS Entry Sequenced Data Set; a VSAM sequential file.

FCP File Control Program; manages files defined to CICS. FCP uses the File Control Table as a source of information about CICS files.

FCT File Control Table; contains an entry for each file that is to be accessed within the CICS region. CICS supports BDAM and VSAM.

ICE Interval Control Element; created by Interval Control to keep track of the information needed to service time requests when the expiration time arrives.

ICP Interval Control Program; provides the time services supported by CICS.

JCP Journal Control Program; provides journal management for the CICS region. Journal Control processes requests to write information to the system log or to any of the user journals defined in the JCT.

JCT Journal Control Table; has one entry for the system log and one for each of the user journals that are to be used during CICS execution. There is room for 99 entries. The first entry is always the system log, and any remaining entries represent user journals. CICS saves recovery information on the system log. Application tasks can save installation-specific recovery information on the system log or a user journal.

KCP tasK Control Program; supervisor of the CICS region, which provides multitasking services. Task Control also contains facilities for resource reservation so that resource use can be serialized. Task Control uses the Program Control Table as a definitive source of information about transactions that can be processed under CICS.

KSDS Key Sequenced Data Set; a VSAM keyed file.

MDT Modified Data Tag; a bit contained in each field's attribute byte. Data fields displayed on a video terminal are preceded by an attribute byte which governs field characteristics. The MDT indicates whether or not the field has been modified. If the field has been modified (MDT is on), the terminal sends the data field back to the host during input operations. If the MDT is off, the field is not returned. The MDT can be set on programmatically, or by the terminal user altering the field.

PCP Program Control Program; manages CICS application programs. Program Control keeps track of program locations, and maintains a resident use count for each program to determine if the program is in use. PCP uses the Processing Program Table as a source of information about CICS application programs.

PCT Program Control Table; contains an entry for each transaction identifier that can be used to initiate a task under CICS. A transaction's entry in the PCT specifies transaction security, priority, and special processing requirements, such as Dynamic Transaction Backout. The first program to process each transaction is also defined. Task Control uses the PCT as a complete source of information about each TRANSID.

PLT Program List Table; defines a collection of application programs to be executed at particular times during CICS execution. Application programs named in a Program List Table for Program Initiation (PLTPI) are automatically executed during CICS startup. Programs named in a Program List Table for ShutDown (PLTSD) are automatically executed during a normal CICS shutdown.

PPT Processing Program Table; contains an entry for each application program or BMS mapset to be used during real time execution of CICS. A program cannot be used under CICS unless it is defined in the PPT. The PPT is used by Program Control as a complete source of information about CICS application programs.

PSW Program Status Word; contains useful debugging information and is provided in a CICS dump resulting from a program check (ASRA). The PSW contains a code indicating the type of program check and the address of the instruction that would have been executed if the abend had not occurred.

RBA Relative Byte Address; a record's address within a file relative to the first byte of the file. RBAs can be used to access data from VSAM KSDS or ESDS files. However, the use of RBAs for KSDS access is not recommended, because record RBAs can change in a KSDS.

RRDS Relative Record Data Set; a VSAM direct file.

RRN Relative Record Number; a record's number relative to the first record in a file. Data records within a VSAM RRDS can be accessed by Relative Record Number.

RUP Recovery Utility Program; a CICS program that executes during an emergency restart of CICS. RUP reads the system log backwards, and collects information about modifications to protected resources by tasks that were incomplete at the time of a system crash. This recovery information is written to the Restart Data Set (DFHRSD) for subsequent backout processing by CICS.

SCP Storage Control Program; manages dynamic storage within the CICS region. Storage Control supports GETMAIN and FREEMAIN requests so that CICS and application tasks can acquire and release dynamic storage.

SIT System Initialization Table; contains information about the CICS system to be initialized. This includes CICS constants such as maximum task value, runaway task interval, system stall interval, and storage cushion size.

SRP System Recovery Program; invoked when a program check or task abend occurs in the CICS region. SRP attempts to recover from the failure by purging offending application tasks. This results in an ASRA dump being written to the CICS Dump Data Set, and a message being written to the terminal operator.

TCA Task Control Area; the main control block used by CICS to govern a task's execution. CICS uses the TCA to keep track of everything that it needs to know about the task.

TCAM TeleCommunications Access Method; TCAM frees CICS from involvement with network management, as the access method runs in its own region and controls and manages the network. TCAM and CICS usually exchange data via sequential data queues.

TCP Terminal Control Program; interfaces with an appropriate telecommunications access method to provide for the exchange of data between CICS application programs and terminals.

TCT The Terminal Control Table; contains an entry defining each of the terminals in CICS's network.

TCTTE Terminal Control Table Terminal Entry; a terminal's entry in the Terminal Control Table.

TCTUA Terminal Control Table User Area; a fixed area of storage within the Terminal Control Table that can be defined for each terminal in the TCT. This area is optional. The TCTUA is limited to 255 bytes, and is available for use by application tasks that execute at the terminal. The ASSIGN command can be used to test the TCTUA length, and the ADDRESS command can be used to obtain addressability to it. The TCTUA is allocated as part of the CICS region, but is untouched by CICS. Therefore, if used by an application, the TCTUA should be cleared when no longer needed. Failure to do so could result in a task finding data values erroneously.

TDP Transient Data Program; provides a general queueing service under CICS. Transient Data queues can be internal to CICS (Intrapartition queues) or available to CICS and other regions in the same machine (Extrapartition queues).

TIOA Terminal Input/Output Area; the buffer used by CICS to pass terminal input to an application task.

TSP Temporary Storage Program; provides a scratch pad facility under CICS. Temporary Storage queues can be used to save application data that are needed temporarily. TS queues can be built in main memory or in a

Temporary Storage Data Set (DFHTEMP) that is dynamically managed by Temporary Storage.

TST Temporary Storage Table; used to define Temporary Storage queues that have particular processing requirements (such as recoverability or security checking).

TUP Trace Utility Program; a batch program that can be used to print the AUX trace data set. Trace information is saved routinely in a memory trace table. The memory trace table is finite in size, and wraparound occurs when the end of the table is reached. If more trace information is needed for debugging purposes than can be kept in the memory trace table, AUX TRACE can be turned on. If AUX TRACE is on, then the information saved in the memory table is also written to the AUX TRACE data set. Trace information in AUX TRACE does not wrap around. Usually traces are required only for complex program bugs or system problems.

TWA Transaction Work Area; a user appendage of the TCA. As such, it is available for use by the application task. The TWA was used extensively for modifiable data in Macro Level CICS programs. However, in Command Level, CICS acquires a dynamic work area (Data Division or DSECT area) that is unique on a task-by-program basis. Therefore, Command Level programs usually save modifiable data in the CICS-provided work area. Thus, the COBOL Command Level program saves data in Working Storage, since there is a unique one for each task.

VSAM Virtual Storage Access Method; more encompassing than other IBM file access methods. There are three types of VSAM files: the KSDS or keyed file, the ESDS or sequential file, and the RRDS or direct file.

VTAM Virtual Telecommunications Access Method; like TCAM, runs in its own region and manages the data communications network. CICS is an application program to VTAM, and relies on VTAM to provide transmission services.

appendix ***E***

CICS Commands

NOTE: This Appendix contains most of the CICS commands, but, command options that are rarely used have been omitted. A "/" between two options indicates that they are mutually exclusive. For a complete list of all CICS commands, consult the CICS Programmer's Reference Command Level.

Command	Description and syntax
ABEND	Abnormally terminates a task and provides a four-character abend code. The abend code is used in a formatted dump that is written to the Dump Data Set, and a message including the abend code is written to the terminal.
	EXEC CICS ABEND ABCODE (4-character code) CANCEL
ADDRESS	Obtains addressabilty to a CICS data area. The options that may be specified include CSA, CWA, TWA, TCTUA, and EIB. The CSA is the main control block of CICS. The CWA is a user appendage of the CSA. The TWA is a user appendage of the TCA. The TCTUA is a user storage area associated with a terminal. The EIB option is used by a LINKed to module to obtain addressability to the EIB.
	EXEC CICS ADDRESS option (pointer/BLL)

Command	Description and syntax
ASKTIME	Requests that CICS either update the EIBDATE and EIBTIME fields with the current date and time, or provide an absolute time which can be formatted with the FORMATTIME command. EXEC CICS ASKTIME ABSTIME (8-byte field-name)
ASSIGN	Requests that CICS provide information to the executing task. The information is placed in a program-specified work area, and can then be tested. EXEC CICS ASSIGN option (data-area)
CONVERSE	Requests a SEND, WAIT, and RECEIVE with a single command. EXEC CICS CONVERSE FROM (data-area) FROMLENGTH (2-byte field-name) / FROMFLENGTH (4-byte field-name) INTO (data-area) / SET (pointer/BLL) TOLENGTH (2-byte field-name) / TOFLENGTH (4-byte field-name) MAXLENGTH (2-byte field-name) / MAXFLENGTH (4-byte field-name)
DELAY	Requests that CICS DELAY a task's execution. EXEC CICS DELAY INTERVAL (hhmmss) / TIME (hhmmss) REQID (request-id)
DELETE	Requests that CICS DELETE a record from a VSAM KSDS or RRDS. EXEC CICS DELETE DATASET (ddname) RIDFLD (field-name) RBA / RRN KEYLENGTH (value) GENERIC NUMREC (2-byte field-name) SYSID (remote-system-name)
DELETEQ TD	Requests that CICS delete an Intrapartition Transient Data queue. EXEC CICS DELETEQ TD QUEUE (queue-name) SYSID (remote-system-name)

Command	Description and syntax

DELETEQ TS	Requests that CICS delete a TS queue that is no longer needed.
	
	EXEC CICS DELETEQ TS
	    QUEUE (queue-name)
	    SYSID (remote-system-name)

DEQ	Requests that CICS release a resource owned by the requesting task.
	
	EXEC CICS DEQ
	    RESOURCE (resource-name)
	    LENGTH (2-byte field-name)

DUMP	Requests that a formatted storage dump be written to the Dump Data Set.
	
	EXEC CICS DUMP
	    DUMPCODE (4-char. code)
	    FROM (data-area)
	    LENGTH (2-byte field-name) / FLENGTH
	     (4-byte field-name)
	    COMPLETE
	    TASK
	    STORAGE
	    PROGRAM
	    TERMINAL
	    TABLES
	    DCT
	    FCT
	    PCT
	    PPT
	    SIT
	    TCT

ENDBR	Requests that CICS terminate a file browse operation.
	
	EXEC CICS ENDBR
	    DATASET (ddname)
	    REQID (browse-id)
	    SYSID (remote-system-name)

ENQ	Requests that CICS reserve a resource on behalf of the requesting task.
	
	EXEC CICS ENQ
	    RESOURCE (resource-name)
	    LENGTH (2-byte field-name)

FORMATTIME	Requests that CICS format an absolute time value obtained with the ASKTIME command. EXEC CICS FORMATTIME ABSTIME (8-byte field-name)

Command	Description and syntax
FORMATTIME continued	YYDDD (field-name) YYMMDD (field-name) YYDDMM (field-name) DDMMYY (field-name) MMDDYY (field-name) DATE (field-name) DATEFORM (field-name) DATESEP (value) DAYCOUNT (field-name) DAYOFWEEK (field-name) DAYOFMONTH (field-name) MONTHOFYEAR (field-name) YEAR (field-name) TIME (field-name) TIMESEP (value)
FREEMAIN	Requests that CICS free a storage area acquired by the requesting task. Only those things acquired explicitly by a task should be FREEMAINed. EXEC CICS FREEMAIN DATA (area-name)
GETMAIN	Requests that CICS dynamically acquire user storage for a task. EXEC CICS GETMAIN LENGTH (2-byte field-name) / FLENGTH (4-byte field-name) SET (pointer/BLL) INITIMG (1-byte field-name)
HANDLE CONDITION	Requests that CICS trap an unusual condition and pass control to a named paragraph in the program where the condition is handled. EXEC CICS HANDLE CONDITION condition (paragraph-name)
IGNORE CONDITION	Requests that CICS ignore an unusual condition and pass control back to the program at the next sequential instruction after the command causing the unusual condition. The programmer can then test the EIBRCODE. EXEC CICS IGNORE CONDITION condition
LINK	Requests that CICS pass control to another application program. When the LINKed to module has completed, the LINKing module is reinvoked at the next instruction after the LINK command.

Command	Description and syntax

LINK
continued
	EXEC CICS LINK
	    PROGRAM (module-name)
	    COMMAREA (data-area)
	    LENGTH (2-byte field-name)

LOAD	Requests that CICS provide the load or entry point address of a program. If the module is not in storage, CICS will load it.
	
	EXEC CICS LOAD
	    PROGRAM (module-name)
	    SET (pointer/BLL)
	    LENGTH (2-byte field-name) / FLENGTH
	      (4-byte field-name)
	    ENTRY (pointer/BLL)
	    HOLD

POST	Requests that CICS acquire and post an ECB to inform the requesting task when an interval of time has expired or a particular wall time has come. It is the responsibility of the task to check the ECB.
	
	EXEC CICS POST
	    INTERVAL (hhmmss) / TIME (hhmmss)
	    SET (pointer/BLL)
	    REQID (request-id)

READ	Requests that CICS read a file record on behalf of the requesting task.
	
	EXEC CICS READ
	    DATASET (ddname)
	    INTO (area-name) / SET (pointer/BLL)
	    LENGTH (2-byte field-name)
	    RIDFLD (field-name) RBA / RRN
	    KEYLENGTH (value)
	    GENERIC
	    SYSID (remote-system-name)
	    DEBKEY / DEBREC
	    GETQ / EQUAL
	    UPDATE

READNEXT	Requests that CICS retrieve the next forward sequential record during a browse operation.
	
	EXEC CICS READNEXT
	    DATASET (ddname)
	    INTO (area-name) / SET (pointer/BLL)
	    LENGTH (2-byte field-name)
	    RIDFLD (field-name) RBA / RRN
	    KEYLENGTH (value)
	    SYSID (remote-system-name)
	    REQID (browse-id)

Command	Description and syntax
READPREV	Requests that CICS retrieve the previous record during a browse operation. EXEC CICS READPREV DATASET (ddname) INTO (area-name) / SET (pointer/BLL) LENGTH (2-byte field-name) RIDFLD (field-name) RBA / RRN KEYLENGTH (value) SYSID (remote-system-name) REQID (browse-id)
READQ TD	Request that CICS read a Transient Data queue record. EXEC CICS READQ TD QUEUE (queue-name) INTO (data-area) / SET (pointer/BLL) LENGTH (2-byte field-name) SYSID (remote-system-name)
READQ TS	Requests that CICS read a Temporary Storage queue record. EXEC CICS READQ TS QUEUE (queue-name) INTO (data-area) / SET (pointer/BLL) LENGTH (2-byte field-name) ITEM (2-byte field-name) / NEXT NUMITEMS (2-byte field-name) SYSID (remote-system-name)
RECEIVE	Requests that CICS pass the requesting task terminal input. EXEC CICS RECEIVE INTO (data-area) / SET (pointer/BLL) LENGTH (2-byte field-name) / FLENGTH (4-byte field-name) MAXLENGTH (2-byte field-name) / MAXFLENGTH (4-byte field-name) NOTRUNCATE
RECEIVE MAP	Requests an input mapping operation so that native mode terminal data can be interrogated and placed into an application program symbolic map area. EXEC CICS RECEIVE MAP (mapname) MAPSET (mapsetname) INTO (data-area) / SET (pointer/BLL) FROM (data-area) LENGTH (2-byte field-name)

Command	Description and syntax
RELEASE	Requests that CICS decrement a program's resident use count.
	EXEC CICS RELEASE PROGRAM (module-name)
RESETBR	Requests that CICS reset a browse pointer.

	EXEC CICS RESETBR
	    DATASET (ddname)
	    RIDFLD (data-area) RBA / RRN
	    GENERIC
	    KEYLENGTH (value)
	    REQID (browse-id)
	    GTEQ / EQUAL
	    SYSID (remote-system-name)

RETRIEVE	Requests that CICS retrieve data stored for the requesting task. The data would have been stored when the task initiation request was made via the START command.

	EXEC CICS RETRIEVE
	    INTO (data-area) / SET (pointer/BLL)
	    LENGTH (2-byte field-name)
	    RTRANSID (4-byte field-name)
	    RTERMID (4-byte field-name)
	    QUEUE (8-byte field-name)
	    WAIT

RETURN	Requests a return to a higher logical level. If executing in a LINKed to program, the return is to the LINKing program. If executing at the highest application logical level, the return is to CICS, and the task is terminated.

	EXEC CICS RETURN
	    TRANSID (nxt-transid)
	    COMMAREA (data-area)
	    LENGTH (value)

REWRITE	Requests that CICS update a record which was previously read with the UPDATE option.

	EXEC CICS REWRITE
	    DATASET (ddname)
	    FROM (data-area)
	    LENGTH (2-byte field-name)
	    SYSID (remote system-name)

SEND	Requests that CICS send a message to a terminal.
	EXEC CICS SEND FROM (data-area)

Command	Description and syntax
SEND continued	LENGTH (2-byte field-name) / FLENGTH (4-byte field-name) ERASE WAIT
SEND CONTROL	Requests that CICS send control information without data to a terminal. EXEC CICS SEND CONTROL ERASE / ERASEUP ALARM FREEKB FRSET CURSOR (value)
SEND MAP	Requests an output mapping operation followed by a transmission of data to a terminal. EXEC CICS SEND MAP (mapname) MAPSET (mapsetname) FROM (data-area) LENGTH (value) DATAONLY / MAPONLY ERASE / ERASEUP CURSOR (value) ALARM FREEKB FRSET
START	Requests that CICS initiate a task based upon time. EXEC CICS START TRANSID (transid) TERMID (terminal-id) INTERVAL (hhmmss) / TIME (hhmmss) REQID (request-name) FROM (data-area) LENGTH (2-byte field-name) SYSID (remote system-name) RTRANSID (4-byte field-name) RTERMID (4-byte field-name) QUEUE (8-byte field-name) NOCHECK PROTECT
STARTBR	Initiates a browse operation. A browse involves reading records sequentially from a specified starting point. EXEC CICS STARTBR DATASET (ddname) RIDFLD (data-area) RBA / RRN

Command	Description and syntax
STARTBR continued	GENERIC KEYLENGTH (value) REQID (browse-id) GTEQ / EQUAL SYSID (remote-system-name)
SUSPEND	Passes control back to CICS so that it can perform multitasking. EXEC CICS SUSPEND
UNLOCK	Releases exclusive control of a record which was read with the UPDATE option, and which is not going to be updated. EXEC CICS UNLOCK DATASET (ddname) SYSID (remote-system-name)
WAIT EVENT	Requests a task delay until an ECB is posted. EXEC CICS WAIT EVENT ECADDR (pointer/BLL)
WAIT TERMINAL	Requests a task delay until a previous terminal output has completed. EXEC CICS WAIT TERMINAL
WRITE	Writes a new record to a data set. EXEC CICS WRITE DATASET (ddname) FROM (data-area) LENGTH (2-byte field-name) RIDFLD (data-area) RBA / RRN KEYLENGTH (value) MASSINSERT SYSID (remote system-name)
WRITEQ TD	Writes a record to a Transient Data queue. EXEC CICS WRITEQ TD QUEUE (queue-name) FROM (data-area) LENGTH (2-byte field-name) SYSID (remote system-name)
WRITEQ TS	Writes a record to a Temporary Storage queue. EXEC CICS WRITEQ TS QUEUE (queue-name) FROM (data-area) LENGTH (2-byte field-name) ITEM (2-byte field-name)

Command	Description and syntax
WRITEQ TS continued	MAIN / AUXILIARY SYSID (remote system-name)

XCTL	Requests a transfer to another program. There is no implied return from the transferred to program.
	
	EXEC CICS XCTL
	    PROGRAM (module-name)
	    COMMAREA (data-area)
	    LENGTH (value)

Attribute Character Summary

Prot	A/N	High Intens	Sel Pen Det	Non Disp PRT	MDT ON	Bits 23	Bits 4567	EBCD	ASCII	Graphic Character
U						00	0000	40	20	ƅ
U					Y	00	0001	C1	41	A
U			Y			00	0100	C4	44	D
U			Y		Y	00	0101	C5	45	E
U		H	Y			00	1000	C8	48	H
U		H	Y		Y	00	1001	C9	49	I
U		–	–	Y		00	1100	4C	3C	<
U		–	–	Y	Y	00	1101	4D	28	(
U	N					01	0000	50	26	&
U	N				Y	01	0001	D1	4A	J
U	N		Y			01	0100	D4	4D	M
U	N		Y		Y	01	0101	D5	4E	N
U	N	H	Y			01	1000	D8	51	O
U	N	H	Y		Y	01	1001	D9	52	P
U	N	–	–	Y		01	1100	5C	2A	*
U	N	–	–	Y	Y	01	1101	5D	29	)
P						10	0000	60	2D	–
P					Y	10	0001	61	2F	/
P			Y			10	0100	E4	55	U
P			Y		Y	10	0101	E5	56	V
P		H	Y			10	1000	E8	59	Y
P		H	Y		Y	10	1001	E9	5A	Z
P		–	–	Y		10	1100	6C	25	%
P		–	–	Y	Y	10	1101	6D	5F	–
P	S					11	0000	F0	30	0
P	S				Y	11	0001	F1	31	1
P	S		Y			11	0100	F4	34	4
P	S		Y		Y	11	0101	F5	35	5
P	S	H	Y			11	1000	F8	38	8
P	S	H	Y		Y	11	1001	F9	39	9
P	S	–	–	Y		11	1100	7C	40	@
P	S	–	–	Y	Y	11	1101	7D	27	'

H = High   P = Protected   U = Unprotected
N = Numeric   S = Automatic skip   Y = Yes

Common COPYLIB Members Used in CICS Programs

```
01   DFHEIBLK.
02      EIBTIME  PIC S9(7) COMP-3.
02      EIBDATE  PIC S9(7) COMP-3.
02      EIBTRNID PIC X(4).
02      EIBTASKN PIC S9(7) COMP-3.
02      EIBTRMID PIC X(4).
02      DFHEIGDI COMP PIC S9(4).
02      EIBCPOSN COMP PIC S9(4).
02      EIBCALEN COMP PIC S9(4).
02      EIBAID   PIC X(1).
02      EIBFN    PIC X(2).
02      EIBRCODE PIC X(6).
02      EIBDS    PIC X(8).
02      EIBREQID PIC X(8).
02      EIBRSRCE PIC X(8).
02      EIBSYNC  PIC X(1).
02      EIBFREE  PIC X(1).
02      EIBRECV  PIC X(1).
02      EIBFIL01 PIC X(1).
02      EIBATT   PIC X(1).
02      EIBEOC   PIC X(1).
02      EIBFMH   PIC X(1).
02      EIBCOMPL PIC X(1).
02      EIBSIG   PIC X(1).
02      EIBCONF  PIC X(1).
02      EIBERR   PIC X(1).
02      EIBERRCD PIC X(4).
02      EIBSYNRB PIC X(1).
02      EIBNODAT PIC X(1).
02      EIBRESP  COMP PIC S9(8).
02      EIBRESP2 COMP PIC S9(8).
02      EIBRLDBK PIC X(1).
```

Figure G-1. DFHEIB.

```
C          01     DFHAID.
C                 02    DFHNULL    PIC   X   VALUE  IS  ' '.
C                 02    DFHENTER   PIC   X   VALUE  IS  QUOTE.
C                 02    DFHCLEAR   PIC   X   VALUE  IS  '_'.
C                 02    DFHCLRP    PIC   X   VALUE  IS  '-'.
C                 02    DFHPEN     PIC   X   VALUE  IS  '='.
C                 02    DFHOPID    PIC   X   VALUE  IS  'W'.
C                 02    DFHMSRE    PIC   X   VALUE  IS  'X'.
C                 02    DFHSTRF    PIC   X   VALUE  IS  'h'.
C                 02    DFHTRIG    PIC   X   VALUE  IS  '"'.
C                 02    DFHPA1     PIC   X   VALUE  IS  '%'.
C                 02    DFHPA2     PIC   X   VALUE  IS  '>'.
C                 02    DFHPA3     PIC   X   VALUE  IS  ','.
C                 02    DFHPF1     PIC   X   VALUE  IS  '1'.
C                 02    DFHPF2     PIC   X   VALUE  IS  '2'.
C                 02    DFHPF3     PIC   X   VALUE  IS  '3'.
C                 02    DFHPF4     PIC   X   VALUE  IS  '4'.
C                 02    DFHPF5     PIC   X   VALUE  IS  '5'.
C                 02    DFHPF6     PIC   X   VALUE  IS  '6'.
C                 02    DFHPF7     PIC   X   VALUE  IS  '7'.
C                 02    DFHPF8     PIC   X   VALUE  IS  '8'.
C                 02    DFHPF9     PIC   X   VALUE  IS  '9'.
C                 02    DFHPF10    PIC   X   VALUE  IS  ':'.
C                 02    DFHPF11    PIC   X   VALUE  IS  '#'.
C                 02    DFHPF12    PIC   X   VALUE  IS  'a'.
C                 02    DFHPF13    PIC   X   VALUE  IS  'A'.
C                 02    DFHPF14    PIC   X   VALUE  IS  'B'.
C                 02    DFHPF15    PIC   X   VALUE  IS  'C'.
C                 02    DFHPF16    PIC   X   VALUE  IS  'D'.
C                 02    DFHPF17    PIC   X   VALUE  IS  'E'.
C                 02    DFHPF18    PIC   X   VALUE  IS  'F'.
C                 02    DFHPF19    PIC   X   VALUE  IS  'G'.
C                 02    DFHPF20    PIC   X   VALUE  IS  'H'.
C                 02    DFHPF21    PIC   X   VALUE  IS  'I'.
C                 02    DFHPF22    PIC   X   VALUE  IS  '¢'.
C                 02    DFHPF23    PIC   X   VALUE  IS  '.'.
C                 02    DFHPF24    PIC   X   VALUE  IS  '<'.
```

Figure G-2. DFHAID.

```
C           01          DFHBMSCA.
C                02      DFHBMPEM    PICTURE X    VALUE  IS   'R'.
C                02      DFHBMPNL    PICTURE X    VALUE  IS   'N'.
C                02      DFHBMASK    PICTURE X    VALUE  IS   '0'.
C                02      DFHBMUNP    PICTURE X    VALUE  IS   ' '.
C                02      DFHBMUNN    PICTURE X    VALUE  IS   '&'.
C                02      DFHBMPRO    PICTURE X    VALUE  IS   '-'.
C                02      DFHBMBRY    PICTURE X    VALUE  IS   'H'.
C                02      DFHBMDAR    PICTURE X    VALUE  IS   '<'.
C                02      DFHBMFSE    PICTURE X    VALUE  IS   'A'.
C                02      DFHBMPRF    PICTURE X    VALUE  IS   '/'.
C                02      DFHBMASF    PICTURE X    VALUE  IS   '1'.
C                02      DFHBMASB    PICTURE X    VALUE  IS   '8'.
C                02      DFHBMEOF    PICTURE X    VALUE  IS   ' '.
C                02      DFHBMDET    PICTURE X    VALUE  IS   '"'.
C                02      DFHBMPSO    PICTURE X    VALUE  IS   '+'.
C                02      DFHBMPSI    PICTURE X    VALUE  IS   '|'.
C                02      DFHSA       PICTURE X    VALUE  IS   'Y'.
C                02      DFHCOLOR    PICTURE X    VALUE  IS   'B'.
C                02      DFHPS       PICTURE X    VALUE  IS   'C'.
C                02      DFHHLT      PICTURE X    VALUE  IS   'A'.
C                02      DFH3270     PICTURE X    VALUE  IS   ' '.
C                02      DFHVAL      PICTURE X    VALUE  IS   'A'.
C                02      DFHOUTLN    PICTURE X    VALUE  IS   'B'.
C                02      DFHBKTRN    PICTURE X    VALUE  IS   'F'.
C                02      DFHALL      PICTURE X    VALUE  IS   ' '.
C                02      DFHERROR    PICTURE X    VALUE  IS   '"'.
C                02      DFHDFT      PICTURE X    VALUE  IS   '"'.
C                02      DFHDFCOL    PICTURE X    VALUE  IS   ' '.
C                02      DFHBLUE     PICTURE X    VALUE  IS   '1'.
C                02      DFHRED      PICTURE X    VALUE  IS   '2'.
C                02      DFHPINK     PICTURE X    VALUE  IS   '3'.
C                02      DFHGREEN    PICTURE X    VALUE  IS   '4'.
C                02      DFHTURQ     PICTURE X    VALUE  IS   '5'.
C                02      DFHYELLO    PICTURE X    VALUE  IS   '6'.
C                02      DFHNEUTR    PICTURE X    VALUE  IS   '7'.
C                02      DFHBASE     PICTURE X    VALUE  IS   ' '.
C                02      DFHDFHI     PICTURE X    VALUE  IS   ' '.
C                02      DFHBLINK    PICTURE X    VALUE  IS   '1'.
C                02      DFHREVRS    PICTURE X    VALUE  IS   '2'.
C                02      DFHUNDLN    PICTURE X    VALUE  IS   '4'.
C                02      DFHMFIL     PICTURE X    VALUE  IS   'D'.
C                02      DFHMENT     PICTURE X    VALUE  IS   'B'.
C                02      DFHMFE      PICTURE X    VALUE  IS   'F'.
C                02      DFHUNNOD    PICTURE X    VALUE  IS   '('.
C                02      DFHUNIMD    PICTURE X    VALUE  IS   'I'.
C                02      DFHUNNUM    PICTURE X    VALUE  IS   'J'.
C                02      DFHUNINT    PICTURE X    VALUE  IS   'R'.
C                02      DFHUNNON    PICTURE X    VALUE  IS   ')'.
C                02      DFHPROTI    PICTURE X    VALUE  IS   'Y'.
C                02      DFHPROTN    PICTURE X    VALUE  IS   '%'.
C                02      DFHMT       PICTURE X    VALUE  IS   'A'.
C                02      DFHMFT      PICTURE X    VALUE  IS   'E'.
C                02      DFHMET      PICTURE X    VALUE  IS   'C'.
C                02      DFHMFET     PICTURE X    VALUE  IS   'G'.
C                02      DFHDFFR     PICTURE X    VALUE  IS   ' '.
C                02      DFHLEFT     PICTURE X    VALUE  IS   'H'.
C                02      DFHOVER     PICTURE X    VALUE  IS   'D'.
C                02      DFHRIGHT    PICTURE X    VALUE  IS   'B'.
C                02      DFHUNDER    PICTURE X    VALUE  IS   'A'.
C                02      DFHBOX      PICTURE X    VALUE  IS   '|'.
C                02      DFHSOSI     PICTURE X    VALUE  IS   'A'.
C                02      DFHTRANS    PICTURE X    VALUE  IS   '0'.
C                02      DFHOPAQ     PICTURE X    VALUE  IS   '"'.
```

Figure G-3. DFHBMSCA.

INDEX

407